Pakistan and Human Rights

Pakistan and Human Rights

Edited by
Satvinder Juss

LEXINGTON BOOKS
Lanham • Boulder • New York • London

Published by Lexington Books
An imprint of The Rowman & Littlefield Publishing Group, Inc.
4501 Forbes Boulevard, Suite 200, Lanham, Maryland 20706
www.rowman.com

86-90 Paul Street, London EC2A 4NE, United Kingdom

British Library Cataloguing in Publication Information Available

Library of Congress Cataloging-in-Publication Data

Names: Juss, Satvinder S. (Satvinder Singh), editor.
Title: Pakistan and human rights / edited by Satvinder Juss.
Description: Lanham : Lexington Books, [2022] | Includes bibliographical references and index. | Summary: "All too often the law in Pakistan interacts with the country's socio-cultural and religious norms. This together with the War on Terror, has led to the increased use of the death penalty, enforced disappearances, the use of Special Criminal Courts, 'honor crimes' and minority rights violations in a way that jeopardizes human rights"—Provided by publisher.
Identifiers: LCCN 2021045355 (print) | LCCN 2021045356 (ebook) | ISBN 9781793646064 (cloth) | ISBN 9781793646071 (epub)
Subjects: LCSH: Human rights—Pakistan.
Classification: LCC KPL2095 .P348 2022 (print) | LCC KPL2095 (ebook) | DDC 342.549108/5—dc23/eng/20211105
LC record available at https://lccn.loc.gov/2021045355
LC ebook record available at https://lccn.loc.gov/2021045356

Contents

Introduction

This groundbreaking publication on *Pakistan and Human Rights* consists of a series of innovative and carefully chosen path-breaking chapters by leading experts and specialists in the field of human rights law. With insightful contributions from a number of young emerging scholars, many of whom based in Pakistan itself, they provide a critical perspective on the legal ordering of human rights issues, at a time when the legitimacy and politics of national regulatory governance over the lives of people is in question as never before. An inquiry into the state of human rights protections in that country is, therefore, all the more compelling. This book is organized into three sections. Part I starts with four chapters that consider a number of salient human rights issues in Pakistan, which stand in their own right. These include addressing the question whether human rights stand diametrically opposed to the need for economic expansion, whether minorities are protected in Pakistan, the societal prevalence of bonded labor and debt bondage, and the right to health in the coronavirus pandemic. Part II examines in a further four chapters the struggle for human rights as it conflicts with sociocultural norms and Islamic law. Examples include the *Quisas & Diyat Ordinance* 1990, the ostracization of the Ahmadi community, the prevalence of "honor crimes" especially against women, and children's rights which are always subject to traditional patriarchal norms. Part III consists of a selection of final four chapters, which though focusing on the application of formal state law, also throw up instances of the systemic existence of a gross violation of human, because such law all too often also interacts with oppressive sociocultural norms to produce a punitive legal system. This section begins with a discussion of the death penalty in Pakistan, followed by enforced disappearances, the use of special criminal courts, and the idiosyncratic practice in the Pakistan

Supreme Court of exercising the *suo motu* jurisdiction to decide cases in a way that gives individuals the greatest latitude.

The scene is set as the volume opens in part I, with a contribution from Uzair Kayani on the *The Law and Economy of Human Rights in Pakistan.* He explains how economic progress and progress in human rights are not antithetical to each other, but rather complementary of each other, in a way that both can become clear governmental priorities. In an erudite analysis, he shows how the benefits of economic reasoning, such as sensitivity to individual preferences, incentives, informational constraints, the importance of accurate measurement and data analysis, and cost-benefit analysis can supplement reasoning about human rights, contrary to what is often believed. This being so, it is important that policy-makers in Pakistan recognize that there is a potential for much greater transparency, rigor, and progress in the areas where both perspectives can support each other, as against areas where they clearly do conflict, since they do not stand diametrically opposed to each other in every case.

Thereafter, the second chapter is a jointly authored piece by Javaid Rehman and Adrija Ghosh on the burning question of *The Plight of Minority Rights in Pakistan.* They confront the question directly as to whether the religious minorities of Pakistan, as the Constitution of Pakistan proclaims, are equal citizens of the country. They ask whether such minorities have fundamental rights guaranteed to them. Are they, in fact, assured about their rights in this respect, or do they face de jure and de facto persecution, victimization, harassment and all the various forms of discriminatory treatment? They pose the question directly to the existing governing party in control today, namely, the *Pakistan Tehark-e-Insaf* (PTI), in order to give this question a contemporary present-day relevance. With that in mind, they focus on the position of religious minorities since August 2018, when the PTI effectively took office as the federal government. Interestingly, their chapter also investigates the impact of coronavirus upon religious minorities and communities of country in a way that provide revealing insights.

Moving away from minority rights, the third chapter examines the plight of ordinary citizens trapped into a life of bonded labor or debt bondage. The contribution is an important one, as there is arguably no more striking a violation of human rights caused in society as a whole than the affliction of poverty among its people. In a piece aptly titled as *Poverty as Deprivation of Human Rights in Pakistan*, Maleeha Sattar and Adnan Sattar consider the position of person who pledge themselves—often with the entire family—to work against an advance payment. In Pakistan, this is known as *peshgi*, and it is one of the most widespread forms of modern slavery in the region, including in India and Nepal. Although the practice is historically rooted in feudal agrarian relations and the caste system, there has been national legislation in

Pakistan, but bonded labor continues to remain all-pervasive in agriculture, as well as in informal sectors of the economy, such as brick making. In this chapter, the authors explain how not just private construction companies but even government departments have been complicit in sustaining this practice. In the building industry, for example, government departments continue to purchase bricks produced under debt bondage and forced labor. Therefore, what is needed, they argue, is a reframing of the problem to include these other actors, since the legal prohibition of bonded labor has not yielded any lasting results. Accordingly, what the authors do here is to conceptualize bonded labor as a market and supply chain failure in terms of a lack of compliance with domestic and international normative standards and socially desirable outcomes. Interestingly, the chapter draws for lessons from the UK's Modern Slavery Act, 2015, as well as the Rugmark Foundation's pioneering work on the licensing and labeling of child-labor-free carpets. Whether their recommendations will be taken into account remains to be seen.

Chapter 4 is on *Pakistan's Constitution and the Right to Health* by Muhammad Danyal Khan, where he considers the right to health at the time of the coronavirus pandemic, given that the Constitution of the Islamic Republic of Pakistan includes the right to life as one of the fundamental rights, but not the protection of health as a fundamental right. As a result, the constitutional courts have interpreted health-related issues under the right to life. However, the post-COVID-19 era demands more to be done, he argues, and this where action on protecting patents on medicines, importing medical equipment, and regulating the health-care services is now so urgently required. He draws upon the constitutional courts of developing countries in Argentina, Brazil, South Africa, Columbia, Nigeria, and India, which have played a pivotal role in protecting the right to health in this way, so as to make it a fundamental right in Pakistan. To this extent, he looks at the interpretative trends of these developing countries with a view to establishing whether these can be of help to the constitutional courts in Pakistan.

Part II, straddling another four chapters, on the tension between Pakistan's sociocultural and religious norms with state law, begins with the fifth chapter by Satvinder S. Juss on *Crime and Punishment in Pakistan* with a particular focus on the 1990 Quisas and Diyat Ordinance. He argues that the Islamic law-based ordinance is flawed and falls short of providing justice where it is most needed, namely, for the dispossessed and powerless. What is needed for there to be realistic fundamental change are alternative interpretations of sharia and the 1990 Ordinance, rather than an outright rejection of these as being incompatible with modern human rights standards, given that the Pakistani government has already proceeded on this basis. This is clear from its recent commitments to the protection of women's rights where the Pakistan government has rejected an interpretation of *fasad-fil-ardz* (mischief on earth) that justifies "honour killings." Judges in Pakistan must also now do the same in their interpretation of Islamic law. After all, when the practice of *quisas* and *diyat* was first implemented in the seventh century, it was in the interests of promoting peace and social harmony, and if current interpretations and application of the law do not achieve that ideal, then it is necessary to return to the original rationale for the existence of such practices before they can be upheld in the Pakistan of the twenty-first century.

Another specific group at risk of human rights violations are the Ahmadis in Pakistan. Yasser Latif Hamdani takes up their cause in chapter 6 with an account of *The Legal Status of Ahmadis in Pakistan*. Although they are much in the news in Pakistan, the Ahmadis are a relatively small community numbering between 0.2 and 2 million. They profess to be Muslims but are considered non-Muslims. The reason for this is that in 1974 Pakistan passed a constitutional amendment to declare them non-Muslims. This was a botched and backhanded attempt by the government of the time to resolve a long-standing theological dispute that existed within the country's Muslim community, at the behest of the hard-line orthodox Muslim clergy. Further restrictions were then introduced in the Pakistan Penal Code 1860 through an ordinance promulgated by the military government of General Zia ul Haq in the 1980s. This has been used to persecute and marginalize the Ahmadi community in Pakistan. What is unique about their persecution is that whereas they identify themselves with the Muslim majority, the majority insists on treating them as non-Muslims. This in turn is then accompanied by violence being meted upon them. Hamdani explains how when no less than ninety-five of them were brutally gunned down in Lahore while praying in May 2010, this blatant act of terrorism was widely applauded by many in the Muslim community at large. When Mian Muhammad Nawaz Sharif condemned the outrage and sent his condolences to "our Ahmadi brothers," he was widely criticized for it. Since then the targeted killing of Ahmadis has become commonplace. Indeed, to be "accused" of being an Ahmadi can result in death and get a person killed. Yasser Latif Hamdani discusses their plight and what needs to be done.

Ahmadis, however, are not the only ones targeted as a group in the wider community. Young women who are thought to have disgraced their families by falling in love or by leaving their husbands in unhappy marriages are targeted with particular vehemence. In an incisive and deeply probing account in chapter 7, under the heading of *Honour Crimes in Pakistan: Unveiling Reality*, Gauhar Neha examines the conflict between Islamic law and the deeply embedded local sociocultural norms in the Pakhtun belt of frontier Pakistan, which has a tenuous relationship with formal law. She looks at the role of the informal *jirga* system which serves to aid and abet outdated cultural practices such as *swara* that have disproportionately marginalized

Pakhtun women for centuries. She ask why are *jirgas* so prevalent in the Pakhtun belt of Pakistan, what impact the mixture of sharia and customary law have on the lives of Pakhtun women, and why the practice of *swara* is so widespread despite steps being taken to eradicate it. She notes how the tribal dynamics of discriminatory practices have over time served to strengthen gendered stereotypes where human rights violations find an easy home. The patriarchal and feudal psyche of the Pakhtun community has also led to the social exclusion of women paving the way to the widespread practice of *sawara*, such that the recently proposed reforms to eradicate such practices must now be urgently implemented.

After that Adnan Sattar provides in chapter 8 a penetrating analysis of another much-neglected area of human rights law, namely, the rights of children. Here he charts children's rights discourse in Pakistan, posing the question of *Taking Children's Rights Seriously: Is Pakistan Ready*? In order to ensure a child's protection from abuse and violence in Pakistan, he asks how the child is positioned in relation to those entrusted with her care. What value is placed on children's interests and wishes in matters that concern them? Has the historical conceptualization of children as property of parents given way to a new understanding of children as subjects? Is the notion of the state's *parens patre* powers to protect children from abuse articulated and operationalized adequately in law and in practice? In order to answer such momentous questions, Adnan Sattar turns for standards of rights protection for children in the Convention on the Rights of the Child (CRC), 1989, in an attempt to locate those standards within Pakistan's own legal framework. He takes the recent case of a maid, ten-year-old Tayyaba, who was subjected to violence at a judge's residence, before examining children's right to freedom from violence and exploitation in the context of family, society, and state power relations. Against this background, he then charts a new way forward.

In the third part of this book, there is consideration of formal law and how it too leads to the gross violation of human rights norms, when it interacts with sociocultural norms and expectations of the community at large, to create a highly punitive system of law. We begin in chapter 9 with *The Death Penalty in Pakistan* by Satvinder S. Juss who notes how initially the death penalty in Pakistan was reserved exclusively for terrorist offenses under the National Action Plan, but that other offenses have now been included as well, of which the most controversial is that for the offense of blasphemy. The result is that an increasing number of people are now being sentenced to be sent to the gallows by the government, with their families having to incur massive costs and social stigma, in the process of attempting to have them released. Juss accordingly first considers the use of capital punishment in the context of international norms and practices around the world. He then analyzes the role of religion and culture in this debate. Finally, he considers the two prominent crimes which carry the death penalty, namely, terrorism and blasphemy, before inquiring into what best explains Pakistan's use and justification of capital punishment.

Not entirely unrelated to the official use of the state of capital punishment is the *Enforced Disappearances in Pakistan* of those regarded as being troublesome, a subject addressed by Reema Omer in chapter 10. She explains how the "enforced disappearance" is an omnibus expression, covering everything from the secret detention and rendition of those accused of terrorism, to the abductions of ordinary people exercising a right to self-determination for a separate state in Balochistan and Sindh, and even to those activists and journalists who have been critical of the state. She makes it clear how in Pakistan enforced disappearances need to be understood as part-and-parcel of other systematic human rights abuses, such as extrajudicial executions, torture, arbitrary arrests, detentions, fair trial denials, and even curbs on freedom of expression. For all who fall in this category, charges of terrorism, sedition, and defamation are levied, so that the evidence points to how enforced disappearances are used as a political tool by the state to silence dissent. Although the Supreme Court of Pakistan has denounced the practice as a "crime against humanity," not a single perpetrator has been held accountable, and enforced disappearances continue.

Closely tied to enforced disappearances is *The Use of Special Criminal Courts in Pakistan* and this is tackled superbly well by Marva Khan in chapter 11. She begins with the elementary question of what basic protections are afforded by the Constitution of Pakistan to a person who finds themselves in the criminal justice system. From Article 10A, which guarantees the right to fair trial and due process, to Article 14 with its right to dignity, the ordinary citizen of the land has much to rely upon. However, a parallel legal system has now emerged under the guise of preventive detention, exercised by military courts and the National Accountability Bureau (NAB). This has led to the subversion of basic rights. Constitutional immunity is granted to the military courts, but although such immunity is not extended to NAB, it still exercises broad punitive powers, without institutional separation of powers within the institution itself. The special court that tried General Musharraf's treason case is also discussed together with its implications. Despite the fact that Article 212B of the Constitution, which allowed for the creation of special courts for the trial of heinous offenses, has now been repealed, the state has only accelerated its efforts of an increasing reliance on special adjudicating mechanisms, which augurs badly for the future.

The rules-based system, which lies at the heart of any legal order, and so characteristic of the well-known canons of the rule of law, is further undermined by what Waris Husain in chapter 12 describes as *The Pakistani Judiciary and the Suo Motu Jurisdiction*. The *suo motu* doctrine, which is to do with an action taken by a court of its own accord, without any request by the parties involved, but which Husain says is unknown in much of the rest of the world, is used with much relish in Pakistan. In his chapter, he states that there has been a reluctance by the chief justices of the country to bind their successors to a rules-based system. Instead, what we have is the existence of a personality-based system in the apex court. This could be one reason, as he points out, why some have referred to Pakistan's top court as the chief justice's court rather than the Supreme Court. In this personality-based system, the ghost of Chief Justice Chaudhry hangs heavily, given that he had advised his junior justices not to create rules which limited *suo motu* jurisdiction of the Court. His worrying rationale is noteworthy. He had "counselled younger judges to consider the time they'd be CJP [Chief Justice of Pakistan] and such [*suo motu*] power would be handy." If that is so, it makes justice dependent on the person who applies the law, rather than the law itself, which is disconcerting coming from the apex court of a country that needs not less law, but more law, for a society that is so custom-bound.

Given the huge range of what has been covered in these chapters, I would like to thank my authors for so readily agreeing to participate in this project and I trust that the readers will find these accounts informative and moving in equal measure. I would like to record my gratitude to my contributors working across different continents, and especially to the acquisitions editor, Becca Beurer, for her patient and unsparing support for the production of this work.

Satvinder S. Juss
July 2021

Part I

Chapter 1

The Law and Economy of Human Rights in Pakistan

Uzair J. Kayani

Pakistan has struggled to provide its people with either human rights protection or economic welfare. Each approach acts as a convenient foil for the other: proponents of human rights argue that "neoliberal economics" has harmed human rights, while economists argue that human rights are internally inconsistent, inflexible, and politically manipulable obstacles to development.[1]

While there are many potential inconsistencies between economics and human rights—discussed in broad terms here—there are also several areas where economic progress and progress in human rights coincide. These are areas where the benefits of economic reasoning, such as sensitivity to individual preferences, incentives, informational constraints, the importance of accurate measurement and data analysis, and cost-benefit analysis, can supplement reasoning about human rights. There is a potential for much greater transparency, rigor, and progress in the areas where both perspectives can support each other versus areas where they conflict. In this chapter, I shall explain some important ways in which human rights and economics interact in academic and policy debates in Pakistan. I will conclude by identifying some pros and cons of each view and offering recommendations on where and how the two can work together.

We will use a somewhat simplistic but common distinction to compare economics and human rights at the surface. Isaiah Berlin distinguished between positive and negative freedom, where negative freedom was freedom from interference (primarily by the state), whereas positive freedom was the removal of hindrances (again, primarily by the state) that prevent a person from achieving her full potential. Berlin and others noted two potential conflicts between these two kinds of freedom: first, positive freedom requires costly action by the government to remove obstacles, and this cost must be borne by the public; the imposition of this cost can sometimes appear as interference with people's property rights, that is, an abridgment of a negative freedom. Second, the meaning of achieving one's potential (in terms of positive freedom) can be controversial in terms of negative freedom, since this presupposes some state of "attained potential" that everyone should reach, regardless of whether one wants to. For example, whether such attainment comprises only literacy, a high school education, college, or graduate study seems unclear, and may be at odds with people's personal preferences over education. Put differently, the implementation of positive rights can sometimes appear paternalistic. For these reasons, there is a broader consensus over negative rights than over positive rights. Admittedly, people make out the distinction between negative and positive freedoms to be more obvious than it is. First, one could argue that negative rights are also somewhat paternalistic: Why should someone be forbidden from "selling" her negative rights? Why should a person not be free to decide whether she wants to sell her right to free speech, equal treatment under the law, or nondiscrimination? Second, the enormous legal system that enforces and secures negative rights already entails massive taxation and redistribution to the officers of the court and the accompanying legal system. Thus, while we will use Berlin's distinction from time to time to make generalizations, it is important to understand that these are imprecise, and should qualified in every situation as needed.

There are important commonalities between the human rights and economics paradigms. First, both human rights and economics focus on human welfare, that is, on bettering people's lives. Second, both fields are rooted in moral theory, with their modern foundations planted in the works of moral and political thinkers such as Adam Smith, Karl Marx, John Stuart Mill, Wilfredo Pareto, Jeremy Bentham, and John Rawls. Third, both perspectives are also hegemonic, in the sense that they propose to describe or prescribe actions and behavior in every sphere of human life. Fourth, both perspectives are predominantly atomistic or individualistic: economics operates from assumptions that individuals are primarily self-interested, whereas human rights law axiomatizes individual rights and entitlements. About here, the similarities start to end. However, these shared underpinnings provide an opportunity to understand both fields more deeply, particularly in the context of Pakistan. The most obvious overlap between the two approaches is the interdisciplinary field of "law and economics" in general and the right to property in particular. The right to private property is a human right that forms the basis of free exchange in an economy. However, even though property rights are a precondition for many economic models, they only form a small part of the voluminous body of human rights recognized by most states. International Human Rights law comprises a myriad of negative rights and positive rights, best illustrated by the International Covenant of Civil and Political Rights (ICCPR) and the International Covenant of Economic, Social, and Cultural Rights (ICESCR), respectively. These rights span issues such as criminal law and procedure, religion, cultural heritage, food, education, and employment. Economics, meanwhile, focuses on questions of trade, markets, infrastructure, taxation and redistribution, finance, incentives, and cost-benefit analysis. On many such questions, the prescriptions of human rights and economics can conflict.

Some reasons for this conflict are epistemic, while others are practical. First, economics models itself after applied mathematics, or the natural sciences. The standard approach in these fields is to minimize the starting assumptions, or axioms, required to deduce a result. In this "scientific" method, a system that rests on more axioms is seen as inferior to one that rests on fewer axioms. In particular, a system that assumes all human rights recognized in international law would be inferior to one that recognizes only the smallest possible number of rights required to explain economic theory. The reason for this Occam's razor approach is that the more assumptions one requires to justify a system, the more restrictive and falsifiable that system becomes: if one hundred assumptions are needed to make a system work, then the system fails if any of those assumptions is relaxed. In the case of economics, these first principles boil down to a set of axioms about individual preferences and numerical utility scales. These assumptions do not require individuals to have any particular commitments to rights or entitlements. Rather, even the construction of rights through social contracts follows from self-interested individuals' private interests.[2] Second, and already suggested by the first distinction, economics is primarily concerned with individuals' *preferences* rather than their *needs*. The idea of specifying needs is sometimes seen as paternalistic, because it depends on some external pronouncement of what people should have rather than their own preferences. The language of needs, which is central in human rights, suggests that there are certain "needed" things that person cannot give up, or acquire from another, regardless of whether she values them personally. In economics, this can look like a restriction on free exchange. Moreover, once some set of rights is identified as "needs," it is difficult to form a consistent system that tells which rights are included in the set of "needs" and which are not. Third, because of the possibility that some persons prefer some things more than others, economics allows for unequal distributions of entitlements. Indeed, most systems of incentives depend on unequal distributions that reward people who produce more value than others. Without such incentives, a system based on self-interest would not produce value for others. This notion of unequal distribution can also conflict with the human rights paradigm, insofar as the latter generally assumes an equal and identical distribution of entitlements.

In these ways, two perspectives that seem to want the same thing—betterment for all people—end up on opposite sides of many policy debates. With the prominence of "law and economics" in the second half of the last century, these differences also erupted in courtrooms over a range of legal issues, ranging from typically economic concerns such as the regulation of businesses, consumer rights, labor rights, corporate entities, price controls, and competition, to human rights concerns such as social security, subsistence wages, health care, due process of law, and nondiscrimination.[3]

While there are many potential inconsistencies between economics and human rights—discussed in broad terms here—there are also several areas where economic progress and progress in human rights coincide. These are areas where the benefits of economic reasoning, such as sensitivity to individual preferences, incentives, informational constraints, the importance of accurate measurement and data analysis, and cost-benefit analysis can supplement reasoning about human rights. There is a potential for much greater transparency, rigor, and progress in the areas where both perspectives can support each other versus areas where they conflict. In this chapter, I shall explain some important ways in which human rights and economics interact in academic and policy debates. I will conclude by identifying some pros and cons of each view and offering recommendations on where and how the two can work together.

I. GOVERNANCE AND INSTITUTIONS IN ECONOMICS VERSUS HUMAN RIGHTS

From a governance perspective, the main difference between the human rights approach and the economic approach is the balance of power among the executive, legislative, and judicial branches of government. Human rights are protected primarily by the judicial system. This is an important difference from economic and development policy, which is primarily implemented by the legislative and executive branches. Even though all branches have significant roles in either domain, human rights are based on laws, whereas most economic decisions are based on government policies.

It follows that an expansion of human rights entails an expansion of judicial power, while an expansion of economic programs entails an increase of executive and legislative power. Since human rights are vague and subject to broad interpretations, they provide a ready avenue for judicial activism. If the judiciary does not have a deeply ingrained tradition of judicial restraint, then it can easily be tempted to maximize its jurisdiction to the extent that a broad interpretation of human rights allows.

This, perhaps, was partly the impetus for the Pakistan Supreme Court's Human Rights Cell, which makes liberal use of the suo motu power. Recent cases provide insight on the expansive scope of Human Rights jurisdiction in Pakistan. *In the Matter of Excessive and Unannounced Load Shedding in Sindh*, 2020 SCMR 1702, the Supreme Court directed K-Electric, a private company, and several government agencies to upgrade their infrastructure and governance processes to improve power distribution in Sindh. In a case *Regarding Colossal Losses Incurred by Pakistan Railways*, 2020 SCMR 1216, the Court directed the chief secretary of Sindh, the Pakistan Railways, and the federal government "regarding the operation of Pakistan Railways and overhauling the Secretariat from top to bottom to ensure that the Railways operate in Pakistan safely." *In the Matter of Slackness in the Progress of Pending Enquiries Relating to Fake Bank Accounts, etc.*, 2019 SCMR 332, the Court created a "Joint Investigation Team" to investigate money laundering, even though preexisting federal agencies such as the National Accountability Bureau and the Federal Investigation Agency were already investigating the same issues. In another "human rights" case, *In the Matter Regarding Appointment of Managing Director, Pakistan Television Corporation*, 2019 SCMR 1, the Supreme Court reviewed the hiring and compensation package of director of a public company. The purpose of these examples is to show that "Human Rights" jurisdiction in Pakistan has grown to encompass a whole host of economic and regulatory activity that is normally controlled by the executive and legislative branches.

A recent rationale for this expansion is the Supreme Court's opinion in *Naimatullah Khan v. Pakistan*, 2020 SCMR 622 ¶ 4, 5:

> Most sacred among [citizens' rights] is the "right to life" and such right to life is not restricted only to the prosecution of a person but the state is required, as mandated in the Constitution, to ensure that all aspects of citizens' life are protected and dealt with by the State. . . . The provision of drinking water, is a right to life; provision of electricity, is a right to life; provision of education, is a right to life; provision of health facility, is a right to life; provision of civic infrastructure and civil infrastructure, is a right to life; so is the subject of transportation of the citizens, is a right to life, for without transportation neither can the citizen get education, engage in his trade, business or profession, nor can a citizen reach the healthcare institutions nor can a citizen obtain necessities of life, like, food, clothes, etc. and such needs keep on going "ad infinitum." The: pivotal thing to be noted is that the State is required to provide citizens, safe, humane and dignified means of travelling, from one destination to another, within and outside the Cities. This is also essential to ensure equality of the citizen and also as a social justice, to eradicate social evils and to promote social and economic well being of the people. The State and its Organs cannot, as per mandate of the Constitution, abdicate, ignore or abandon this most important function of theirs and leave the citizens to fend themselves, which only drives the citizen towards anarchy.

A larger scope for judicial action on human rights will create a heavier workload for the courts, and this will require greater funding for the entire judicial system. The cost of adjudicating human rights raises the issue of the optimal scope of jurisdiction, or the optimal size of the judicial system.

One perspective on the optimal size of the judicial system focuses on the cost of producing law. This perspective suggests that the optimal size of the judiciary is the point at which it is operating at its minimum average cost: that is, the point at which its increasing returns to scale are equal to its disutilities from scale. The average cost of a judicial system depends on it fixed and variable costs. Fixed costs may include the building of more courts, the creation of more salaried positions for administrative and judicial support, and maintenance costs for any systems needed to deal with the heavier caseload. Variable costs include court delays in particular cases, difficulties in obtaining and vetting evidence, varying degrees of cooperation from other public organs, and hours spent on hearing and deciding complex cases. Utilities from scale arise, for example, where a larger stock of judicial precedents allows for the easy disposition of future cases; deeper judicial experience and greater diversity among judges lead to better-reasoned opinions; a larger judiciary is able to decide cases that a smaller system would be unable to cope with; and greater specialization in the judiciary allows for quicker, expert adjudication on a range of issues. On the other hand, disutilities from scale arise if there are too many cases for the lower judiciary to hear, or for the superior judiciary to review; if it is prohibitively costly for information on precedents and rulings to be disseminated across the larger judiciary; if courts become more bureaucratized to deal with the heavier caseload, and therefore less adaptable to evolving legal problems or developments; or more fundamentally, if jurisdiction simply expands into areas that courts are inept at dealing with, such as price controls or positive rights that are subject to on fiscal and political constraints that the judiciary is either unaware of or insensitive to.

A second perspective looks at the judiciary as one means of dispute resolution among many others, such as civil servants or legislators, community traditions or cultural devices, alternative dispute resolution, or self-help. From this perspective, the optimal size of the judiciary is the point at which the judicial system only resolves those disputes that it can decide more efficiently than these alternative systems. Efficiency here increases in the quality of the judgment (i.e., the extent to which the judgment makes people better off) and decreases in the cost of arriving at that judgment. The underlying economic theory is Oliver Williamson's theory of the firm, which distinguishes between transaction costs and organizational costs. An organization can generally decide between producing a service or product in-house or purchasing it from the market. Analogously, the judiciary can often choose between deciding a dispute itself, or outsourcing it to the executive, the legislature, or an alternative forum of resolution. For firms, the decision between these options depends on whether organizational costs—such as the costs of training and monitoring employees—exceed transaction costs—such as the costs of finding an outside supplier and contracting with it. In the case of the judiciary, the organizational costs are largely similar: training judicial officers in the type of dispute, subject matter, and sensitivities involved, and ensuring both the dissemination of and compliance with new decisions. The analog for transaction costs are the additional legal problems that decision making by alternative fora may engender, and the opportunity cost of deciding those cases in courts, such as the benefits of precedents, consistency, a cooperating state machinery, and reasoning that is open to public scrutiny. Some key advantages of the judicial system are the reach of a judgment as a binding or persuasive precedent; access to the formidable machinery of the state in implementing decisions; predictability, consistency, and transparency of decisions because of publicly available judgments; and greater legitimacy because of the constitutional system. Disadvantages arise where the judiciary lacks expertise, such as in cases involving complex scientific, financial, or industrial concerns; where judges lack perspective, such as issues affecting minorities or vulnerable groups that are not represented in the judiciary; and where the black letter law has become unwieldy and cumbersome, such that court process has grown more ornery than available alternatives.

The positive human rights exemplified by the ICESCR are an obvious interface for human rights and economics. In the Constitution of Pakistan, most positive rights are distinguished from fundamental rights, and dubbed "Principles of Policy" instead. Articles 37 and 38 contain such positive rights as education; economic aid to the poor; humane work conditions; equitable distribution of wealth; food and clothing for subsistence; and health care. Though laudable on paper, these principles appear to have a second-class status in the Constitution: under Article 30 (2), "The validity of an action or of a law shall not be called in question on the ground that it is not in accordance with the Principles of Policy, and no action shall lie against the State or any organ or authority of the State or any person on such ground."

Unlike fundamental rights, these principles of policy are explicitly subject to the availability of resources. Constitution, Article 29 (20), "In so far as the observance of any particular Principle of Policy may be dependent upon resources being available for the purpose, the Principle shall be regarded as being subject to the availability of resources."

This distinction in the Constitution provides a basis for applying cost-benefit analyses to positive, as opposed to negative, rights. However, this distinction has not caused the judiciary to develop a greater interest or expertise in cost-benefit analysis. On the contrary, an important precedent in public interest litigation appears to erase the distinction between fundamental rights and principles of policy in matters of suo motu jurisdiction. The Lahore High Court recently interpreted the landmark case of *Benazir Bhutto v. Pakistan*, PLD 1988 SC 416, as follows:

The apex Court went further and added that fundamental rights include not only the rights enumerated in Chapter 1 of Part II of the Constitution but also those envisaged by Article 2A and the Principles of Policy in Chapter II of Part II. It said:

> While construing Article 184(3), the interpretative approach should not be ceremonious observance of the rules or usages of interpretation, but regard should be had to the object and the purpose for which this Article is enacted, that is, this interpretative approach must receive inspiration from the triad of provisions which saturate and invigorate the entire Constitution, namely, the Objectives Resolution (Article 2A), the Fundamental Rights and the Directive Principles of State policy so as to achieve democracy, tolerance, equality and social justice according to Islam.[4]

There are several examples of judicial decisions that seem to cause significant economic harm, such as the *Reko Diq* case,[5] suo motu notice of private school fees,[6] and the suo motu action to build the Diamer Bhasha dam.[7]

A counterintuitive effect of the constitutional distinction between principles of policy and fundamental rights—so far as it survives now—is that the explicit mention of resource constraints for the principles can lead courts to ignore resource constraints when fundamental rights are involved. While the Constitution also subjects many fundamental rights to constraints, such as national security, limiting legislation, and the sublimely vague "glory of Islam," these are not resource constraints. This distinction between the principles of policy and fundamental rights can lead to the pernicious tendency to seek some idealized notion of justice "though the heavens may fall." Such a tendency can constitutionalize absurdity.

Positive rights are an especially precarious area for judicial control. Judges are less equipped to make decisions than the policy-making branches of government. Accordingly, questions of positive rights should be nonjusticiable, that is, "outsourced" to the other branches. As the Constitution suggests, positive rights are explicitly subject to resource constraints, and the allocation and use of public resources are primary domains of the legislature and the executive respectively. Common law courts and lawyers such as Pakistan's are not trained to make governmental decisions, such as budget allocations, price controls, trade policy, or national defense. The Constitution vests authority for such decisions in the president and parliamentarians, who, unlike judges, are accountable to the people. Even the most minimal conception of a representative democracy requires that this be so.

Historically, the Pakistani judiciary has swung between extremes in the exercise of its jurisdiction. Until the late 1980s, courts were perhaps excessively deferential, under the so-called doctrine of necessity attributed to Hans Kelsen: that in some extreme circumstances (such as existential emergencies), an organ of the state may be forced to act without legal authority, or against existing law. This narrow emergency exception arises in all common law systems, typically on pressing issues of national security. However, Pakistani courts stretched the exception to swallow the rule. In a series of notorious cases, including *Pakistan v. Maulvi Tamizuddin Khan*, PLD 1955 FC 430, *Pakistan v. Dosso*, PLD 1958 SC 533, and *Bhutto v. Chief of Army Staff*, PLD 1977 SC 657, the Court refused to intervene in violations of fundamental rights, abrogations of constitutions, and military coups. However, since 2008, when the government of Parvez Musharraf ended, courts have swung in the opposite direction, with multiple chief justices making aggressive use of the suo motu powers of Article 184 (3) and the Court's "human rights" cell to intervene in a plethora of policy issues.[8] Both extremes are harmful to the judiciary in particular and the government in general. To see this, we need to understand how reputations affect institutions.

In economics, the importance of "reputation effects" is studied primarily in Game theory. We will intuitively sketch out the basic game theory model to understand how reputation effects may apply to a judicial system that seeks a maximal human rights agenda.

II. BUILDING A CONSENSUS IN ECONOMICS VERSUS HUMAN RIGHTS

There is a great diversity of views on, or interpretations of, human rights. Three reasons for this diversity are the vagueness of specific rights, the sovereign powers of states to determine their own laws, and cultural differences among societies that favor some interpretations of rights over others.

There are also diverse views on economics such as neoclassical, Keynesian, welfare, evolutionary, Marxist, and behavioral theories. However, all of these approaches are shared across the world rather than varying across cultures or countries. Thoughts on economic progress and development appear to have a clearer overlapping consensus over what needs to happen, what should be avoided, and how things should be measured.

The fact that multifarious legal, welfare, and moral systems can all comply with human rights requirements suggests that beyond a limited space where all of these disparate systems overlap, the content of human rights is ambiguous. Such ambiguity is often indispensable in building consensus, as any students of legislation will recognize. Ambiguity assists in building consensus precisely because it does not force sovereign states to deviate from their preferred policies. However, while vagueness helps build political consensus, it also creates a space for the judiciary to modify that consensus, by interpreting the vague language in the ways that it prefers rather than the ways that the legislature or executive intended. Human rights law thus creates a Scylla and Charybdis for the other branches: if they commit to language that is too specific, then they cannot build a consensus across nations and cultures; however, if they use ambiguous language, they cannot prevent the courts from using their powers to interpret law to force unintended policy changes anyway. Expanded judicial enforcement of human rights can prove onerous for the legislative and executive branches. This is especially true if judicial decision making is mercurial. Since the scope of human rights (both negative and positive) is so large, a very large swath of legislative and executive activity would require a review that entails significant uncertainty and speculation about how courts might intervene.

The theory of incomplete contracts can help us understand another quandary of human rights law. The political leaderships of states enter into incomplete (i.e., vague and abstract) human rights treaties to be able to reach a consensus, while maintaining enough flexibility to pursue their policies and respond to unforeseen contingencies that may implicate these treaties in the future. However, once these contingencies and policy issues arise domestically, the gaps and ambiguities in contracts are slowly replaced by binding court judgments that may defeat the purpose of the original ambiguities. The best hope of avoiding such an outcome is that the domestic are more closely aligned with, or respectful of, state policies and objectives than other nations are. Our own courts are likelier to understand our cultural and political realities than a foreign government. However, this too can prove optimistic in systems where courts have a weak tradition of deference to other branches.

In Pakistan, human rights have also proven especially controversial because of the state's deep suspicion of nongovernmental organizations (NGOs). For example, in 2015, the Interior Minister was quoted as saying that "there are several NGOs operating in Pakistan without any specific agenda and some of them were engaged in 'anti-Pakistan' activities."[9] In 2017, the provincial government of Punjab shut down several NGOs for anti-state activities.[10] In July 2020, the Lahore High Court enjoined the Punjab government from pressuring NGOs to register and disclose extensive information under the Punjab Charities Act of 2018.[11] This crackdown on NGOs, then, is a live issue that has significant implications for human rights protection in Pakistan. The economic analysis of NGOs is relatively sparse. One view is that NGOs arise when the state is unable or unwilling to supply public goods. A typical scenario is where the state fails to budget adequately for public goods such as education, health care, or access to justice. A second view is that

NGOs are easier for donors to monitor and supervise than sovereign states. Programs implemented directly through states have to account for inefficiencies and incentive problems in the public sector, such as corruption, shirking, and inadequate human resources. A third perspective is that NGOs have cross-community (and in some cases, cross-country) networks and expertise in their fields, which provide significant advantages over state agencies in implementing programs.

From each of these perspectives, one can make a strong case for NGO involvement in human rights work in Pakistan.

However, the element of foreign funding and control of NGO work has proved controversial in Pakistan. This is another distinction between human rights work and economic development work: NGOs focused on development work almost invariably work with the domestic government, since their priorities are generally aligned; however, NGOs operating in the human rights space often work with private entities, since a substantial portion of their work concerns communities that the government has either ignored or actively suppressed. NGOs that do not work with the government are likelier to fall under suspicion, whether for genuine reasons, or for their failure to patronize government officials who expect some sort of quid pro quo. Recently, the government has imposed onerous registration and disclosure requirements on charities and other NGOs to keep closer tabs on their work. Many NGOs have also been denied No Objection Certificates, and have had to leave the country.[12] In 2015, the federal government framed a policy to regulate international nongovernmental organizations (INGOs)[13] that required strict registration and monitoring. Under Article 5.9 of the policy, "There will be regular and effective monitoring of INGOs' activities and work throughout Pakistan. MOI will periodically update relevant authorities about the status and areas of operation / of INGOs enabling them to ensure effective vigilance on INGOs." Under Article 5.11, "Involvement in any activity inconsistent with Pakistan's national interests, or contrary to Government policy, will lead to cancellation of registration. Likewise, INGOs shall not take part or assist in any kind of political activities, conduct research or surveys unrelated to their TORs."

III. MACRO VERSUS MICRO ANALYSIS IN ECONOMICS AND HUMAN RIGHTS

Both human rights and economics have to confront conflicts between what is best for an individual and what is best for society. Economics analyzes this conflict through concepts such as externalities, public versus private goods, holdout problems, regulation of monopolies and monopsonies, and systems to mitigate market failures. These concepts recognize that in numerous cases, individual interests lead to social harm, and provide models and devices to curb or deny private interests for public gain. This is the general domain of macroeconomics as opposed to microeconomics.

In the case of human rights, "macro-rights," or communitarian values, are far less developed than micro (i.e., individual) right. The main document that recognizes these rights is the International Covenant on Economic, Social, and Cultural Rights (ICESCR). Like the Principles of Policy in Pakistan's Constitution, Article 2 of the ICESCR also explicitly recognizes resource constraints, and recommends the progressive realization of economic rights. However, the ICESCR largely qualifies or sidesteps the most vexing issues in communitarianism: issues where the community's preferences are diametrically opposed to those of an individual exercising a fundamental right. This vacillation was perhaps necessary to ensure that the ICESCR and ICCPR were consistent. Under domestic law, communitarianism appears similarly stunted. Because of a long-standing focus on the individual, common law precedents in most countries do not provide a strong basis for communitarian claims. Judicial doctrines do set limits on rights where these rights can substantially harm the public interest. However, there are two problems with private versus public interests in the human rights domain that are not prominent in economics. First, the judicial weighing of private and public interests is less likely to rely on empirical knowledge, such as prices, values, and projections, since this sort of information is often not available (or in the case of some abstract rights, even knowable). The weighing of a human right against national security, for instance, often proves to be an unconvincing and dubious exercise in conjecture and speculation. Second, while human rights are occasionally weighed against the state's interests, they are very rarely weighed against communitarian rights or interests. The rough analog for communitarian interests in the economy is a person's competitors, who seek access to the same rights and privileges, but are being injured by that person's behavior. However, human rights are predominantly individual rights, and often at odds with communal sensibilities and expectations. This disjunction between individual and communal rights has led critics to complain that the focus of human rights on individuals rather than communities is peculiar to "classical liberalism," culturally conditioned, and an imposition on other systems of rights and values.

Communitarianism[14] is a (very) rough analog for macroeconomics in the domain of human rights. The communitarian perspective focuses on the rights and entitlements of communities rather than individuals. Scholars such as Michael Sandel and Charles Taylor have argued that the classical liberal view—which animates much of human rights law—misunderstands the connection between an individual and her community. The rights that an individual needs or enjoys depend on, and spring from, the community that she is embedded in. The individual is not an atomistic actor, separate from and surrounded by other atomistic actors; rather, her values, beliefs, commitments, and understandings arise from her embeddedness in the values and norms of her community.

Human rights law does recognize communitarian rights that can be characterized as social or cultural rights, particularly in the ICESCR. Communitarian priorities vary across societies, just as macroeconomic priorities vary across economies. However, communitarianism is more relativistic than macroeconomics, in that its prescriptions about what communities should value are weak. Much communitarian theory is apparently descriptive rather than prescriptive. The prescriptive content is often presented indirectly, as a description of more or less desirable outcomes in different societies.

As a constitutionally Islamic state, Pakistan is especially sensitive to communitarian versus individual values.[15] This tendency can lead a state to adopt a primarily communitarian approach to human rights that is inconsistent with that of most other, individual-centric states. Typical conflicts arise on issues of free speech versus cultural or religious sensibilities, and gender discrimination versus traditional roles.

IV. MEASUREMENT IN ECONOMICS VERSUS HUMAN RIGHTS

Historically, it has proven difficult to measure progress on human rights. There are several reasons for this. First, human rights are not directly quantifiable; second, different countries disagree on their interpretations of various rights; third, the absence or presence of a right in formal law does not always correspond to its implementation of protection in practice; fourth, many observable outcomes that improve with better human rights protections can also be improved for other reasons, such as economic progress or discriminatory divisions of resources; fifth, the level of disaggregation required to tell whether specific groups have fared worse than others can itself create human rights conflicts because they impede on rights of privacy, human dignity, and nondiscrimination, among others; and sixth, the vast amounts of information required to empirically record human rights practices are prohibitively expensive to collect and validate. To help address these and related problems, in 2012, the United Nations Office of the High Commissioner on Human Rights published "Human Rights Indicators: A Guide to Measurement and Implementation." However, the guide recognizes these limitations and struggles to move beyond surveys, dates, numbers of detentions, and educational or health care outcomes, and so on. These measurable indicators are useful to measure legislative and executive activity or socioeconomic progress, but they are not reliable indicators for human rights. One is forced to make several inferential leaps, or to disprove all possible alternative hypotheses, to be able to (still tentatively) attribute these changes to human rights protections.

There have nevertheless been notable efforts in measuring human rights. The Human Freedom Index (HFI),[16] copublished by the Cato and Fraser Institutes, purports to compare levels of negative freedom across countries. It gives equal weight to what it calls "personal freedom" and "economic freedom." The former comprises civil rights that are typical of the bills of rights in various constitutions, such as Part II (Articles 8 through 28) of the Constitution of Pakistan. The latter includes rights to property, free exchange, fair competition, and choice. These two indices are averaged to obtain the HFI. The HFI assigned Pakistan an average "human freedom" rating of 5.69 out of 10 in 2019. This was lower than the global average rating of 6.93, and the ratings of neighboring China (6.17), India (6.64), Bangladesh (5.77), Sri Lanka (6.41), and Nepal (6.51). This means that Pakistan ranked 140th out of 162 countries. On personal freedoms, it ranked 140, while on economic freedoms, it stood 136th. This placed Pakistan and Myanmar as the lowest ranked countries in an already underperforming South Asia. Table 1.1 shows Pakistan compared with neighboring countries in 2018 on both personal and economic freedoms, with a highest possible score of 10 in each category. Each type of freedom is broken into several categories (shown here), and each category is further subdivided into subcategories.

A second widely used metric is Freedom House's Freedom in the World Index,[17] which measures (among other things) a "Global Freedom Score," comprising civil liberties (with a maximum score of 60) and political rights

Table 1.1 Personal Freedoms (HFI 2020)

Country\ Category	*Rule of Law*	*Security and Safety*	*Movement*	*Religion*	*Association, Assembly, and Civil Society*	*Expression and Information*	*Identity and Relationships*
Pakistan	3.3	6.5	4.2	3.5	6.3	7.9	5.8
India	4.3	8.1	6.7	5.0	6.3	6.3	8.3
Sri Lanka	4.3	7.3	10	7.4	8.0	7.9	3.2
Bangladesh	3.1	7.0	6.7	5.7	6.3	7.5	1.7
Brunei	6.2	8.3	4.2	–	–	5.0	1.7
Nepal	4.3	9.1	8.3	6.6	8.1	7.1	6.7
Singapore	7.7	9.6	8.3	6.2	5.1	7.5	7.3

Source: Ian Vásquez & Tanja Porčnik. The Human Freedom Index 2020. Washington, DC: Cato Institute, Fraser Institute, and Friedrich Naumann Foundation for Freedom; 2020.

Report in PDF format and data in xlsx, csv, and other formats available online at https://www.cato.org/human-freedom-index/2020

The table is drawn from the xlsx data file.

Table 1.2 Economic Freedoms (HFI 2020)

Country\ Category	*Size of Government*	*Gender Legal Rights Adjustment*	*Legal System & Property Rights*	*Sound Money*	*Freedom to Trade Internationally*	*Regulation*
Pakistan	7.7	0.7	3.8	6.6	5.7	6.5
India	7.2	0.8	5.1	8.3	5.7	6.5
Sri Lanka	8.8	0.9	5.1	8.1	5.4	7.0
Bangladesh	8.1	0.8	3.0	6.9	5.6	6.6
Brunei	3.3	0.8	5.4	8.6	7.1	8.5
Nepal	6.9	0.8	4.6	6.9	6.6	7.4
Singapore	7.3	1.0	7.7	9.8	9.4	9.0

Source: Ian Vásquez & Tanja Porčnik. The Human Freedom Index 2020. Washington, DC: Cato Institute, Fraser Institute, and Friedrich Naumann Foundation for Freedom; 2020.

Report in PDF format and data in xlsx, csv, and other formats available online at https://www.cato.org/human-freedom-index/2020

The table is drawn from the xlsx data file.

(with a maximum score of 40). These two scores are simply added to generate a Global Freedom Score out of 100. The subcategories of civil liberties are freedom of expression and belief; associational and organizational rights; rule of law; and personal autonomy and individual rights. The subcategories of political rights are electoral process; political pluralism and participation; and functioning of the government. The 2020 scores for Pakistan and selected neighboring countries are shown in table 1.3.

We see immediately that there are important differences between the HFI and Freedom in the World ratings. The former ranks Singapore first overall, whereas the latter rates India the highest. There are at least two reasons for this disparity. First, the HFI is composed of numerous data sets from disparate sources, whereas the Freedom in the World Index is composed of the

Table 1.3 Freedom in the World Scores 2020

Country\Category	*Political Rights*	*Civil Liberties*
Pakistan	16	22
India	34	37
Sri Lanka	22	33
Bangladesh	15	24
Brunei	7	21
Nepal	25	31
Singapore	19	31

Source: Ian Vásquez & Tanja Porčnik. The Human Freedom Index 2020. Washington, DC: Cato Institute, Fraser Institute, and Friedrich Naumann Foundation for Freedom; 2020.

Report in PDF format and data in xlsx, csv, and other formats available online at https://www.cato.org/human-freedom-index/2020

The table is drawn from the xlsx data file.

assessments of in-house and regional experts, based on mostly nonempirical sources such as "news articles, academic analyses, reports from nongovernmental organizations, individual professional contacts, and on-the-ground research."[18]

These survey or meta-analysis-based ratings are not readily amenable to statistical analysis. A meta-analysis, such as the one used for the HFI, requires some objective method of choosing and combining some data sets rather than others that were available and could have filled the same role. Meanwhile, opinion-based surveys like the Freedom in the World Index are heavily reliant on a sample of opinions that may not be representative of the relevant population. For these reasons, even these relatively well-known ratings do not allow for reliable data-based judgments that we would need to craft recommendations or identify gaps.

An attractive feature of the capabilities approach discussed in the next section is that—like the economic or development approach, and unlike the human rights approach—it emphasizes goals that are easier to measure and compare: literacy, social security, access to health care, and so on.

V. TELEOLOGY IN ECONOMICS VERSUS HUMAN RIGHTS

Though the ends sought by human rights and economics are similar at a high level of, generally, human betterment—what those ends entail and how we might reach them are seen differently in each field. Even if there are limitations on human rights data, we can still learn from the human rights perspective what kinds of information the development or economic perspective lacks. In particular, development data focuses on achievements or attainments, such as the extension of a service, entitlement, or resource to a certain number of people (e.g., training on forensic investigations for 5,000 investigators). The human rights perspective, on the contrary, focuses on the people not yet protected by a right. Put differently, the assumption in human rights is that everyone must have a particular right, and that the failure to universalize it is a failure. This perspective creates different incentives from development, where the assumption is often (though not always) that the resource being provided is a facility rather than a right. Another advantage of the human rights approach is that it seeks more permanent advances, such as protections secured by constitutions, statutes, and case law. A particular economic milestone can easily be reversed, because it is an achievement reached at a particular time (say health care coverage or literacy); however, a human right is typically enshrined in national and international law, and is expected to survive into perpetuity.

The other side of the coin is that there is a tendency in both law and moral theory to veer into absolutism: all good things must be pursued and protected at all times, and every delay in promoting a good is a failure. In the real world, we often have to choose among various goods, and it is possible to make these choices in better or worse sequences. Sequencing, or scheduling, matters. Both human rights and development, done properly, enhance social welfare. However, development and the protection of rights are perpetual tasks: no state can claim to have perfect economic development or perfect rights protection. Perpetual investments in these domains force us to make difficult choices: at any given time, should the government invest five billion rupees in educating police officers against torture or in training electricians to build and maintain better grid stations? In general, we would want to make the choice that secures the greatest benefit for the least cost at a given point in time. The answer to that question changes across time, depending on what we have already done. Infrastructure development may be cheaper at a time of lower wages or lower resource costs; police training may be cheaper at a time when connectivity and other infrastructure allows the state to easily reach far flung police stations and monitor their work. To simplify, it is easy to imagine cases where spending equally on infrastructure and human rights training will attain a certain goal in ten years; whereas spending only on infrastructure for three years, and then spending only on human rights training the next three years, will attain the same goal in six years. Progress in one domain can make progress in the other easier or more efficient.

This problem of sequential choices arises when we compare human rights protections in developing versus developed countries. Many European nations were able to extract enormous economic value from colonialism and war. Similarly, the United States was able to accumulate wealth and build a base for industrialization on the back of slave labor. These same nations were subsequently able to provide human rights protections that are generally stronger than those enjoyed elsewhere. Egregious abuses of rights were able to provide an economic base to build institutions, infrastructure, and systems that could eventually improve governance, private behavior, and social progress. It is in fact doubtful that international law in general or international human rights law in particular would even exist without the economic and institutional support provided by the West.

It is not clear that developing countries will do better to leapfrog or reverse this sequence. Without the economic base that aggressive development provides, the state cannot build a strong tax base to support its institutions. It cannot provide sufficient incentives against corruption, shirking, and other antisocial behaviors. For such reasons, some scholars have argued that the human rights agenda favors rich states, whereas development programs favor poor states.

Implicit in the argument that we should sequence, or prioritize, some kind of progress before others is the assumption that progress in certain domains can be weighed against, or traded for, others. This is natural in economics, but appears strange in a human rights context. At the crux of this disagreement is the idea of alienable versus inalienable rights. Can a person lose or alienate a right for some time in order to secure another facility or right first? Several economists have criticized human rights on the basis that many of these rights are inalienable. There has been a steady movement toward making human rights alienable. Examples include nondisclosure agreements, where a person sells her freedom of speech; arbitration clauses, where a person sells her right to due process of law; and independent contracting arrangements, where a person sells her rights to the minimum wage and employment benefits, and so on. These are typical examples of transactions that would be more expensive, and, therefore, less attractive, if such loopholes did not exist.

A seminal article in law and economics by Calabresi and Melamed[19] provides the standard view on the alienability of rights (or, in their terms, entitlements). Where person A commits an action that affects person B, there are six standard legal regimes to regulate this action: (i) person B has a right to stop person A's action, but can freely choose to allow A's action; (ii) person A has a right to perform the action, but can freely choose not to act; (iii) person B has a right against A's action, but A can act without B's consent and compensate B for the infringement; (iv) Person A has a right to act, but B can stop the action without A's consent and compensate A; (v) person B has a right against the act, and cannot allow this act, even if she wants to; and (vi) person A has a right to act and cannot give up this right, even if she consents. Cases (i) and (ii) allow for a voluntary exchange: the parties have to mutually agree to trade rights; this is called a property rule. Cases (iii) and (iv) allow for involuntary exchange, one party can infringe the other's rights, but must pay a price or compensation that is set by society (e.g., by a court); this is called a liability rule. Cases (v) and (vi) do not allow for an exchange; in these cases, the right involved is inalienable as a matter of law. This is largely the case with human rights. To choose between these approaches, students of law and economics use Ronald Coase's concept of transaction costs.[20] These are the costs of reaching an agreement to exchange rights or entitlements, such as the costs of bargaining, writing up terms, searching for potential sellers and buyers, and so on. When transaction costs are low, the property rule is best, since only the preferences of the people holding or wanting a right matter. When transaction costs are high, the liability rule is best, since a court or third party can provide a neutral value of the right more efficiently (or cheaply) than the parties can on their own. Finally, when transactions impose costs on others or are against public policy (e.g., negative externalities that cannot be compensated for) then inalienability is the best rule, since neither a voluntary transaction nor a valuation of the total harm is possible.

The case for the inalienability of human rights is that these rights are essential to ensure that any individual is free and secure in the decisions that she makes and the transactions that she undertakes. These human rights, then, are preconditions for the functioning of a market in particular and society in general. A person who does not have the freedom of thought and action, or the access to a fair system of dispute resolution that human rights provide will be unable to function as an autonomous individual.

Classical economics thinks of alienability as a good thing, since this allows people to exchange rights (or any goods) voluntarily. In this way, rights can be assigned to those that value them the most without a government having to figure which rights to give to whom. This is a basic logic of a free market. However, an influential effort to bridge the gap between human rights and economics chooses the opposite position. This is the "capabilities" approach of Amartya Sen. Traditionally, while most negative human rights are considered inalienable, most economic rights are considered alienable and transferable (in the sense that one can choose to exercise these rights or give them away, for example, by declining to own a home or seek employment). The capabilities approach argues that certain economic and social rights are also inalienable, and are perhaps as necessary (if not more so) for social welfare than most negative rights. These economic rights, called capabilities, are the necessary preconditions for freely exercising both negative and positive human rights: education, health care, shelter, and some level of social security. The argument goes that without these basic capabilities, other rights are difficult or impossible to exercise to the full benefit of the individual.

The Supreme Court appears amenable to this "capabilities" approach. In a human rights case *Regarding Alarming High Population Growth Rate in the Country*, 2019 SCMR 247, the Court reasoned that "fundamental rights such as the right to free speech and information are of no use to those struggling with hunger, malnutrition, and starvation. Economic prosperity is thus a sine qua non for the implementation of all fundamental rights[.]"

VI. CONCLUSION AND RECOMMENDATIONS

Although proponents of human rights and economics share a commitment to bettering individual and collective lives, they use very different reasoning, and often find themselves at loggerheads. In this chapter, I have surveyed some salient differences. First, from a governance perspective, both approaches have different implications for the separation of powers. The human rights approach expands the power of the judiciary, whereas the economic approach counsels for small government in general, and a focus on more democratic institutions, such as the market or a representative parliament in particular, since these institutions are designed to gather representative views from society rather than the extreme views of contesting litigants in an adversarial trial. In Pakistan, there are two governance-related reasons for caution in expanding the human rights program. First, Pakistani courts have shown a willingness to adopt maximal interpretations of rights—particularly the right to life in Article 9 —and the introduction of broadly worded human rights is an invitation to further judicial expansion. This may add to the workload of an already overburdened judiciary, further politicize the judiciary, and withdraw political power from a historically weak parliament. Second, the Pakistani Supreme Court has liberally used its suo motu power under Article 184(3) to create a "Human Rights Cell"[21] that has already evidenced a tendency to take and decide cases that have not been litigated in lower courts, and that seem only tangentially linked to human rights. In some of these cases, there is little evidence or cross-examination. This exercise strips the judiciary of important legitimacy, because there is no lower court litigation, little opportunity for appeal or review, and a high chance of error, given the low level of information available with the Court.

My recommendations from a governance perspective are for the Supreme Court to severely restrain its suo motu jurisdiction under 184(3), and likewise for the high courts to severely reduce their original jurisdiction based on fundamental rights under Article 199 (1) (C). The decision to leapfrog courts of first instance, or to take up a matter where there is no case or controversy, should be a very rare exception—akin to the declaration of an emergency or the impeachment of a head of state—and not a norm. Courts are simply not designed for policy making, or for representing the electorate's will. I further recommend more restrictive definitions of broad human rights language in judicial opinions. Sweeping interpretations of these rights will tend to erode democratic power and thrust courts into a political space where they have no democratic legitimacy.

Second, from a sociopolitical perspective, it is more difficult to build either national or international consensus over human rights than over economic policy. Cultural differences appear to be more salient in the human rights space, and the fact that human rights are typically most valuable to persecuted and vulnerable groups make them politically less attractive than economic progress that will typically benefit the powerful the most. This is admittedly a sad reality, but it should not force us to deny or delay the limited gains from economic development. I suggest that we should generally prioritize gains that are achievable with the least resistance—that is, at least cost—whether they are economic, social, or political. The histories of developed countries show us that even severe infringements of human rights are, to a significant degree, reversible in the medium to long term.

Third, macro-level thought in human rights needs to be taken seriously, particularly in extremely complex environments like Pakistan. Human rights jurisprudence in particular, and court reasoning in general, must move away from doctrinal or black letter law to an ex ante, forward-looking, consequential mode of reasoning. If consequences had been kept in mind, we would not have seen the judicial hubris that recent courts have displayed in expanding the idea of human rights to cover massive swaths of government policy making under the judicial umbrella. The examples discussed in this chapter represent significant departures from human rights jurisprudence, and place the court in a policy-making role that it cannot legitimately or practically fulfill. Judgments that the state is unable to enforce are likely to create a culture of impunity. We should also concede that there are communitarian values in many societies that may well require courts to interpret human rights in different ways, rather than importing precedents from abroad. Macroeconomics teaches us that severe interventions in the otherwise "free" market are sometimes necessary to avoid a general economic collapse. We should expect that the same sorts of interventions can sometimes be necessary for other individual freedoms—including human rights—as well. The point with human rights, as with zealous free market economics, is that we need to be pragmatic, flexible, and keenly aware of future effects, rather than dogmatic and faithful to the past (particularly others' pasts).

Fourth, to make meaningful progress in human rights, we need to keep and evaluate ourselves against meaningful data. An enormous number of positive and negative individual rights are on the books in Pakistan, but these have not resulted in the levels of protection that are comparable to countries with fewer protections. This focus on the written laws rather than their force, or implementation, is a symptom of poorly informed decisions. A cursory survey of even the core fundamental rights enshrined in the Constitution should have taught us ages ago that the primary focus of human rights law must be on implementation. Implementation, in turn, requires the institutional buy-in and support of the executive branch—the police and the civil service. No number of judicial notices or decisions can secure such support. The main problems with human rights in Pakistan are administrative problems that require empirical data on actions, incentives, bottlenecks, and accountability in the executive branch. Executive action is more amenable to empirical analysis than litigation is, and data-driven recommendations for implementation have to come from within the executive branch that can own and implement them. Put differently, the focus of human rights law in Pakistan should be administrative law rather than substantive rights.

Finally, we should resist the impulse toward absolutism in human rights. We need to remind ourselves that in every common country, the meanings of various rights have evolved over time in response to societal realities and circumstances. Human rights have always been "traded off" at times of national need, not merely through derogation in times of emergency, but also through restrictive interpretations in times of peace. It may well be necessary to reinterpret the due process of law in a context where courts are severely overburdened by a backlog of cases. It may be necessary to reinterpret the freedom of religion in a context where religion has been more politicized than in secular countries. It may prove critical to employ ex post facto laws where legal cover was specifically created to allow socially or economically destructive actions.

Some of these recommendations likely appear extreme. However, they must be understood in the context of a country that has failed to make meaningful progress in human rights over seventy years. Even core economic decisions in Pakistan's past have not been in line with the basic economic thinking outlined earlier. However, the expansion of the judiciary into these policy-making areas under the garb of "human rights" is likely to do more harm than good. This is not because of some malice or legal incompetence, but simply because the nature and structure of the judicial branch do not allow it to solve problems of an executive or legislative nature. A pragmatic, "economic" approach to human rights should help the judiciary avoid these pitfalls, and specialize exclusively in the areas and on the questions where it is the most efficient actor.

NOTES

1. *See, for example,* Manuel Couret Branco, *Economics Versus Human Rights* (Routledge 2009).
2. *See, for example,* Kenneth C. Binmore, *Game Theory and the Social Contract: Just Playing* (MIT Press 1998).
3. *See, for example,* Gary S. Becker, *The Economic Approach to Human Behavior* (Uni. Chicago Press 1978).
4. Muhammad Suleman v. Station House Officer, PLD 2020 Lahore 534 ¶ 12, (*citing* Benazir Bhutto v. Pakistan, PLD 1988 SC 416).
5. 2012 SCMR 773
6. Civil Appeal No. 1095/2018 (Supreme Court of Pakistan).
7. Zafarullah Khan v. Pakistan, 2018 SCMR 1621.
8. Examples such as school fees and Reko Diq, etc. Are discussed elsewhere in this chapter. *See also,* Waris Husain, *The Judicialization of Politics in Pakistan* (Routledge 2018).
9. Aoun Sahi, *Our "Anti-State" NGOs,* The News On Sunday (21 June 2015), available online at https://www.thenews.com.pk/tns/detail/558860-our-anti-state-ngos

10. Rana Tanvir, *"Anti-State Activities"- Punjab Shuts Down Several NGOs*, The Express Tribune (21 January 2017), available online at https://tribune.com.pk/story/1302265/anti-state-activities-punjab-shuts-several-ngos

11. Newspaper Staff Reporter, *Govt Barred from Coercing NGOs for Re-registration*, Dawn (28 July 2020), available onine at https://www.dawn.com/news/1571495

12. *See, for example,* Deutsche Welle, *Pakistan Orders 18 Foreign-funded NGOs Out of the Country* (4 October 2018), available online at https://www.dw.com/en/pakistan-orders-18-foreign-funded-ngos-out-of-country/a-45761398

13. Ministry of the Interior, *Policy for Regulation of International Non-Governmental Organizations in Pakistan, 2015.*

14. *See* Daniel Bell, *Communitarianism,* in *The Stanford Encyclopedia of Philosophy* (Fall 2020 edition), Edward N. Zalta ed., available online at https://plato.stanford.edu/cgi-bin/encyclopedia/archinfo.cgi?entry=communitarianism

15. *See, for example,* Filippo Dionigi, *Islamism as Communitarianism: A Comparative Analysis*, in *Hezbollah, Islamist Politics, and International Society. Middle East Today* (Palgrave 2014).

16. The Cato Institute, *The Human Freedom Index*, online at https://www.cato.org/human-freedom-index-new

17. The Freedom House, *Freedom in the World Index*, online at https://freedom-house.org/countries/freedom-world/scores

18. Freedom House, *Freedom in the World Research Methodology*, online at https://freedomhouse.org/reports/freedom-world/freedom-world-research-methodology

19. Guido Calabresi & Douglas Melamed, *Property Rules, Liability Rules and Inalienability: One View from the Cathedral*, 85 Harv. L. Rev. 1089 (1972).

20. *See, for example,* James E. Krier & Stewart J. Schwab, *Property Rules and Liability Rules: The Cathedral in Another Light*, 70 N.Y.U. L. Rev. 440 (1995).

21. The Supreme Court of Pakistan: Human Rights Cell, online at https://www.supremecourt.gov.pk/human-rights-cell/

Chapter 2

The Plight of Minority Rights in Pakistan

Javaid Rehman and Adrija Ghosh

INTRODUCTION

Much ink has been spilled over analyzing the minorities "question" of Pakistan.[1] In revisiting this "question," the present chapter attempts to address one fundamental question: Are the religious minorities of Pakistan, as the Constitution of Pakistan proclaims, equal citizens of the country with all fundamental rights guaranteed and assured or do they face de jure and de facto persecution, victimization, harassment, and all forms of discriminatory treatment? In examining this core question, the role and positioning of the current government, *Pakistan Tehark-e-Insaf* (PTI), are vitally important; the chapter, therefore, considers the position of religious minorities since August 2018, when the PTI effectively took office as the federal government. The chapter also investigates the impact of coronavirus upon religious minorities and communities of country.

Pakistan's population figures are shrouded in controversy, although the more reliable figures suggest that the country has a population of over 200 million inhabitants and is now the fifth most populous in the world.[2] An official census completed in 2017—which was controversial in its genesis—recorded a population of 212,742,631.[3] These population figures were immediately contested as under-representative of the ethnic and religious minorities of Pakistan. According to the 2017 census figures, while 96.28 percent of Pakistan's population consists of Muslims, Christians and Hindus represent 1.59 percent and 1.60 percent of the population respectively.[4] Ahmadis, like other religious minorities, claim underrepresentation in the official figures, which currently suggest their population—spread across Pakistan—as 0.22 percent of the entire population.[5] In addition to the officially recognized religious minorities, Pakistan also faces a serious and substantial sectarian conflict: the country is ridden with sectarian strife with frequent deadly conflicts between the Sunni majorities Muslims and the minority Shias. Officially, Pakistan has refused to provide any figures of Muslims sects, although unofficial figures suggest that the majority Sunnis consist of approximately 80 percent and the minority Shias represent between 10 percent and 20 percent of the total population. This chapter briefly examines the Sunni–Shia conflict with the contemporary persecution of the Hazara Shia community of Pakistan.

This chapter has been divided into five sections. After this introductory section, section II presents a brief analysis of how Mohammad Ali Jinnah, the founder and first governor general of Pakistan, had approached the minorities "question" and how Pakistan's constitutional and international treaty ratification processes have responded to this debate. Section III, which is further subdivided into a number of subsections, examines in detail the contemporary state practices and the impact of laws and policies on religious minorities. Section IV critically analyzes the position of the Shia minority, focusing in particular upon the Hazara Shias. The final section, section V, offers a number of concluding observations.

IT WAS NOT ALL THAT BAD IN THE GOOD OLD DAYS

Notwithstanding the fact that religious identity had formed the genesis of the struggle for an independent state for the Muslims of British India and the campaign for Pakistan was built around the two-nation theory—the assertion that Hindus and Muslims constituted two distinct, irreconcilable nations—the Pakistan movement itself was not led by the rigid Islamic orthodoxy. The architects of the Muslim majority state were educated liberals and democrats who neither had the knowledge nor the interest in the rigid implementation of the sharia within Pakistan. Charismatic leaders such as Mohammed Ali Jinnah, Sir Mohammad Allama Iqbal, and Chaudry Zafar-Ullah Khan had visions of establishing a tolerant and democratic society with freedom of religion as its cornerstone.[6] The official position was reiterated by the founder and first governor general Mohammed Ali Jinnah in his speech to Pakistan's Constituent Assembly on August 11, 1947. He said:

> You are free: you are free to go to your temples, you are free to go to your mosques or to any other places of worship in the State of Pakistan. You may belong to any religion, caste or creed—that has nothing to do with the business of the State . . . We are starting with this fundamental principle that we are all citizens and equal citizens of one State. . . . Now, I think we should keep that in front of us as our ideal and you will find that in course of time Hindus would

> cease to be Hindus and Muslims would cease to be Muslims, not so in the religious sense, because that is the personal faith of each individual, but in the political sense as citizens of the State.[7]

Jinnah was a great proponent of freedom of religion and belief as well as minority rights: in order to avoid any illusion that Pakistan's domestic laws and international affairs were to be determined by the *sharia*, Jinnah appointed in his first cabinet a Dalit or untouchable Hindu, Jogendra Nath Mandal, as law minister and Pakistan's international and foreign affairs was handed over in the custody of Chaudry Zafar-Ullah Khan, an Ahmadi as foreign minister. All of Pakistan's constitutional manifestations, in particular the current constitution, *the Constitution of the Islamic Republic of Pakistan*, 1973, provide for a number of fundamental rights including the freedom to profess religion and to manage religious institutions (Article 20), safeguard educational institutions in respect of religion (Article 22), equality of all citizens before the law (Article 25), nondiscrimination on the basis of religion, race, caste, sex, and residence in access to public places and services (Article 26) and preservation of language, script, and culture (Article 28). Internationally, Pakistan has made numerous commitments to international human rights and minority rights standards. This is affirmed by Pakistan becoming a party to the International Bill of Human Rights.[8] Indeed, Pakistan supported for the adoption of the Universal Declaration of Human Rights (1948), Article 18 of which provides for freedom of religion or belief. The declaration was adopted with forty-eight votes in favor and none against, with only Saudi Arabia the only Muslim majority states among the eight states abstaining from the vote. At the time of ratification of the International Covenant on Civil and Political Rights (ICCPR) in April 2008, Pakistan entered a reservation inter alia to Article 18, a provision of the covenant which provides for the right to freedom of religion or belief bringing the international treaty in line with Article 20 of the Constitution of the Islamic Republic, 1973. In September 2011, Pakistan withdrew the majority of the reservations to the ICCPR, including those to Article 18 of the ICCPR.

In addition, Pakistan has also ratified the Convention against Torture,[9] the International Convention on the Elimination of All forms of Racial Discrimination,[10] Convention on Elimination of All forms of Discrimination Against Women,[11] the Convention on the Rights of the Child[12] and the Convention on the Rights of the Persons with Disabilities.[13] The international bill of rights, alongside all other aforementioned human rights instruments, contains guarantees of equality of all persons inter alia regardless of religion or belief and equality of treatment and protection of all individuals. At the same time, Pakistan has refused to offer a standing invitation for all UN Special Procedures of the Human Rights Council to visit Pakistan to monitor and report on the practical implementation of international human rights obligations.

WHAT HAPPENED TO QUAID'S VISION? THE REPRESSION OF MINORITY RIGHTS

In light of Pakistan's constitutional manifestations, its international human rights commitments and state's frequent stance in support of Muslim minorities internationally—most notably within India and within the Western world—one would assume that domestically, Pakistan is firmly committed to upholding rights of its religious minorities.[14] At the very least, the assumption would be that the laws of Pakistan would be nondiscriminatory and members of religious minorities would be equal before the law and would have equal opportunities in education, employment, and public services. In reality, nothing could be further from the truth as religious minorities suffer from discrimination, exclusion, and ostracization.[15] Among the numerous issues facing religious minorities, the following represent the key contemporary concerns.

Blasphemy Laws

Chapter XV of the Pakistan Penal Code 1860 (as amended) lists in Sections 295–297 a series of offenses "relating to Religion."[16] Prior to the commencement of Zia-ul-Haq's Islamization process, the Pakistan Penal Code attached criminal sanctions to a number of activities. These were injuring or defiling places of worship with intent to insult the religion of any class,[17] deliberate and malicious acts intended to outrage religious feelings of any class by insulting its religion or religious beliefs,[18] disturbing religious assembly,[19] trespassing on burial places,[20] and uttering words with deliberate intent to wound religious feelings.[21] These offenses were designed to apply for the protection of sentiments of all religions, and were on the whole applied objectively.

From 1980 onward and throughout the period of General Zia's military dictatorship, there was a rapid expansion to the blasphemy offenses in the Penal Code. Unlike the preexisting provisions within the Pakistan Penal Code that were equally applicable to all religions or beliefs, General Zia inducted the blasphemy provisions with a specific objective: this was not the maintenance of public order or provision of equal protection to all religions or belief but this was to promote a certain kind of orthodoxy, to politicize religion and in this process undermine the rights of religious minorities.[22] The first amendment to Chapter XV of the Penal Code was made in 1980, with the incorporation of Section 298-A. The section provides as follows:

> Whoever by words, either spoken or written, or by visible representation, or by any imputation, innuendo or insinuation, directly or indirectly, defiles the sacred name of any wife (Ummul Mumineen), or members of the family (Ahle-bait), of the Holy Prophet (peace be upon him), or any of the righteous Caliphs (Khulafa-e-Rashideen) or companions (Sahaaba) of the Holy Prophet (peace be upon him) shall be punished with imprisonment of either description for a term which may extend to three years, or with fine, or with both.

In 1982, further measures were introduced through Ordinance 1 of 1982 which inserted Section 295-B into the Penal Code. Section 295-B provides for the following additional offenses:

> Whoever wilfully defiles, damages or desecrates a copy of the Holy Qur'an or of an extract therefrom or uses it in any derogatory manner or for any unlawful purpose shall be punishable with imprisonment for life.

In 1984, Ordinance XX of 1984 inserted Section 298-B and Section 298-C to the Penal Code. Ordinance XX was targeted specifically at the Ahmadi community, and it has had the most serious impact on their fundamental right to existence and identity.[23] In 1986, through Criminal Law (Amendment Act) 111 of 1986, a new clause was introduced in the Pakistan Penal Code. The most substantial offense, with the most serious consequences is provided in Section 295-C:

Use of Derogatory Remarks, Etc., In Respect of the Holy Prophet:

> Whoever by words, either spoken or written, or by visible representation or by any imputation, innuendo, or insinuation, directly or indirectly, defiles the sacred name of the Holy Prophet Muhammad (peace be upon him) shall be punished with death, or imprisonment for life, and shall also be liable to fine.

Originally designed as an alternative, death penalty was deemed mandatory after the Federal Shariat Court had ruled in 1990 that the alternative punishment of life was repugnant to the injunction of Islam.[24] However, within the same judgment, the Federal Shariat Court had also made of the following pronouncements: "295–C should be amended to make 'the same acts or things when said about other Prophets, also an offence with the same punishment as suggested above' and that Blasphemy under section 295–C was an 'intentional or reckless wrong,' and required the requisite *mens rea* of 'intention, purpose, design, or at least foresight.' "[25]

In the absence of the federal government taking any action, this Federal Shariat Court's interpretation of S.295–C has become binding upon all courts of Pakistan. Regrettably, while the alternative punishment of imprisonment is no longer valid, a deliberate decision has been made by Pakistani courts not to follow the Federal Shariat Court's explicit injunction of the necessity of establishing "intention, purpose, design, or at least foresight" and wholly treat the offense with Section 295-C as pertaining to the realm of strict liability. In addition, Pakistan's blasphemy laws and their paraphernalia suffer from a range of flaws and weaknesses as accusations of blasphemy can be launched spuriously with the accusers not being legally required to present actual evidence of blasphemy;[26] the system, as such, does not carry penalties for false accusations of blasphemy, encouraging allegations based on personal vendettas, enmities or pure and simple hatred for non-Muslims.[27] More alarmingly, the heavily politicized nature of the blasphemy laws also presents a very serious concern due to their inherent ambiguity and lack of specificity; the prosecution of offenses under Section 295-C provides a significant example of vague provisions that are being misapplied with convictions leading to death penalty.

Section 295-C represents a draconian law not only because of the mandatory death sentence that is attached to its violation, but the provisions that constitute a criminal offense of Section 295-C are poorly drafted engendering considerable legal uncertainty. The use of terminology such as "words, either spoken or written, or by visible representation or by any imputation, innuendo, or insinuation, directly or indirectly" provide considerable ambiguity of legal language. Similarly, the meaning of the term "defile" is vague and uncertain. The International Commission of Jurist has observed that

> [t]he vague and overbroad wording of section 295–C of the Pakistan Penal Code, which criminalizes words, representations, imputations, innuendos, or insinuations, which directly or indirectly, defile "the sacred name of the Holy Prophet," has allowed prejudices, religious leanings and personal predilections of judges to shadow their judgments, calling into question their impartiality. This bias is apparent in the conduct of judges during blasphemy proceedings, and also their judgments. These concerns are magnified further by the requirement under Pakistani law that judges presiding over first instance trials in 295–C cases be Muslim. The provision, when coupled with the vagueness of the law, all but invites the types of partiality . . . and is inconsistent with the rights to trial before an independent and impartial court.[28]

The vague nature of Section 295-C has allowed manipulative segments within the society to target and abuse the vulnerable religious minorities of Pakistan. Fabricated and falsified evidence has been used to register First Information Reports (FIRs) and to secure the death convictions. Examples abound as the history of spurious claims leading to convictions is long and protracted. In the now-infamous case of Aasia Bibi, Ms. Bibi was working as a farmhand in Ittan Wali, a village 60 miles west of Lahore. During her work in the fields, she was asked by a landlord to fetch water. She complied, but the other women she was working with—all Muslims—refused to touch the water bowl and drink the water: as it had been touched by a Christian, it was considered to be "unclean."[29] Subsequently, a Muslim mob was initiated in Sheikhupura. Ms. Bibi was taken to the police station, and blasphemy charges were framed against her: she was prosecuted under Section 295-C of the Pakistan Penal Code for insulting the Prophet and, on November 7, 2010, she was sentenced to death (by hanging) by the local court of Sheikhupura.[30] A few days later, the Lahore High Court restrained both the then Pakistan president Zardari and the late Punjab governor, Salman Taseer, from pardoning her or from taking part in any activity aimed at securing pardon for her. Governor Taseer was shot dead on January 4, 2011, in Islamabad, by one of his own police bodyguards, Mumtaz Qadri. The governor had backed a private member's bill in parliament, to amend the blasphemy law in an attempt to reduce the prospects of any miscarriages of justice and remove the punishment of the death penalty it can carry with it.[31] But when Qadri killed the governor in 2011, he was hailed by many as a hero, and lawyers in Islamabad's District Courts garlanded him when he was taken there for hearings. He was sentenced to death by a trial court in October 2011. However, Judge Pervez Ali Shah who passed the sentence was forced to leave the country due to threats by extremists and he has not been heard since.[32] This is indicative of the judicial environment in Pakistan where the judiciary is harassed or intimidated. In the case of Salman Taseer, justice appears to have prevailed as his murderer, Mumtaz Qadri, was hanged on February 29, 2016, around 4:30 a.m. at Adiala Jail in Rawalpindi.[33] Aasia Bibi remained in prison for nearly ten years, charged and convicted to a death sentence for contravening the provisions of S.295-C of the Pakistan Penal Code. Her eventual acquittal by Pakistan's Supreme Court in October 2018, nevertheless, highlighted this law's draconian nature as a strict liability offense and disproportionate punishment dispensing mandatory death sentence. Blasphemy laws have been used as a tool to abuse religious minorities (and indeed other human rights defenders) for even an accusation of blasphemy could trigger mob violence and brutality against the alleged blasphemer—in its 2018 judgment in the *Aasia Bibi case*, the Supreme Court noted that "[S]ince 1990, 62 people have been murdered as a result of blasphemy allegations, even before their trial could be conducted in accordance with law."[34]

The situation during the currency of the PTI government has unfortunately worsened with a number of extra-judicial killings of individuals who are alleged to have blasphemed. Currently, at least seventeen people are on death row, convicted of blasphemy offenses, and many others are serving life sentences for related offenses. More broadly, Pakistan retains and continues to implement the death penalty for offenses which under international law are not regarded "as most serious crimes." A country with one of the world largest death row numbers, around 8,000 persons including children (including those from religious or ethnic minority backgrounds) and with rampant corruption in the criminal justice machinery, there is an urgency to introduce a moratorium on all executions and to address injustice inherent in the current blasphemy laws.

Forced Conversions and Forced Marriages

A great violation of human dignity is exhibited through forcible conversions and forced marriages of non-Muslim girls and women. In the absence of precise numbers, Pakistani NGOs such as the Movement for Solidarity and Peace have estimated that around 1,000 Hindu and Christian girls are kidnapped, forced to convert to Islam and forcibly married, or sold into prostitution, annually in Pakistan.[35] The law enforcing agencies fail to take action against these men, with evidence that they are complicit in supporting such criminal activities and also pressurize the victims and their families not to lodge formal complaints. More generally, there is abundance of evidence of corruption and nepotism within police and all law-enforcing agencies. According to the 2018 Report produced by the Commonwealth Initiative for Freedom of Religion or Belief, the

> police will often either refuse to record an [First information Report] FIR or falsify the information recorded on the FIR, thus denying the families involved the chance to take their case and complaints any further. The lack of an FIR or the misrepresentation of information means that the family are unable to seek further justice in law courts, as an FIR is the vital first stage in the Criminal Procedure Code. Police are also often lethargic in attempting to recover a girl who has been abducted, thus allowing the conversion and marriage to take place. Both the lower courts and the higher courts of Pakistan have displayed bias and a lack of adherence to proper procedures in cases that involve accusations of forced marriage and forced conversions [and in such cases] the judiciary is often subjected to external influences, such as fear of reprisal and violence from extremist elements.[36]

There is frequent failure to investigate the circumstances in which conversions have taken place and to inquire about the age of the girl in question. These girls are usually left in the custody of their kidnappers throughout the trial process and are placed under intense pressure to deny that any abduction or rape has taken place and to claim that the conversion took place of their own free will.[37] Minority girls forcibly converted and married are often also under legal marriageable age, which according to the Child Marriage Restrain Act 1929 is 16 years for girls and 18 years for boys. Some of the victims are forcibly married to men much older than themselves and these men are already married. The girls are used for sexual gratification of these abductors and sometimes sold for prostitution or sexual slavery afterward. Vulnerable minority girls and their guardians are denied justice in the criminal justice system. The abductors and those engaged in forced conversions and marriages use political influence or (false) religious arguments to justify their actions and pressure the police not to register cases against them. Pakistan has committed to eliminate child, early, and forced marriages by 2030, and has also accepted obligations inter alia through a number of international instruments to end child abductions, forced and early marriages of girls. However, there has been a complete failure to incorporate these international obligations into domestic law or implement these in practice. The constant fear of abductions and forcible conversions of young Hindu and Christians girls forces their parents to arrange early marriages for their daughters (sometimes child marriages) resulting in early pregnancies, increased child mortality and poverty.

To address some of these issues, in November 2016, the Sindh Provincial Assembly unanimously passed the Sindh Criminal Law (Protection of Minorities) Bill which, inter alia, makes forcibly converting a minor a criminal offense and recommends a five-year punishment for perpetrators and three years for facilitators. However, due to political opposition from a single religious party with no representation in the Sindh Assembly at that time, the bill failed to receive the approval of the governor and, therefore, did not enter the statute books. A similar bill introduced within Pakistan National Assembly, Child Marriages (Restraint) Amendment Bill 2019, which raises the minimum age of marriage in Pakistan, has been stalled and failed to become law because of the opposition from the Pakistan government.

Discrimination and Persecution of Minorities

Religious minorities, in particular, Hindus, Christian, and the Ahmadis suffer from the worst form of discrimination and persecution. This is reflected in almost all segments of public and private life. Because of historic patterns of discrimination and ostracization, Hindus and Christians remain at the bottom rung of the educational and socioeconomic ladder. The most humiliating jobs—jobs which majority Muslims would not perform—are frequently reserved for Christians and Hindus. A significant proportion of the Hindus within the province of Sindh are the so-called untouchables, the scheduled caste Hindus. As *harees*, these scheduled caste Hindus form part of the landless bonded laborer of the province of Sindh.[38] Sindh's agricultural wealth, to a large extent, has depended on the intensive and strenuous work of the bonded laborer in producing hugely profitable cash crops such as sugarcane. While huge profits are made by the wealthy landlords, this landless bonded laborer community consisting of substantial number of scheduled caste Hindus continues to suffer from abject poverty. They remain tied to the land where they are forced to work literally as slaves. The landlords ensure that these bonded laborers and their future generations remain illiterate and unable in any manner to challenge the unfair system of exploitation. The National Assembly of Pakistan abolished bonded labor through the Bonded Labour Abolition Act 1992. However, the banned practices continue to thrive in many parts of Sindh; officials remain reluctant to interfere for fear of incurring the wrath of powerful ruling families.

Lower caste Hindus or Dalits in Pakistan had converted to Christianity in order to escape discrimination based on caste hierarchy. However, even now, the descendants of those lower caste Hindus who have converted to Christianity find themselves being employed as sweepers and manual scavengers, who traditionally form the lowest rung of the caste ladder in Hinduism, being considered as untouchables. The Muslims refuse to work as cleaners and most of this work is reserved for Christians.[39] The Christian and Hindu minorities are also deprived of educational and employment opportunities; their working opportunities are confined to those sectors which will not be undertaken by the majority Muslims. Discrimination against religious minorities is promoted through school textbooks which stigmatize non-Muslims and with distorted historical facts, portray non-Muslims as inferior to Muslims. In the worst cases, some textbooks include hate materials and actively encourage discrimination or violence against religious minority groups. The Pakistani Minorities Teachers Association and others, particularly Ahmadi organizations, have produced a vast amount of research identifying materials in textbooks containing discriminatory and hate materials against minorities. The current PTI government's emphasis on a Single National Curriculum is an attempt to impose upon religious minorities, religious values and beliefs that are contrary to their faith and also violate the provisions of Article 22(1) of the Constitution of Pakistan.

Discrimination against Hindus, Christians, and, in particular, the Ahmadis is also featured significantly in many Pakistani classrooms. Minority students are routinely subjected to physical and psychological ill-treatment, including being segregated, bullied, teased, beaten, and pushed toward conversion. There are consistent reports that teachers often turn a blind eye to this discrimination or, in many cases, participate in it. Segregation policies have also been practiced in a number of schools, including in some cities where school officials have prohibited Christian or other non-Muslim pupils from drinking water or using lavatories reserved for Muslim students. In one particularly horrific case, a Christian schoolboy was murdered by his own class fellows for drinking water from a "Muslim" cup, on a particularly hot day. Meanwhile, the class teachers stood by, allowing this tragedy to unfold.[40]

With the onset of COVID-19 since March 2020, Hindus and Christians in Pakistan have been discriminated against, in the disbursement of aid.[41] In late March, reports of discrimination against Hindus and Christians by the NGO Saylani Welfare International Trust emerged from Karachi and Sindh.[42] In Karachi, the NGO was said to have skipped Christian households when distributing ration/food cards.[43] Further, it appears that Hindus have been excluded from the distribution of government food aid.[44] Anecdotal evidence also shows that Christians, in several areas of Lahore, Karachi, and Punjab, have not been allowed to access rations distributed by the government.[45] These reports led to the United States Commission on International Religious Freedom (USCIRF) issuing a press release decrying the denial of food aid to Hindus and Christians in Pakistan.[46]

Recent reports have highlighted the increased threat that Pakistan's sanitation workers are facing in light of the COVID-19 pandemic striking the country. The dangerous and menial sanitation jobs are specifically reserved for religious minorities in the Sunni-dominated society, and Christians make up some 80–90 percent of the sanitation workforce. They are severely underpaid, they work in dangerous conditions, and they are rarely, if ever, provided with the safety equipment necessary to perform their duties. There is now a risk of removal from employment of Christian sanitary workers. There is also a risk of Christian women (who work in private homes) to be removed from their employment—many Muslims regard Christians as unclean and, therefore, would not allow them in their houses.

SECTARIANISM AND THE ISSUE OF SHIA MINORITY COMMUNITIES IN PAKISTAN

As noted above, although there are no official figures, according to unofficial statistics, Shias account for about 10–20 percent of the Muslim population of Pakistan.[47] While Shias were not originally targeted (except in the case of localized and one-off incidents) because of their religious beliefs, sectarian violence against Shias has intensified since the late 1970s, and has now come to be a mainstay in the political, social, and religious life of Pakistan.

It must, however, be noted that the division between Shias and Sunnis dates back to 632 AD, when differences arose with regard to the question of succession, given that Prophet Muhammad (peace be upon him) had died without a male heir and had not given instructions as to who should succeed him as the Caliph or the leader of the Islamic faith.[48] Despite the Shia-Sunni divide in Islam, until the 1970s, the sectarian violence against Shias was not the order of the day in Pakistan. However, since 1970s, Shias have become the main victims of sectarian violence and anti-Shia militancy has come to dominate public life.

It was primarily General Mohammad Zia-ul-Haq's policy of Islamization that deepened the Shia-Sunni sectarian divide in Pakistan, by alienating the Shias.[49] General Haq's attempts to create an Islamic state modeled on Arabized Islam or Wahhabism, following the Deobandi Sunni tradition, led to widespread dissatisfaction among, and protests from the Shia community.[50] Particularly, the attempts to Islamize the legal system by imposing the Hanafi Sunni *fiqh* was not conducive to maintaining amity and peace between the two sects.[51] Setting up of the Federal Shariat Court, Islamization of banking system, Islamization of education (especially madrassa education), the introduction of discriminatory rules and regulations governing job applications, and the use of blasphemy laws to discriminate against and harass minorities, created serious tensions between Shias and Sunnis.[52] The compulsory imposition of *zakat* (compulsory charity tax deducted by the government) was another bone of contention.[53] This was against Shia beliefs and tradition, which regarded the payment of *zakat* or giving of charity to be a voluntary, private matter.[54]

It may also be noted that the Shia-Sunni conflict in the 1980s was essentially a proxy war between Shia Iran and Sunni Saudi Arabia.[55] Consumption of Jihadi literature from Afghan training camps and the inflow of Saudi money and weapons led to the Islamization of education and student politics, with madrassas regularly producing radicalized recruits.[56] Politico-religious parties acquired money, weapons, and training from Afghan camps during the Afghan civil war, backed and sponsored by Saudi Arabia.[57] The Sipah-e-Sahaba (SSP), an anti-Shia jihadi militia, which received support from the Saudis and the Zia government, was formed in 1985 and became the main vehicle for anti-Shia militancy and the aggressive promotion of Sunni Islam.[58]

The intervention of Shia Iran encouraged the mobilization and political radicalization of the Shia community. Backed by Iran, Shias responded to Sunni extremism by forming their own militant organizations.[59] Thus, General Zia's policy of Islamization and the Iranian Revolution in 1979 spurred the Shia community, which was hitherto a moderate community, into radical politics.[60] This in turn further prompted the Sunni radicals and militants to adopt violent activism, and, in some instances, terrorism.[61]

It has also been observed that class tensions and socioeconomic conditions fuelled the rise of sectarian violence and discord.[62] The poor migrants who came to Pakistani Punjab after 1947, majorly Sunni Muslims, remained poor, socially and economically backward and neglected. The SSP gave the rural poor a political platform; co-opted the narrative of socioeconomic difference and class divide, and turned it into sectarian conflict.[63] This is why the Jhang district in Punjab, where Shias have traditionally been rich landowners, saw maximum violence in the 1980s.[64] Sectarian hatred was fanned and mobilized for political gain by politico-religious parties, and even by secular parties, which adopted a policy of appeasement of religious lobbies, to retain political power.[65]

Governments, both military and civilian, that came after General Zia, have either tolerated or tacitly enabled sectarian violence and extremism. The SSP was allowed to participate in electoral politics (until 2002, when it was banned by General Musharraf's government) and its support was utilized to form governments. For instance, Benazir Bhutto's government did not carry out its promise of stopping all funding to madrassas, which had become the epicenters of sectarian extremism and militancy, and instead an SSP leader was made the minister of fisheries in the Punjab government.[66] General Musharraf, who had also vouched to put an end to sectarian violence, did not take any steps beyond the superficial.[67] The Deobandi Sunni militant organizations continue, even now, to have links to politico-religious parties.[68] Banned organizations continue to function under new names or despite the existence of bans.

This sectarian tension between Sunnis and Shias has resulted in a spate of targeted killings of Shia professionals and officials such as doctors, lawyers, businessmen, and so forth; assassinations of political and religious leaders; bombings in public places, at social gatherings, and near places of worship of Shia Muslims; enforced disappearances;[69] and hate speech.[70] Shia pilgrims traveling to and from Iran have also been victims of militant attacks.[71] The South Asia Terrorism Portal estimates that between 2001 and June 2018, 2,693 Shia Muslims were killed and 4,847 were injured in 471 instances of terrorist and sectarian violence.[72]

The Hazaras are the most vulnerable among Shias. A majority of Hazaras are Shias and their identifiable Mongoloid features and their ghettoization in Quetta, Balochistan, makes them even more vulnerable to targeted attacks.[73] The Human Rights Commission of Pakistan in its report titled "State of Human Rights in 2019" observed that despite the deployment of security forces to protect the Hazara Shia community, nearly 500 Hazaras were killed and 627 injured in just 5 years.[74] Hazara's need for security protection has led to further ghettoization and has impeded their ability to live a normal life.[75] The constant threat to their lives has affected their economic and educational opportunities. They live in constant fear.[76]

Despite the killings and attacks against Shia Muslims having become more frequent and bloodier in the recent years, the Pakistani state has failed to respond in a meaningful manner. Hardly ever does the police properly investigate such incidents. Arrests are rare and charging of suspects and their conviction is even more infrequent. There has also been no attempt to put an end to campaigns and venomous propaganda, whether in schools, public places, and on social media, spewing hate against Shia Muslims, who are deemed to be heretics and apostates by Sunni extremists. The Pakistani government's overall response reflects "incompetence, indifference, or possible complicity."[77] As such, the Pakistan government can be described to be unable and unwilling to protect the Shias.[78] The Pakistan intelligence, military, and administrative authorities are arguably also complicit in the sectarian violence.[79]

The Lashkar-e-Jhangvi (LeJ) (a violent breakaway faction of the SSP) has repeatedly proclaimed its intent to wipe out Shia "infidels" and is responsible for several attacks against Shias.[80] However, its leader, Malik Ishaq was never brought to justice despite having been arrested and implicated in several cases of killings and murders. In 2011, the Pakistani Supreme Court released him on bail as it claimed that the prosecution had failed to furnish sufficient evidence against him.[81] He was acquitted by the court in thirty-four out of forty-four cases and released on bail for the remaining ten.[82] Thereafter, despite a spate of arrests and periods of detention, he was never convicted,[83] and was ultimately killed in an encounter in 2015.[84] Similar instances of the judiciary, due to its lack of independence and fear of retaliation, failing to curb sectarian violence and bring the perpetrators to justice, are well known.[85]

There has been an evident failure on the part of the PTI government to deal with this situation. During the period between August and October 2020, the anti-Shia propaganda in Pakistan came to a head. Rampant use of blasphemy laws against Shias during the month of Muharram,[86] anti-Shia demonstrations in Karachi,[87] and instances of vitriolic speech by Sunni extremists, spewing sectarian hatred was reported widely in the international media.[88] This goes to show that the sectarianism in Pakistan is an issue that needs to be reckoned with. A facet of the significant human rights implications of the sectarianism was clearly reflected in the stigmatization of the Shia community, especially the Hazara Shias during the COVID-19 public health crisis.

The COVID-19 virus was referred to as the "Shia virus."[89] Shia pilgrims returning from Iran were quarantined in extremely poor conditions.[90] The Hazara Shias were particularly racially profiled and blamed for bringing the virus into the country.[91] Subsequently, two federal ministers, Zulfikar Bukhari and Ali Zaidi, both belonging to the Shia community, were targeted and blamed by the Ahl-e-Sunnat Wal Jamaat (ASWJ) (a banned sectarian organization which is essentially the SSP functioning under a new name) chief for allowing pilgrims from escaping quarantine and spreading the virus.[92]

The USCIRF, in a press release, condemned the stigmatization of Hazara Shia Muslims minorities in Pakistan, as a result of insinuations that they purportedly had brought COVID-19 into the country.[93] Even prior to the announcement of the lockdown, by a notification on March 12, 2020, staff belonging to the Hazara Shia minority group were barred from going to work by the inspector general of police in Balochistan, Quetta.[94] On March 13, 2020, the Water and Sanitation Authority also issued a notification forbidding the movement of employees belonging to the Hazara tribe out of Hazara neighborhoods.[95] These notifications had to be withdrawn on account of public protests by Hazara representatives in the Balochistan Assembly.[96] However, similar instances of discrimination have not been reported in public institutions such as civil hospitals and State Bank of Pakistan, Hazara employees were unofficially asked not to come to work.[97]

There is no significant evidence to suggest that Hazara Shia pilgrims returning from Iran—one of the first countries after China to have seen a severe outbreak of the virus—themselves flouted security protocols and mandatory quarantine at Taftan.[98] It is to be noted that while those who had traveled to Iran for recreation, business, or education were allowed to return home on being screened by thermal guns, Hazara Shia pilgrims were put in poorly kept and unhygienic quarantine camps[99] in the border town of Taftan.[100] The living conditions were poor and there was a severe lack of medical facilities, with no testing or medicines even for people who had begun to show symptoms.[101] Additionally, the conditions were not conducive to isolation and disease prevention, with no running water and lax regulations governing movement, resulting in people entering marketplaces and walking around the town. Hence, the spread of the virus among the Hazara Shia pilgrims was a massive failure on the part of the government, at both the provincial and federal levels.[102] Despite this, it is the community that has been targeted and blamed for the spread of virus, despite being only a small portion of persons that had entered Pakistan from COVID-affected countries.[103]

CONCLUSIONS

The role of Islam within Pakistani political framework and the rights of religious minorities are two issues that have consistently remained preeminent in Pakistan's checkered constitutional framework. In its nearly seventy-four years of history as a sovereign state, Pakistan has continued to suffer from an "ideological schizophrenia."[104] This schizophrenia is reflected on the one hand from extreme religious influences and continued attempts to either enforce "Nizam-e-Mustafa" propagated by the late General Zia-ul-Haq or the currently fashioned ideal of establishing the "State of Medina." On the other hand, Pakistan portrays itself as a state that champions minority rights and fully respects human rights of all its citizens. Indeed, Pakistan criticizes the growth of "Islamophobia" in the Western world and a consistent theme within its domestic and foreign policy is the support for the Kashmiri Muslim minorities of "occupied" Indian Kashmir.

During Zia's time, religious moralities were transposed into Pakistan's legal and constitutional framework, in the form of inter alia Hudood laws, separate electorates, and blasphemy laws, which continue to have serious repercussions and implications upon religious minorities to this day. The situation of religious minorities has not improved since the demise of the Zia regime: if anything, during the current PTI government there are far greater concerns in terms of discrimination and persecution of various minority communities. This study has examined in considerable depth the highly devastating impact of blasphemy laws, the continuing forced conversions and forced marriages of young Christian and Hindu girls and the discrimination and neglect of religious minorities in the key areas of education and employment. Religious minorities have been targeted, harassed, and victimized since the start of the COVID-19 pandemic, with these vulnerable communities facing further ostracization, marginalization, and extreme poverty.

In this milieu of denial of the rights of religious minorities, Pakistani state has also failed to deal with the increasing sectarian strife. The observations made by the Human Rights Commission of Pakistan in this regard are pertinent. The commission notes that

> the federal and provincial governments have had a tendency to blame "enemies of the country" for attempting to "create unrest in Pakistan to achieve their nefarious designs." This is a widely repeated sentiment among Pakistani politicians. However, this approach ignores how sectarianism is also a homegrown problem in Pakistan, with a sort of constitutional support given to narrow Sunni majoritarianism to the exclusion of all other modes of interpreting Islam. It also ignores how the problem of sectarianism requires not merely security interventions, but broader political ones which establish the right of Shias and others like Ahmadis, Hindus, and Christians to be part of Pakistan.[105]

NOTES

1. See, for example, J Rehman, *Weaknesses in the International Protection of Minority Rights* (The Hague: Kluwer Law International) 2000; SS Ali and J Rehman *Indigenous Peoples and Ethnic Minorities of Pakistan* (Routledge: London) 2001; J Rehman, 'Minority Rights and the Constitutional Dilemmas of Pakistan' (2001) 19(4) *Netherlands Quarterly of Human Rights*, 417; J Rehman, 'Nation-Building in an Islamic State: Minority Rights and Self-Determination in the Islamic Republic of

Pakistan' in J Rehman and S Breau (eds.) *Religion, Human Rights and International Law* (The Hague: Martinus Nijhoff Publishers) 2007, 409–439.

2. *Pakistan Population*, Worldometer, https://www.worldometers.info/world-population/pakistan-population/ (last accessed 13 October 2019).

3. *2017 Census of Pakistan*, Wikipedia, https://en.wikipedia.org/wiki/2017_Census_of_Pakistan (last accessed 10 October, 2020).

4. *Population by Religion*, https://www.pbs.gov.pk/sites/default/files/tables/POPULATION%20BY%20RELIGION.pdf (last accessed 10 October, 2020).

5. Ibid.

6. L Collins and D Lapierre, *Freedom at Midnight* (London: Collins) 1975, 102; also see A Jalal, *The Sole Spokesman: Jinnah, The Muslim League and the Demand for Pakistan* (Lahore: Sange-meel Publishers) 1992.

7. Mohammad Ali Jinnah, Address to the First Constituent Assembly, 11 August, 1947.

8. Consisting of the Universal Declaration on Human Rights adopted 10 December 1948; the International Covenant on Civil and Political Rights, adopted 16 December, 1966 and ratified by Pakistan 17 April 2008 and the International Covenant on Economic and Social Rights adopted, 16 December, 1966 and ratified by Pakistan, 23 June 2010.

9. *Convention against Torture and Other Cruel, Inhuman or Degrading Treatment or Punishment,* New York, 10 December 1984 United Nations, *Treaty Series*, vol. 1465, p. 85. (ratified 23 June, 2010).

10. *International Convention on the Elimination of All Forms of Racial Discrimination*, New York, 7 March 1966, United Nations, *Treaty Series*, vol. 660, 195, CERD/C/66/Add.10, para 8. (ratified 21 September, 1996).

11. International Convention on the Elimination of All forms of Discrimination against Women, New York, 18 December 1979, United Nations, *Treaty Series*, vol. 1249, p. 13. (Accession 12 March, 1996).

12. *Convention on the Rights of the Child,* New York, 20 November 1989, United Nations, *Treaty Series*, vol. 1577, p. 3. (ratified 12 November, 1990).

13. *Convention on the Rights of Persons with Disabilities,* New York, 13 December 2006, UN Doc. A/61/488. (Ratified 5 July, 2011).

14. On the subject of 'Islamophobia' and 'defamation of religions' see J Rehman and SE Berry 'Is "Defamation of Religions" Passé? The United Nations, Organisation of Islamic Cooperation, And Islamic State Practices: Lessons from Pakistan' (2012) 44 *George Washington International Law Review* 431.

15. See *Report of the All-Party Parliamentary Group for International Freedom of Religion or Belief and the All-Party Parliamentary Group for the Pakistani Minorities*, September 2019 https://appgfreedomofreligionorbelief.org/media/190918-Full-Report-Religious-Minorities-of-Pakistan-Report-of-a-Parliamentary-Visit.pdf (last accessed 15 November, 2020).

16. See Chapter XV, Pakistan Penal Code (1860) (XLV of 1860) [6 October 1860] https://www.oecd.org/site/adboecdanti-corruptioninitiative/46816797.pdf (last accessed 10 October, 2020).

17. Section 295.

18. Section 295-A.

19. Section 296.

20. Section 297.

21. Section 298.

22. H Esmaeili, I Marboe and J Rehman, *The Rule of Law, Freedom of Expression and Islamic Law* (Oxford: Hart Publishing) 2018, 153.

23. For further analysis see Rehman and Berry (n 14) 457–467.

24. *Muhammed Isamail Qureshi v Pakistan* PLD 1991 FSC 10.

25. Ibid.

26. United States Commission on International Religious Freedom (USCIRF), *USCIRF 2016 Annual Report: Pakistan*, 114 https://www.uscirf.gov/sites/default/files/USCIRF%202016%20Annual%20Report.pdf (last accessed 5 November, 2021).

27. Ibid., 114.

28. International Commission of Jurists, *On Trial: The Implementation of Pakistan's Blasphemy Laws* (Geneva: ICJ) 2015, 34.

29. See Human Rights Commission of Pakistan (HRCP) Report, *State of Human Rights in 2010*, (Lahore: 2011) 55, 134 http://hrcp-web.org/publication/book/annual-report-2011-urdu/ (last accessed 10 October, 2020); *Asia Bibi, Pakistan Blasphemy Case Defendant, Death Sentence Handed Down*, Huffington Post, 25 May 2011 http://www.huffingtonpost.com/2010/11/11/asia-bibi-pakistan-blasph_n_782297.html (last accessed 15 November, 2020); F Hassan, 'Blasphemy in Pakistan', (2012) 28(1) *Peace Magazine*, 19.

30. J Perlez, *Pakistani Sentenced to Death May Get a Pardon*, NY Times, 22 November 2010 http://www.nytimes.com/2010/11/23/world/asia/23pstan.html (last accessed 10 October, 2020); *Christian woman sentenced to death in Pakistan for blasphemy*, The Telegraph, 9 November 2010, http://www.telegraph.co.uk/news/religion/8120142/Christian-woman-sentenced-to-death-in-Pakistan-for-blasphemy.html (last accessed 15 November, 2020); FL Rue, *Petition for Asia Bibi on its way to one million signatures*, 20 January 2012 http://christiannewsbuzz.com/2012/01/petition-for-asia-bibi-for-release-reaches-half-a-million/ (last accessed 15 November, 2020); *Fear for Pakistan's death row Christian woman*, BBC News, 6 December 2010 http://www.bbc.co.uk/news/world-south-asia-11923701 (last accessed 15 November, 2020).

31. *Pakistan Minorities Minister Shahbaz Bhatti shot dead*, BBC News, 2 March 2011, http://www.bbc.co.uk/news/world-south-asia-12617562 (last accessed 15 November, 2020).

32. *Salman Taseer murder: Killer's appeal denied*, BBC News, 7 October 2015, http://www.bbc.co.uk/news/world-asia-34467603 (last accessed 15 November, 2020).

33. *Taseer's Killer Mumtaz Qadri Hanged*, Dawn, 2011, https://www.dawn.com/news/1242637 (last accessed 15 November, 2020).

34. *Mst Asia Bibi v The State* Crl.A. No.39-L of 2015, para 12.

35. See Movement for Solidarity and Peace, *Report on Forced Marriages and Forced Conversions in the Christian Community of Pakistan*, Movement for Solidarity

and Peace, 2014, 2 http://d3n8a8pro7vhmx.cloudfront.net/msp/pages/162/attachments/original/1396724215/MSP_Report_-_Forced_Marriages_and_Conversions_of_Christian_Women_in_Pakistan.pdf?1396724215 (last accessed 14 October, 2020).

36. Commonwealth Initiative for Freedom of Religion or Belief, Forced Conversion and *Forced Marriages in Sindh, Pakistan*, CIFORB, The University of Birmingham, 2018, 9–10 https://www.birmingham.ac.uk/documents/college-artslaw/ptr/ciforb/forced-conversions-and-forced-marriages-in-sindh.pdf (last accessed 15 November, 2020)

37. Ibid.

38. Urdu word pronounced as *harees*, meaning landless bonded labor.

39. Z Shaukat, *Faces of discrimination*, The News on Sunday, 5 January 2020 https://www.thenews.com.pk/tns/detail/592949-faces-of-discrimination (last accessed 25 May, 2020).

40. *Pakistan, when Christians die for a glass of water*, La Stampa, 18 September 2017 https://www.lastampa.it/vatican-insider/en/2017/09/18/news/pakistan-when-christians-die-for-a-glass-of-water-1.34421819?refresh_ce (last accessed 1 November, 2020).

41. *Christians and Other Minorities in Pakistan Denied COVID-19 Aid*, Persecution.org, 15 May 2020 https://www.persecution.org/2020/05/15/christians-minorities-pakistan-denied-covid-19-aid/ (last accessed 30 May, 2020).

42. *COVID-19: Hindus denied food supplies in Pakistan's Karachi*, Business Standard, 30 March, 2020 https://www.business-standard.com/article/news-ani/covid-19-hindus-denied-food-supplies-in-pakistan-s-karachi-120033000041_1.html (last accessed 23 April 2020); S Khokhar, *Coronavirus: Karachi NGO denies food to poor Hindus and Christians*, AsiaNews, 30 March 2020 http://asianews.it/news-en/Coronavirus:-Karachi-NGO-denies-food-to-poor-Hindus-and-Christians-49699.html (last accessed 23 April, 2020).

43. Ibid.

44. Hindus denied food supplies (n 42); *Discrimination amid pandemic, Pakistan refuses to give food to Hindus as Covid-19 rages*, ANI, 1 April 2020 https://www.aninews.in/news/world/asia/discrimination-amid-pandemic-pakistan-refuses-to-give-food-to-hindus-as-covid-19-rages20200401123439/ (last accessed 23 April, 2020).

45. *Pakistan: Christians denied aid during Covid-19 crisis*, Church in Chains, 8 April 2020 https://www.churchinchains.ie/news-by-country/south-asia/pakistan/pakistan-christians-and-other-minorities-denied-aid-during-covid-19-crisis/ (last accessed 23 April, 2020); *COVID-19: Pak minorities face discrimination at the hands of authorities*, WION, 8 April 2020 https://www.wionews.com/south-asia/covid-19-pak-minorities-face-discrimination-at-the-hands-of-authorities-291369 (last accessed 23 April, 2020); *Over 100 Christian Families Denied Food Aid Amid COVID-19 Crisis in Pakistan*, Persecution.org, 7 April 2020 https://www.persecution.org/2020/04/07/100-christian-families-denied-food-aid-amid-covid-19-crisis-pakistan (last accessed 23 April, 2020).

46. *USCIRF Troubled by Denial of Food Aid to Pakistani Hindus and Christians*, USCIRF, 13 April 2020 https://www.uscirf.gov/news-room/press-releases-statements/

uscirf-troubled-denial-food-aid-pakistani-hindus-and-christians (last accessed 23 April, 2020).

47. *World Directory of Minorities and Indigenous Peoples - Pakistan: Shi'a and Hazaras'*, Minority Rights Group International, June 2018 https://www.refworld.org/docid/5ba0af627.html (last accessed 29 October, 2020); The Oxford Dictionary of Islam, *Pakistan, Islam in*, Oxford Centre for Islamic Studies, http://www.oxfordislamicstudies.com/article/opr/t125/e1809?_hi=1&_pos=1 (last accessed 29 October, 2020).

48. S Pruitt, *Islam's Sunni-Shia Divide, Explained*, History, 31 July 2019 https://www.history.com/news/sunni-shia-divide-islam-muslim (last accessed 29 October 2020).

49. AK Behuria, 'Sunni-Shia Relations in Pakistan: The Widening Divide', (2004) 28(1) *Strategic Analysis,* 179.

50. E Murphy, *Islam and Sectarian Violence in Pakistan: The Terror Within* (New York: Routledge), 2019, Ch. 5–6.

51. Ibid.

52. *The State of Sectarianism in Pakistan: Asia Report N°95*, International Crisis Group, 8 April, 2005, 10 https://www.crisisgroup.org/asia/south-asia/pakistan/state-sectarianism-pakistan (last accessed 23 November, 2020).

53. F Grare 'The Evolution of Sectarian Conflicts in Pakistan and the Ever-Changing Face of Islamic Violence', (2007) 30(1) *South Asia: Journal of South Asian Studies*, 127–143, 128.

54. Ibid.

55. M Ahmar, 'Sectarian Conflicts in Pakistan', (2008) 9(1) *Pakistan Vision* 1-19, 5.

56. Grare (n 53), 134.

57. Ibid.

58. International Crisis Group (n 52), 11.

59. Murphy (n 50).

60. Grare (n 53), 128–129.

61. Ibid.

62. Ibid., 131–132.

63. Ibid.

64. Ibid.

65. Ibid.

66. Ibid., 134–136.

67. Ibid.

68. CC Fair, 'Explaining Support for Sectarian Terrorism in Pakistan: Piety, Maslak and Sharia', (2015) 6(4) *Religions*, 1137–1167, 1139.

69. S Karmani, *The story of Pakistan's "disappeared" Shias*, BBC News, 31 May 2018 https://www.bbc.co.uk/news/world-asia-44280552 (last accessed 15 November, 2020).

70. F Mihlar, *Everything has shattered'—rising levels of violence against Shi'a in Pakistan*, Briefing, Minority Rights Group International, 2014 https://www.ecoi.

net/en/file/local/1192801/1788_1403517042_pakistan-briefing-june-2014.pdf (last accessed 15 November, 2020).

71. Ibid.

72. *Shias killed in Pakistan since 2001*, South Asia Terrorism Portal https://www.satp.org/satporgtp/countries/pakistan/database/Shias_killed_Pakistan.htm (last accessed 15 November, 2020).

73. See UK Home Office, *Country Policy and Information Note Pakistan: Hazaras*, November 2019, 7 https://www.ecoi.net/en/file/local/2020583/Pakistan_-_Hazaras_-_CPIN_-_v2.1__November_2019_.odt (last accessed 23 November, 2020); *US Commission on International Religious Freedom (USCIRF)*, USCIRF 2019 Annual Report: Pakistan https://www.uscirf.gov/sites/default/files/2019USCIRFAnnualReport.pdf (last accessed 23 November, 2020).

74. *Human Rights Commission of Pakistan, State of Human Rights in 2019*, 2020, 176-177 http://hrcp-web.org/hrcpweb/wp-content/uploads/2020/04/REPORT_State-of-Human-Rights-in-2019-20190503.pdf (last accessed 30 October, 2020); see also *Timeline: Hazara killings in Balochistan*, Dawn, 11 January 2013 https://www.dawn.com/news/777973/timeline-hazara-killings-in-balochistan (last accessed October 30, 2020) (Timeline of attacks targeting the Hazara Shi'a community between 2001 and February 2013).

75. Human Rights Commission of Pakistan (n 74), 176–177.

76. Ibid.

77. *Pakistan: Arrest, prosecute sectarian killers*, Human Rights, 13 May 2015 https://www.hrw.org/news/2015/05/13/pakistan-arrest-prosecute-sectarian-killers (last accessed 30 October, 2020).

78. KK Shahid, *What Role Does the State Play in Pakistan's Anti-Shia Hysteria?*, The Diplomat, 17 September 2020 https://thediplomat.com/2020/09/what-role-does-the-state-play-in-pakistans-anti-shia-hysteria/ (last accessed 30 October, 2020); US Commission on International Religious Freedom (USCIRF), *USCIRF 2013 Annual Report: Pakistan*, 4 https://www.uscirf.gov/sites/default/files/resources/Pakistan%20 2013(1).pdf (last accessed 30 October, 2020).

79. Shahid (n 78).

80. *Pakistan: Rampant Killings of Shia by Extremists Disarm, Prosecute Militants, Protect Hazara Community*, Human Rights Watch, 29 June 2014 Watch https://www.hrw.org/news/2014/06/29/pakistan-rampant-killings-shia-extremists (last accessed 30 October, 2020).

81. *USCIRF 2013 Annual Report: Pakistan* (n 78), 5.

82. Ibid.

83. Mihlar (n 70).

84. M Ishaq, *Pakistan Sunni militant chief killed by police*, BBC News, 29 July 2015 https://www.bbc.com/news/world-asia-33699133 (last accessed 30 October, 2020).

85. A Tripathi, 'Pakistan: Sectarian targets', (2013) 12(4) *South Asia Intelligence Review Weekly Assessments & Briefings*; B Shah, *The trouble convicting LeJ's Malik Ishaq*, Foreign Policy, 19 August 2014 https://foreignpolicy.com/2014/08/19/

the-trouble-convicting-lejs-malik-ishaq/ (last accessed 30 October, 2020); *USCIRF 2013 Annual Report: Pakistan* (n 78), 5.

86. Shahid (n 78).

87. Ibid.

88. SM Baloch and H Petersen, *Pakistani Shias live in terror as sectarian violence increases*, The Guardian, 21 October 2020 https://www.theguardian.com/world/2020/oct/21/pakistani-shias-live-in-terror-as-sectarian-violence-increases (last accessed 30 October, 2020)

89. JA Mirza, *COVID-19 fans religious discrimination in Pakistan*, The Diplomat, 28 April 2020 https://thediplomat.com/2020/04/covid-19-fans-religious-discrimination-in-pakistan/ (last accessed 30 October, 2020)

90. Ibid.

91. Ibid.

92. *Anti-Shia bigotry in times of coronavirus*, Naya Daur, 19 March 2020 https://nayadaur.tv/2020/03/anti-shia-bigotry-in-times-of-coronavirus/ (last accessed 30 October, 2020)

93. *USCIRF troubled with targeting of Hazara Shi'a in Pakistan amid coronavirus Lockdown*, USCIRF, 31 March, 2020 https://www.uscirf.gov/news-room/press-releases-statements/uscirf-troubled-targeting-hazara-shi-in-pakistan-amid (last accessed 23 April, 2020).

94. *Inspector General of Police, Balochistan*, Quetta, 'Order', 12 March 2020 https://www.bolaq.org/wp-content/uploads/2020/03/Police-notification.jpg (last accessed 23 April, 2020).

95. Water and Sanitation Authority, Quetta, 'Order', 13 March 2020 https://www.bolaq.org/wp-content/uploads/2020/03/WASA-notification.jpg (last accessed 23 April, 2020).

96. HR Changezi, *Corona virus, Pakistan, and the deep-seated racial biases*, Bolaq, 30 March 2020 https://www.bolaq.org/2020/03/corona-virus-pakistan-and-the-deep-seated-racial-biases/ (last accessed 30 October, 2020).

97. Mirza (n 89).

98. Although it is suggested by local authorities that some ran away and could not be traced. See A Amir, *Who is responsible for the disaster in Taftan?*, The Friday Times, 20 March 2020 https://www.thefridaytimes.com/who-is-responsible-for-the-disaster-in-taftan/ (last accessed 23 April, 2020).

99. H Petersen and SM Baloch, *Pakistan coronavirus camp: No facilities, no humanity*, The Guardian, 19 March 2020 https://www.theguardian.com/world/2020/mar/19/pakistan-coronavirus-camp-no-facilities-no-humanity (last accessed 23 April, 2020).

100. Amir (n 98).

101. Peterson and Baloch (n 99).

102. Amir (n 98).

103. JA Mirza, *Pakistan's Hazara Shia minority blamed for spread of Covid-19*, Institute of Development Studies, 17 April 2020 https://www.ids.ac.uk/opinions/

pakistans-hazara-shia-minority-blamed-for-spread-of-covid-19/ (last accessed 23 April, 2020)

104. O Noman, *Pakistan: A Political and Economic History since 1947* (London: Kegan Paul International, London), 1990, 3.

105. Human Rights Commission of Pakistan (n 74), 176.

Chapter 3

Poverty, Bonded Labor, and Unaccountable Supply Chains

The Case of Brick Kiln Workers in Pakistan

Maleeha Sattar and Adnan Sattar

This stained light, this night-bitten dawn
This is not the dawn we yearned for.
This is not the dawn . . .

—Faiz Ahmed Faiz[1]

Bonded labor or debt bondage, where a person pledges himself—often with the entire family—to work against an advance payment (*peshgi* in Urdu), has been described as one of the most widespread forms of modern slavery.[2] Particularly prevalent in India, Pakistan, and Nepal, the practice is historically rooted in feudal agrarian relations and the caste system. Despite national legislation and Pakistan's international human rights commitments, bonded labor continues to pervade agriculture and is also found in informal sectors of the economy, most notably, brick making.[3] The phenomenon is usually understood narrowly as a problem of unscrupulous employment practices, involving helpless workers and exploitative employers. Conversations about bonded labor mostly involve the same story and repeat the same assumptions. Such portrayals miss out on some crucial aspects of the problem. This chapter attempts to widen the debate by illustrating how several actors, including private construction companies, public agencies and government departments, and ordinary citizens are complicit in sustaining the practice by purchasing bricks produced under debt bondage and forced labor. Such reframing of the problem is also called for because the legal prohibition of bonded labor and litigation have not yielded lasting results.

We conceptualize bonded labor as a market and supply chain failure in terms of a lack of compliance with domestic and international normative standards and socially desirable outcomes. Various stages are mapped out in brick-making supply chain, which are characterized by a lack of government regulation, informality, and the use of intermediaries and subcontracting. We argue that effectively addressing bonded labor requires more robust preventative measures as well as clearing up the brick-making supply chain through amendments in public procurement law, labeling of bricks as being compliant with human rights standards, and consumer mobilization for ethical purchasing. In nudging the debate toward a new direction, the chapter draws insights from other contexts, such as the UK's Modern Slavery Act, 2015, and the Rugmark Foundation's pioneering work in licensing and labeling child-labor-free carpets.

I. INTRODUCTION

It is estimated that up to 4.5 million people work on brick kilns across Pakistan, majority of whom are trapped in debts.[4] The presence of *peshgi* or the initial loan of money itself does not necessarily amount to a relationship of debt bondage.[5] Majority of brick kiln workers earn meager income on piece rate (number of bricks produced). The nature and length of services that the workers are required to render to the employer remain ill-defined. Being illiterate, they may also incur deductions from their already meager income due to false accounting. These factors combined with the absence of a social safety net create a situation where the repayment of *peshgi* remains forever out of the worker's reach. Worse still, brick kiln workers are driven to accrue additional debts to finance sickness and injury and life events such as weddings and funerals. As a result, they are trapped in a vicious cycle of indebtedness and beholden to their "employers." The poverty which the brick kiln workers experience can be seen as a quintessential state of "unfreedom" in the sense described by Amartya Sen.[6] The condition of brick kiln workers is also marked by deprivations of "elementary capabilities" needed for survival and for escaping poverty.[7]

Bonded labor on brick kilns (*bhattas*) has a significant gender dimension to it. As loans are negotiated between the male head of the family and the middleman (*jamadar*) recruiting workers on behalf of the employer, women's labor is rendered invisible although they work alongside men in brick fields, especially in Sindh and Punjab Provinces.[8] Women also bear the burden of household chores and looking after sick children and male members of the family. Since majority of workers migrate from villages to urban or semi-urban areas where brick kilns are located, women have the additional burden of adjusting to unfamiliar and sometimes hostile surroundings.[9] The kind of privations these women suffer on daily basis are hard to capture on multidimensional accounts of poverty let alone the traditional poverty lines measured by headcount ratio or based on per capita income or consumption.[10] Women's poverty, it needs to be recognized, is more than an economic status. It is also based on patriarchal power relationships between men and women.[11] Children, both boys and girls, sometimes as young as 10 or 11, help out parents as they make unbaked bricks, a category of workers known as *patheras*. Older male children are known to take up more strenuous tasks of stacking and unloading the bricks.

In 1992, following a Supreme Court ruling in a pioneering public interest litigation case, Pakistan's Parliament adopted the Bonded Labour System (Abolition) Act, prohibiting the practice of employing bonded labor.[12] In theory, every bonded laborer stood freed and discharged from any obligation to pay debts. The Act made forcing anyone to work in bondage a crime punishable with imprisonment for a term extending up to five years. In the 1990s, human rights groups, particularly the Bonded Labour Liberation Front and the Human Rights Commission of Pakistan, successfully filed petitions in courts releasing hundreds of workers from bondage. However, the victory turned out to be short-lived. Many workers returned to brick kilns as they could not find an alternative source of income. To freed workers, their bonded status had at least offered an insurance of sorts "to the effect that they and their children would be considerably less likely to die of hunger in a situation of crisis."[13] Further, a number of brick kiln owners simply prevented laborers from escaping in the first place by using force and bribing police officials who could report on them. In following years, many cases of bonded labor involving cruel and degrading conditions came to light. However, not a single employer was convicted.[14] In 2017—a quarter of a century after bonded labor was declared unconstitutional by the Supreme Court—the UN Committee on Economic, Social and Cultural Rights expressed concern about the shortfalls in the implementation of the Bonded Labour System (Abolition) Act, 1992, in its concluding observations on Pakistan's initial report on the implementation of the International Covenant on Economic, Social and Cultural Rights (ICESCR). Referring to Article 7 of the ICESR, which enshrines the "right of everyone to the enjoyment of just and favourable conditions of work," the committee lamented that

> the practice of bonded labour continues to exist, particularly in the brick kiln and agriculture sectors; that perpetrators of violations of the Act are rarely punished because few judges in the lower courts are aware of the Act and because of the complicity of the police; and that the lack of other means of living for workers in such situations push them back into a cycle of debt bondage.[15]

In 1995, the government had notified the Bonded Labour Abolition Rules, instructing provincial governments to carry out inspections of places where bonded laborers were suspected to be and to set up vigilance committees in every district to identify, free, and rehabilitate bonded laborers.[16] In 2001, the government adopted a "National Policy and Plan of Action for the Abolition of Bonded Labour and the Rehabilitation of Freed Bonded Labourers."[17] The plan earmarked an amount of 100 million rupees to provide relief packages and vocational training to freed workers and to raise awareness on bonded labor. The Plan of Action included training of labor inspectors and police officials and setting up of complaint cells at the district and provincial levels.[18] However, these laudable plans never saw the light of the day.[19]

Against the backdrop of the 18th constitutional amendment, devolving significant legislative powers to provinces, provincial assemblies have, in recent years, enacted new laws prohibiting bonded labor.[20] However, in substantive terms, the provincial laws simply reproduce the provisions of the 1992 Bonded Labour Abolition Act. In 2016, the province of Punjab adopted the Prohibition of Child Labour at Brick-Kilns Act 2016, which diverges from the 1992 Act in that it seeks to regulate the system of advance payments instead of outlawing it altogether. The law prohibits the employment of children under the age of 14 at brick kilns while setting out the conditions of employment for other workers, including 15- to 18-year-olds.[21] Taking a more pragmatic approach toward the issue of advance payments, the law obligates the employer to specify the amount of presage in the employment contract.[22] It lays down 50,000 rupees as the maximum amount of *peshgi* which a brick kiln owner can offer to a worker.[23] The same year, the Punjab government launched an "Elimination of Child and Bonded Labour Project" to be implemented in phases across thirty districts of the province. The project involves provision of nonformal education and vocational training to the children of brick kiln workers, and helping the worker acquire national identity and social security cards. To what extent the project achieves the stated aim of "breaking the cycle of poverty" and "empowering" the bonded workforce in the brick-making industry is yet to be seen. Further, the project design is short on synergies with relevant areas of public policy and service delivery, such as poverty alleviation and health care.

NGO efforts on the ground have concentrated on providing legal aid to bonded laborers, running nonformal education centers, and enrolling children in mainstream schools. Action Aid, Society for the Protection of the Rights of the Child (SPAARC), Trocaire and other organizations have done commendable work activating and supporting the work of the District Vigilance Committees (DVCs). However, experience to date suggests that such interventions rarely survive beyond the project duration. The DVCs go dormant as soon as external funding dries up. Children who enroll in schools following NGO campaigning often drop out when projects are wound up. Critics have also taken issue with the composition of the DVCs as they include people "who benefit from debt bondage," namely brick kiln owners.[24] One innovative project launched by the American Centre for International Labour Solidarity (Solidarity Centre) sought to introduce "decent work" in brick kilns through the registration of bonded laborers with official social security and old age benefits schemes and certification of "model brick kilns" as a prequalification for procurement of bricks by public sector agencies and construction companies. The latter component of the project never got off the ground as "implementing partners" were heavily invested in the time-consuming task of negotiating for fair wages and improved working conditions with kiln owners.[25]

Without wishing to undermine well-meaning NGO initiatives, we take the view that past efforts have bypassed some crucial dimensions and dynamics of bonded labor in Pakistan's brick-making industry. It is argued that a lasting change in terms of reducing the incidence of bonded labor warrants an understanding of the phenomenon as embedded within local political economy and the market. In particular, we need to focus attention toward monitoring and regulating the supply or product chain of brick making. Some observers insist that Pakistan already has the requisite laws to combat bonded and child labor. On the contrary, we would like to suggest that there is a glaring blind spot in the legal and policy framework. Worryingly, the government itself is complicit in sustaining bonded labor on brick kilns. The bricks turned out under the system of debt bondage are purchased and used not only for private construction but for public infrastructure development as well. In other words, the state takes away from one hand what it gives from the other in the form of the legal prohibition of bonded labor. Significantly, procurement law at the federal and provincial levels in Pakistan is silent on the need for clearing up bonded, forced or child labor from the supply chain of brick making—or any industry for that matter. Private builders or public departments are under no specific legal obligation to apply human rights, social or environmental criteria in supplier evaluation.

As mentioned earlier, the question of bonded labor has traditionally been framed as a dyadic conflict between hapless workers and unscrupulous employers. That amounts to a simplistic and reductionist reading of the problem. In reality, government agencies, private architects and builders, as well as ordinary citizens are equally complicit when they purchase the unethically produced bricks. It is time to acknowledge this uncomfortable truth.

The political economy and supply chain analysis presented in this chapter seeks to map out significant actors and drivers at various stages of brick-making process from the procurement of raw material and recruitment of workers to the wage system to the sale of the final product in the retail market.

Taking a cue from innovative projects in other sectors globally, we build a case for shifting the focus toward mobilizing consumers of bricks and putting in place a policy framework for ethical procurement as a means of reducing the incidence of bonded and child labor in brick-making industry.

II. DEFINING BONDED LABOR

The term "bonded labor" is often used interchangeably with "debt bondage."[26] The 1956 UN Supplementary Convention on Slavery, the Slave Trade and Institutions and Practices defines "debt bondage" as "the status or condition arising from a pledge by a debtor of his personal services or of those of a person under his control as security for a debt, if the value of those services as reasonably assessed is not applied towards the liquidation of the debt or the length and nature of those services are not respectively limited and defined."[27] Article 7(b) of the Supplementary Convention characterizes debt bondage as a "servile status" and obligates state parties to implement national provisions to abolish it. Implicit in this definition is the recognition that not all work rendered against a loan of money is bonded labor. However, when such work or service is incommensurate with advance payment, or where there is no reasonable prospect of the debt being repaid, it turns into bonded labor or debt bondage.

Debt bondage as practiced in Pakistan's brick-making industry straddles two other normative and legal concepts, namely slavery and forced labor. The 1926 *Convention to Suppress the Slave Trade and Slavery*, also known as the *Slavery Convention*, defines slavery as "the status or condition of a person over whom any or all of the powers attaching to the right of ownership are exercised."[28] Bonded labor within Pakistan's brick-making industry can be characterized as slavery within the terms of the *Slavery Convention* in that brick kiln owners are known to sell and exchange workers. Sometimes, an existing owner will transfer workers to another kiln in exchange for the payment of the "debt" on behalf of workers by another owner. The workers will then be obliged to supply labor at the new kiln for an indefinite period of time. Occasionally, based on old kinship ties or the need for on-farm labor, an agricultural landowner may give refuge to brick kiln workers, becoming a guarantor for loan repayment.[29] Beyond the legal definition, there are other core characteristics of slavery which we might want to look at before categorizing a labor arrangement as a form of slavery. As Kevin Bales and others have suggested, focusing on "economic exploitation" and the "maintenance of violent control" helps avoid "the notion that state-sanctioned or legal slavery is 'true slavery.' "[30] On this approach, when considering a potential case of modern slavery, it is important to ask the following questions: "Is this person paid nothing beyond subsistence?," and "can this person walk away, or are they under violent control?"[31] While brick kiln workers are not an undifferentiated mass, many of them are paid subsistence wages. Second, bonded laborers do not have an option to simply walk away from an exploitative situation. At best, they can hope to have their debts transferred to another owner or a landlord.

The question of violent control brings us to the classification of debt bondage as a form of compulsory or forced labor, known locally as *baigar*. The 1930 ILO *Convention concerning Forced or Compulsory Labour* (ILO Convention No. 29) defines it as "all work or service which is exacted from any person under the menace of any penalty and for which the said person has not offered himself voluntarily."[32] As regard the first element of the definition, it has to be noted that workers on most, if not all, brick kilns live under surveillance. Owners invariably employ the services of a watchman (*chowkidar*) who is tasked to make sure that workers do not attempt to escape. The fact that most brick kilns workers live on site works to the advantage of the owner. The *jamadar* or the recruiter is under an obligation to track down and return to the owner any worker who runs away. According to the ILO, "even when no violence has occurred at their own kilns, workers were aware of incidents at other kilns" where attempts to escape were met with a penalty in the form of violence by the owner or his agents.[33] There have been cases where police actually helped brick kiln operators track down runaway workers and even implicate them under false charges.[34] That provides a poignant illustration of how Pakistan's criminal justice system works to the advantage of the powerful and discriminates against the socioeconomically disadvantaged and already vulnerable individuals.[35] With regard to the second element of the definition, that is, absence of voluntariness, on surface, brick kiln workers pledge their services against a debt willingly. However, it is questionable whether contracts made under conditions of extreme hardship, and involving unfair wage arrangements, can be characterized as "voluntary." Debt bondage in brick making lends itself to be seen as forced labor due to poor working conditions and the absence of clearly defined contractual terms. That is more so the case when it comes to women since they do not enter into a contract with the employer at all. Rather, it is male brick makers who commit members of their families, including women, to work against a loan of money.

The international prohibition of debt bondage, slavery and forced labor is echoed in Article 11 of the Constitution of Pakistan.[36] The same article forbids the employment of "a child below the age of fourteen years" in "any factory or mine or any other hazardous employment."[37] These prohibitions represent one side of the normative framework needed to guide action on the ground. The other side includes positive obligations embodied in domestic and international human rights guarantees. In setting up the normative criteria for "cleaning up" the brick-making supply chain, reference can be made to international labor standards identified as being core in the 1998 ILO Declaration on Fundamental Principles and Rights at Work.[38] They are freedom of association and the effective recognition of the right to collective bargaining; the elimination of all forms of forced or compulsory labor; the effective elimination of child labor; and the elimination of discrimination in respect of employment and occupation.[39]

Overlapping the "core" international labor standards is the concept of "decent work" advanced by the ILO in 1999. "Decent work" is conceptualized as involving four components: employment, social protection, workers' rights, and social dialogue. Employment here covers work of all kinds and applies not just to workers in the formal economy but also to unregulated wage workers. It also refers to adequate opportunities for work, remuneration and safety at work and healthy working conditions. Social protection entails adequate support in times of injury and sickness and old age. The two other components emphasize the social relations of workers: the fundamental rights of workers (freedom of association, nondiscrimination at work, and the absence of forced labor and child labor); and social dialogue, in which workers exercise their right to present their views, defend their interests and engage in discussions to negotiate work-related matters with employers and authorities. Combining the two mutually reinforcing concepts, that is, "decent work" and "core labor standards," we would get the following set of criteria for monitoring and regulating the brick-making supply chain:

i) Employment: opportunities for work, remuneration and safety at work and healthy working conditions;
ii) Social protection: social security and old age benefits or pension cover;
iii) Freedom of association and social dialogue: right to form and join unions, right to collective bargaining and to negotiate with authorities and employers; and
iv) Absence of forced labor, bonded labor, and child labor.

III. THE BRICK-MAKING SUPPLY CHAIN

A supply chain or a commodity chain outlines the sequence of activities and processes required to bring a product from its raw state to the finished goods sold to the consumer. Adapted from Jennifer Hurley and Doug Miller's analysis of the global garment industry, the supply chain analysis presented here maps out various tasks and actors involved in Pakistan's brick-making industry.[40] Brick making is not an export-oriented industry. Nonetheless, just like the garment industry, it involves raw material sourcing, intermediary roles, manufacturing, and retail. A simplified supply chain of bricks in Pakistan (depicted in figure 3.1) is characterized by informality and lack of governmental regulation, cost saving, and the use of intermediaries, and subcontracting at every stage. Consequently, there are entry points for improved governance at various stages or tiers with a view to eliminating bonded labor and advancing human rights.

Land Acquisition and Recruitment of Workers

The lowest tier in the brick-making supply chain involves the acquisition of land, construction of a labor colony (comprising small mud houses) and a

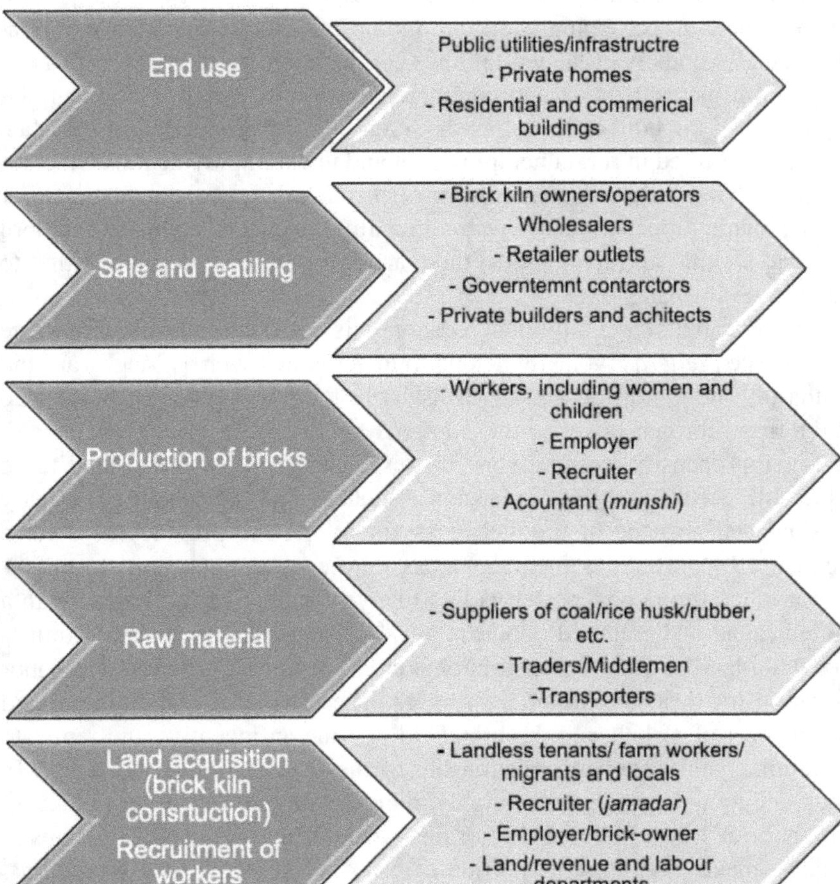

Figure 3.1. Supply Chain of Bricks in Pakistan. *Figure created by authors based on literature review and key informant interviews in Sindh and Punjab Province.*

brick kiln, and the recruitment of workers. The brick kiln operators usually obtain land (about 10 acres in size) on a lease from local land owners for a period extending from two years to up to ten years.[41] Operators seldom register the kilns as industrial units, bypassing tax net and labor and environmental regulation. Government officials from land and revenue departments look the other way as land owners and operators are politically well-connected and have the resources to buy off local and provincial administration. Over the years, some brick kiln owners have accumulated enough wealth to own multiple kilns in the same area.[42]

The recruitment of workers is carried out by a middleman or subcontractor known as a *jamadar*. Majority of workers who work on the brick field, preparing and molding unbacked bricks *(patheras)*, come from the ranks of landless peasants or evicted tenants. That is especially the case in Punjab and Sindh where sharecropping is still common in agriculture, and where relatively small numbers of landed families continue to own large tracts of land. While farm mechanization and commercialization of agriculture has gradually loosened the hold of feudal mode of agricultural production in Pakistan, it has also resulted in rural unemployment and underemployment. As in colonial times, the landless in contemporary Pakistan are a "social residue."[43] For evicted sharecroppers, who were traditionally dependent upon the landlord for basic welfare and livelihoods, there are few options except migrating to urban or peri-urban areas.[44]

The brick-making recruitment economy is also intertwined with caste system. The *patheras* typically belong to lower castes such as Meghwars and Kohlis in Sindh and Sheikhs and Musalis in Punjab. Typical of those who suffer from chronic poverty, the *patheras* are likely to have "low assets" and have propensity to engage in "distress selling."[45] They also tend to be vulnerable across multiple dimensions, such as lack of schooling, quality housing, and absence of productive assets. While the presence of diverse occupation opportunities in urban areas may enable many poor to graduate out of "extreme poverty," it is less likely to happen in rural areas with a limited range of livelihood opportunities.[46] Landlessness, social discrimination and a lack of access to institutional credit serve as push factors in labor migration for these classic brick workers. The offer of a cash advance and the prospect of a shelter at the brickfield provide an incentive and replicate the familiar master-servant relationship of the feudal political economy. In Sindh and Punjab, *patheras* invariably migrate with entire families to take up work at brick kilns. Religious minorities—Hindus in Sindh and Christians in Punjab—make up a sizeable portion of brick workers, especially *patheras*. The *jamadar* usually recruits people from his own clan or *baradari*. While this arrangement allows him to manage the workforce efficiently and to tract down runaway workforce, it does not offer a guarantee that the workers will be treated fairly. The recruiter's loyalty lies primarily with the brick-kiln operator whom he depends for his own livelihood.

Another category of workers, *jalaiwalas*, that is, those who undertake the hazardous task of firing the kiln and baking bricks, are also typically migrants. Other workers, namely *kharkars* (who transport unbaked bricks to the kiln from the brickfield) *bharaiwalas* (who load and stack up bricks in the kiln), and *nikasiwalas* (who unload baked bricks) are recruited locally. All workers obtain some amount of loan at the time of recruitment although the mode of remuneration differs by the category of workers (more on this shortly). It is crucial to note that the workers do not receive a written contract upon recruitment. Specific details of the nature of work and the length of services remain undefined. Additionally, although the middlemen or *jamadars* play a vital role in brick-making economy, they operate beyond the pale of labor law or any sort of government regulation. A recruiter does not need a license to operate or to complete any paperwork before hiring workers. The system also allows kiln operators to evade liability for debt bondage by outsourcing the recruitment process to the middlemen.

Raw Material Sourcing

In addition to labor and land, other inputs that need to be mobilized for brick making are coal, clay, and rice and maize husk for co-combustion with coal. To reduce the price of inputs, some brick operators add in hazardous substances such as discarded rubber and plastic. Clay is usually dug out from the brickfield. Land-lease agreements specify the depth to which kiln operators can dig up the land. That is meant to ensure that the value of the land does not depreciate over time due to excessive digging and extraction. Apart from that internal arrangement between the land owner and the brick kiln operator, there is no evidence of environmental standards such as the "polluter pays principle" embodied in the Pakistan Environmental Protection Act, 1997, being applied to brick-making industry. The law empowers Environmental Protection Agencies (EPAs) to order the closure of or impose administrative penalties on industries emitting pollution in excess to National Environmental Quality Standards.[47] There are no documented cases of the provincial EPAs taking action against brick kiln operators.

The main suppliers of coal are mines situated in Sindh, Balochistan, and parts of Northern Punjab, especially district Chakwal. Brick operators do not purchase coal directly from coal mines. The supply chain involves a number of actors such as authorized sellers or agents, resellers and transporters. There are profit margins for every actor along the supply chain. Brick kiln operators sometime cite soaring prices of coal as the reason why they are not able to pay decent wages to workers. As part of the Solidarity-Centre-supported program referred to earlier, SPAARC (one of the "implementing partners") attempted to incentivize brick kiln owners in Hyderabad by helping them obtain coal at almost 40 percent less than the market rate. That was achieved by undercutting a long chain of middlemen and obtaining coal directly from an authorized agent.[48] However, such initiatives are difficult to sustain and replicate in the absence of state intervention in the market as a means of ensuring compliance with legal norms and standards. There is also a counter-narrative to brick kiln operators' assertion that unaffordable prices of coal compel them to keep wages low. Owners in Multan, for example, maintain that they procure coal originating in Sindh and Balochistan at prices as high as 4,000 to 4,500 per ton. However, activists on the ground report that coal for brick kilns in Multan comes from Chakwal at far lower rates. In some cases, coal is supplied by truckers who essentially transport industrial or agricultural produce from Punjab to Balochistan and bring along coal on their way back to recover fuel charges.[49]

More thorough research is required on the possibility of phasing out coal as an input in brick kilns and replacing it with biomass and other forms of renewable energy. Most owners are of the view that where biomass such as rice or maize chaff and cow dung is used, the quality of the finished product is nowhere as good as that of coal-based bricks. Some activists on the ground would challenge that assertion, citing the fact that the key to quality is maintaining a certain level of temperature in chimneys where bricks are fired rather than the input used per se.[50] In recent years, some brick kilns have adopted what is known as zigzag technology, which uses smaller quantities of coal and burns them more efficiently. The technology, however, falls short of making a switch to renewables. While it may increase productivity from the perspective of brick kiln owners, the impact on workers' health and the environment is questionable.

Production of Bricks

The production process involves several stages from digging of clay to mixing it with water, to molding mud bricks, transporting sun-dried bricks to the kiln, stacking them inside the kiln, firing the kiln, taking the prepared bricks out, and loading them for transportation. Depending on the size of the kiln and the number of workers, a kiln will produce anywhere between 400,000 to a million bricks in a *chakkar* or a cycle spanning no more than 40 to 60 days.[51] *Patheras*, almost exclusively migrants, work on the first stage of the production, preparing and molding mud bricks from early morning to late evening Saturday through Wednesday. Women and children help out in the process. Dried bricks are transported on donkey carts by locally hired *kharkars*. Inside the kiln, working under the supervision of a *mistri* or a supervisor, *baharaiwalas* stack up the bricks for baking. The bricks are covered in baked brick dust and fired inside the kiln typically by four to five male *jalaiwals*, who are mostly migrants. In about a week's time, baked bricks are removed, sorted for quality, and stacked up by both locally hired *nikasiwalas* and *patheras.* Male children, especially adolescents, are frequently involved in *bharai* (stacking bricks in the kiln) and *nikasi* (unloading baked bricks).

Jalaiwalas are paid a monthly salary. The other categories of workers are employed on piece rate. The actual wages paid are substantially less than the officially notified rate. An amount is subtracted on account of debt repayment and faulty bricks. Each brick kiln has an accountant (*munshi)*, who makes the deductions and keeps an account of wages paid. Being indebted and illiterate, most workers are not in a position to argue with the *munshi* on the question of wages. The inability to read the account books leaves workers vulnerable to manipulation.[52] The wage system based on *peshgi* and piece rate serves a dual purpose for the kiln operator. First, it allows the operator to keep a control over the workers' output. Despite harsh conditions, workers are obliged to produce a maximum number of bricks to work toward debt repayment and earning a reasonable wage. Second, low piece rate ensures that workers continue to accumulate further debts and remain bonded for as long as it serves the operators' interests. The debts are not waived even in the case of sickness or death of a worker. Rather they get passed on to other members of the family.[53]

Every year, kilns close during the monsoon season when it is not possible to prepare and sun-dry the bricks. Operators also shut business for a few weeks every four or five months to stabilize the prices. The logic behind this move is that an abundant supply of bricks would suppress the market price and reduce the profit margin for the operators. However, as a rule, brick kiln workers are not allowed to take up seasonal agricultural or other form of temporary employment during these lean periods. Restrictions on seasonal work are clearly designed to keep the workers in bondage and close off avenues of alternative sources of livelihood. Some major cities in the Punjab Province, especially the provincial capital, Lahore, suffer high levels of smog in winter owing largely to the burning of crop stubbles. Since brick kilns add to smog, the government has, in recent years, ordered temporary closure of brick kilns during late autumn and winter. There has been no parallel measure to compensate workers for lost income or to provide them with alternative livelihoods.[54]

Apart from some isolated examples, such as All Sindh Mahnatkash Welfare Bhatta Mazdoor Union based in Hyderabad, brick kiln workers are not unionized, and consequently, unable to negotiate wages and working conditions collectively. Brick making exposes workers, especially children, to a range of health hazards such as scorching heat, dust, and coal emissions.[55] *Jalaiwalas* work inside the kiln handling fire without any protective gear. Yet, the concept of occupational safety is alien to the brick-making industry. According to the ILO, Pakistan currently has 330 labor inspectors for the entire country, evidently an absurdly low number to cover such a large country. Any sort of labor regulation within brick making is further precluded by the fact that most kilns are unregistered and operate beyond the pale of the law.

Sale and Retailing

Finished bricks are sold through a number of channels. The local retailers, who procure bricks from the kiln operators, have a profit margin of around 20 percent after adding in costs of transporting bricks from kilns to retail outlets. For example, as of summer 2020, the market price of bricks in Lahore was around rupees 12,000 per 1,000 bricks. The retailers purchase it at around rupees 7,000 at source. The market price of bricks varies significantly from one district to another. To illustrate, a supply of bricks costing rupees 12,000 in Lahore would sell at around rupees 7,000 in Multan. However, provincial government set a uniform minimum wage for brick kiln workers across the province. From the perspective of brick kiln operators, the price differential reflects the higher cost of production in Lahore, incurred primarily on land leasing. Yet, it could be argued that larger commercial centers have a greater demand for bricks, allowing producers to expand the scale of production and reducing the average cost of production. There is considerable force in that argument that minimum wages should be revised upward for the provincial capitals to let the workers benefit from the higher operating profits that brick kiln operators enjoy there.

Individual consumers also purchase bricks direct from kilns at concessional rates. Contractors working on private construction and public sector infrastructure place orders in advance and procure bricks on credit. Private architects and engineers also source bricks from retail outlets or contractors. Most significantly, large and registered kiln operators bid directly to supply bricks for public sector projects such as construction of footpaths and pavements, school and dispensary buildings, and offices. Other operators bid in partnership with professional contractors and builders. The government of Pakistan established the Public Procurement Regulatory Authority in 2002.[56] The stated aim of the authority is to "improve governance, management, transparency, accountability and quality of public procurement of goods, works and services."[57] The rules notified by the authority in 2008 speak to the need for transparency in public procurement but remain silent on assessing supply chains for bonded or forced labor or other human rights violations.[58] The same pattern is repeated in provincial public procurement laws.[59] The Khyber Pakhtunkhwa Public Procurement Regulatory Authority

Act, 2012, provides in Section 16 that all "procurements shall be carried out in accordance with such Code of Ethics as may be prescribed." Section 17 further stipulates that "notwithstanding anything contained in this Act, the international obligations of Government arising out of bilateral or multilateral Agreements including Treaties, financing agreements, or agreements by Government shall continue to remain and be valid, binding and operative." However, no "Code of Ethics" or specific guidelines have been issued requiring public agencies to clean up forced or bonded labor from their supply chains.[60] As a consequence, a brick-making unit, which employs child labor and pays workers less than the officially prescribed minimum wage, can still bid for public sector orders as long as it meets formalities such as registration and tax-filer status. Contractors and builders bidding for public sector projects do not have to demonstrate that they source bricks from kilns which do not employ forced or child labor. Consequently, public agencies commissioning construction work, or the contractors bidding for official projects, are least concerned about the conditions under which bricks are produced.

Using public procurement to promote supply chain compliance with social, environmental, and labor laws is an established practice in parts of the world. Pakistan has yet to catch up with the trend.[61] For example, in line with the *European Union Directive 24/14*, the British Parliament passed the Public Services (Social Value) Act 2012, which requires public bodies in England and Wales to consider how the services they commission and procure might improve the economic, social, and environmental well-being of the area. The Parliament passed the Modern Slavery Act, 2015, which obligates certain commercial entities to disclose the steps that they have taken to identify the use of forced labor and human trafficking in their supply chains and in their own businesses.[62]

End Use

It has been said of modern slavery that it "creeps into products like a poison, tainting and polluting them in a way that is difficult to see."[63] Globally, there have been documented cases of slavery and forced labor in the production of cocoa, coffee, cotton, sugar, iron, rugs and carpets, iron and steel, and gold and diamonds. In Pakistan, the pavements we walk on, public sector schools that our children study in, and in many cases, the homes we live in are made up of bricks produced under debt bondage and forced labor.

Since bricks are not an exported commodity, there has been little international pressure on producers and suppliers to clean up the supply chain. Brick-making industry can be contrasted with football manufacturing in Sialkot, Pakistan's hub of sports goods industry, where business came under sustained pressure through the 1990s to eliminate child labor from the supply chain. Before the launch of the ILO sponsored Atlanta Project in 1997, football stitching was typically outsourced through a chain of subcontractors to home-based units, relying heavily on child labor. Consumer outrage in the West at media reports on child labor led national and international companies to collaborate in transferring stitching from villages to regulated factories in the city and replacing child labor with adult labor. The project, although hailed widely as a success story, has not been without its critics. It has been pointed out, for example, that many children moved to other occupations and family incomes declined as a result of the project.[64] While remaining alert to the need for ensuring education opportunities for children and improved livelihood sources for adults, we can learn from the Atlanta project and other precedents where the mobilization of end users can help remove human rights violations from a supply chain. One strategy successfully employed in other sectors to clear up supply chains is the labeling of products as being complaint with social standards.[65] For example, Rugmark Foundation, a non-profit organization established in 1994 inspects and licenses carpet looms. To be eligible for a Rugmark logo and license, manufacturers promise not to employ children under 14 years of age and to pay adults a minimum wage. Carpet makers also agree to allow Rugmark's inspectors to examine their looms and workers at any time.[66]

IV. CONCLUDING REMARKS

In light of the foregoing discussion, it is suggested that combating bonded labor in brick making requires a set of strategies that are in tune with the economic and social determinants of debt bondage and the political economy of brick making in Pakistan. There is a need to recognize the various stages in brick-making supply chain and strategize interventions at every stage to uphold human rights and labor standards. Working on site to improve occupational safety, unionizing workers, and providing children with education opportunities is, no doubt, an important task. It is equally vital, however, to take a bigger view of the picture. Debt bondage is likely to survive in one form or another as long as it works to the economic advantage of land owners, kiln operators, and various other actors and intermediaries along the supply chain. The key to effecting a lasting change is to render debt bondage socially unacceptable and economically untenable. One way of achieving this is to incentivize compliance with human rights and social criteria as a requirement for supplying material to public sector agencies. Under the proposed legislative change, all federal, provincial and local government departments would be obligated to ensure that the supply chains of products and service they procure are free of bonded labor and comply with core labor standards.

The course of action being proposed here does not negate the importance of other initiatives on the ground. Rather, it complements them and seeks to address some of their shortcomings. For example, several NGOs have lobbied for the registration of brick kilns with provincial governments. That is a necessary first step. However, as mentioned earlier, mere registration as an industrial unit may bring a kiln within the tax net but it does not necessarily translate into compliance with human rights and labor standards. A substantive change in that direction would require a transformed public procurement framework linked with the evaluation of bidders and suppliers based on social criteria. Similarly, even registered brick kiln operators outsource recruitment and the *peshgi* system to middlemen who operate informally beyond the pale of labor law. There is thus a need to register and monitor not just brick kilns but intermediaries, such as recruiters of bonded workforce, something extant NGO programs seem to have overlooked.

Partnerships need to be built with professional groups, such as architects and builders, to make sure that they source bricks from "clean" and human rights compliant units. A mechanism of certifying and labeling bricks as bonded and child labor-free and consumer mobilization for ethical purchasing could, in time, shift the business case in favor of upholding human rights standards.

On the lower tier of the supply chain, which involves recruitment of workers, there is a need to rejuvenate debate and activism on agricultural land reform in Pakistan given that landlessness is known to be one of the major determinants of debt bondage.[67] To address the root causes of bonded labor, linkages need to be forged with social safety programs, simultaneously with a critical engagement with the design and efficacy of those programs. In 2008, the government of Pakistan initiated the Benazir Income Support Programme (BISP), as its flagship social safety program. Through BISP, the government paid unconditional cash transfers to eligible families based on a "poverty scorecard."[68] The BISP also offered health insurance to its beneficiaries (*Waseela-e-Sehat*), provided vocational training opportunities (*Waseela-e-Rozgar*), and access to interest-free financial support *(Waseela-e-Haq).* On some evaluations, the program had no discernible effect in reducing poverty based even on the evidently narrow measure of headcount poverty.[69] The program was not found to have improved education and health outcomes in a significant manner either.[70] Further, there is no evidence of BISP, or its successor social safety net program launched in 2019, *the Ehsaas Programme*, having targeted bonded laborers in brick making and those at risk of falling into bondage.[71] Bringing brick kiln workers within the pale of cash transfer and other social safety programs could be an important step toward creating an enabling environment in which their capabilities are enhanced and their range of choices expanded.

Although this chapter has made an attempt to pull together existing literature and insights from the field, more in-depth research is required in a number of areas. For example, further research is needed to understand the technical feasibility of greening brick production by replacing coal with bio mass and other renewable forms of energy. Under the United Nations Climate Change Framework, developed countries can finance emission-reduction projects in developing countries to earn certified carbon credits in support of emission reduction targets. Pakistan has yet to attract funding under this arrangement, known as the Clean Development Mechanism. Similarly, while we stress the need for engaging professional associations of architects and builders to promote ethical purchasing, further research would be needed to map out relevant associations and their social dynamics.

Finally, NGO and donor-sponsored work in the area of bonded and child labor has previously invited critiques on the grounds of alleged insensitivity to workers' own concerns and agency.[72] It is vital, therefore, that research and practice in this area is built on dialogue and consultations with brick kiln workers, including women and children.

NOTES

1. Translated by Daud Kamal. See *The Unicorn and the Dancing Girl: Poems of Faiz Ahmad Faiz, with Original Text /translated by Daud Kamal; Selected & Edited by Khalid Hasan* (Allied Publisher 1988).

2. Kevin Bales, Zoe Trodd and Alex Kent Williamson, *Modern Slavery: The Secret World of 27 Million People* (One World 2009) 33.

3. See Isabelle Guérin, 'Bonded Labour, Agrarian Changes and Capitalism: Emerging Patterns in South India', (2013) 13 (3) *Journal of Agrarian Change* 405–423; and Akhil Patel, 'Disposable People: New Slavery in the Global Economy', (2000) 22 (3) *Human Rights Quarterly* 867–872.

4. Faras Ghani, 'The spiraling debt trapping Pakistan's brick kiln workers', *Aljazeera*, 21 October 2019. Available: https://www.aljazeera.com/features/2019/10/21/the-spiralling-debt-trapping-pakistans-brick-kiln-workers/. Accessed: 10 November 2020. For earlier estimates, see Anti-slavery International, *Poverty, Discrimination and Slavery: The Reality of Bonded Labour in India, Nepal and Pakistan* (Anti-slavery 2008) 7.

5. Ali Khan, 'Peshgi without Bondage: Reconsidering the Links between Debt and Bonded Labour', (2010) 22 (3) *Cultural Dynamics* 247–266.

6. Conversely, development is to be understood as 'a process of expanding the real freedoms that people enjoy'. That entails removing factors that limit individual freedoms – factors such as poor economic and social opportunities, systematic social deprivation, and restrictions on political participation. Amartya Sen, *Development as Freedom* (OUP 2011) 3.

7. Amartya Sen, 'Capability and Well-being,' in Martha Nussbaum and Sen (eds.), *The Quality of Life* (Clarendon Press 1993) 30–53. See also Amartya Sen, 'Human Rights and Capabilities' 2005 (6) 2 *Journal of Human Development* 151–166.

8. The situation is different in more culturally conservative Khyber Pakhtunkhwa and Balochistan provinces where cultural norms frown upon women taking up manual labor in public places.

9. While there have been media reports of sexual abuse of female brick kiln workers, according to an assessment by the Pakistan Institute of Labour Education and Research (PILER) and International Labour Organisation (ILO), such cases are rare. However, as the assessment notes, women might be reluctant to speak out on such sensitive subjects perhaps because of fear of retaliation by brick kiln owners or their agents. See PILER/ILO, 'Unfree Labour in Pakistan: Work, Debt and Bondage in Brick Kilns' (ILO 2004) 18–19.

10. See Government of Pakistan/UNDP, *Multidimensional Poverty in Pakistan* (GoP 2016). The concept of multidimensional poverty and multidimensional poverty index is based on the Alkire Foster method developed by Sabina Alkire and James Foster of Oxford Poverty and Human Development Initiative. Measuring multidimensional poverty involves taking into account the different types of deprivation that individuals experience at the same time, such as a lack of education or employment, or poor health or living standards. Available: http://www.ophi.org.uk/research/multi-dimensional-poverty/alkire-foster-method/

11. See Sandra Fredman, 'Women and Poverty–A Human Rights Approach', (2016) 24 (4) *African Journal of International and Comparative Law* 494–517.

12. *Darshan Masih v the State*, PLD 1990 SC 513. Turning into a written petition a letter written to then chief justice, the court declared the practice of bonded labor unconstitutional and directed the government to introduce a legislation prohibiting the practice.

13. Werner Menski, Introductory Overview in Menski, Ahmad Rafay Alam and Mehreen Raza Kasuri *Public Interest Litigation in Pakistan* (Pakistan Law House 2000) 1–21. 9.

14. Kevin Bales, *Ending Slavery: How We Free Today's Slaves* (University of California Press 2007) 18, 189.

15. Committee on Economic, Social and Cultural Rights, 'Concluding Observations on the initial report of Pakistan', UN Doc. E/C.12/PAK/CO/1, 20 July 2017, para 45.

16. In 1996, brick kiln owners approached the Federal Shariat Court invoking Article 203-D of the Constitution and claiming that some provisions of the Bonded Labour Abolition Act (1992) were un-Islamic. The court dismissed the petition. See *Syed Shabbir Hussain Kazmi and others v. Government of Punjab and others* PLD 2006 FSC 1.

17. Ali Khan, 'Bonded Labor in Pakistan', in Beate Andrees and Patrick Belser (eds.), *Forced Labor: Coercion and Exploitation in the Private Economy* (Lynne Rienner 2009) 51–70, 51.

18. HRCP/ILO, *Abolition of Bonded Labour in Pakistan* (2003) 11.

19. Anti-slavery International (n 4) 20.

20. See, for example, the Punjab Bonded Labour System (Abolition) (Amendment) Act 2012 and the Khyber Pakhtunkhwa Bonded Labour System (Abolition) Act, 2015.

21. The law defines the child as 'a person who has not completed the fourteenth year of age'. See Section 2€.

22. Section 3, Punjab Prohibition of Child Labour at Brick Kilns Act, 2016. For a contextualized approach to the question of advance payments or *peshgi* in the context of domestic work, see Harris Gazdar and Ayesha Khan, 'Bonded Labour in Domestic Work and Begging', in Ayaz Qureshi and Ali Khan (eds.), *Bonded Labour in Pakistan* (OUP 2016) 126–143.

23. Section 4, The Punjab Prohibition of Child Labour at Brick-Kilns Act, 2016.

24. Anti-slavery International (n 4) 20.

25. Solidarity Centre, 'Mobilizing International Donor Support for Decent Work in Brick Kilns Industry: Formative Assessment and Recommendations Report', July 2014 (Unpublished Document).

26. Anti-slavery (n 4) 6.

27. Article 1 (a).

28. Article 1

29. A. Ercelawn and M. Nauman, 'Debt Bondage at Brick Kilns in Pakistan' in Ayaz Qureshi and Ali Khan (eds.), *Bonded Labour in Pakistan* (OUP 2016) 23–42, 32. See also PILER/ILO (n 9) 17.

30. Bales, Trodd and Williamson (n 2) 32.

31. Ibid 33.

32. Article 2(1), The 1930 ILO Convention concerning Forced or Compulsory Labour (ILO Convention No. 29).

33. PILER/ILO (n 9) 17.

34. Ali Qazilbash, 'Beyond Setting at Liberty: A Legal Study of Bonded Labour in Pakistan', in Qureshi and Khan (n 23) 1–22. 19–20.

35. For a recent overview, see HRCP/FIDH, 'Punished for Being Vulnerable: How Pakistan Executes the Poorest and the Most Marginalized in Society', October 2019. An insightful discussion of how the powerful influence and manipulate state institutions in Pakistan, see Armytage, Rosita. 'An Evolving Class Structure? New Perspectives on Pakistan's Political Economy', (2019) 9 *State, Class and Social Change* 153.

36. Article 11 (1) reads: 'Slavery is non-existent and forbidden and no law shall permit or facilitate its introduction into Pakistan in any form'.

37. Article 11 (2).

38. Tonia Novitz, The European Union and International Labour Standards: The Dynamics of Dialogue between the EU and the ILO, in Philip Alston (ed), *Labour Rights as Human Rights* (OUP 2005) 214–241.

39. These principles correlate broadly to certain fundamental ILO Conventions, namely: Conventions 87 and 98 on Freedom of Association and Collective Bargaining (1948 and 1949); Conventions 29 and 105 on the Elimination of All Forms of Forced and Compulsory Labour (1930 and 1957); Convention 138 on the Minimum Age for Admission to Employment (1973); Convention 182 on the Worst

Forms of Child Labour (1999), and ILO Conventions 100 and 111 on the Elimination of Discrimination in Respect of Employment and Occupation (1957 and 1958).

40. Jennifer Hurley with Dough Miller, 'The Changing Face of the Global Garment Industry', in Angela Hale and Jane Wills (eds.), *Threads of Labour: Garment Industry Supply Chains from the Workers' Perspective* (Blackwell 2006) 16–39.

41. Ercelawn and Nauman (n 29) 23.

42. PILER/ILO (n 9) 3.

43. Jan Breman, *Labour Bondage in West India: From Past to Present* (OUP 2007) 49.

44. Nicholas Martin, 'The Political Economy of Bonded Labour in the Pakistani Punjab', (2009) 43 (1) *Contributions to Indian Sociology* 35–59.

45. Lohana, Hari Ram, 'Poverty dynamics in rural Sindh, Pakistan', Chronic Poverty Research Centre Working Paper 157 (2009), p. 34.

46. G. M. Arif and F. Bilquees, 'Chronic and Transitory Poverty in Pakistan: Evidence from a Longitudinal Household Survey', (2007) 46 (2) *The Pakistan Development Review* 111–127.

47. Section 11, Pakistan Environment Protection Act, 1997.

48. Solidarity Centre (n 25) 9.

49. Ibid, p. 10.

50. Ibid.

51. Sabur Ghayur and Zeeshan Ghayur, 'Economics of Decent Work in Brick Making', February 2014 (Solidarity Centre) 11.

52. It is pertinent to note here that adult literacy is not a policy priority in Pakistan. Apart from isolated NGO initiatives there is currently no large-scale adult literacy program. According to the latest figures, literacy rates by provinces stand as follows: Balochsitan, 40 percent; Khyber Pakhtunkhwa, 55 percent; Sindh 57 percent; and Punjab (64 percent). See Pakistan Social and Living Standards Measurement Survey 2018-2019. Available: http://www.pbs.gov.pk/content/pakistan-social-and-living-standards-measurement. Accessed: 6 November 2020.

53. Ercelawn and Nauman (n 29) 33.

54. 'Workers hold demo against brick kilns closure', *Dawn,* 4 November 2020.

55. Muhammad Zakria Zakar et al., '"Nobody Likes a Person Whose Body Is Covered with Mud": Health Hazards Faced by Child Laborers in the Brick Kiln Sector of the Okara District, Pakistan', (2015) 47 (1) *Canadian Journal of Behavioural Science* 21–28.

56. Established under the Public Procurement Regulatory Authority Ordinance 2002.

57. See Public Procurement Regulatory Authority Pakistan: http://www.ppra.org.pk/ . Accessed: 10 November 2020.

58. See Section 4, Public Procurement Authority Rules, 2008. S. R. O. 805(I)/2008.

59. See the Punjab Procurement Regulatory Authority Act 2009, and Khyber Pakhtunkhwa Public Procurement Regulatory Authority Act, 2012. The Khyber Pakhtunkhwa Act.

60. References to the prohibition of forced and bonded labor and other human rights obligations were also conspicuously absent in the 'National Procurement

Strategy – 2013-2016' put out by the federal government's Public Procurement Regulatory Authority.

61. John Howe, 'The Regulatory Impact of Using Public Procurement to Promote Better Labour Standards in Corporate Supply Chains' in Kate Macdonald and Shelley Marshall (eds.), *Fair Trade, Corporate Accountability and Beyond: Experiments in Globalising Justice* (Ashgate 2010).

62. See Section 57, Part 6, Modern Slavery Act, 2015.

63. Bales (n 14) 18

64. Ali Khan, *Representing Children: Power, Policy and the Discourse on Child Labour in the Football Manufacturing Industry of Pakistan* (OUP 2007) 198–199.

65. For an overview, see Subrata Sarkar, 'Market-Based Initiatives to Combat Child Labour: Social Labelling Considerations and Policy Implications', (2000) 25 (4) *Management and Labour Studies* 262–271.

66. Bales, Trodd and Williamson (n 2) 158.

67. Nadeem Malik, 'Bonded Labour in Pakistan', (2016) 6 *Advances in Anthropology* 127–136.

68. The poverty scorecard is based on a range of indicators, such as the household size, education status, agricultural landholding, housing and toilet facilities, and livestock ownership.

69. See 'PIDE Policy Viewpoint: 'Unconditional Cash Transfer and Poverty Alleviation in Pakistan BISP's Impact on Households' Socioeconomic Wellbeing', No. 18, 2020. Available: https://www.pide.org.pk/pdf/Policy-Viewpoint-18.pdf

70. Zahid Mumtaz and Peter Whiteford, 'Social Safety Nets in the Development of a welfare System in Pakistan: An Analysis of the Benazir Income Support Programme', (2007) (39) 1 *Asia Pacific Journal of Public Administration* 16–38. 21.

71. The strategy document for the Ehsaas programme mentions 'labourers' as one of the target groups, but not bonded labouers specifically. This is problematic considering that sectors such as brick making known for a high incidence of bonded labor who suffer from chronic poverty can be easily identified. See, Government of Pakistan, 'The multi-sectoral and multi-stakeholder Ehsaas Strategy'. Available: https://www.pass.gov.pk/userfiles1/files/Strategy_Ehsaas_for_online_consultation.pdf. Accessed: 14 November 2020.

72. See, for example, Ali Khan (n 64).

Chapter 4

Pakistan's Constitution and the Right to Health

Muhammad Danyal Khan

COVID-19 is a test for our societies, and we are all learning and adapting as we respond to the virus. Human dignity and rights need to be front and centre in that effort, not an afterthought.

—Michelle Bachelet, UN High
Commissioner for Human Rights[1]

The post-COVID-19 world will demand from the world around us much more in protecting the right to health. General Comment no. 36 of the Human Rights Committee (HRC) calls the member states to International Covenant on Civil and Political Rights (ICCPR) to interpret the right to life in its wider meaning that includes positive states' obligations toward health.[2] When in April 2006, Pakistan presented its candidature for the elections of the Human Rights Council, it committed to ratification of core human rights treaties. While it ratified the International Covenant on Economic, Social and Cultural Rights (ICESR), and signed the ICCPR, it has not ratified the latter. However, it is the ICESR which contains within it the right to health, pointing out in Article 12 that "the State Parties to the present covenant recognise the right of everyone to the enjoyment of the highest attainable standard of physical and mental health." Nevertheless, a total of 115 states, the Constitution of Pakistan does not include protection of health among the fundamental rights.[3] The focus of this chapter, therefore, is on the scope for constitutional innovations in Pakistan. In cases of *Miss Shehla Zia and others vs. WAPDA*[4] and *Syed Mansoor Ali Shah vs. Government of Punjab*,[5] the constitutional courts have interpreted the scope of the right to life in a wider sense to protect the issues related to health. By analyzing the judgments of constitutional courts during the years 2017–2020, the article assesses the effectiveness of treating the issue of health under the right to life. It will demonstrate how for a country like Pakistan, the way ahead lies in protecting the right to health by learning from transnational experiences elsewhere, as examples exist here of how constitutional courts have found permanent solutions to protecting health as fundamental right.

INTRODUCTION

The role of the judiciary has been growing in protecting the right to health under the scope of the right to life in Pakistan. This study will analyze the role of constitutional courts in interpreting health-related issues under the right to life. Moreover, the study will suggest how constitutional courts can play their role to further establish the human rights framework of health-related issues. Recent suo motu action by the Supreme Court of Pakistan on the issue of COVID-19 has attracted different responses.[6] The world after the COVID-19 episode will be different from now, so will be the status of protecting the right to health. Pakistan has been the signatory of several international treaties that calls for or places obligations for protecting both physical and mental health. International legal scholarship has started anticipating that the issue of health will become more relevant toward fulfilling international legal obligations once the current pandemic is over.[7] The study analyzes the limitations and potentials for Pakistan to fulfill the health-related legal obligations at national and international levels.

The recent outbreak of the coronavirus (COVID-19) is not only a test for human advancement in medical sciences but is also a reality check for human rights and the right to health. The Access to Medicines Index Report 2018 finds that almost 2 billion people face several issues accessing basic health-care facilities.[8] The deprivation causes pain, fear, and violation of human rights. The demand for protection of the right to health has been interpreted as a moral or ethical obligation of the states. The issue is often tied with the available economic resources at the state level and philanthropic activities in Pakistan. Not including health among fundamental rights leaves it as a moral demand. In the post-COVID-19 era, the states will have to do more to meet the demands of international human rights standards, demand from local populations, and international organizations.

The issue of health is interpreted under the right to life, in countries, where it is not included in constitutional rights. Article 6(1) of ICCPR confers the right to life as an inherent right of everyone.[9] The right to life is one of the essential human rights for the realization of all other human rights. The HRC calls for wider interpretations of the right to life that includes the protection of health care in relation to pandemics, reducing infant mortality, and increasing life expectancy.[10] This may include the enforcement of health-related issues under the scope of the right to life. Creating the scope of enforcing the right to health under the right to life can help effectively solving the issue and forming an international consensus on protecting the right to health. Apart from life-threatening diseases, the right to health is part of the International Convent on Economic, Social and Cultural Rights (ICESCR), a binding international human rights document. The covenant obligates member states to work individually and through international cooperation for realization of rights mentioned under the covenant. Likewise, health-related human rights obligations may also find space under the domain and scope of article 15 of ICESCR that binds member states to recognize the right of everyone to enjoy the benefits of scientific progress and its application. In this way, the health-related issues may become part of enjoying the benefits of scientific progress. Apart from the International Bill of Rights, human rights obligations for the protection of health are found in various international and regional treaties. Among fundamental characteristics of human rights is their indivisibility.

Pakistan, having at the very least ratified the ICESR, owes certain health-related international legal obligations. It now has a duty to protect the right to health of its citizens. The legal obligations to protect the right to health are tripartite in their essential nature; the duty to respect, protect, and fulfil.[11] Under the duty to respect, Pakistan needs to refrain from all measures undermining access to health-related human rights standards.[12] It has an obligation to respect health vis-à-vis any conflicting rights or policies.[13] The duty to respect also includes the provision of the right to health in an indiscriminate way protecting all vulnerable factions of societies such as women, children, prisoners, and seriously ill people. The second part of the legal obligations of the member states includes protecting health from all countermeasures by third parties. This includes ensuring the standards of health from all social, cultural, and corporate third parties that may impact the access.[14] The third tier of the legal obligations requires the fulfillment of the obligations by recognizing and enforcing health as a human right in their legal systems.[15] This includes necessary legislation, enforcement, and effective interpretation by the respective state organs. Furthermore, it requires positive measures by the state to ensure that it takes all necessary steps to realize the right to health as a part of human rights.

The Constitution of the Islamic Republic of Pakistan includes the right to life as one of the fundamental rights.[16] As the Constitution does not include protection of health as a fundamental right, the constitutional courts have interpreted the health-related issues under the right to life such as in *Miss Shehla Zia and others vs. WAPDA*[17] and *Syed Mansoor Ali Shah vs. Government of Punjab*.[18] However, the post-COVID-19 era demands that much more be done. By providing space to the right to health among the constitutional rights, the government of Pakistan can bargain tangible concessions in relation to conflicting obligations such as protecting patents on medicines, importing medical equipment, and regulating the health-care services. The constitutional courts in several developing countries such as Argentina,[19] Brazil,[20] South Africa,[21] Columbia,[22] Nigeria,[23] and India[24] have played a pivotal role to protect the right to health by interpreting it under the available provisions of national and international laws. The judiciary can play its constitutional role in establishing the protection of health as a fundamental right in Pakistan. Therefore, it is time not only to do more to protect the right to health. The chapter will focus on the role of constitutional courts in establishing the right to health under the scope of the right to life, its limitations, and establishing the right to health as a constitutional right in Pakistan. In this regard, the study will include the interpretative trends that can help the constitutional courts in Pakistan.

HOW TO INTERPRET HEALTH-RELATED ISSUES UNDER THE RIGHT TO LIFE?

The right to life is the most prominent of all human rights. The content of the right to life does not mention the right to health as a part of the right to life.[25] However, in cases of a life-threatening disease such as COVID-19, access to health-care facilities becomes a necessary condition for survival.[26] In this way, the laws, policies, enforcement of various rights that restrict any essential aspect of health may affect the fundamental notion of the right to life.[27] The HRC adopts the same approach by demanding member states to avoid restrictive interpretation of the right to life and asks member states to take all necessary steps for increasing life expectancy, reducing child mortality, and overcoming epidemics.[28] As per the interpretation of the HRC, cases of diseases such as HIV/AIDS, cancer, TB, and other infectious diseases shall contribute to dealing with the issues of child mortality and life expectancy. The domain of the right to life may include the right to health as part of the obligations of the member states to ICCPR.[29]

Recently, General Comment No. 36 of the HRC has started a new era for health-care facilities as part of human rights obligation under the scope of the right to life.[30] The committee has the mandate to supervise and facilitate enforcement of rights under the ICCPR in the member states. The committee, with the fiat of authoritative interpretation, requires the member states to abandon narrow interpretation of the right to life that only includes negative states' obligations. The committee finds that the scope of the right to life includes both acts and omissions to prevent premature and unnatural death. Moreover, the obligations related to the right to life extend to the sustenance of life with dignity.

The member states, in the light of General Comment no. 36, are under obligation to protect the right to life with dignity through the positive steps that include protection of health for people suffering from life-threatening diseases.[31] While interpreting the right to life with reference to health, the comments stress on the text of the provision that includes that no one is arbitrarily deprived of his life.[32] The comments interpret that denial of health facilities to a person suffering from life-threatening diseases fall under the scope of the right to life. The member states of ICCPR are under obligation to ensure they respect, protect, and fulfill their liabilities by legislating, enforcing, and interpreting as part of the right the health under the right to life.

The health-related issues, in life-threatening cases, may fall under the right to life. The right to life may enhance the enforcement standards of the right to health. Moreover, the ICCPR is effective for its Optional Protocols which enhance its enforceability. The text of the ICCPR regarding the right to life provides universal protection of human life and calls all signatories to protect an individual against arbitrary deprivation of it.[33] The right to life is fundamental to all human rights and is substantively explained and granted by the ICCPR. Moreover, the right to life is essential for enjoying other human rights. The right to life is non-derogable. The text of Article 4 of the ICCPR calls it an inherent right that one owns with birth and this why some of the writers claim it as a part of *Jus Cogens*, a rule of international law that is compulsory for all states.[34]

Scholars argue that the scope of the right to life only extends the deprivation of life without due process of law.[35] Moreover, death by hunger, lack of food, health, and access to medicine does not fall under the scope of the right to life.[36] The restrictive interpretation of the right to life focuses on keeping its effective enforcement as including housing, health, food, and other life necessities will make the domain of the right to life wider and less enforceable.[37] Therefore, the domain of the right to life is the protection of life itself. Interpretative trends among human rights scholars focus negative duty on states not to infringe on individuals the right to life. Positive aspects of duties such as providing all necessities of life will not fall under the domain of the right to life of the ICCPR.[38]

Interpretations of the right to life by the HRC go a step ahead from classical approaches. For instance, Article 2 of the ICCPR put a positive duty on member states to ensure and respect all human rights enumerated in the document. It is further stressed that member states are under obligation to make their laws, executive set-ups, and judicial interpretations in line with international human rights standards. The same article of the covenant puts duties on states to "take necessary steps, under their constitutional processes and with the provisions of the covenant to adopt those laws or measures to give effect to the rights recognised in the present covenant."[39] The following paragraph, if critically evaluated, puts positive duty to act beside negative duty to apply restraint on power. Positive duty is exploiting states' constitutional framework and making laws effective for the protection of the right to life. Moreover, life cannot be taken in isolation with the health facilities. We may take the example of COVID-19, AIDS, cancer, malaria, and other life-threatening diseases where denial of health care is the denial of the right to life.[40] The right to life is accomplished by the protection of all other human rights enumerated in the ICCPR and the ICESCR. General Comments 6 of the HRC reflected upon the flexible interpretation of the right to life in the following words:

> The Committee has noted that the right to life has been too often narrowly interpreted. The expression "inherent right to life" cannot properly be understood in a restrictive manner, and the protection of this right requires that States adopt positive measures. In this connection, the Committee considers that it would be desirable for States parties to take all possible measures to reduce infant mortality and to increase life expectancy, especially in adopting measures to eliminate malnutrition and epidemics.[41]

The comment calls the member states to take positive measures through their constitutional process to protect the right to life. Among increasing life expectancy and reducing child mortality, measures to eliminate malnutrition, and the epidemic is relevant to the issue of access to medicine.[42] In the case of life-threatening diseases, the issue of protection of health becomes relevant to the right to life. The member states to the ICCPR have a positive duty to respect, protect, and fulfill the right to life. Keeping in view these arguments, states are under obligation to legislate, administrate, and interpret the issue of access to life-saving health interventions as a matter of protecting life itself.[43]

JUDICIAL INTERPRETATION OF THE RIGHT TO HEALTH UNDER THE RIGHT TO LIFE

In the case of the recent outbreak of COVID-19, the inaccessibility to healthcare facilities is a violation of the right to life, and human dignity. For example, during childbirth, many women lose their lives to uncontrolled bleeding. To avoid bleeding during childbirth, a drug named prophylactic uterotonics may treat the blood loss that is the biggest contributor to maternal mortality.[44] The issue of child mortality relates to the issue of access to medicines. The issue connects health facilities with the right to life and human dignity. Article 6 of the Convention on Rights of Child (CRC) includes the protection of the right of every child as an inherent right.[45] It is pertinent to mention that the provision calls all member states to take all necessary positive steps for protecting the life of a child concerning both pre-birth and later issues. There are cases from the developing countries where the courts have found that inaccessibility of health-care facilities falls under violation of the right to life and human dignity.

These judicial interpretations indicate that the inaccessibility of necessary health-care facilities connects to the right to life. In this regard, the decision based on ECHR in *Travares v. France* is very significant in explaining this.[46] The Appellant's wife died in a French hospital during childbirth for several medical issues. The claimant argued that the negligence of the hospital staff constituted a violation of Article 2 (1) of the ECHR that includes the right to life for everyone. Although, the case did not get the merits of remedies as the defendant contended that they followed all necessary medical standards.[47] However, the judge found that the state must take all necessary positive measures for protecting the right to health in connection to the right to life.[48] The judgment found that the states are bound to both positive and negative obligations which include avoiding loss of life as well as taking all necessary positive steps to save lives from arbitrary loss.[49] The provision grants everyone a guarantee of life. The examples from the European interpretation of human rights mention that the issue of health connects to life when it comes to a life-threatening disease. Moreover, health-care facilities are an integral part of health care and facilities related to health.

In *Social and Economic Rights Action Center & the Center for Economic and Social Rights v. Nigeria*, the decision included several human rights obligations and their interdependence. The commission fixed responsibility on the Nigerian government for failing to protect the right to life for its inability and violation of the right to health as the result of the activity of oil companies in Ogoniland.[50] The commission tested the obligation of the state on the criteria to respect, promote, and fulfill their commitments to guaranteed rights. Resultantly, the commission found that the state has violated its obligations by not protecting the domestic population from the oil exploration activities and their impact on the right to life, health, and other related rights.[51] The inability of Nigeria was interpreted as a violation of Article 4 (1) of the Banjul Charter that provides everyone the right to have respect for life. The commission ordered to stop the impact of oil exploration on the local population. The commission recommended the government to protect the population from physical attacks on the lives of the people and these examples demonstrate that the African Commission on Human Rights does not segregate between the right to health and life. A similar approach is found by the International Association for Hydro-Environment Engineering and Research (IAHR) in *Mendes v. Brazil* where the commission interpreted that the right to life is interconnected with all other human rights in the charter.[52]

The commission found that it is a violation of Article 4 of the convention not to protect its populations from arbitrary loss of life.[53] The findings of the court demonstrate that the right to health and life are closely connected. The issue of accessing the health-care facilities, when it leads to arbitrary loss of life, demands the member states to Banjul Charter to respect, promote, and fulfill their positive obligations.

The preamble of the Bolivian Constitution interconnects various human rights stating:

> A State based on respect and equality for all, on principles of sovereignty, dignity, interdependence, solidarity, harmony, and equity in the distribution and redistribution of the social wealth, where the search for a good life predominates; based on respect for the economic, social, juridical, political and cultural pluralism of the inhabitants of this land; and on collective coexistence with access to water, work, education, health and housing for all.[54]

The text of the preamble explains that a good life depends on respect for various human rights by the state. The Bolivian Constitution of 1967 also includes various positive aspects of the state obligations related to the right to life. The Constitutional Tribunal of Bolivia interpreted access to medicines to HIV/AIDS infected patients under the scope of the right to life.[55] The tribunal found that it is the obligation of the state under the right to life to provide necessary medicines in chronic illness that may lead to loss of life.[56] The Constitution of Columbia provides the right to health for everyone. The right also includes a guarantee of protecting life with dignity. The protection of dignity includes the obligation of the state to protect its population against diseases such as cancer, AIDS, and other health conditions that may impair the enjoyment of life with dignity.[57]

The arguments try to establish that the scope of the right to life is widening in both international and national legal frameworks. The interpretation of the right to life is getting wider interpretation by including the protection from the life-threatening disease under the domain of the right to life. The obligations must include the positive obligation of providing health-care facilities when it is a case of life-threatening disease.

HOW DID THE COLUMBIAN CONSTITUTIONAL COURT HELP TO ESTABLISH THE PROTECTION OF HEALTH AS A RIGHT?

Columbia remains a success story in helping the state to recognize the right to health as a constitutional right. Under constitutional jurisdiction, the court ordered the Ministry of Health and other health establishments to provide health-related remedies to twenty-two claimants in different cases.[58] Apart from ordering the treatment of the claimants, the court asked the Columbian government to amend laws in a way that does not obstruct the right to health of individuals. To deal with the issue in the transitional period, the court demanded the government to expedite investing resources and evaluating health-related services provided by the private companies.[59] The decision has helped in evolving the status of the right to health as a constitutionally guaranteed right. The case can guide states like Pakistan toward recognizing the right to health as a constitutional right.

To include the right to health in the Columbian Constitution of 1991, the legislature has adopted Law 1751 during 2015 that includes the right to health as a constitutionally guaranteed right. It is pertinent to note that the adoption of the law was the result of several dozen judicial interpretations of health-related obligations during decades' long judicial activism. Resultantly, the court ordered the state of Columbia to include the right to health among constitutionally guaranteed human rights.[60] The court used its *tutela* action as its function to order the government to protect the right to health of the claimants effectively.[61] The *tutela* stands for the protection of human rights using writ jurisdiction. The Columbian Constitution gives power to the courts. Through writ petition, an individual can invoke the jurisdiction of the court on the question of violation of human rights. The petitioner has to contend that no alternate remedy is available, and the action or inaction may result in a violation of constitutionally guaranteed rights of the individual.[62] The special judges of the constitutional court of Columbia decide the *tutela* action.

Deciding twenty-two cases related to *tutela* action, the Columbian Constitutional Court made the famous decision T-760 during 2008.[63] The decision discussed several judicial interpretations related to various aspects of the right to health in the past. The court found that the *tutela* action of the plaintiffs is maintainable as the human rights are interconnected. The court found that there is a multifaceted correlation between rights to the health of vulnerable people with the right to life. The court referred to various international legal instruments and the obligations of the state of Columbia toward these treaties.[64] The decision mentioned that the state, by the virtue of its obligations toward Article 12 of the ICESCR, is under obligation to respect, protect, and fulfill its health-related obligations. The decision also benefited from the interpretation of the right to health in General Comments No. 14 of the CESCR. The decision not only provides a remedy to the plaintiffs but also settles the question of the status of the right to health.

The decision of the Columbian Court remains a guideline for all developing and less-developed countries where the right to health is not part of constitutionally guaranteed rights or its enforcement remains ineffective. The decision settles the principle of human rights indivisibility, interconnected charter, and core obligation of the developing countries toward human rights ideals.[65] The decision also does not agree with the reliance on the scarce economic resources and progressive realization of the right to health as economic and social rights. The litigation in Pakistan under various constitutional rights is providing a transitional remedy; however, the study suggests that the right to health should be included among fundamental rights.[66] The judicial role will further pave the way for legislative and policy reforms as it happened in the Columbian example.

THE SCOPE OF INTERPRETING THE RIGHT TO HEALTH UNDER THE RIGHT TO LIFE IN PAKISTAN

The Constitution of the Islamic Republic of Pakistan, 1973, does not include specific provisions to guarantee the right to health and other rights that are closely connected to life and dignity.[67] Therefore, the constitutional courts in Pakistan have interpreted health and environment-related issues under the right to life. During the year 1994, the Supreme Court of Pakistan interpreted the right to life in a wider sense that includes the positive duties of the state toward the right to life. The committee in its General Comments No. 06 and 36 have called the member states not to interpret the right to life in the narrower sense that only includes negative obligations. The authoritative comments from the committee are adopted by the constitutional courts in Pakistan.

The Constitution of Pakistan is including various rights among fundamental rights. In 2010, the 18th Amendment to the Constitution brought in the right to education; however, the right to health has not been established as a fundamental or constitutional right.[68] As the right to health is not included among the constitutional rights, the protection of health and related services are interpreted under the right to life.

During the year 1994, the Supreme Court of Pakistan interpreted the issues related to the impact of the environment on health under the scope of the right to life.[69] In *Shehla Zia versus Wapda*, the findings of the judgment found that Article 9 of the Constitution of the Islamic Republic of Pakistan provides that no person shall be deprived of life or liberty without due process of law.[70] While interpreting the right to life, the court obligated the state with necessary positive steps for protecting life by taking all necessary measures to stop any impact on life. The case involved the possible health and environmental effects of electromagnetic waves from the grid station on the nearby population. The court interpreted the possible health and environmental effects under the scope of the right to life and dignity of human life. The court found that:

> Article 9 of the Constitution provides that no person shall be deprived of life or liberty save in accordance with law. The word life is very significant as it covers all facts of human existence. The word life has not been defined in the Constitution but it does not mean nor can be restricted only to the vegetative or animal life or mere existence from conception to death. Life includes all such amenities and facilities which a person born in a free country is entitled to enjoy with dignity, legally and constitutionally.[71]

To further include the positive obligations of the member states, the Supreme Court included the reference to Article 14 of the Constitution that sets the right to dignity of human life. The judgment finds that "Article 14 provides that the dignity of man and subject to the law the privacy of home shall be inviolable. The fundamental right to preserve and protect the dignity of man under Article 14 is unparalleled and could be found only in few Constitutions of the world."[72] The wider interpretation of the scope of the right to life supplements various aspects of human life missing from the list of constitutional rights. Therefore, the wider scope of the right to life covers the protection of human life, health, environment, and other necessities for the dignified existence of human life.

The High Court of Punjab Province, in the case of Shehla Zia and Syed Mansoor Ali Shah vs. Government of Punjab,[73] discussed the question of the hazardous impact of air pollution on the lives of the people living in Lahore city. The judgment ordered the government to take all necessary steps for protecting the environment based on the right to life and human dignity. Another positive aspect of the judgment is that it not only relies on national laws but also includes the reference to the Stockholm Treaty 2001, which focuses on the protection of human health from air pollution.[74] The judgment once again calls for the wider interpretation of the scope of the right to life to address issues related to health.[75] These two judgments have opened a way to address the issues related to human life and its dignity that includes the right to health.

The scope of protecting the right to life in Pakistan may be wider as the word "life" is not defined in the constitutional document. This provides an interpretative scope to the constitutional courts to decides on matters connected to the existence of human life. Moreover, the courts have supplemented the idea of life with dignity. This can play a pivotal role in setting the human rights framework for the right to health. The following part will analyze selected judgments during 2017–2020 to highlight the constitutional framework for the protection of the right to health as a developing or indirect constitutional right. The analysis of the cases will be in descending order.

Government of Sindh versus Secretary Health Department 2020 SCMR 1

After the outbreak of the COVID-19, the challenge for the government was to use available resources optimally. The governments were trying to avoid the obligations in relation to health-care measures to curb the spread of COVID-19 for the reason of scarce economic resources. The recent judgment from the Supreme Court of Pakistan has interpreted the scope of health-related issues under the right to life. The case originally involved the domain of federal and provincial legislative authority over health and related issues.[76] The Constitution of Pakistan is federal. It defines legislative lists for both center and the provinces. The court while interpreting the obligation of the government toward protecting health and related issues commented that the protection of health is an integral part of the right to life.[77] The case law settles that:

> Art. 9—Right to life—Scope—Right to healthcare—Right to life undoubtedly entailed the right to healthcare which meant that everyone had the right to the highest attainable standard of physical and mental health and this comprised of access to all kinds of medical services including but not limited to hospitals, clinics, medicines and services of medical practitioners which must not only be readily available and easily accessible to everyone without discrimination, but also of high standard—Federal Government had an obligation to carry out all necessary steps to ensure realization of this goal.[78]

The judgment from the apex court of Pakistan has comprehensively defined the components of the state obligations toward the protection of health under the scope of the right to life. The components of the right to health care delineated in the verdict are in line with Article 12 of the ICESCR.[79] The obligations of the state are toward protecting both the physical and mental health of the citizens.[80] Moreover, the judgment includes provision of health-related facilities as a condition to the right to life.[81] A critical analysis of the findings in the judgment points that the wider interpretation of the right to life by the constitutional courts is beneficial in protecting those aspects of life not covered specifically by the fundamental rights in the Constitution.[82] The judgment introduces the interpreting trends for considering the right to health under the scope of the right to life.

Aamir Lutuf Ali Zardari versus Province of Sindh 2019 CLC 224

The judgment comes from the High Court of the province of Sindh. The petitioner through public interest litigation asked the constitutional court to protect the health-related services under the scope of the right to life. The judgment interprets the scope of the right to life as under:

> Arts. 9 & 24—Term "life"—Scope—Health care includes the meaning of the term "life" and not restricted to mere the vegetative or animal life or mere existence from conception to death but it (life) includes all such amenities and facilities which a person born in a free country is entitled to enjoy with dignity, legally and constitutionally.[83]

The judgment defines the obligations of the provincial authorities in relation to health-related facilities in the province.[84] Further, the decision of the court mentions that the provincial government must work in its maximum capacity to ensure the protection of health under the scope of the right to life. The court interprets the protection of health as an essential and integral part of the right to life. According to the interpretation of the court, a life should include the life with dignity and availability of necessities of life.[85] The findings in the case have paved the way for establishing the right to health as a part of the state's positive obligations.

Asghar Laghari versus Federation of Pakistan 2018 CLD 424

In this case, the issue involved the access to clean drinking water. The judgment coined a terminology of "water justice" under the scope of the right to life. The judgment relied on the case of *Shehla Zia versus Wapda* and chose for the wider interpretation of the right to life.[86] The court found that the right to life cannot stand in isolation to the basic necessities of life.[87] These include the provision of clean drinking water. The judgment argues that the provision of water is a part of the overall protection of the conditions necessary for the existence of life. For these reasons, the state has obligations toward its citizens to provide the clean drinking water as well as protecting the overall climate necessary for the protection of the right to life and human dignity as per the right to life.[88] The judgment is significant in recognizing that the human rights are fundamentally interconnected where the enforcement of one is connected to others.[89] The judgment decides that the interpretation of the right to life may cover various economic and social rights. The wider interpretation of the right to life, in the findings of the court, creates space for the issue of health as it is an integral part of protecting life especially in diseases such as COVID-19, cancer, TB, malaria, and other life-threatening diseases.

Messer GETZ Pharma versus Federation of Pakistan PLD 2017 Sindh 157

The fundamental question in the case was the high price of a drug to treat hepatitis C, Sofosbuvir. The case practically connected the scope of the right to life with health as an economic, cultural, and social right. The judgment mentions that Article 12 of the ICESCR establishing the right to health is integrally connected to the right to life.[90] The judgment mentions:

> Arts. 9 & 14—Right to health—Scope—Unlike 115 countries of the world, the Constitution of Pakistan does not explicitly recognize the "right to health"—Right to life is enshrined under Art. 9 of the Constitution and when it is read with Art.14 of the Constitution, which grants right to "dignity of man" the same gives birth to the "right to health" as a fundamental right—Such "right to health" is also covered by several international human rights instruments, including International Covenant on Economic, Social and Cultural Rights (ICESCR) ratified by Pakistan on 17-4-2008, which recognizes the right of nationals to the enjoyment of the highest attainable standard of physical and mental health.[91]

The findings of the court acknowledge that the right to health is not included among the constitutional rights in Pakistan. However, the protection of health can be interpreted under the right to life and dignity of human life. The judgment stresses that the dignity of human life cannot be maintained without the protection of health.[92] Pakistan has ratified the covenant and the obligations include protection of highest standards of both mental and physical health.

The judgment is significant toward recognizing the health-related issues under the scope of the right to life. The judgment has presented a detailed analysis of Pakistan's and international laws concerning the health facilities. The findings of the court mention that the patent laws in Pakistan should be interpreted in a way that creates harmony with the standards of protecting health. The judgment analyzes the duty of the state toward respecting, protecting, and fulfilling their obligations in relation to the right to health mentioned in the Article 12 of the ICESCR.[93] Furthermore, the judgment specifies that ensuring the availability of essential medicines as mentioned by the World Health Organisation (WHO) is the obligation of the government. It is worth noting that the judgment decides that the covenant is legally binding on the government of Pakistan.[94]

The judgment acknowledges access to medicines as a derivative right under Article 9 that forms the right to life for everyone. The domain of access to medicines is interpreted under Article 14 of the Constitution of the Islamic Republic of Pakistan.[95] The findings recommend reading of both Articles and understanding their sole objective to protect not only adverse steps against life but also the protection of human life with dignity.[96] The court decided that the right to health in a way exists as a derivative right among the constitutional rights. Interpretation of right to life along with right to human dignity may include the protection of health and access to medicines. The court concludes that the provision of affordable medicines forms as a part of the right to life.[97] Along with the availability of affordable medicines under the scope of the right to life, the court requires the government to use the flexibilities in the Trade-Related Aspects of Intellectual Property Agreement (TRIPS Agreement) and Doha Declaration to protect access to medicines against patent protection.[98]

THE LIMITATIONS OF INTERPRETING THE RIGHT TO HEALTH AS AN ENTITLEMENT UNDER THE RIGHT TO LIFE IN PAKISTAN

Pakistan follows the framework of the Common Law System where the judiciary holds constitutional authority to develop law through its interpretative trends. The Constitution of Pakistan provides a mandate to the constitutional courts for guarding the observance of fundamental or constitutional rights. Article 184 (3) of the Constitution empowers the Supreme Court to pass an order or decision in case of an issue related to the protection of public interest or fundamental rights as explained in Article 199 of the constitution. The text of Article 199[99] explains how the high courts of relevant provinces can play their constitutional role in upholding the rule of law and compliance to the constitutional rights.

The noninclusion of the right to health among the constitutional rights and its interpretations by the courts under the right to life has not protected the standards of health. The analysis of the judgments interpreting the right to life for protecting the right to health makes the provision remote and less effective. For instance, the judgments on the issues of access to water, air quality, and health are advisory where the state authorities can avoid the enforcement on account of limited resources available and the overall economic capacity of the state. Moreover, tying various economic, cultural, and social rights to the right to life cannot be an effective way to protect them. Although Pakistan is a signatory to the ICESCR, however, the country has recorded the reservation that the state will perform its obligations as per the availability of economic resources.[100] The reservations include that Pakistan will progressively work for realizing the economic, social, and cultural rights. The reservation has been part of General Comments by the Committee on Economic, Cultural, and Social Rights (CESCR). The committee has further explained the difference between inability and non-willingness toward performing obligations related to the rights in the covenant. Moreover, the committee has explained the core obligations. In case of the right to health, General Comments No. 14 mentions that the member states have a positive obligation to ensure access to Essential Medicines as prescribed by the WHO. The case of *GETZ Pharma versus Federation of Pakistan* decides in a similar manner.

The arguments reflect that the status of the right to health is evolving in Pakistan. The health-related issues are interpreted as the obligations under the right to life. This derivative status may work as a transitional solution; however, the long-term way out is including the right to health as a constitutional right.

CONCLUSION

The study analyzed the transitional way of protecting health under the scope of the right to life by the constitutional courts and concludes that the permanent solution lies in including the right to health among fundamental rights. Moreover, the study has proposed the role of constitutional courts in establishing the right to health among the fundamental rights in Pakistan. Examination of the recent judgments from the constitutional courts reveals that the judiciary has played its role in interpreting health-related issues under the scope of the right to life as a transitional solution. However, the courts' findings and instructions to the governments are interpreted in a way that gives certain flexibility to the state authorities with the view of available state capacity.

The status of the right to health as an indirect right under the scope of the right to life has not been effective in protecting the standards of health. The constitutional courts have certain discretion in applying the scope of the right to life and human dignity to protect health. Interpreting the right to health under the domain of the right to life has not been effective. Therefore, the study has presented the example from Columbian constitutional courts where the judiciary played its role to establish the right to health among fundamental rights. Post-COVID-19 era will require the member states of the international community to do more for protecting the right to health. To fulfill international human rights obligations along with national needs, the constitutional courts of Pakistan may require the state to include health among constitutional right.

NOTES

1. Michelle Bachelet (UN High Commissioner for Human Rights), 'Coronavirus: Human rights need to be front and centre in response' (6 March 2019) https://www

.ohchr.org/EN/NewsEvents/Pages/DisplayNews.aspx?NewsID=25668&LangID=E accessed 17 March 2020.

2. Para 36 of General Comments No. 36 of the Human Rights Committee mention, "The right to life is a right which should not be interpreted narrowly. It concerns the entitlement of individuals to be free from acts and omissions that are intended or may be expected to cause their unnatural or premature death, as well as to enjoy a life with dignity"; United Nations Human Rights Committee, General Comment No. 36 on Article 6 of the International Covenant on Civil and Political Rights – Right to life, para 26; UN Human Rights Committee (HRC), *CCPR General Comment No. 6: Article 6 (Right to Life)*, 30 April 1982 https://www.refworld.org/docid/45388400a.html accessed 16 September 2019.

3. Dr Sania Nishtar, 'Health and the 18th Amendment; Need for a national structure' http://www.heartfile.org/pdf/Health_18Amendment_draft.pdf accessed 21 April 2020

4. *Miss Shehla Zia and others vs. WAPDA [PLD 1994 Supreme Court 693].*

5. *Syed Mansoor Ali Shah vs. Government of Punjab 2007 C L D 533.*

6. (Suo Moto Action Regarding Combating the Pandemic Of Corona Virus (COVID-19) S.M.C. 01/ 2020 https://www.supremecourt.gov.pk/downloads_judgements/s.m.c._1_2020_20042020.pdf accessed 21 April 2020.

7. Michael Igoe, Vince Chadwick, 'After the pandemic: How will COVID-19 transform global health and development? (13 April 2020) https://www.devex.com/news/after-the-pandemic-how-will-covid-19-transform-global-health-and-development-96936 accessed 21 April 2020.

8. Access to Medicine Foundation, Access to Medicine Index 2018.

9. International Covenant on Civil and Political Rights (adopted 16 December 1966, entered into force 23 March 1976) 999 UNTS 171, Article 6 (1).

10. Prof. Javaid Rehman mentions 'reduction in infant mortality' as inherent right under article 6 (1) of ICCPR. Further, it is observed that "The term 'inherent' as used in article 6 (1) connotes a positive and broad obligation including, for example prevention of wards and reduction in infant mortality." Reduction in infant mortality requires access to medicines and in this way access to medicine may be interpreted on analogical grounds for facilitating access to medicine in life-threatening diseases under article 6 (1) of ICCPR; Javaid Rehman, *International Human Rights Law* (Pearson Education Ltd, 2010) 93.

11. UN Committee on Economic, Social and Cultural Rights (CESCR), *General Comment No. 14: The Right to the Highest Attainable Standard of Health (Art. 12 of the Covenant)*, 11 August 2000, E/C.12/2000/4, para 12.

12. Ibid.

13. Joo-Young Lee, *A Human Rights Framework for Intellectual Property* (Ashgate, 2015) 130.

14. Ibid.

15. Patrick L. Wojahn, 'A Conflict of Rights: Intellectual Property under Trips, the Right to Health, and Aids', (2001) 6 UCL *Journal of International Law and Foreign Affairs* 465–497.

16. The Constitution of Islamic Republic of Pakistan, Article 9.

17. *Miss Shehla Zia Case (n-4).*

18. *Syed Mansoor Ali Shah Case (n-5).*

19. Viceconte, Mariela Cecilia vs the State Ministry of Health and Social Action https://www.globalhealthrights.org/wp-content/uploads/2014/01/ENGLISH-Viceconte-Argentina-1998-English-2.pdf accessed 27 November 2019.

20. Brazil's Constitution of 1988 with Amendments through 2014, Article 196 states, "*Health is the right of all and the duty of the National Government and shall be guaranteed by social and economic policies aimed at reducing the risk of illness and other maladies and by universal and equal access to all activities and services for its promotion, protection and recovery.*"

21. Minister of Health v Treatment Action Campaign (TAC) (2002) 5 SA 721 (CC), https://www.escr-net.org/caselaw/2006/minister-health-v-treatment-action-campaign-tac-2002-5-sa-721-cc accessed 21 November 2019.

22. Decision T-760 of 2008, https://www.escr-net.org/caselaw/2009/decision-t-760-2008 accessed 20 November 2019; Aquiles Ignacio Arrieta-Gómez, 'Realizing the Fundamental Right to Health through Litigation: The Colombian Case', (2018) *Health and Human Rights Journal* https://www.hhrjournal.org/2018/06/realizing-the-fundamental-right-to-health-through-litigation-the-colombian-case/ accessed 20 November 2019.

23. *Social and Economic Rights Action Center & the Center for Economic and Social Rights v. Nigeria; Viceconte, Mariela Cecilia v. the State Ministry of Health and Social Action.*

24. Smity v State of West Bengal [1996] AIR 2426 SC; Ilias Bantekas, Lutz Oette, *International Human Rights Law And Practice* (Cambridge University Press, 2011) 380; Brigit Toebes, 'International Health Law: An Emerging Field of Public International Law', (2015) 55 (3) *Indian Journal of International Law* 299–328.

25. Health and Human Rights Resource Guide, 'How is Access To Medicines a Human Rights Issue?' https://www.hhrguide.org/2017/06/09/access-to-medicines-and-human-rights/ accessed 15 November 2019.

26. Stephen P. Marks, 'Access to Essential Medicines as a Component of the Right to Health" in Health: A Human Rights Perspective' https://cdn1.sph.harvard.edu/wpcontent/uploads/sites/580/2012/10/marks_access_to_essential_medecines-2009.pdf accessed 16 November 2019., Alicia Ely Yamin, 'Not Just a Tragedy: Access to Medications as Right under International Law', (2003) 21 *Boston University International Law Journal* 325–371, 331.

27. United Nations Human Rights Committee, General Comment No. 36.

28. United Nations Human Rights Committee, General Comment No. 36 on Article 6 of the International Covenant on Civil and Political Rights – Right to life, para 5; UN Human Rights Committee (HRC), *CCPR General Comment No. 6: Article 6 (Right to Life)*, 30 April 1982 https://www.refworld.org/docid/45388400a.html accessed 16 September 2019.

29. Ibid.

30. Ibid.

31. Ibid.

32. Ibid.

33. Ray Monihan, Richard Smith, 'Too Much Medicine? Almost Certainly', (2002) *British Medical Journal* 324–859, 324.

34. Ibid.

35. Holger Hestermeyer, *Human Rights and the WTO: The Case of Patents and Access to Medicine* (Oxford University Press 2008) 115–116.

36. Holger P. Hestermeyer, 'Access to Medicine as Human Rights' http://www.mpil.de/files/pdf2/mpunyb_hestermeyer_8.pdf accessed 6 November 2018.

Ibid.

37. Hestermeyer (n-35) 115–116.

38. Ibid.

39. Ibid.

40. Alicia Ely Yamin, 'Not Just a Tragedy: Access to Medications as Right under International Law', (2003) 21 *Boston University International Law Journal* 325–371, 331.

41. UN Human Rights Committee (HRC), *CCPR General Comment No. 6: Article 6 (Right to Life)*, 30 April 1982 https://www.refworld.org/docid/45388400a.html accessed 2 September 2019

42. Ibid.

43. Ibid.

44. Health and Human Rights Resource Guide, 'How is Access To Medicines a Human Rights Issue?' https://www.hhrguide.org/2017/06/09/access-to-medicines-and-human-rights/ accessed 15 November 2019.

45. Convention on the Rights of the Child (Adopted and opened for signature, ratification and accession by General Assembly resolution 44/25 of 20 November 1989), Article 6.

46. Rebecca J. Cook, Bernard Dickens, 'Human Rights Dynamics of Abortion Law Reform', (2003) 25 *Human Rights Quarterly* 1–59.

47. Ibid.

48. Ibid.

49. Ibid.

50. *Social and Economic Rights Action Center & the Center for Economic and Social Rights v. Nigeria (Communication No. 155/96)* https://www.escr-net.org/caselaw/2006/social-and-economic-rights-action-center-center-economic-and-social-rights-v-nigeria accessed 17 November 2019.

51. Ibid.

52. James L. Cavallaro, et al., *Doctrine, Practice, and Advocacy in the Inter-American Human Rights System* (Oxford University Press, 2019) 349.

53. Ibid.

54. Bolivian Constitution 2009, Preamble.

55. Health and Human Rights Resource Guide (n-44).

56. Health and Human Rights Resource Guide (n-44).

57. Health and Human Rights Resource Guide (n-44).

58. Aquiles Ignacio Arrieta-Gómez (n-22).

59. Decision T-760 of 2008, https://www.escr-net.org/caselaw/2009/decision-t-760-2008 accessed 20 November 2019.

60. Ibid.
61. Ibid.
62. Ibid.
63. Ibid.
64. Ibid.
65. Ibid.
66. Ibid.
67. Dr Sania Nishtar (n-3) 1.
68. Sania Nishtar et al., 'Health Reform in Pakistan: A Call to Action' (2013) 391 (9885) *The Lancet* 2291–2297.
69. Ibid.
70. Ibid.
71. *Miss Shehla Zia and others vs. WAPDA [PLD 1994 Supreme Court 693] 714.*
72. Ibid. 715.
73. Ibid.
74. Ibid
75. Ibid.
76. *Government of Sindh Versus Secretary Health Department 2020 SCMR 1.*
77. Ibid.
78. Ibid.
79. Ibid.
80. Ibid.
81. Ibid.
82. Ibid.
83. *Aamir Lutuf Ali Zardari versus Province of Sindh 2019 CLC 224.*
84. Ibid.
85. Ibid.
86. *Asghar Laghari versus Federation of Pakistan 2018 CLD 424.*
87. Ibid.
88. Ibid.
89. Ibid.
90. *Messer GETZ Pharma versus Federation of Pakistan PLD 2017 Sindh 157.*
91. Ibid.
92. Ibid.
93. Ibid.
94. Ibid.
95. Ibid.
96. Ibid.
97. Ibid.
98. Ibid.
99. "199. Jurisdiction of High Court.—(1) Subject to the Constitution, a High Court may, if it is satisfied that no other adequate remedy is provided by law,—(a) on the application of any aggrieved party, make an order—(i) directing a person performing, within the territorial jurisdiction of the Court, functions in connection with the affairs of the Federation, a Province or a local authority, to refrain from doing

anything he is not permitted by law to do, or to do anything he is required by law to do; or(ii) declaring that any act done or proceeding taken within the territorial jurisdiction of the Court by a person performing functions in connection with the affairs of the Federation, a Province or a local authority has been done or taken without lawful authority and is of no legal effect; or(b) on the application of any person, make an order—(i) directing that a person in custody within the territorial jurisdiction of the Court be brought before it so that the Court may satisfy itself that he is not being held in custody without lawful authority or in an unlawful manner; or(ii) requiring a person within the territorial jurisdiction of the Court holding or purporting to hold a public office to show under what authority of law he claims to hold that office; or(c) on the application of any aggrieved person, make an order giving such directions to any person or authority, including any Government exercising any power or performing any function in, or in relation to, any territory within the jurisdiction of that Court as may be appropriate for the enforcement of any of the Fundamental Rights conferred by Chapter 1 of Part II.(2) Subject to the Constitution, the right to move a High Court for the enforcement of any of the Fundamental Rights conferred by Chapter 1 of Part II shall not be abridged".

100. UN Treaty Collection https://treaties.un.org/pages/ViewDetails.aspx?src=IND&mtdsg_no=IV-3&chapter=4&clang=_en accessed 13 January 2021.

Part II

Chapter 5

Crime and Punishment in Pakistan

Satvinder S. Juss

INTRODUCTION

It is trite that the legal system in Pakistan is ponderously slow, poorly resourced, and plagued by corruption. So much so that there is a popular Punjabi saying in the country to the effect that *May God save even my worst enemy from disease and a court case.*[1] Indeed, in 2014, Imtiaz Gul, in an article in Pakistan's *Express Tribune*, estimated that around 2 million civil and criminal cases were pending in the courts every year, 75 percent of which were being handled by just 900 magistrates.[2] This leads to a judicial paralysis which means that it can take years for a case to be prosecuted.[3] The Pakistani Penal Code[4] also does not recognize or authorize plea bargaining, which is seen to be morally dubious, prioritizing administrative interests over justice and potentially encouraging innocent people to plead guilty to avoid harsher punishment.[5] This contributes to the stagnation of the system. Indeed, at best, no more than 26 percent of all criminal suspects, including terrorists (who are tried in a separate and theoretically more stringent court[6]), are ever convicted.[7] With the system so overburdened, those before the courts often have to needlessly attend court proceedings daily for months on end or even years just to have simple issues, such as land transfers, settled. The failure of the secular state legal system means that these hapless citizens are driven to turn toward local religious courts and tribal councils (*jirgas*) where issues are handled more swiftly.[8] However, while these courts have the merit of relative efficiency and expediency, they offer a traditional interpretation of justice. More worryingly, they invariably endorse illegal practices such as *karo kari* killings (a form of premeditated honor killing which originated in rural and tribal areas of Sindh, Pakistan) and *vani*[9] (i.e., a custom in some parts of Pakistan whereby young girls are given in marriage or servitude).

In this scenario, state law in Pakistan is often regarded as an imposition, put in place by the British during colonial times before 1947. As such, it is perceived as being alien to local tradition and traditional Islamic codes. This is why sharia law, based on Islamic injunctions, is regarded as truer to the values of Pakistani people. It is also why the sharia-compliant laws in the *Quisas* and *Diyat* met with such great support among the people of the country.[10] *Quisas* imply "retaliation in kind," such as an "eye for an eye," as form of retributive justice, whereby the punishment is one which is analogous to the crime. *Diyat* is different, being a financial compensation paid to the victim or heirs of a victim in cases of murder, bodily harm, or property damage. It is an alternative punishment to *quisas* (which is based on equal retaliation). Since Pakistanis have little loyalty to state law, they have little compunction when it comes to undermining it. The ineffectiveness of state law is exacerbated by the general population's attempt to undermine it to their advantage. The allegiance of the people to kin groups and the family is more important. The people's primary loyalty is to their relations. The desire to evade state strictures leads to high levels of corruption.[11] As a consequence, it is far easier to say that where an issue only involves members of the same family or kin group, justice can and should be meted out within that same family with no outside involvement from the state. Justice becomes a private and personal matter.

It is not a question of civil (or even criminal) law between the individual and the state. It is this belief that leads to "honor killings" going unaddressed. In these *karo kari* cases, men and women are punished and sometimes even killed for sexual infractions (such as extramarital sex or marrying outside of a kin group), which is seen as "dishonouring" a family.[12] *Diyat* can also be exploited in these cases since the guardians or next of kin of dead girls can order their murders but also have the power to excuse their killers.[13] The custom of *vani*, where young girls are given in marriage as compensation for crimes committed, also continues to be prevalent in some tribal areas, and indeed could be interpreted as a form of *diyat*, although the practice itself is illegal and punishable with a prison sentence of at least three years and a fine of 500,000 rupees.[14] In the event, this is how the Pakistani system debunks the Western one, where the modern state is subject to a single legal code, which is expressed through a set of absolute rules. Instead, there are strong local courts (*jirgas*), particularly in rural areas, and these give Pakistanis a choice between state law and local tribal law.[15] This results in the creation of a "negotiated nature" of law and power,[16] which is facilitated by the high levels of corruption in Pakistan, so that most questions of justice are settled through negotiations (by paying *diyat* or bribes) because the very character of the legal system is so fluid. Even so, the system of *Quisas* and *Diyat* in the 1990 Ordinance is flawed and falls short of providing justice where it is most needed, namely, for the dispossessed and powerless. That being so what this chapter sets out to argue is that for there to be realistic fundamental change, alternative interpretations must be sought in both the sharia and the 1990 Ordinance, rather than an outright rejection of these as is sometimes advocated by reformers in the West, on grounds that such laws are incompatible with modern human rights standards. Such an approach is realistic, it is argued here, because the Pakistani government has already proceeded on this basis when making recent commitments to the protection of women's rights, by rejecting an interpretation of *fasad-fil-ardz* (mischief on earth) that justifies "honor killings." Since judges in Pakistan have enormously wide discretion in the interpretation of Islamic law, they must also now do the same. This is because when the practice of *quisas* and *diyat* was first implemented in the seventh century, it was in the interests of promoting peace and social harmony. Current interpretations and application of the law do not achieve that ideal. It is, therefore, necessary to return to the original rationale of such practices. This will enable us to extrapolate meaningful principles of law and justice today which can properly apply in a Pakistan of the twenty-first century. This chapter will first consider the origins of *Quisas* and *Diyat*, then the *Quisas* and *Diyat* Ordinance of 1990, before considering its misuse and exploitation. It will then consider the delicate question of honor killings in the context of three cases, namely, of *Samia Shaheed*, of *Shahzeb Khan*, and of *Raymond Davis*. It will then look at how the anti-terrorism court is drawn into the investigation of perfectly ordinary crimes, before asking why justice is so elusive under the 1990 Ordinance. Finally, it will evaluate the ordinance in the context of modern needs before reaching firm conclusions about what needs to be done in the future.

1. ORIGINS OF *QUISAS* AND *DIYAT*

Quisas and *diyat* in the Quran are based on a law of equality. This refers to "the free for the free, the slave for the slave, the woman for the woman." But there are exceptions to this principle of equality, so that the victim's relatives are expressly enjoined that "if any remission is made by the brother of the slain then grant any reasonable demand and compensate him with handsome gratitude," and the perpetrator's family are reminded not to forget that "this is a concession and a Mercy from your Lord." The underlying rationale lies in the ultimate well-being of society so "that ye may restrain yourselves."[17] In this way, *diyat* is a peaceful substitute for vengeance. Both *quisas* and *diyat* are meant for managing and limiting the bloodshed of the vicious tribal blood feuds, given that these were so common during the time of the Prophet Mohammed.[18] Under the Quran, there are two kinds of homicide: deliberate and accidental. *Quisas* is put forward as the standard punishment for deliberate homicide, unless the *wali* (the victim's heirs or closest relatives) accept a *diyat* payment. Alternatively, for an accidental killing, the murderer should pay *diyat* automatically unless the victim's heirs renounce their claim to it.[19] In this way, *Quisas* neatly fit into the tiered system of Islamic law where the top tier of crimes are *Hudud* crimes, established explicitly under the Quran, as crimes not against your fellow man, but against God.[20] Here there are six *Hudud* crimes: theft, adultery, false accusations of adultery, alcohol consumption, apostasy, and highway robbery.[21] The Quran prescribes harsh punishments for *Hudud* crimes such as flogging, amputation, and lashings as well as stoning and beheading.[22] *Quisas*, on the other hand, comprise the middle tier of Islamic crimes, in that whereas *Hudud* crimes are premised on transgressions against God, *Quisas* are crimes against men and include wounding or murder, both intentional and accidental.[23] Due to this nature of *Quisas* crimes, they are actionable by the victim or their family, with punishment being on a retaliatory eye-for-an-eye basis.[24] However, victims and their families do have the right to forgive the crime or accept monetary compensation ("blood money") in lieu of a reciprocal punishment.[25] Then there are the bottom tier of crimes under Islam. These are *Ta'zir* (i.e., to punish) as the third of the three major types of punishment prescribed by sharia Islamic law as *Hadd* or *Hudud, Quisas*, and then *Ta'zir*. Whereas the punishments for the *Hadd* or *Hudud* are fixed by the *Quran* or *Hadith* (as "defined by God"), and whereas *Quisas* allow "equal retaliation" in cases of intentional bodily harm, what *Ta'zir* refers to are punishments for offenses where neither the *Quran* nor the *Hadith* prescribe a specific punishment. *Ta'zir* punishments, therefore, work as forms of "moral chastisement" for all types of crimes which are neither *Hudud* or *Qisas*.[26] As a result, *Ta'zir* crimes are often decided by rulers or courts and punishments usually include lashing, imprisonment, or fines.[27]

To understand the practice of *quisas* and *diyat*, one needs to turn to its origins in pre-Islamic tribal law. Compensation mechanisms here were established in order to encourage peace in a way that "did not establish hierarchical punishment, but rather institutionalised and contained revenge" within a system of regulated negotiations,[28] in a largely familial and tribal context of many crimes. Pardoning an offender, or negotiating compensation, was an invaluable means of cultivating harmonious relations between rival groups, who remained in inevitable contact with each other afterward, where what was required was the diminishing of feelings of vengefulness between them.[29] This speaks to a private, family, or tribal-based understanding of conflict and resolution, which many in Pakistan can identify with, not least where questions of family honor are implicated. This is why amendments to the Pakistan Penal Code (PPC) made by the *Quisas* and *Diyat* Ordinance prevent *quisas* being claimed by any *wali*, who is a direct descendent of the offender, by instead decreeing that the claim to *quisas* should be relinquished by the payment of *diyat*.[30] This allows for violent intrafamilial feuds to be settled without further bloodshed.[31]

Westerners, of course, find this all too often hard to accept. For the non-Muslim observer in the West, sharia law or Islamic law "evokes strong emotions," as Berger points out, because for them "it denotes a system of medieval times that imposes a harsh code of behaviour sanctioned by draconic punishments," even though for many Muslims "it represents a system that promotes goodness and justice."[32] To be precise, however, Berger identifies three different "notions" of sharia: sharia as ideology, sharia as a legal science, and sharia as applied throughout the twentieth century in countries like Pakistan. Of these, the latter is the most noteworthy because this is when Islamic law began to be reintroduced into secular legal systems toward the end of the twentieth century. This is why simply translating sharia as "Islamic law" is something which "does not do credit to sharia" because "Sharia is more than law; it is a code of conduct for the everyday life of the Muslim." This is why, "[w]hen a Muslim therefore claims to be favourable to sharia, he or she does not necessarily mean that sharia needs to be implemented as a system of state law" since "[i]t may very well mean that he refers to living everyday life as a good person."[33] This is why Western perceptions often lack the nuance that is needed to understand sharia. The truth is that sharia does not work as "law" in the Western sense of a system of rules designed to regulate society and to govern conflict resolution. Instead, sharia is a scientific legal system. It is based on the interpretation (*ijtihad*) of scripture by Islamic scholars. It is not a word-for-word translation from the Quran and the *sunnah* (which means "habitual practice," referring to the body of the traditional social and legal custom and practice of the Islamic community) neither of which detail laws in explicit detail.[34] There are a small number of laws which are specifically described in scripture, but most laws now known as sharia are *fiqh* (i.e., the theory or philosophy of Islamic law based on the teachings of both the Quran and the traditions of the Prophet), that is to say, interpretations or individual conclusions only. This means that they "may change with time and place, depending on needs and circumstances."[35]

This suggests that the sharia system of religious law is, in its original iteration, fundamentally pluralistic, because any interpretation can only be a probable conclusion, and not an absolute one. In addition, since Islam does not acknowledge any formal clergy, any literate individual can study and interpret religious law by themselves. Like many aspects of Pakistani law, therefore, sharia is inherently pliant. This emphasis on interpretation implies that general concepts of "peace" and "goodness" as set out in Islamic teachings could legitimately be taken into account when interpreting religious teachings as law. This would be in line with the way in which literal iterations of Islamic laws expressed in the seventh century are taken into account in modern readings. This freedom of interpretation, as Berger explains, has produced a fascinating range of results, from the radical teachings of al-Qaeda to equally radical liberal conclusions by Muslim feminists.[36] This is why there is no one good way to define sharia. The closest approximation of sharia would, in its emotional sense, be as "justice."[37] Both sharia and Western legal systems share the same commitment to this ideal. Both struggle with the issue of defining what is "justice." Although the concept of "justice" in many Muslim countries may be at variance with human rights standards in the West, sharia in itself is not *prima facie* the root of the problem.

2. THE *QUISAS* AND *DIYAT* ORDINANCE OF 1990

The modern Pakistani legal system owes its essential origins to the common law tradition when the country obtained independence from Britain in 1947, but as it has not been significantly updated since its inception, this has contributed to the obfuscation of the legal process in Pakistan.[38] This legal system as constructed in 1947 was largely secular. Yet, there remains an ongoing debate about the extent to which Islam should be the driving force behind it in Pakistan. Under General Zia-al-Huq's regime, new Islamic courts were introduced on a parallel level with secular courts. This was ostensibly to "remind the secular courts and other institutions of government of the centrality of Islam," but emphasizing Islamization was also a way for leaders to consolidate their power by finding a common ground which pulls groups of people or political parties together.[39]

This is how "the Islamization of law" is used in Islamic countries to refer to an official program of replacing laws of Western origin with laws based on Islamic sources. In Pakistan, this is also used to refer to the creation of entirely new laws based on Islamic injunctions. In truth, the process of Islamization in Pakistan began after the death of Mohammed Ali Jinnah in 1948 and with the introduction of the Objectives Resolution in 1949. This deliberately did not advise in favor of the Islamization of the laws of Pakistan. However, it nevertheless was ambiguous enough in its advice, that people should live their lives in accordance with the teachings of Islam, that it came to be used as justification for such Islamization.[40] All three Pakistani Constitutions use the Objectives Resolution embodying the common provision that no law should be made that is "repugnant to the holy *Qur'an* and *sunnah*." However, this ambiguous wording has been manipulated by different groups in the promotion of Islamization. This is most vividly seen in the case of the introduction of *Quisas* and *Diyat* law.[41]

These were introduced by means of declaring that the PPC and the Code of Criminal Procedure were "repugnant" to Islamic teachings because these codes did not recognize blood money or pardons by a deceased's next of kin as options in a murder case. In fact, the only options provided in Islamic texts for dealing with murder cases were *quisas* (retaliation), *diyat* (blood money), or pardon.[42]

General Zia al-Huq's program of Islamization included the establishment of sharia courts to review Pakistani laws for their "repugnancy" to Islam. These courts could recommend the amendment of any law that they found to be repugnant in this sense and Chapter 16 of the PCC was brought under review in this manner in October 1979 in the case of *Gul Hassan Khan v. Government of Pakistan*. Khan and another petitioner who had been accused of murder had both arranged compromises according to Islamic law with the heirs of their victims, but these were not recognized by state law. They, therefore, sought to have the existing Pakistani Penal Code declared to be repugnant because it failed to provide for the teachings of Islam in this case.[43] The Peshawar sharia court found in favor of the petitioners and further expanded the scope of the review to all of Chapter 16 of the PPC, referring to the "urgency" of Islamization, and thus marking the beginning of the drive to formally reintroduce *diyat* into the Pakistani legal system. In 1990, *Quisas* and *Diyat* were finally formally reintroduced to the Pakistani Penal Code, incorporating a "long neglected but not forgotten doctrine into the largely secular legal system of the modern state" and generating an essential tension between "the empowerment of the victim and the needs of the state."[44]

The process by which the *Quisas* and *Diyat* Ordinance was first introduced and then formally incorporated into Pakistani law was that these provisions were initially introduced through the Criminal Law Amendment Ordinance VII of 1990. This became popularly known as *Qisas* and *Diyat* Ordinance (QDO) signed off in October 1990 by President Ghulam Ishaq Khan, during the caretaker government headed by Prime Minister Ghulam Mustafa Jatoi. However, the ordinance was then re-promulgated over twenty times. This is because the constitutional life of an ordinance is four months. It was only seven years later, during the government of Mian Nawaz Sharif in 1997, that it became an Act of Parliament, covering all offenses against human body as provided for in *Qisas* and *Diyat*.[45] Unsurprisingly, in these circumstances, others believe that "because of its omissions and ambiguities, the *Quisas* and *Diyat* Ordinance will not, in itself, create a definitive shift in the theory of punishment. Rather it will establish greater discretion and flexibility for judges who oversee its implementation."[46] Nevertheless, there remain dangers in a system where judicial discretion holds so much power, because these create opportunities for discrimination and corruption, as well as the possibility of instability and unaccountability.[47]

The *Quisas* and *Diyat* Ordinance could, therefore, be absorbed with varying levels of success in different areas of Pakistan. In rural and tribal regions, settlements in battery and murder cases were apparently already quite common. Settlements of this sort were not officially upheld by the state pre-1990, but nevertheless effectively brought an end to many disputes because the witnesses (who were usually family members of the deceased) would often change their stories once they had been compensated with *diyat* payments. Therefore, there is reason to believe that the implementation of the *Quisas* and *Diyat* Ordinance would have very little material effect in rural areas, other than to bestow judges with the power to officially accept or reject settlements that have been made.[48] It is the urban areas of Pakistan which have long moved away from the agrarian, land-based social structures of the kind that existed when *quisas* and *diyat* were first established in the Quran. *Quisas* and *diyat* mostly rely on the assumption that murders and assaults arise from situations such as disputes over water or land, or blood feuds between tribes that live in close proximity. Maintaining local harmony in such situations so as to avoid a cycle of revenge was indeed best achieved through *quisas* and *diyat* as against modern conceptions of retributive "justice." On the other hand, the kind of violence that occurs in urban spaces is frequently more anonymous and random, and here "the consequences of a pardon may be that the offender disappears into the anonymity of urban life and is therefore more likely to victimise another stranger than to attack the same family."[49] It is the potential for this system to be more easily manipulated which likely lead the courts and law drafters to maintain the option of *tazir* (discretionary penalty) and *fasad-fil-ardz*[50] (corruption on earth).

The law in the *QDO* currently draws attention to *qatl-i-amd*. This refers to any person who causes the death of a person by doing an act with the intention of causing death or bodily injury or by doing an act knowing that his act is so imminently dangerous that it in all probability will cause death. Such a person is said to be committing *qatl i-amd.* The law also refers to *badl-i-sulh* (i.e., mutually agreed compensation according to sharia). The way the rules work out is as follows. First, under Section 308(1) where an offender who is guilty of *qatl-i-amd* is not liable to *quisas* (retaliation) "he shall be liable to *diyat*" (blood money). However, Section 309(1) then allows for a "waiver" of quisas *qatl-i-amd* so that "an adult sane *wali* may, at any time and without any compensation, waive his right of quisas." Thereafter, it is clear from Section 310 that the law allows for the *compounding of qisas (Sulh) in qatl-i-amd* by the party offended against, so that "[i]n the case of *qatl-i-amd,* an adult sane *wali* may, at any time on accepting *badl-i-sulh*, compound his right of quisas." There is, however, a strict prohibition on such a party not to demand a "female" so that "a female shall not be given in marriage or otherwise in *badal-i-sulh.*" Indeed, Section 310A even goes further and imposes a penalty in such cases. It makes it clear that "[w]hosoever gives a female in marriage or otherwise compels her to enter into marriage, as *badal-i-sulh, vani* or *swara* or any other custom or practice under any name, in consideration of settling a civil dispute or a criminal liability, shall be punished with imprisonment." This imprisonment "may extend to seven years but shall not be less than three years" but in addition, such a person "shall also be liable to fine of five hundred thousand rupees."

What, however, will be the value of the diyat? This is set out in Section 323(1), so that "[t]he Court shall, subject to the Injunctions of Islam as laid down in the Holy Qur'an and Sunnah and keeping in view the financial position of the convict and the heirs of the victim, fix the value of diyat which shall not be less than the value of thirty thousand six hundred and thirty grams of silver." Viewed at from the standpoint of modern times, this is clearly an anachronism. The current value of silver in Pakistan is 617Rp/10 grams.[51] The current minimum diyat payment is, therefore, approximately 1,873,212Rp (£11,473.42 or $14,792.76).[52] But the average monthly income in Pakistan was only $148 ($1,776 pa) in 2015.[53] The result is that the minimum threshold placed on diyat payments acts so as to limit the potential for settlement,[54] so that poorer and less wealthy offenders cannot benefit from diyat. This was well demonstrated in the case of *Haji*.[55]

This arose when in the United Arab Emirates, in 2017, a Pakistani man, Haji, who was working in Ras al Khaimah accidentally ran over and killed another man who had been sleeping under the wheels of his truck. Haji could not afford the Dh100,000 *diyat* payment requested by the courts in agreement with the dead man's family. His insurance company refused to help, and he, therefore, spent seven months in prison in Ras Al Khaimah. The payment was eventually, however, covered by four anonymous donors, after Haji's story was featured on the website of *Emarat Al Youm*, a UAE newspaper. The appeal was sponsored by a state-sponsored project named "Faraj Box," which aids prisoners who cannot afford to pay fines or monetary compensations. This particular UAE case aptly demonstrates the payment of *diyat* in a claim of accidental death, arising under Sections 318–322 of the PPC. The families of both men lost a breadwinner. The payment of *diyat* compensated and supported the family of the victim in a way that the cold comfort of "vengeance" or "justice" would not have done. At the same time, it allowed Haji to be released from prison and to return to providing for his own family. Thus, the option of *diyat* played an important role in a justice system which must care for both victims (by ensuring that they or their families feel compensated or avenged for violent crimes against them or their families) and for the state by deterring people from committing violent crimes in the first place. In this case, Haji's inability to pay the full amount of *diyat* makes it clear that the financial penalty was a genuine punishment for him and likely a deterrent against murder for non-wealthy individuals.

The PPC also retains provisions which ensure that the state maintains the power to supersede private agreements in cases where the offense is regarded to have been "outrageous to the public conscience, or if the offender is considered a potential danger to the community, or if the offense has been committed in the name or on the pretext of honour." This is contained under the principle of *fasad-fil-ardz*, meaning "mischief on earth,"[56] so that under Section 311, notwithstanding the provisions of Section 309 and 310, "the Court may, having regard to the facts and circumstances of the case, punish an offender against whom the right of qisas has been waived or compounded with death or imprisonment for life or imprisonment of either description for a term of which may extend to fourteen years as *ta'zir*." The expression *fasad-fil-arz* is enormously wide. Not only shall it include "the past conduct of the offender" or even "the brutal or shocking manner in which the offense has been committed which is outrageous to the public conscience," but also cases where "the offender is considered a potential danger to the community." Given that all killers can be understood to be a "potential danger to the community," judges have the discretion in cases of their own choosing (which may include the preservation of "honor") to prevent the waiving of *quisas*. Thankfully, however, Section 311(F) of the PPC appears to-date to have been rarely invoked. One reason for this is the "interpretation provision" in Section 338 of the PPC, which is to the effect that "[i]*n the interpretation and application of the provisions of this Chapter, . . . the Court shall be guided by the Injunctions of Islam as laid down in the Holy Qur'an and Sunnah.*"

3. MISUSE AND EXPLOITATION

However, while the *Haji* case demonstrated how diyat can be applied effectively in a twenty-first-century context, other cases tell a sorry tale. They demonstrate how easily it is to manipulate the ordinance. Three notable cases can be examined: (i) the murders of *Samia Shaheed* who was killed by her father and ex-husband because of her remarriage to a man they considered to be unsuitable; (ii) the murder of *Shahzeb Khan*, a university student killed by a group of wealthy young men after a fight; and (iii) the murder by Raymond Davis, where the American authorities and Pakistani security services colluded to allegedly exploit the system to secure Davis's release by pressuring the families of his victims to accept large financial settlements in return for dropping a case which had extremely worrying international security implications. In all three cases, it could be argued there was at least some motivation in the killers' belief that they would be able to avoid retribution. These three cases make it clear that the "negotiated nature" of the law in Pakistan as established by the *Quisas* and *Diyat* Ordinance renders the law ineffective in deterring people from committing violent crimes, by prioritizing the offenders over the victims and their families. In the words of one prosecutor in the Pakistani legal system, "the accused is the favorite child of the law."[57]

Shahzeb Khan[58]

Shahzeb Khan was a student who was shot and killed by a group of young men in 2012, after an argument.[59] The Khan family pardoned their son's killers (under suspected duress), but after negotiation from prosecutors the Supreme High Court (SHC) upheld the original prison sentence, claiming that the killing amounted to an act of terrorism. This is because, although the intention behind the attack was not one of terrorism, the murder had achieved the same effect because of the reaction to the case by the public and in the media.[60] The case was transferred and retried in the Pakistani Anti-Terrorism Court (ATC). In the ATC, the opportunity for an out-of-court financial settlement was not available. In August 2016, the lawyer of the killer's family filed a criminal review application in the Sindh High Court (a local court) claiming that the killer, Shahrukh Jatoi, had been a juvenile at the time of the murder and should not, therefore, have been subject to terrorism charges. The Sindh High Court concluded that killing arose out of a "personal vendetta," and set aside the sentence handed out in the ATC. As such, it ordered that the case be retried in sessions court. The accused were released on bail in November 2017.

However, the Pakistani Supreme Court then ordered that this ruling should be overturned and insisted that the killers be rearrested or issued with Exit Control Orders which would prevent them leaving the country. The Sindh High Court, however, continued to defy the orders of the court, saying that they have no obligation to uphold High Court rulings which are unlawful, and as of August 2018, the case had still not been concluded.[61] One obvious reason for this impasse is that the Jatois are a prominent Pakistani family who are extremely wealthy and part of one of the biggest tribes in the Baloch region, so they have an extremely strong support base. The case illustrates just how vulnerable the laws regarding *diyat* are to exploitation by those who are rich and powerful. This case is a vivid illustration of how the option of being simply able pay *diyat* contributes to a sense of entitlement and invincibility by the powerful that is associated with their wealth and influence. The reality is that the very presence of *diyat* in the legal system emboldens wealthy individuals to commit violent crimes. They may rightly believe that they can easily avoid retribution.

Yet, this overlooks the fact that crimes like murder are not merely private disputes. They are civil crimes and offenses against society. Pakistani law incorporates the Islamic idea of *fasad-fil-ardh* (crimes which have an impact on wider society). As in the ATC, in cases where *fasad-fil-ardh* is held, it is surely arguable that punishment must be administered by the state irrespective of any private agreement or payment of *diyat*. If *tazir* and *fasad-fil-ardh* were exercised more often, it would ensure that the wealthy and well-connected cannot happily buy their way out of punishment, thus preventing the justice system "from decaying into a simple money equation."[62]

Samia Shahid[63]

Samia Shahid was killed by her first husband, Mohammad Shakeel (who was also her first cousin). She had already divorced him in a sharia court in the UK. However, this was without the permission of her father. This omission apparently "tarnished the honor of her family." After her divorce, she married another man. Not only was he not a member of her extended family, but he was not a Sunni Muslim either like herself but a Shia Muslim. This only enraged her father and ex-husband. All may well have remained well for her, however, were it not for the fact that Shahid was then persuaded to travel to Pakistan to meet her father and Shakeel. They hoped to pressure her into abandoning her second husband, Mukhtar Syed Kazam, and return to Shakeel. When she refused to do so, Shakeel and her father decided to kill her the night before she was to leave Pakistan and return to the United Kingdom.

According to the police report, Shahid was held down by her father as she tried to escape Shakeel's house who then strangled her. Shahid's father asked for a postmortem examination to be carried out two hours after his daughter's death. It seems that he wanted the cause of death to be established as murder as quickly as possible so that Shakeel could be charged with murder and he could then exploit Pakistan's laws regarding *diyat* and, as his daughter's *wali* (guardian), arrange a compensation payment for her death from Shakeel. Shakeel would then be set free. However, this well-arranged plan was frustrated by the arrival from the UK of Shahid's second husband, Kazam, who arrived in Pakistan after her death and filed a criminal complaint against her family, which promptly lead to a police investigation. Although, in this case, justice was served but this type of event is not uncommon in Pakistan. The fact that the power to forgive the killer, and even waive the payment of *diyat* is reserved to the *wali* of the victim (in this case the father), all too often means that for many women, those who ordered their deaths are also those with the power to ensure that the killer walks free.[64]

Raymond Davis[65]

Of the three cases, the case of Raymond Davis is the most extreme example of the application of diyat to satisfy the interests of the powerful party and the most well known in Pakistan. In 2011, Raymond Davis was a military contractor in Lahore. He was acting as security detail for CIA operatives. They were actually secretly working in Pakistan. While stuck in traffic one day, Davis saw two armed men, later identified as Faizan Haider and Mohammed Faheem, pull up in front of him on a motorbike. According to him, he saw one of them point a gun at him. Davis shot and killed one of the men and then shot the second man in the back as he tried to run away. A third man was killed when he was hit by a US consulate vehicle speeding to the scene to try and rescue Davis. Davis spent several weeks in prison while the American government tried to obtain diplomatic immunity for him. He was eventually released after the families of his victims were paid *diyat* of a reported $2.4 million. The payment was made by the Pakistani authorities. They apparently used the money from the public treasury, although the American government seemed to imply that they would reimburse the money to their Pakistani counterparts. Unsurprisingly, the handling of the case caused huge anger and there were widespread protests in Pakistan. In 2017, a lawyer named Tariq Asad filed a petition in the Islamabad High Court seeking information about who exactly paid the *diyat* money to the families of the victims. Considering the furious reaction to the case in Pakistan, and the suicide of Faheem's wife following the event, it seems unlikely that an agreement could have been reached between the families and the US government without a certain amount of duress.[66] Yet, this contradicts the terms of *diyat* which is required to be by mutual consent.

In this particular case, the Americans had first tried to obtain diplomatic immunity for Davis. It was only after this failed that an agreement was sought between Davis and the families of his victims. That agreement was then only achieved after the warring political factions in Pakistan realized that they be unable to hold Davis to ransom in their own power struggles.[67] In the process, Pakistan was described in a leading English weekly as America's "schizophrenic buddy," due to its inability to traverse the inconsistency and uncertainty generated by the infighting of different political factions.[68] There emerged huge anti-American feeling in the country. The Davis murder case is the most striking example of how *diyat* has become a convenient bargaining chip which works to the advantage of the perpetrator of the crime rather than as a tool for justice. Indeed, Pakistan police and state institutions actively encourage parties to settle matters out of court, thus reducing their own investigative and prosecution work. This means that it is in the interests of law enforcement agencies to persuade parties to accept *diyat* agreements, and this is so even when they are clearly illegal under Section 311 of the PPC.[69]

4. HONOR KILLINGS

The PPC explicitly excludes murders in the name of honor from its provisions for settlement.[70] However, although the so-called honor killings are illegal in Pakistan, they still happen with alarming frequency. This is despite new legislation in 2016 that introduced a recommended sentence of twenty-five-year imprisonment for honor killings.[71] The problem is that the decision as to whether a murder was an honor killing or a "regular" murder remains at the judge's discretion. If family members can convincingly argue that a killing occurred as the result of another issue, such as a land dispute, *diyat* is still viable as a substitute for *quisas*, and no minimum prison sentence is enforceable.[72] The Quisas and Diyat Ordinance grants families, as the heirs of the victim, the power to compromise and forgive. This would not be so bad were it not for the fact that many of these killings are committed by, and indeed, with the consent of the very same family members, to whom diyat is technically payable, as was so dramatically illustrated by the *Samia Shahid* case. Small wonder, therefore, that it has been argued that the *Quisas* and *Diyat* Ordinance should be completely removed from the PPC otherwise the perpetrators of honor killings will always be able to escape retribution.[73] The risk is there, in the words of the human rights lawyer Hina Jilani, because:

> Killings are [regarded as] private offenses, against the individual, not the state, so who will bring and pursue the charges of murder? If the father or brother kills a woman, the family of the girl will not pursue the case, as in their eyes no wrong has been done . . . the prosecution case collapses in almost all the scenarios of an honour killing: In *karo-kari* cases there is no aggrieved party to pursue the case, society as a whole approves of the killing . . . If a brother kills his sister on the ground of honour, her guardian, her father[,] can forgive his son.[74]

Palo has placed this view within a wider culture of Islam's "male-dominated interpretations of concepts like female chastity and male authority [which] reinforce[s] an Islamic culture of male dominance."[75] To give sharia law constitutional and legal backing by means of the *Quisas* and *Diyat* Ordinance was to legitimize inherently patriarchal customs, ensuring that the female experience of justice will remain fundamentally and inescapably discriminatory as long as the ordinance persists. Even more perversely, the potential financial gains available may act as an incentive for men to contrive claims of immoral behavior against their spouse or female relative which "justify" an honor killing and allow them to claim monetary compensation.[76] This is a clear example of a way in which the ordinance actively fails to promote stability, instead effectively encouraging crime. Indeed, the ordinance, by allowing a victim's heirs to pardon their murder, implicitly condones honor killings, and is, therefore, fundamentally discriminatory and contrary to the Pakistani Constitution which guarantees that all citizens are equal before the law.[77]

Nafisa Shah has more recently endorsed Palo after extensively reviewing the ways in which the *Quisas* and *Diyat* Ordinance makes it possible for families to carry out honor killings without fearing retribution. She concludes that the ordinance effectively acts as an endorsement of such practices and empowers local judges to rule in a way which reinforces cultural norms of gender inequality. It seems hard to disagree with Palo's observation that Pakistani authorities work behind "a shield of cultural relativism" on the assumption that "because this inhumane, gender oppressive form of punishment is accepted by Pakistani society, the judicial system should also permit it."[78] The same logic is essentially applied to the *Quisas* and *Diyat* Ordinance, which, because of its origins in Islamic custom, claims a kind of cultural protection making it difficult to dispute its validity. This ensures that any measure designed to restrict the ordinance's power will always be regarded as an essential condemnation of Islamic practice. Yet, there must be a way, as Rachel Ruane has argued, of finding "alternative interpretations [of Islam] that can combine both traditional understandings of Islamic law with fundamental principles of human rights."[79] The fact that this has still not been done is a failure of judicial imagination. Curiously, it is not a failure of sharia itself.

5. THE ANTI-TERRORISM COURT

Pakistan's Anti-Terrorism Act of 1997 is notoriously ambiguous. It allows terrorism charges to be laid against political activists and human rights defenders. Prosecutors are enabled to all too easily "circumvent the regular criminal courts and clog anti-terrorism courts with ordinary crimes,"[80] with the result that the anti-terrorist court, like ordinary Pakistani courts, suffers from increasing judicial paralysis.[81] Under the Ant-Terrorism Act, 1997,[82] terrorism is defined so widely in Section 4(6)(1) *inter alia*, as to include not just "the use or threat of action" that "is designed to coerce and intimidate or overawe the Government or the public or a section of the public or community" but also "to create a sense of fear or insecurity in society," as well as "for the purpose of advancing a religious, sectarian or ethnic cause." The Pakistani constitution is already known to be ambiguous and the Pakistani legal codes are easy to manipulate.[83] Given that the definition of terrorism offered here is so extremely broad it can easily be extended to include ordinary murders if the Supreme Court so chooses[84] without any constitutional restraint being imposed.

The dangers of this happening were exhibited in the *Shahzeb Khan* murder case (considered above), where prosecutors exploited the ambiguous definition of terrorism in the Pakistani Anti-Terrorism Act, and had Khan's case transferred to the ATC. The justification for this decision bears consideration. It was that "since the incident had created a 'sense of helplessness' in the people" because it had "attracted the attention of public at large," being widely covered by the media, that the threshold of terrorism had been met, "regardless of the absence of motive to create 'terror' in society."[85] However, the Jatoi family successfully petitioned the courts to release Shahrukh Jatoi (one of the killers) on the grounds that the offense was not terrorism but based on a personal disagreement. No wonder that in a comment in the Pakistani *Express Tribune*, Sharukh Jatoi's lawyer is said to have declared, "[t]he Constitution is an empty vessel and judges pour meanings in them,"[86] demonstrating how vulnerable Pakistani justice is to the beliefs of individual judges and their own interpretations of scripture. Time and time again one finds evidence of how the courts fail to interpret both the scripture and legislative provisions like *fais-fil-ardz* in a fair and consistent manner, thus allowing justice to be avoided. The *Shahzeb Khan* murder case amply demonstrates how the penal code is not robust enough to properly manage murder cases. In this case, prosecutors obviously felt that in order to ensure that Khan's killers received prison time, it was necessary to find a way of trying the case in the tougher anti-terrorism court, which has the power to override private agreements between killers and the heirs of their victims. Facts had to be manipulated. This made it possible for the killers to be released. Yet, such a circumvention of the jurisdiction of the ordinary criminal court also weakened the Anti-Terrorism Act, which is frequently resorted to by prosecutors in an effort to ensure that even perpetrators of "normal" crimes cannot avoid punishment, because of delays been caused. So bad is the situation that the Pakistani government itself has "cited [. . .] delays in the Anti-Terrorism Court (ATC) proceedings as a 'failure' of civilian courts to provide expeditious justice."[87] Going to and fro, from one court to the other, is not quite the "negotiated nature" of justice in Pakistan Anatoly Lieven had referred to, but something far more sinister and insidious—it is a calculated exercise in avoiding justice altogether.

6. WHITHER JUSTICE?

If a system of criminal law is to be judged as a means to an end, and not an end in itself, then it must be tested against a standard of efficacy, as Wasti argues,[88] given that "[p]unishment, an evil, is not a desirable act in itself" and that "averting the recurrence of the offence is not only the prime objective but the sole permissible purpose of inflicting a criminal punishment."[89] Pakistan and the *Quisas* and *Diyat* Ordinance fall short of this standard of "efficacy" for justice systems. The introduction of the *Quisas* and *Diyat* Ordinance changed the role of the state in the prosecution of murder cases, which became a facilitator of the "fair passage of the case through the courts."[90] The problem is that the law provides exemptions in imposition of *quisas*. As for the *diyat*, this is often exploited. So the ordinance only contributes to a "deterioration of the situation of law and order," with the Pakistani justice system hovering between its harshest and softest elements, uncompromisingly incorporating some of the toughest elements of Islamic law, but lacking the rigor to properly enforce these laws, in a way that the system is genuinely equal, as was manifestly intended in the inception of these laws in the Quran.[91]

Ultimately, state power is maintained, because although *quisas* and *diyat* increase victim empowerment by allowing the punishment for a violent crime to be dictated by the victim or the victim's heirs, so long as the exculpatory clauses regarding *tazir/ fasad-fil-arz* remain, the power available to the victims or their families is necessarily tempered. In this way, the state ultimately retains control of the penal system, as judges retain the right to overrule private agreements. Moreover, Section 338G of the ordinance allows for legislative change to be carried out to further the aims of the ordinance, in accordance with Islamic ideology.[92] What Pakistan has succeeded in doing after 1990 is to discard a system "which, in theory, provided consistency in prosecutions and sentencing, and [replaced] it with a regime that bestows great discretion on the judiciary," but which necessitates a high level of regular scrutiny to ensure that the system remains fair.[93] However, the dogged persistence of "honor" killings in Pakistan, and the fact that the well-heeled escape justice only confirms that the current level of scrutiny is insufficient.

In fact, the *Quisas* and *Diyat* Ordinance is also destabilizing of the rule of law. From the outset, it fails first to prevent crimes from being committed. Once committed, it then falls short in exacting justice. The prevention and punishment of crime are the twin pillars of any justice system. The *Quisas* and *Diyat* Ordinance demonstrably fail on both fronts. It does not end there. There is constant negotiation between local, religious, and state legal systems. There are then subsequent negotiations in the opportunity being given to victims and their families as to how they choose the manner of punishment. On top of this, there is official corruption which renders the entire system inherently unstable and unpredictable, with individual judges given wide berth to engage in personal interpretations of scripture as and how they want, but often in a way which discriminates against women. The result of this decentralization of the legal system is "the government [retreating] from its own accountability."[94] The result is that the failure of the Pakistani government to develop "a fair and consistent pattern of overseeing the quisas and diyat process" has led to "confusion and inequity [which . . .] result in society's disillusionment with judicial arbitration."[95] In fact, the changes made to the legal system in 1990 drastically curtailed the execution of justice in the country with the Supreme Court's conviction rate dropping from 79 percent in 1984 to 35 percent in 2000.[96] Such has been the race to the bottom that by 2014 this number has since fallen still more to 26 percent.[97]

7. EVALUATION OF THE ORDINANCE

Sadly, much international commentary swiftly morphs into criticism of "Islamic law," which many Muslims see as being indistinguishable from criticism of Islam itself. The lashing of a young Nigerian woman named Bariya Magazu for committing *zina* (a sexual offense) is a case in point.[98] Magazu had become pregnant out of wedlock. She claimed she had been raped. Her lawyers had been granted an appeal date in a higher sharia court, thus successfully postponing the flogging pending the result of the appeal. The ensuing international outcry at the injustice of punishing the victim of a rape was, however, layered with generic criticism of Islamic law and Islamic customs regarding sexual conduct. Many commentators declaimed that sharia law to be inherently inhumane and illegitimate. Magazu fell victim to a backlash in Pakistan. Contrary to what the international community had hoped, the date for Magazu's flogging was brought forward. It was carried out a week before the planned appeal. Local officials proudly declared that they would ignore any human rights-based appeals for clemency. They would only be "willing to consider arguments made from the point of [view of] Muslim laws."[99] Flogging is an extreme and cruel form of punishment. It subjects the victim to inhuman and degrading treatment in violation of international law. It should be outlawed for its own sake. However, in Magazu's case, the criticism of Islamic laws from non-Muslims in the West exacerbated her predicament. It drove the local governor to order that the punishment be brought forward for fear that "an appeal would be successful or that public outcry would prompt the Nigerian [federal] government to intervene."[100] In the result, for the beleaguered Bariya Magazu, the invocation of "human-rights standards" was of no protection but instead placed her in even more danger.

This is, therefore, a clear illustration of how foreign governments and NGOs should desist from declaring that Islamic law to be alien to human right standards, for this creates a false dichotomy, which only serves to exacerbate the division between the two.[101] Once sharia law is characterized as being incompatible with human rights standards, any calls for reform will be presented as a choice between being "pro-rights" or "pro-Islam," and this is counterproductive in that it fails to protect vulnerable individuals.[102] In the case of Bariya Magazu, there was a far easier route available to follow because the punishment of rape victims for *zina* is explicitly forbidden by all schools of Islamic law and in her case sharia was not the root of her punishment.[103] The problem is that many Muslim societies retain traditional power structures. They are deeply patriarchal. They continue to rely heavily on the reproductive capacities of women's bodies. Such societies regard female sexuality as something to be tightly guarded and rigorously controlled. This is why there are extremely harsh punishments for any sexual infraction.[104] On top of this are the deeply ingrained misogynistic attitudes which lead to the phenomena of rape and victim-blaming. Yet, it needs emphasizing that this is not a uniquely Islamic issue. It is tied to societal factors. These attitudes are, nevertheless, fostered by the wide scope within Islam for the interpretation of scripture.

The same may be said of the *Quisas* and *Diyat* Ordinance. The ordinance is clearly vulnerable to exploitation. It has been shown to be particularly valuable to the wealthy wishing to escape justice, or to the families of honor-killing victims. However, honor killing is not unique to Pakistan. The rich trying to buy their way out of justice is also far from being a specifically Muslim issue. Indeed, the *Quisas* and *Diyat* Ordinance does not explicitly condone either of these misuses. In fact, there are provisions within the ordinance giving judges the power to overrule private agreements where this is deemed appropriate. One such case is where they believe the motivation for a murder to be the preservation of "honour." Without societal change, the problems will persist and the Pakistani government will have little incentive for reevaluating the ordinance.

8. CONCLUSION

The interrogation of laws based on Islamic teachings is more potent today than perhaps ever before because many Islamic teachings exist in an "uneasy tension with modernity."[105] The situation is compounded by the fact that the harsh punishments of the seventh century found in a literal reading of the Quran and sunnah have been all too easily exploited by misogynists and extremists so that these texts have been used to justify slavery, rape, and mass-murder by groups like al-Qaeda, the Taliban, and ISIS.[106] It is something which haunts the word "sharia," and which observant Muslims are perpetually hounded with in non-Muslim medias. It is, however, counterproductive to dismiss all products of sharia in this way, not least because it strengthens the case of extremist groups like ISIS. What is needed is engagement with extremist ideologies in intellectual terms. Dismissing them out-of-hand carries with it the implication that such extremist interpretation is the only interpretation of Islamic law. In so doing, all that is achieved is that Muslims are presented with a stark choice between modernity and their faith which is erroneous. Muslim governments, like Pakistan, have little incentive to reevaluate their sharia-compliant laws, even when that is necessary in the *Quisas* and *Diyat* Ordinance, which, in practice, permits behavior that strays from Islamic teachings. That is why for there to be realistic change, sharia must be "taken on its own terms and regarded as something to work with rather than an obstacle to be removed."[107]

That is not to say that religiously ordained injustice should be overlooked, but where there is injustice based on Islamic teachings, it is "unnecessarily provocative" to question sharia—God's law—or suggest that it should be subject to change.[108] The more viable option is to go along with Islamic scholars who themselves readily accept that *fiqh*—different interpretations of what sharia should mean in the real world, based on study of the Quran and the sunnah—is inherently pluralistic, fallible, and subject to questioning. Changes to sharia-based laws in Pakistan should take as their model Pakistan's 2006 Women's Protection Act that amended the conditions for *zina* trials and discarded the conditions for rape prosecutions.[109] What is interesting about these changes is that they were affected by criticism of the accuracy of the *fiqh* interpretation, under which four witnesses were to confirm a rape, on grounds that this was an inaccurate understanding of the sharia. In this way, "using only established, uncontested women's *fiqh* rights, it is . . . possible for classical, un-reformed, Islamic law to do much of the heavy lifting in improving the lives of many Muslim women."[110]

This chapter argues that the same attitude could and should be applied to the *Quisas* and *Diyat* Ordinance. For there to be realistic and successful change, it is altogether too simplistic to characterize the sharia basis of the 1990 Ordinance as flawed and inadequate. What must be sought instead are justifications for reformed view, whether this be in the sharia or in the ordinance, as it currently exists. After all, the Pakistani government has already done this, given recent commitments to the protection of women's rights in their attempts to reduce numbers of honor killings in the name of honor as *fasad-fil-ardz* (mischief on earth) crimes, and judges must be encouraged to do the same. Greater emphasis must be placed on the spirit in which *quisas* and *diyat* were originally conceived in the seventh century, which was for the purpose of promoting peace and social harmony, which the ordinance fails to do in its current iteration. Change will not come easily. Quite aside from the problems of disputing sharia-based laws, the issues which obfuscate the delivery of justice in the implementation of the *Quisas* and *Diyat* Ordinance also afflict every other institution in Pakistan. Civil and political life in

Pakistan is consistently arrested by the opposing tensions of Islamic values, traditional tribal custom, the hangover from of British colonial practices, as well as having to be a key player in the global war on terror.[111] Indeed, the introduction of the ordinance into the Pakistani Penal Code in 1990 was part of an ongoing process of Islamization, which served a specific political agenda, and failed to recognize the ways in which Pakistan had changed. It hardly needs reminding how the social and economic realities of modern-day Pakistan are fundamentally different from those under which *quisas* and *diyat* were first practiced, thus unnecessarily creating an ongoing tension between scripture and twenty-first-century society. Religious edicts destabilize the Pakistani state. Legislation for greater rigor exists in the provision for *fasad-fil-ardz* but it is easily circumvented, and there needs to be greater accountability of judges for their failure to use the law as it stands.

Whereas discretion is an element in all power, the individual discretion of judges should be properly structured, and not be at large as it is presently. The state intervenes to ensure parity for all in the eyes of the law. Justice should not be rendered so vulnerable to manipulation, bribery, and prejudice. The paying of *diyat* by high-profile figures (which has included the US government) to escape retribution only serves to show that what we have here is a punitive system which works not to the advantage of the victim, but the perpetrator of crime. This works if the seventh-century Islamic ideal of law, being used promoting peace and social harmony, is to be taken to mean that it should maintain the interests of the rich and powerful in society over those that are weak and dispossessed, but this is not what Islamic law originally envisioned. Such a view goes against the spirit of these laws. *Diyat* in particular recognizes that "retribution" in the form of *quisas* may not be adequate compensation for a family that has lost a marriageable daughter, or an individual who has lost the use of an arm and can no longer work. This is why what is needed is an empowered and fair judiciary which can limit opportunities for exploitation, so that there is genuine compensatory justice.

In the spirit of Islamic teachings, the exploitation of *diyat* by the wealthy must be considered to be as repugnant to the Quran and the sunnah as the failure to provide proper compensation for a victim or their family. In this time of widespread global challenges to religious practice, Muslim states are naturally cautious of stepping away from sharia law and, therefore, seemingly from Islam itself. However, the current method of application of the *Quisas* and *Diyat* Ordinance in Pakistan does not serve the state or the people adequately. An alternative future must be envisioned in Pakistan. A future where gender bias and class bias do not stand in the way of the constitutional guarantee of parity before the law—and this will be a future which succeeds in forging sophisticated connections and coalitions between traditional Islamic beliefs and the values of modernity in a changed Pakistan.

NOTES

1. Anatol Lieven, *Pakistan: A Hard Country* (London: Penguin, 2012) pg. 107.

2. Imtiaz Gul, 'Terror Crime and the Tardy Justice System', *Express Tribune* (July 1, 2014), http://www.tribune.com.pk/story/729778/terror-crime-and-the-tardy-justice-system/ see also Sabir Shah, Judiciary and Prosecution in India and Pakistan, NEWS INT'L (Dec. 12, 2013), http://www.thenews.com.pkfTodays-News-13-27236-Judiciary-and-prosecution-in-India-and-Pakistan

3. Peter G. Strasser, 'The Evolving Pakistani Criminal Justice System: A Study of the Raymond David Matter', *Tulane Journal of International and Comparative Law* (Vol. 23, Issue 1: Winter 2014), pp. 107–150 (pg. 117).

4. See, The Pakistan Penal Code (Act XLV of 1860) as found at pakistani.org http://www.pakistani.org/pakistan/legislation/1860/actXLVof1860.html#f126 And corroborated by The Pakistan Penal Code as found at OECD.org https://www.oecd.org/site/adboecdanti-corruptioninitiative/46816797.pdf, and The Criminal Law (Amendment) Act, as printed in *The Gazette of Pakistan*, No. M-302, L.7646 (Islamabad, 11th April 1997) http://www.na.gov.pk/uploads/documents/1324604341_299.pdf

5. *Id.*

6. See section 8. 'Impact of Quisas and Diyat on the Anti-Terrorism Court'.

7. Strasser, *supra* note 4, at pg. 120.

8. Lieven, *supra* note 2, at pg. 106.

9. Kashif Zafar, 'Is the local justice system a menace?' *The Express Tribune* (5th May 2014) https://tribune.com.pk/story/704253/is-the-local-justice-system-a-menace/

10. Lieven, *supra* note 2, at pg. 28.

11. Lieven, *supra* note 2, at pp. 86–87.

12. *Id.* at pp. 91–92.

13. See section 7. 'Misuse and exploitation – Samia Shaheed'.

14. PPC *supra* note 1, at Section 310A. Shamsul Islam, 'The custom of vani: Tit-for-tat, the tribal way', *Express Tribune* (28th March, 2014) https://tribune.com.pk/story/688205/the-custom-of-vani-tit-for-tat-the-tribal-way/

15. Lieven, *supra* note 2, at pg. 87.

16. *Id.* at pg. 27.

17. Yusuf Ali Qur'an, pg. 71.

18. Tahir Wasti, 'Islamic Law in Practice: The Application of Qisas and Diyat Law in Pakistan' *Yearbook of Islamic and Middle Eastern Law* (Vol. 13: 2006–2007) pp. 97–106 (pg. 104)

19. *Id.* at pp.104–105.

20. Quran, 5:33–34.

21. See generally Mohamed El-Awa, *Punishment in Islamic Law* (American Trust Publications, 1982).

22. Vogel, 'The Trial of Terrorists under Classical Islamic Law' (n 77), 59.

23. Quran, 4:92.

24. Quran, 5:45; Jeffrey Walker, 'The Rights of the Accused in Saudi Criminal Procedure' (1993) 15 *Loyola of Los Angeles International and Comparative Law Review* 863, 868.

25. Quran 4:92; Rudolph Peters, *Crime and Punishment in Islamic Law* (Cambridge University Press, 2006), 186–187.

26. Vogel, 'The Trial of Terrorists under Classical Islamic Law' (n 77), 60.

27. Ibid, 56.

28. Evan Gottesman, 'The Re-emergence of Quisas and Diyat in Pakistan', *Columbia Human Rights Law Review* (Vol. 23, Issue 2: Summer 1992), pp. 433-462 (pp. 443–444).

29. *Id.* at pg. 444.

30. PPC *supra* note, at Sections 306 and 308.

31. Please see section 3. 'Official Reintroduction of Quisas and Diyat in 1990'.

32. Maurite Berger, 'Sharia – A Flexible Notion', *Rechtsfilosofie en Rechtstheorie* (Vol. 35, Issue 3, 2006), pp. 335–345.

33. Berger, *supra* note 24, at pg. 336.

34. Berger, *supra* note 24, at pg. 337.

35. Berger, *supra* note 24, at pg. 338.

36. Berger, *supra* note 24, at pg. 340.

37. Berger, *supra* note 24, at pg. 344.

38. Strasser, *supra* note 4, at pg. 136.

39. John T. Philipsborn, 'Unsteadily to Centre Stage: An Overview of Pakistan's Justice', *Judicature* (Vol. 85, Issue 5: March-April 2002), pp. 228–236 (p. 230).

40. Wasti, *supra* note 18, at pp. 99–101.

41. *Id.* at pp. 100–101.

42. *Id.*

43. Gottesman, *supra* note 20, pp. 437–439.

Gul Hassan Khan v Government of Pakistan

- Two petitioners, Gul Hassan Khan and Noor Alam Khan, were convicted of murder and sentenced to death, but both arranged compromises with the heirs of their victims and were subsequently pardoned by the heirs.
- This agreement was **not recognized** by the Pakistani Penal Code or the Criminal Procedure Code at the time. The petitioners sought to have provisions of the acts therefore declared repugnant to the Injunctions of Islam, complaining specifically about section 302 of the PPC and section 345 of the CPC.
    - **PPC Section 302** stated that "Whoever commits qatl-i-amd shall be punished with death or imprisonment for life and shall also be liable to fine." The problem with this section, according to the judge in the Peshawar sharia court, lay in its failure to allow for pardon or settlement by the victim's heirs in the way that is described as one of two possible means of dealing with a murder case in the Qur'an. (Gul Hassan Khan, P L D 1980 at Peshawar 15).

- **CPC Section 345** listed all offenses which may be settled but omits murder. As a result, section 345(7), which states, "No offence shall be compounded [settled] except as provided by this section" denies the heirs of murder victims the right to settle.
- **CPC Section 381** also omitted the heirs' right to pardon those sentenced to death: "When the sentence of death passed by a Court of Session is submitted to the High Court for confirmation, such Court of Session shall, on receiving the order of confirmation or other order of the High Court thereon, cause such order to be carried into effect by issuing a warrant or taking such other steps as may be necessary." **Both sections 345 and 381 were amended by the *Quisas* and *Diyat* Ordinance.**

44. *Id.* at pg. 434.**

45. Waseem Ahmad Shah, 'Pros and Cons of Quisas and Diyat law', *Dawn* online (16th September 2013) https://www.dawn.com/news/1043236

46. Gottesman, *supra* note 20, at pp. 433–434.

47. *Id.* at pg. 434.

48. *Id.* at pg. 457.

49. *Id.* at pg. 457.

50. See for example, Muhammad Sohail and Ataullah Khan Mahmood, "Islamic Criminal Jurisprudence on the offence of Trafficking in Persons: An interpretation of Fasad Fil Arz and Hadd Offence", *Pakistan Journal of Islamic Research* (Vol. 20, Issue 2_11, 2020, pp. 107–114) esp. at pp. 110–112.

51. Urdu Point News, Pakistan, daily Silver rate 9th August 2018, https://www.urdupoint.com/business/silver-rates-in-pakistan.html

52. Bloomberg News online currency converter, 9th August 2018, 1250 BST https://www.bloomberg.com/markets/currencies

53. CEIC statistics https://www.ceicdata.com/en/indicator/pakistan/monthly-earnings

54. Gottesman, *supra* note 20, at pg. 442.

55. Ahmed Shabaan & Ras AL Khaimah, 'Four donors pay Dh100,000 blood money for Pakistani prisoner's release in RAK', *Kahleej Times* (7th March 2018) https://www.khaleejtimes.com/news/general/four-donors-pay-dh100000-blood-money-for-pakistani-prisoners-release-in-rak

56. Waseem Ahmad Shah, 'Pros and Cons of Quisas and Diyat law', *Dawn* online (16th September 2013) https://www.dawn.com/news/1043236

57. Suzanna Koster, Pakistan's Travesty of Justice, GLOBAL Post (Oct. 6, 2011), http://www.globalpost.com/dispatch/news/regions/asia-pacific/pakistan/l11005/pakistan-justiceterrorism-qadri-taseer-blashphemy-law (quoting a Pakistani prosecutor).

58. Quamber Zaidi, 'Shahzeb Khan Murder: SC dismisses review petition filed by accused Sharukh Jatoi' *Geo TV News* (5th March 2018) https://www.geo.tv/latest/184853-shahzeb-khan-murder-sc-dismisses-review-petition-filed-by-shahrukh-jatoi

59. AFP, 'Eyewitnesses say Shahrukh Jatoi shot Shahzeb Khan', *Geo News TV* (11th January 2013) https://www.geo.tv/latest/83725-eyewitnesses-say-shahrukh-jatoi-shot-shahzeb-khan

60. Naeem Sahoutara, 'Shahzeb murder case: SC orders names of Shahrukh Jatoi, three others to be placed on ECL', *The Express Tribune* (13th January 2018) https://tribune.com.pk/story/1607883/1-shahzeb-murder-case-sc-orders-shahrukh-jatoi-three-others-placed-ecl/ See Section 7. The Impact of the Quisas and Diyat Ordinance on the Pakistani Anti-Terrorism Court.

61. Hasnaat Mailk, 'SC asks locus standi of civil society challenging SCH ruling in Shahzeb murder case', *The Express Tribune* (31st January 2018), https://tribune.com.pk/story/1622982/1-sc-asks-locus-standi-civil-society-challenging-shc-ruling-shahzeb-murder-case/

62. Saad Rasool, 'Blood Money', *Nation*, News, Columns (21 December 2017) https://nation.com.pk/31-Dec-2017/blood-money

63. Details all taken from Jon Boon, 'Samia Shahid's father allegedly hoped to use blood money laws to get away with murder', *Guardian*, News, World, Pakistan (6th September 2016) https://www.theguardian.com/world/2016/sep/06/samia-shahid-father-alleged-hoped-to-use-blood-money-laws-to-get-away-with

64. Nafisa Shah, *Honour and Violence: Gender Power and Law in Southern Pakistan* (New York: Berghahn Books, 2016), pp. 101–104.

65. Details of the case all taken from the following: Raymond Davis and Storms Reback, *The Contractor: How I Landed in Pakistani Prison and Ignited a Diplomatic Crisis* (Dallas, TX: Benbella, 2017).

Omar Waraich, 'Pakistan: How Sharia Freed American Ray Davis', *Time* (16th March 2011) http://content.time.com/time/world/article/0,8599,2059330,00.html Anon. 'Blood for money for blood', *Economist,* Asia, Banyan blog (3rd May 2012) https://www.economist.com/banyan/2012/05/03/blood-for-money-for-blood

66. Malik Asad, 'Who paid blood money to Raymond Davis's Victims?', *DAWN* (13th July 2017) https://www.DAWN.com/news/1344997/who-paid-blood-money-to-raymond-davis-victims

67. Imtiaz Gul, 'Pakistan Couldn't Give Davis Immunity Even If It Wanted To', *Foreign Policy* (Feb. 23, 2011), http://southasia.foreignpolicy.com/posts/2011/02/23/pakistan-couldn-tgive.davis-immunityevenif it wanted-to. Strasser tells us that 'Davis was caught up in a power struggle between President Zardari and the political rulers of Punjab-the Sharif family. For some, the Davis case provided a golden opportunity. There was speculation that by fuelling the anger on the street against both President Zardari and the United States, various groups could use this incident of the "American Rambo" to inflame public opinion and bolster their own popularity.'

68. Bina Shah, 'Saving Private Raymond' *DAWN* (Feb. 24, 2011), http://www.DAWN.com/ news/608535/saving-private-raymond

69. Nazish Brohi, 'The state and *diyat*', *Dawn* online, (3rd January 2018) https://www.dawn.com/news/1380426/the-state-and-diyat

70. PPC *supra* note 1, at Section 302.

71. Saroop Ijaz, ''Honour Killings Continue in Pakistan Despite New Law', *Human Rights Watch, Dispatches* (25th September 2017) https://www.hrw.org/news/2017/09/25/honor-killings-continue-pakistan-despite-new-law

72. Malik Asad, 'Loopholes persist in 'honour killing' bill', *DAWN* online (24th July 2016) https://www.hrw.org/news/2017/09/25/honor-killings-continue-pakistan-despite-new-law

73. Stephanie Palo, 'A Charade of Change: Quisas and Diyat Ordinance Allows Honour Killings to Go Unpunished in Pakistan', *U.C. Davis Journal of International Law & Policy* (Vol. 15, Issue 1 Fall 2008), (pp. 93–109), pg. 94.

74. Amnesty International, Pakistan: Violence Against Women in the Name of Honour, Al Index ASA 33/017/1999, at 50 (Sept. 22, 1999), available at http://web.amnesty.org/library/index/engasa330171999

75. Mazna Hussain, "Take My Riches, Give Me Justice": A Contextual Analysis of Pakistan's Honor Crimes Legislation, 29 HARV. J. L. & GENDER 223,233 (2006)

76. Palo, *supra* note 60, at pg. 101.

77. *Id.* at pp. 102–103. Also Pakistani Constitution arts. 25(1)-(2) (1973).

78. Palo, *supra* note 60, at pg. 103.

79. Rachel A. Ruane, Murder in the Name of Honor: Violence Against Women in Jordan and Pakistan, 14 EMORY INT'L L. REV. 1523, 1523 (2000).

80. Reema Omer, 'Defining Terrorism', *Geo TV News* online (26th June 2018) https://www.geo.tv/latest/200591-defining-terrorism

81. Imtiaz Gul, 'Terror, crime and the Tardy Justice System', *The Express Tribune* (1st July 2014) https://tribune.com.pk/story/729778/terror-crime-and-the-tardy-justice-system/

82. Text of the Anti-Terrorism Act (1997) as found at ilo.org https://www.ilo.org/dyn/natlex/docs/ELECTRONIC/81777/88943/F435058093/PAK81777.pdf

83. Wasti, *supra* note 18, at pp. 100–101.

84. Reema Omer, 'Defining Terrorism', *Geo TV News* online (26th June 2018) https://www.geo.tv/latest/200591-defining-terrorism

85. Reema Omer, 'Defining Terrorism', *Geo TV News* online (26th June 2018) https://www.geo.tv/latest/200591-defining-terrorism

86. Hasnaat Mailk, 'Shahzeb Khan Murder: Top court rejects Shahrukh Jatoi's review petition', *Express Tribune* (5th March 2018) https://tribune.com.pk/story/1651634/1-shahzeb-khan-murder-top-court-rejects-shahrukh-jatois-review-petition/

87. Reema Omer, 'Defining Terrorism', *Geo TV News* online (26th June 2018) https://www.geo.tv/latest/200591-defining-terrorism

88. Wasti, *supra* note 18, at pg. 101.

89. *Id.* at pp. 102–103.

90. *Id.* at pg. 105.

91. *Id.* at pp. 105–106.

92. ***338-G. Rules:*** *The Government may, in consultation with the Council of Islamic ideology, by notification in the official Gazette, make such rules as it may consider necessary for carrying out the purposes of this Chapter.*

93. Gottesman, *supra* note 20, at pg. 459.

94. *Id.* at pg. 460.

95. *Id.*at pg. 461.

96. Nazish Brohi, 'The state and diyat', Dawn online, 3rd January 2018, https://www.dawn.com/news/1380426/the-state-and-diyat

97. Strasser, *supra* note 4, at pg. 120.

98. Asifa Quraishi, 'What if Sharia Weren't the Enemy: Rethinking International Women's Rights Advocacy on Islamic Law', *Columbia Journal of Gender and Law* (Vol. 22, Issue 1 2011), pp. 173–249.

99. Quraishi, *supra* note 91, at pp. 185–186.

100. Quraishi, *supra* note 91, at pg. 188.

101. Quraishi, *supra* note 91, at pg. 176.

102. Quraishi, *supra* note 91, at pg. 186.

103. Quraishi, *supra* note 91, at pg. 184.

104. Ayaan Hirsi Ali, *Heretic: Why Islam Needs a Reformation Now* (New York: Harper Collins, 2015), pp. 146–147.

105. Hirsi Ali, *supra* note 97, at pg. 16.

106. Rukmini Callimachi offers a concise and interesting explanation of how ISIS uses the Qur'an and sharia to justify and spread their ideology in her podcast *Calipahte.* In particular she illustrates how this academic religious discourse is deeply appealing to the kinds of young Islamic men and woman whom ISIS recruits, their uncompromising and unilateral return to the values of 7th century Islam seemingly eliminating the issues of reconciling Islamic values with modern life. Rukmini Callimachi - *Caliphate* [podcast] (2018) https://www.nytimes.com/interactive/2018/podcasts/caliphate-isis-rukmini-callimachi.html

107. Quraishi, *supra* note 91, at pg. 202.

108. Quraishi, *supra* note 91, at pg. 204.

109. Quraishi, *supra* note 91, at pp. 208–209.

110. Quraishi, *supra* note 91, at pg. 218.

111. Hussain Nadim, 'Neither Friend nor Foe: Pakistan, the United states and the War in Afghanistan', Lowly Institute *Analyses*, 28th September 2017, https://www.lowyinstitute.org/sites/default/files/documents/Nadim%20-%20Pakistan%2C%20the%20United%20States%20and%20the%20war%20in%20Afghanistan_WEB.pdf

Chapter 6

The Legal Status of Ahmadis in Pakistan

Yasser Latif Hamdani

THE AHMADIS

Ahmadis are a relatively small community in Pakistan numbering between 0.2 to 2 million.[1] They profess to be Muslims but are considered non-Muslims by the rest of the Muslim sects almost unanimously. In 1974, Pakistan passed the second constitutional amendment to declare them non-Muslims for the purposes of law and Constitution. In doing so, the government of the time claimed to have resolved a long-standing theological dispute that existed in the Muslim community of South Asia. Later, further restrictions were introduced in the Pakistan Penal Code, 1860, through an ordinance promulgated by the military government of General Zia ul Haq in the 1980s. The restrictive community-specific ordinance has been used to persecute and often marginalize this community in Pakistan. The Ahmadi persecution is quite unique in the sense that the community identifies itself as part of the Muslim majority but the majority insists on excluding them from its ranks. This is coupled with violence, most notably on May 28, 2010, when ninety-five community members were gunned down in Lahore while praying in an act of terrorism. While it was a case of terrorism, the act was widely applauded by many sections of the society. When a former prime minister, Mian Muhammad Nawaz Sharif, condemned the incident and sent his condolences to "our Ahmadi brothers," he was widely criticized for having a soft corner for the Ahmadis. Target killing of the community is rampant and even the "accusation" of being an Ahmadi can get a person killed. Ahmadis also face widespread social stigma and the discrimination against them is a popular one.

THEOLOGY

To understand the full animosity that other Muslim sects feel toward Ahmadis, it is important to understand the religious career and claims of Mirza Ghulam Ahmad. He was born on February 13, 1835, in the town of Qadian in Punjab under the Sikh Empire. After his family lost their lands at the hands of the Sikhs, Ahmad was employed as a clerk in Sialkot in the 1860s where he first came across Christian missionaries who he began debating on the issue of religion. Later, when Ahmad moved back to Qadian, he often took up the challenges of Christian missionaries in Batala and earned high praise from the Muslim community for his skill in these debates. By 1882, Ahmad claimed the status of a divinely ordained reformer within Islam and on March 23, 1889, he formally founded the Ahmadi community by asking his followers to take a *baiyait* (allegiance) on his hand, which is a form of religious allegiance. The nature of Ahmad's claims was twofold:

> Ahmad claimed that he was promised Messiah and Mahdi. As a corollary to this claim, he also claimed that contrary to the orthodox Muslim belief that Jesus ascended to heavens alive and would return in the end days, Jesus had died in old age after migrating to the Kashmir valley in India. Ahmad claimed that Jesus had been taken off the cross by Pontius Pilate and had subsequently recovered before taking a journey out of Israel. Ahmad also claimed that the Islamic concept of Dajjal or anti-Christ referred not as much to one person but the materialistic system of the west.[2]

He claimed that while Prophet Muhammad was the "Khatim-un-Nabiyeen," the term "Khatim" in the Quran meant perfection and not final. Therefore, while Prophet Muhammad was the greatest of the prophets and was the last law-bearing messenger of God, prophethood could continue in the Islamic tradition provided that such a prophet would be subordinate to the law of Islam, that is, Zill-e-Nabi or shadow of the Prophet. Ahmad claimed that he was such a prophet who had come to renew and rejuvenate the spirit of Islam and to defend it against the onslaught of religious challenges from the West and the East.[3]

These claims were immediately resisted by the Sunni and Shia Muslim religious leaderships for different reasons and Ahmad and his followers were declared non-Muslim by the Sunni scholars. Ahmad passed away in 1908 and his first successor as the head of the movement was Hakim Nooruddin, titled Khilafa Awal by all Ahmadis. In 1914, Hakeem Nooruddin also passed away and the question of succession arose again. Nooruddin had appointed Ahmad's eldest son Mirza Bahiruddin Mahmood as the Khalifa Saani. Here, however, a faction led by Maulana Muhammad Ali of Lahore broke away.

The original movement was based out of Qadian and the seceding faction was based out of Lahore. There was also a major doctrinal difference. Lahori Ahmadis did not believe that Mirza Ghulam Ahmad was a claimant to prophethood. Qadiani Ahmadis, however, even more staunchly held on the idea of Zill-e-Nabi or Shadow Prophet.

Ahmadis and Pakistan

Both subsects of the Ahmadi movement were also active in what became Pakistan Movement. Bashiruddin Mahmood played an active role in Indian Muslim politics of the late colonial period. In the summer of 1931, he founded the All India Kashmir Committee.[4]

Ahmadis had a special relationship with M. A. Jinnah, the founder of Pakistan, primarily through his aide and confidante Zafrullah Khan, who was an Ahmadi. Certain Muslims[5] tried to press on Jinnah to close the membership for Ahmadis and to not let them in the Muslim League. A Khoja Shia, the Punjabi Sunni Muslim bias against Ahmadis meant little to Jinnah. He certainly saw no reason to allow this theological issue to create a new sectarian issue within the Muslim League.

By not defining the word "Muslim," Muslim League had tried to sidestep a long-standing issue of who constitutes a Muslim. In 1944, *Dawn*, Jinnah's own newspaper, reported that Jinnah had assured Ahmadis the same treatment as any other sect of Islam:

> Mr M A Jinnah was pleased to assure him that according to the latest constitution of the All India Muslim League, there was no bar to the members of the Ahmadiyya Community joining the Muslim League and that as members of the Muslim League they would be entitled to such privileges as are enjoyed by members of other various sects of Muslims.[6]

On May 23, 1944, Jinnah was asked a question in Srinagar regarding the status of Ahmadis in the Muslim League and the Muslim Conference. He explained that the Muslim League was open to all Muslims and that people of Kashmir should not raise these sectarian questions. Jinnah was pressed again on the issue and he answered: "Who am I to declare a person non-Muslim who calls himself a Muslim?"[7]

After Pakistan was created, riots against the Ahmadis broke out in 1953. The main thrust of the protesters was that Zafrullah Khan be removed from the post of foreign minister and Ahmadis be declared non-Muslim. The riots were put down, not before martial law was imposed on the city of Lahore. This led to the Munir Kayani Commission into the Punjab disturbances which asked the poignant question, that is, who is a Muslim, a question that

Ulema were unable to answer at the time. The things were to take an entirely different turn in 1974. Riots broke out again and the matter was then put to the Parliament which voted to pass the 2nd Amendment, declaring Ahmadis non-Muslims for the purposes of law and Constitution. Ten years after the passage of the 2nd Amendment in 1974, the military regime of General Zia-ul-Haq promulgated an ordinance that made unlawful for Ahmadis to "pose" as Muslims.

1974 Amendment and the 1985 Amendment Order

In 1974, the whole National Assembly was converted into a committee of inquiry and it was left to Yahya Bakhtiar, the attorney general, to plead the case against Ahmadis. Ironically, the issue as framed by the learned attorney general was not as much as the finality of Prophethood but the Ahmadis' attitude toward other Muslims. A lengthy cross-examination was carried out on the question of Ahmadis' view of other Muslim sects. Mirza Nasir Ahmad, the third caliph of the Ahmadi community, responded to this by saying that while all Muslims were part of the Islamic community, only those who believed in the claims of Mirza Ghulam Ahmad were true Muslims. This statement eventually was what the National Assembly seized upon and the constitutional excommunication was a foregone conclusion.

The argument of both Ahmadi delegations was: whatever the personal views of a sect within Islam, the state had to remain neutral and respect each sect's interpretation. In other words, if a person professes to be a Muslim, the matter becomes one between him and God Almighty. The first Ahmadi delegation led by Mirza Nasir Ahmad put forward that there were two definitions of Muslims: one, the political category whereby all sects should be considered within the "Millat-e-Islamia" and the second, a religious category that is to be left to each Muslim sect and would not be the business of the state. Only this way can be an endless conflict with regards to takfir after takfir could be avoided and political unity of the Muslim peoples be ensured. Instead of addressing these issues, Yahya Bakhtiar, the then attorney general, repetitively attacked Ahmadis on essentially two counts, that is, Ahmadis' views on other sects and on Ahmadis' insistence on being counted as a separate sect or group of Muslims. By making the whole proceeding about Ahmadis' religious beliefs and not the question of law, that is, whether the state had any right to interfere in the individual's religious beliefs, Mr. Bakhtiar and the PPP conceded a point that hitherto the Pakistani state had refused to concede to the clergy, that is, a majority can decide the beliefs of a minority constitutionally.

It was also the first time that the copyright analogy was invoked by the attorney general, when he compared the issue of religious identity to be akin to copyrights of corporations under law. This would later be one of the arguments used by the Supreme Court of Pakistan in its famous judgment that we discuss in the latter part of this chapter. The legislature—which comprised mostly people unschooled in theology and law—passed the 2nd Amendment to the Constitution, which stated the following:

> A person who does not believe in the absolute and unqualified finality of the Prophethood of Muhammad (peace be upon him) the last of the Prophets, or claims to be a prophet, in any sense of the word or of any description whatsoever, after Muhammad (peace be upon him), or recognizes such a claimant as a prophet or a religious reformer, is not a Muslim for the purposes of the Constitution or law.

Here it is important to consider the phrase "prophet or a religious reformer." Within its ambit included not just the Ahmadis of the Qadiani Jamaat who considered Mirza Ghulam Ahmad a prophet but also Lahori Ahmadis who did not consider him a prophet but a religious reformer. This was because while Lahori Ahmadis had made it clear that they neither considered Mirza Ghulam Ahmad a prophet nor did they consider those who did not believe in Ahmad's claims to be non-Muslims, their belief that Mirza Ghulam Ahmad was a religious reformer was deemed enough to include them in a category of non-Muslims.

Obviously, the 2nd Amendment had not directly named Ahmadis and had qualified the definition with the phrase "purposes of Constitution or law." Thus, the amendment had focused on the legal identity and not ventured into determining the ontic identity of Ahmadis or any other such groups which may fall into this category in the future. General Zia-ul-Haq's regime sought to rectify this with the Third Constitution (Amendment) Order of 1985 when it substituted the definition of "Muslim" with the following:

> *In the Constitution and all enactments and other legal instruments, unless there is anything repugnant in the Subject or context—*
>
> a) *"Muslim" means a person who believes in the unity and oneness of Almighty Allah, in the absolute and unqualified finality of the Prophethood of MUHAMMAD (PBUH), the last of the Prophets, and does not believe in, or recognize as a prophet of religious reformer, any person who claimed or claims to be a prophet, in any sense of the word or of any description whatsoever, after MUHAMMAD (PBUH); and*
>
> b) *"non-Muslim" means a person who is not a Muslim and include a person belonging to the Christian, Hindu, Sikh, Buddhist or Parsi community, a person of the Qadiani group or the Lahori group (who call themselves*

"Ahmadis" or by any other name), or a Bahai, and a person belonging to any of the Scheduled Castes."

One of the criticisms that had come to fore after the second amendment was that it only provided a definition for who is not a Muslim. Till 1985, Ahmadis were considered non-Muslim only to the extent of the Constitution, that is, the bar on a non-Muslim to become president or prime minister. General Zia's amendment order created two new definitions, that is, the definition of a Muslim and the definition of a non-Muslim. The words "constitution" or "law" were jettisoned. Muslim and non-Muslim as defined after the introduction of the Third Constitution (Amendment) Order of 1985 were, therefore, not just legal identities but ontic identities, with new class of non-Muslim identity imposed not just on "Qadiani group or Lahori group (who call themselves 'Ahmadis' or by any other name)" but also on Christian, Hindu, Sikh, Buddhist, or Parsi communities as well as Bahais and a purely caste-based community within the Hindus, that is, scheduled castes (even though no such schedule exists under the Pakistani Constitution). One need not crib too much about the use of the term "community" versus "a person" or "a Bahai" beyond saying that it indicates that while the communities mentioned in the first part of the new definition were established before the advent of Islam, while an Ahmadi or a Bahai were seen to have emanated out of it and after.

1984 Ordinance

Before the Third Constitution (Amendment) Order 1985 came the Ordinance XX of 1984 (1984 Ordinance). This indicates that the Third Constitution (Amendment) Order 1985 was promulgated to give 1984 Ordinance legal cover. The history of the 1984 Ordinance is somewhat murky but it was keeping with the general trend of Islamization undertaken by General Zia's military regime. It is not clear who drafted this and the aforesaid Third Constitution (Amendment) Order 1985. One suspect was Sharifuddin Pirzada, the legendary counsel of the regime and the attorney general, but he denied any role in its authorship. In an interview with Sadia Saeed, he claimed that he had told General Zia that Jinnah had refused to declare Ahmadis non-Muslim and that he at least considered Jinnah to be the authority on the matter.[8] A more likely candidate for authorship is Raja Zafarul Haq, the current PMLN leader, who was at the time very close to General Zia ul Haq. In any event, Ordinance XX of 1984 added the following provision to the Pakistan Penal Code 1860:

298-B. Misuse of epithets, descriptions and titles, etc., reserved for certain holy personages or places:

Any person of the Quadiani group or the Lahori group (who call themselves 'Ahmadis' or by any other name who by words), either spoken or written, or by visible representation- refers to or addresses, any person, other than a Caliph or companion of the Holy Prophet Muhammad (peace be upon him), as "Ameer-ul-Mumineen", "Khalifatul- Mumineen", Khalifa-tul-Muslimeen", "Sahaabi" or "Razi Allah Anho";

refers to, or addresses, any person, other than a wife of the Holy Prophet Muhammad (peace be upon him), as "Ummul-Mumineen";

c) *refers to, or addresses, any person, other than a member of the family "Ahle-bait" of the Holy Prophet Muhammad (peace be upon him), as "Ahle-bait"; or*
d) *refers to, or names, or calls, his place of worship a "Masjid"; shall be punished with Imprisonment of either description for a term which may extend to three years, and shall also be liable to fine.*

(2) any person of the Qaudiani group or Lahori group (who call themselves "Ahmadis" or by any other name) who by words, either spoken or written, or by visible representation refers to the mode or form of call to prayers followed by his faith as "Azan", or recites Azan as used by the Muslims, shall be punished with imprisonment of either description for a term which may extend to three years, and shall also be liable to fine.

298-C. Person of Quadiani group, etc., calling himself a Muslim or preaching or propagating his faith: Any person of the Quadiani group or the Lahori group (who call themselves 'Ahmadis' or by any other name), who directly or indirectly, poses himself as a Muslim, or calls, or refers to, his faith as Islam, or preaches or propagates his faith, or invites others to accept his faith, by words, either spoken or written, or by visible representations, or in any manner whatsoever outrages the religious feelings of Muslims shall be punished with imprisonment of either description for a term which may extend to three years and shall also be liable to fine.[9]

This hit at the very root of religious practice, profession, and propagation, which is a guaranteed fundamental right under Article 20. It may be pointed out that in both Ordinance XX of 1984 and the Third Constitution (Amendment) Order 1985, the word "Quadiani" is misspelt. The correct spellings would be Qadiani because it comes from the Indian town of Qadian, where Mirza Ghulam Ahmad started his mission. While the meaning is clear from the qualification in brackets "who call themselves 'Ahmadis' or by any other name", it is something more than *vitium clerici*. After all, if the Ahmadi community refuses to be identified as "Quadiani" even if they were to be identified as Qadiani, that is, pertaining to Qadian or as followers of Mirza Ghulam Ahmad of Qadian, does that void both the constitutional definition and the law as laid down by Sections 298 B and C? In any event, this point was never raised in any litigation that followed after this law was brought on the books and it has been taken for granted that the odd phrasing of the law refers to the Ahmadis.

For the main Ahmadi group, that is, which is referred to as the Quadiani group, the law had serious consequences. Mirza Tahir Ahmad, the fourth caliph of the community, put the position before the community's council and pointed out that so long as he lived in Pakistan, it would be impossible for him to carry out his duties. It was then decided that he would move to London, where at the Al Fazl Mosque, the community's new headquarters were established. This law continues to be the main tool for anti-Ahmadi clerics to use for persecution of the Ahmadis.[10]

Passports and National Identity Cards

In the 1980s, Pakistan introduced a religion column on the Pakistani passport. Every Pakistani now had to declare his or her faith on the passport, presumably to ensure that no non-Muslim travels to Mecca or Medina, which is barred by Saudi and Islamic law. At some point, and the exact origin of this is unclear, the passport forms were amended to include the following declaration for all "Muslims," defined by the Constitution, as mandatory:

- *I am Muslim and believe in the absolute and unqualified finality of the prophethood of Muhammad (peace be upon him) the last of the prophets.*
- *I do not recognise any person who claims to be a prophet in any sense of the word or of any description whatsoever after Muhammad (peace be upon him) or recognise such a claimant as prophet or a religious reformer as a Muslim.*
- *I consider Mirza Ghulam Ahmad Quadiani to be an imposter nabi and also consider his followers whether belonging to the Lahori or Qadiani group to be Non-Muslim.*[11]

The first two clauses of the declaration conform to Article 260 of the Constitution. Clause III, however, requires every "Muslim" to not only declare Ahmadis non-Muslim but to declare the founder of the community an "imposter nabi." In other words, central to Muslim citizenship of the Pakistani state, both Mirza Ghulam Ahmad and Ahmadis form the main plank. Arguably, this amounts to a censure on every non-Ahmadi Muslim in Pakistan and is unjustified restriction on freedom of conscience and religion.

A similar requirement was added to the National Identity Card ("NIC") form. Even though the NIC itself does not mention the religion of an individual citizen, it is nonetheless required on the application form. In 2019, a new requirement was added to the NIC form whereby every Pakistani citizen, other than a "Muslim," has to affirm that he or she is not a Muslim. This is aimed at specifically curtailing Ahmadis' rights further by forcing them to declare themselves non-Muslim. The Constitution of Pakistan does not require an Ahmadi to accept that he or she is a non-Muslim. The right of an Ahmadi to claim to be a Muslim is arguably protected by Article 20.

The Electoral Question

Elections in Pakistan from 1985 to 1999 were held on the basis of separate electorate for minorities. However, in 2002, Pakistan reverted to joint electorate. This should have meant that all citizens of Pakistan would be on the same electoral roll without distinction of religion or community but an exception was made for Ahmadis. While they were allowed to vote as part of the joint electorate system, their voting list has been drawn up separately, to ensure that they cannot pass themselves off as Muslims. This discrimination is an unacceptable position to the Ahmadis and Ahmadis have boycotted all elections since 1985, first because they were assigned non-Muslim seats and then after 2002 because they are put on a supplementary non-Muslim list.

In 2017, the government of Pakistan, no doubt under pressure from the UN Human Rights Council by virtue of Pakistan's accession to the International Covenant on Civil and Political Rights, decided to rectify the situation in the Elections Act 2017. For Muslims, the Declaration and Oath was changed to Declaration. In the first line of the Declaration, the words "I swear" were changed to "I believe." Toward the bottom of the Declaration, instead of "solemnly swear," the words were changed to "solemnly affirm." It was the repeal of 7(b) by which the government now tried to consolidate lists of Ahmadis and non-Ahmadis into one. It was designed to resolve the dilemma of having a separate list for Ahmadis, when everyone else was on the same joint electorate list. It would have restored effectively the right of Ahmadis to vote without compromising on their conscience but such a situation was obviously unacceptable to religious parties. Without getting into the complex politics that sparked protests against the PMLN government, already reeling from the Panama verdict that had removed Prime Minister Nawaz Sharif from office, suffice to say that a religious group was comfortably installed at the Faizabad interchange between the twin cities of Islamabad and Rawalpindi. Ultimately, the government folded and the Elections Act 2017 was amended again to ensure that the separate list is restored along with the oath in its original form. Ahmadis were once against left in the lurch.

Fundamental Rights and Legislative Restrictions

Article 8 of the Constitution of 1973 states:

1) Any law, or any custom or usage having the force of law, in so far as it is inconsistent with the rights conferred by this Chapter, shall, to the extent of such inconsistency, be void.
2) The State shall not make any law, which takes away or abridges the rights so conferred and any law made in contravention of this clause shall, to the extent of such contravention, be void.

The restrictions or abridgment is envisaged within the articles delineating fundamental rights themselves. For example, Article 19, which promises freedom of speech and press, can be abridged "any reasonable restrictions imposed by law in the interest of the glory of Islam or the integrity, security or defence of Pakistan or any part thereof, friendly relations with foreign States, public order, decency or morality, or in relation to contempt of court, 33[commission of] 33 or incitement to an offence." Article 20 makes religious freedom "subject to law, public order and morality." However, the abridgment cannot completely read out what the fundamental right originally provides. This becomes important as we consider case law that upheld the Ordinance XX of 1984.

Objectives Resolution and Article 20 of the Pakistani Constitution

The Objectives' Resolution which is a substantive part of the Constitution through Article 2-A reads:

> Wherein adequate provision shall be made for the minorities to *freely* profess and practice their religions and develop their cultures. (Emphasis added)

Under Articles 4 and 25 of the Constitution, all citizens are equal before law and subject to protection against discrimination based on religion, gender, and ethnicity. All minorities ought to be similarly placed therefore, and all protections guaranteed to other minorities must be extended to Ahmadis. On the contrary, Ahmadis have been placed on separate electoral lists unlike Hindus, Christians, Buddhists, and other non-Muslims. This is a discrimination that is designed to systematically alienate them from the country's mainstream polity. They are also required to give a declaration that they are non-Muslims when acquiring a national identity cards and passports, which is unconscionable for the community.

20. Freedom to profess religion and to manage religious institutions.—Subject to law, public order and morality—

a) *every citizen shall have the right to profess, practise and propagate his religion; and*
b) *every religious denomination and every sect thereof shall have the right to establish, maintain and manage its religious institutions.*

Article 20 of the Pakistani Constitution says, subject to law, public order and morality that every citizen has the right not just to profess and practice his religion but also to propagate it. To profess and propagate would constitute the free exercise clause. Propagate arguably something more. Under the US Constitution, the idea of propagation of one's faith is not protected under free exercise clause but rather the free speech clause. In this way, arguably, the Pakistani Constitution's equivalent "free exercise clause" is more expansive than the free exercise clause under the US Constitution's first amendment, in light of the word "propagate" though the First Amendment with its free speech clause covers propagation. The free exercise clause in the US Constitution concerns itself with core religious belief and the case law under it distinguishes between belief and action.

Article 20 of the Pakistani Constitution on the other hand speaks very clearly of profession, practice, and propagation, arguably all three of which are actions. This is an important distinction which will become even more so when we consider the fact that US case law was specifically used by the Supreme Court of Pakistan to uphold the 1984 Ordinance as constitutional by 2 to 1 decision in *Zaheeruddin v the State*. It is, therefore, important to look at some of the cases involving the issue of Ahmadis' right to self-identify as Muslims in Pakistan's judicial history.

Case Law on Religious Freedom and Ahmadis

The first major case on the issue of Ahmadis and their status as Muslims came in the late 1960s when Ahmadis had not been declared non-Muslims yet. Agha Shorish Kashmiri was a renowned journalist and poet from the Majlis-e-Ahrar-e-Islam who had also been active in the efforts to declare Ahmadis non-Muslim in Pakistan. In *Agha Shorish Kashmiri* case, the High Court of West Pakistan held:

> The whole burden of argument of petitioner's learned counsel was that Ahmadis are not a sect of Islam and the petitioner's right to say so is guaranteed by the Constitution. The learned counsel over-looks the fact that Ahmadis as Citizens of Pakistan are also guaranteed by the Constitution the same freedom to profess and proclaim that they are within the fold of Islam. How can the petitioners

deny to others what they claim for themselves is beyond our comprehension? Certainly not by terrorizing them. The question at the root is how far the petitioners and others like-minded can in law prevent the Ahmadis from professing that notwithstanding any doctrinal differences with the other sects of Islam they are as good followers of Islam as anybody else who calls himself a Muslim.[12]

The second major case on the issue comes in 1978, four years after the community had in fact been declared non-Muslim vide the 2nd Constitutional Amendment. In *Abdur Rahman Mubashir* case, the Lahore High Court held:

> The dispute between the Muslims of Indian subcontinent and the followers of Mirza Ghulam Ahmad, who are commonly called Ahmadis or Qadianies, is not of recent origin. It is as old as the claim of Mirza Ghulam Ahmad to prophethood, despite his belief in the holy Qur'an and Sunnah.—he tried to reconcile his claim to prophethood with his purported belief in finality of Prophethood of Muhammad (PBUH)—He claimed that he had, though a prophet, not brought any Sharia of his own and that the appearance of a new prophet without new Shariat was not contrary to and did not detract from the doctrine of finality of prophethood of Muhammad. Except for some other minor differences the Qadianis do believe in the mission of Prophet Muhammad (PBUH), and the Holy Qur'an and the Traditions.[13]

This latter case was significant because it was the first attempt by a religious group to raise the issue of the status of Ahmadis before a judicial forum after the 2nd Amendment was passed. This is how the High Court summarized the complaint and responded to it:

> It is alleged in paragraph No. 2 of the plaint that the defendants' place of worship is known as a mosque (Masjid) and they perform prayer in it which resembles the prayer in Shariat and includes Azan, Namaz, Qyam, Sajood, Ruku,' reading of the Qur'an, saying Darood-o-Salam on the Holy Prophet and invoking benediction. It is further alleged in paragraph No. 5 that a mosque is a place of worship which is exclusive for the Muslims and no infidel has a right to construct it or to make his places of worship resemble it (mosque) in any manner or make his place of worship face Ka'ba. A mosque in short is inaccessible in Islam to those beyond its pale.
>
> Similarly, Namaz and other modes of prayer are provided only for Muslims. No non-Muslim can carry on prayer in the manner in which the Muslims perform them. Namaz is also a Shair that is a rite and a ceremony exclusively reserved for the Muslims and a person calling the Azan consequently must be a person belonging to the Islamic faith. Except for some other minor differences the Qadianis do believe in the mission of Prophet Muhammad (PBUH) and the

> Holy Qur'an and traditions. In this view they call their places of worship as Masjid, they perform prayers (Namaz) in the manner ordained for the adherents of Qur'an and call their congregation to prayer by shouting Azan. The prayer in the plaint that they should be barred from constructing their mosque as facing Ka'aba or by imitating the construction of Muslim mosque or calling Azan or offering their prayers in the manner of Muslims and performing prostration and Tash'had will amount to interfering with their religion, which Islam, as a religion of tolerance does not allow.
>
> On the other hand Islam leaves the non Muslims free to profess and practice their religion. Although the Islamic Law cannot be applied to non-Muslims in general, my answer to the above question would be in the affirmative. The reason is that like Muslims, this section of non-Muslims claims to be bound by the Law of Qur'an and Sunnah. In such circumstances, I have no manner of doubt left that at least those non-Muslims who profess to be bound by the same Law as the Muslims, will also be bound by similar principle of justice, equity and good conscience. Consequently, the Muslim Law shall apply to them.[14]

All of this changed with the Ordinance XX of 1984 which sought to criminalize the idea that Ahmadis could claim to be bound by the same law as Muslims. The ordinance was challenged in various constitutional writ petitions and criminal appeals. *Zaheeruddin v. State*[15] is the seminal Supreme Court case in Pakistan's judicial history on the Ahmadi issue, which upheld the Ordinance XX of 1984 as being constitutional. The case law that the Supreme Court relied on in its 2-1 judgment, quite ironically, was US case law under the free exercise clause of the First Amendment to the United States. The main case that the honorable justices relied on was *Reynolds versus United States*.[16]

The First Amendment to the US Constitution reads: "Congress shall make no law respecting an establishment of religion, *or prohibiting the free exercise thereof.*" By way of comparison here is the Article 20 of the Pakistani Constitution: "Subject to law, public order and morality—(a) every citizen shall have the right to profess, practise and propagate his religion." Even if we were to overlook the obvious difference that the United States is a secular state regulating freedom of religion by limiting exercise to core belief as opposed to action, which is expressly allowed under Pakistan's Islamic constitution, the issue becomes one of manifest legal sophistry. The Reynolds's case, it must be recalled, dealt with the issue of polygamy. The law in question was the Morril Bigamy Act of 1862. This law itself had a very interesting history given that Abraham Lincoln who had signed it into law had nevertheless allowed Brigham Young, founder of Salt Lake City, the second president of the Church of Latter Day Saints, that is, Mormons and the first governor of Utah Territory, a go ahead to ignore the law altogether in his exchange for his cooperation in the Civil War. George Reynolds, a member of the Church of LDS, presented himself as a test case. He was married twice to Mary Ann Tudenham and Amelia Jane Schofield and furnished evidence to this effect to the US attorney. The case made it to the US Supreme Court where the Court upheld his conviction by declaring that there was a distinction between religious belief and action and that the latter could validly be used to penalize certain actions. It rejected the religious duty argument based on this distinction. Polygamy, therefore, is unlawful in the United States.

Now the question arises as to whether this legal view could have any bearing under Pakistani Constitution when speaking of religious freedom, especially of the Ahmadi community? Ordinance XX of 1984 makes it unlawful for Ahmadis to not only profess to be Muslims but practice their faith and ultimately to propagate it, all constitutional rights afforded by the Pakistani constitution. This view, as per majority opinion, that a distinction exists between religious belief and action cannot be relevant to Pakistan with its Article 20 and the Objectives' Resolution in its restored post 18th Amendment form as will be explained below. It certainly becomes meaningless when we consider the minorities' clause from the Objectives Resolution which is a substantive part of the Constitution under Article 2-A: "Wherein adequate provision shall be made for the minorities freely to profess and practise their religions and develop their cultures." Developing cultures is not merely religious belief but is manifestly religious action. Ordinance XX of 1984 cannot be rationally, linguistically, constitutionally and legally sustained under the Pakistani law on this ground at all.

The Supreme Court further observed in the *Zaheeruddin* case:

> The fundamental right, relevant here, is the "freedom to profess religion" but it has been made "subject to law, public order and morality." The Courts of other countries, which have similar fundamental rights, have held that this right embraces two concepts; freedom to believe and freedom to act. Some of them held the former to be absolute but others said that, that too was subject to law etc. However, all are agreed that the latter in the nature of things, cannot be absolute. According to them, conduct remains subject to regulation for the protection of the society. So the freedom to act must have appropriate definition to preserve the enforcement of that protection. The phrase "subject to law," on the other hand, does neither invest the legislature with unlimited power to unduly restrict or take away the Fundamental Rights guaranteed in the Constitution, nor can they be completely ignored or bypassed as non-existent. A balance has thus to be struck between the two, by resorting to a reasonable interpretation, keeping in view the peculiar circumstances of each case.[17]

Notwithstanding the argument that Pakistani Constitution allows religious action, even if we accept this transposition of US case law to Article 20, an ordinance that specifically targets one community or class cannot be called "general" or "nondiscriminatory" at the outset. The balance that has to be struck can easily be deduced. It is clear that a state may not unduly suppress free communication of views, religious or others under the guise of conserving desirable conditions. It is also quite clear that in so far as *Cantwell* case is concerned, the Pakistani Supreme Court misapplied the ratio of the judgment. Sections 298 B and 298 C of the Pakistani Penal Code clearly violate the ratio of this case as well as the principle so laid down namely that freedom of belief is absolute. Belief is not something necessarily unspoken. An Ahmadi's belief that he or she is a Muslim is central to his creed. By forcing an Ahmadi to declare that he in fact is not a Muslim, the freedom of belief and not just freedom to act are being violated.

The Pakistani Supreme Court also relied on *Jones v. City of Opelika.*[18] Here the issue dealt with the city of Opelika in Alabama charging Jones, a member of the Jehovah's Witnesses, of selling books without license and thereby violating an ordinance. This was ultimately challenged in the Supreme Court and Justice Reed wrote the majority opinion:

> There are ethical principles of greater value to mankind than the guarantees of the Constitution to the personal liberty which are beyond the power of government to impair . . . There is to be noted too, a distinction between non-discriminatory regulations of operations which are incidental to the exercise of religion from the freedom of speech or the press and those which are imposed upon the religious right itself of unmixed dissemination of information . . . If we were to assume, as is here argued, that the licensed activities involve religious rites, a different question would be presented. These are not taxes on free will offerings. But it is because we view these sales as partaking more of commercial than religious or educational transactions that we find the ordinances, as here presented, valid.

Here again we see the same distinction being applied between action and belief. We must consider a number of other US Supreme Court cases. The first is *Minersville School District v. Gobitis.*[19] According to Jehovah's Witnesses, the salute to an earthly emblem such as the US flag was unfaithfulness to God. Accordingly, Walter Gobitis, a member of the community in Minersville known for its hostility to Jehovah's Witnesses, asked his children not to salute the flag at school. They were expelled from school. The district judge in the case ruled in favor of the Gobitis children. The school board then appealed the decision and was met with a similar decision from the Third Circuit of the US Court of Appeals. Finally, the school board filed a writ of *certiorari* in the Supreme Court that was heard in 1940. In an 8-1 decision, the US Supreme Court ruled that flag salute was a secular policy. Justice Felix Frankfurter wrote the opinion:

> National unity is the basis of national security. To deny the legislature the right to select appropriate means for its attainment presents a totally different order of problem from that of the propriety of subordinating the possible ugliness of littered streets to the free expression opinion through handbills. Conscientious scruples have not, in the course of the long struggle for religious toleration, relieved the individual from obedience to a general law not aimed at the promotion or restriction of religious beliefs.[20]

It must be stated here that a secular national purpose was being ascribed to regulation of religious belief. Yet, a few years later, the US Supreme Court overturned this opinion in *West Virginia State Board of Education v. Barnette*[21] by relying on the freedom of speech clause of the first amendment. Here the issue was almost identical to the *Gobitis* case. The US Supreme Court held:

> One's right to life, liberty, and property, to free speech, a free press, freedom of worship and assembly, and other fundamental rights may not be submitted to vote; they depend on the outcome of no elections . . . If there is any fixed star in our constitutional constellation, it is that no official, high or petty, can prescribe what shall be orthodox in politics, nationalism, religion, or other matters of opinion or force citizens to confess by word or act their faith therein.[22]

This encapsulates the counter-majoritarian spirit of the US Supreme Court. The application of any of US case law that has to be in other jurisdictions has to keep in mind this key feature and function of the US Supreme Court and its approach to protection of minorities. The decision in the *Zaheeruddin* case by the Pakistani Supreme Court was majoritarian and religious populist in its approach to the issue.

Pakistani Supreme Court also relied on *Cox v. State of New Hampshire*.[23] This case dealt with a statute in New Hampshire that prohibited unlicensed parades:

> The sole charge against the appellants was that they were "taking part in a parade or procession" on the public streets without a permit as the statute required. They were not prosecuted for distributing leaflets or for conveying information by placards or otherwise, or for issuing invitations to a public meeting or for holding a public meeting or for maintaining or expressing religious beliefs. Their right to do any one of these things apart from engaging in a "parade or procession" upon a public street is not here involved and the question of the validity of a statute addressed to any other sort of conduct than that complained of is not before us. The authority of a municipality to impose regulations in order to assure the safety and convenience of the people

> in the use of public highways has never been regarded as inconsistent with civil liberties, but rather as one of the means of safe-guarding the good order upon which they ultimately depend. As regulation of the use of the streets for parades and processions is a traditional exercise of control by local government, the question in a particular case is whether that control is exerted so as not to deny or unwarrantedly abridge the right of assembly and the opportunities for the communication of thought and the discussion of public questions immemorially associated with resort to public places. No interference with religious worship or the practice of religion in any proper sense is shown, but only the exercise of local control over the use of streets for parades and processions.[24]

The action here deals with a parade and a procession. The time and place of a parade and procession is within the legitimate purview of state regulation. Nevertheless, the Pakistani Supreme Court's use of this judgment was as spurious and unthinking as all the other case law from the US jurisdiction. Similar reliance was placed on *Hamilton v. Board of Regents of University of California*[25] and *Commonwealth v. Plaisted*.[26] The *Hamilton* case upheld University of California's right to impart military training on able-bodied students. The US Supreme Court in this case held that training in military science was not the same as religious instruction and, therefore, did not violate the Constitution. The *Plaisted* case is also dealt with regulation and not restriction. Therefore, American case law used by the Pakistani Supreme Court is entirely misapplied in the *Zaheeruddin* case. There is no other conclusion one can draw except that in its zeal to double down on persecution against the Ahmadis, Pakistani Supreme Court left no stone unturned and drew inferences that just do not logically follow from the case law presented. Indeed, it exposes the limitations of transnational application of case law across jurisdictions. Contrary to the counter-majoritarian role of the US Constitution, Pakistan's Supreme Court has invented a new test and that is the law and order situation that may be caused by feelings of outrage on part of the majority community. This subjection of a fundamental right to law and order and that too based on outrage caused to a majority community is tantamount to reading out the fundamental right to religion as a whole.

In 2018 came the judgment of the Islamabad High Court in the *Maulana Allah Wasaya* case.[27] Justice Shaukat Aziz Siddiqui writing the opinion stated:

> From the historic account, it is clear that a continuous demand has been raised for the identification of Ahmadis on identity cards and passports. No doubt, by promulgation of Ordinance, 1984 important steps were taken to restrain them

> from using certain Islamic epithets, but what if a Qadiani conceals his real identity? What if a Qadiani by concealing his real identity reaches the high Constitutional office(s)? What if a person while deceiving the state reaches to the highest sensitive post(s)? What if a person or persons, deceiving the Constitution and law, threatens and breaches the security and integrity of the State? It is often said that for every wrong, there is a remedy. What is the remedy for the people of Pakistan against such deception and disloyalty? It is time and again held that the laws are made to prevent the wrongs for the greater cause of public good, but what laws have been enacted to counter such wrong.

In other words, the High Court felt that Ahmadis should not be allowed into any sensitive posts of the state. The presumption here is that Ahmadis are a security risk. The judgment did not stop here. It ruled that even the name Ahmadis could not be used by Ahmadis:

> Undoubtedly, 7th September, 1974 when the Parliament unanimously carried the 2nd Amendment Bill was a big occasion . . . unfortunately certain enactments could not be taken to supplement the Constitution amendments. On the contrary, Qadianis through different devices and maneuvering tried their best to frustrate the objects of 2nd amendment. After declaring Qadianis (both Groups) as non-muslims there should have been some steps for their separate identity, recognition, and scrutiny, as Qadinais are not like other minorities (non-Muslims) who can easily be identified through their appearance, names, beliefs and mode of prayers. On the contrary Qadianis have same names, appearance and even their prayers are like Muslims, therefore, confusion about their separate identity resorted to declare them non-Muslims but the purpose could not have been achieved e.g. name "Ahmad" is somewhat specified for Qadianis and the basis of same they are also termed as Ahmadis which cannot be permitted. Name "Ahmad" refers to the Holy Prophet Hazrat Muhammad (PBUH) who besides other holy books has been addressed by the Allah Almighty in the Holy Quran with this name. Muslims are possessive about this name, and in first interaction or introduction name of an individual indicates about the religion of any person.

It also called for the "Qadiani" or "Mirzai" to be added to the names of individuals, that is, for identification. This is reminiscent of Nazi Germany and yellow star:

> Therefore, it is only in the fitness of things that Qadianis may be referred to as Ghulaman-e-Mirza/Mirzai etc. but not as Ahmadis, which term/reference may confuse them with Muslims who believe in the finality of the prophethood of Hazrat Muhammad (PBUH). Qadianis should not be allowed to conceal their identity by having similar names to those of Muslims, therefore, they should

> be either stopped from using name of ordinary Muslims or in the alternative Qadiani, Ghulam-e-Mirza or Mirzai must form a part of their names and be mentioned accordingly.

Obviously, Justice Siddiqui saw no need for legal sophistry and reliance on American jurisprudence to pen a judgment which strips Ahmadis of their fundamental rights as citizens of Pakistan.

Noncitizens

So, in conclusion, what is the legal status of Ahmadis in Pakistan? It is a penal offense for Ahmadis to identify themselves as Muslims, call their "places of worship" mosques, perform the ritual call for prayer and in recent years even celebrate Eid, especially the ritual sacrifice or propagate their faith in anyway or even publish their literature which is proscribed as "hate literature." Other than the fact that a modern nation-state has no business defining who is or isn't a Muslim, for all practical purposes Ahmadis are additionally denied the fundamental rights guaranteed to every citizen of Pakistan, including but not limited to freedom of speech and freedom of religion. Section 298-C of the Pakistan Penal Code is frequently used by religious groups to further limit their freedoms and persecute them. With forms of national identity cards requiring an explicit declaration from them saying that they are non-Muslim means that they are deprived of almost all citizenship rights. If the judgment in *Allah Wasaya* case is implemented, Ahmadis might be required to take on Qadiani or Mirzai as last names and even forced to stop using the term "Ahmadi." Therefore, it would not be an exaggeration to say that Ahmadis are not just a forced minority in Pakistan but also *de facto* noncitizens unless they accept they are non-Muslims.

NOTES

1. Exact number of Ahmadis is unknown because the details of the recent census have not been announced.
2. Adamson, I., 1989. Mirza Ghulam Ahmad of Qadian.
3. Ibid.
4. Kumar, Radha (2018). Paradise at War: A Political History of Kashmir. New Delhi: Aleph. pp. 25–26. ISBN 9789388292122.
5. Most notably Majlis-e-Ahrar-e-Islam.
6. Dawn 4 May 1944 Dawn. 'From the Past Pages of Dawn: 1944: Seventy Years Ago:Membership for Ahmadiyyas.' May 4, 2014. https://www.dawn.com/news/1104077.

7. Saeed S, Politics of Exclusion: Muslim Nationalism, State Formation and Legal Representations of the Ahmadiyya Community in Pakistan (Dissertation at University of Michigan) https://deepblue.lib.umich.edu/bitstream/handle/2027.42/78803/sadia_1.pdf?sequence=1 accessed on 1 April 2020

8. Saeed S, Politics of Exclusion: Muslim Nationalism, State Formation and Legal Representations of the Ahmadiyya Community in Pakistan (Dissertation at University of Michigan).

9. Pakistan Penal Code 1860 (as amended by Ordinance XX of 1984).

10. See for instance: https://www.amnesty.org/download/Documents/184000/asa330031994en.pdf

11. Passport application form and NIC Form – NADRA Regulations 2002 and Amendment Regulations 2018.

12. PLD 1969 Lahore 289.

13. Abdur Rahman Mubashir PLD 1978 Lah 113.

14. Ibid.

15. Zaheeruddin v. State 1993 SCMR 1718.

16. Reynolds v United States, 98 US 145 (1878).

17. Zaheeruddin v. State 1993 SCMR 1718.

18. Jones v. City of Opelika, 316 U.S. 584 (1942).

19. Minersville School District v. Gobitis, 310 U.S. 586 (1940).

20. Ibid.

21. West Virginia State Board of Education v. Barnette, 319 U.S. 624 (1943).

22. Ibid.

23. Cox v. New Hampshire, 312 U.S. 569 (1941).

24. Ibid.

25. Hamilton v. Board of Regents of University of California (1934) 293US 245.

26. Commonwealth vs. Plaisted.(1889) 148 Mass 375.

27. PLD 1919 Islamabad 62.

Chapter 7

Honor Crimes in Pakistan

A Human Rights Critique of Swara *Practice*

Neha Ali Gauhar

INTRODUCTION

> *Maal da sarra zar, au sar da namusa (Sacrifice wealth to save head, sacrifice head to save honour).*
>
> —Pakhtu proverb

At the age of 4, Asma has little understanding of the enormity of her loss. As a young girl, she has lost what she identifies as home; a remote, rugged village situated in the Pakhtun belt. Unknown to her, her fate rests in the hands of *Jirgamaar*,[1] as notions of Pakhtunwali[2] confirm the finality of *jirga* decisions, and challenging these would risk social boycott and culturally imposed dangers. The elders of the community have assembled in a *Hujra*, the space where men meet, to resolve a dispute which stemmed from the escape of Asma's sister from her abusive marital home after many long years marked with anguish and suffering in silence.

Playing in the courtyard, Asma's gaze fixed on the young, helpless animal as it struggles to resist its fate. The act of a goat being sacrificed is a ritual symbolizing that a decision has finally been reached. The *jirga* has decided that Asma will be tied in wedlock with her sister's husband as compensation under the customary practice of *swara*. That day, Asma's youthful innocence and childhood were sacrificed along with the animal.[3]

For Asma and numerous other young girls and women in Pakistan, this patriarchal social construct is deeply embedded into cultural narratives that have made the lives of women synonymous with brutality. A recent study concluded that 77 percent of marriages in Pakistan were fixed under customary practices including *swara*.[4] Asma was one of the very few fortunate young girls who escaped the cruelty of the *jirga*'s decision, as unacknowledged heroes of her family decided to fight for her. However, her story doesn't have a happy ending, as the protracted battle against outdated and deadly customs took with it the lives of her beloved *Baba* (father) and brother, coercing her widowed mother to take her and her eleven siblings to go into hiding.

The premise of this chapter is to examine the conflict between Islamic law and local sociocultural norms in the Pakhtun belt and its interrelation with formal law. In doing so, the role of the informal *jirga* system cannot be denied in aiding and abetting outdated cultural practices such as *swara* that have disproportionately marginalized Pakhtun women for centuries. Therefore, it is central to the theme of this chapter to discuss the historical roots of legal pluralism in Pakistan that have, over time, legitimized the existence of these non-state quasi-legal bodies. In particular, the following questions will be addressed: Why are *jirgas* prevalent in the Pakhtun belt of Pakistan? What impact does the admixture of sharia and customary law have on the lives of Pakhtun women? Why is the practice of *swara* widespread despite recent steps taken by local socio-legal actors to eradicate it?

This chapter aims to examine the position of women in the Pakhtun society drawing up on the tribal dynamics of discriminatory practices that trigger multi-factoral human rights violations that have strengthened gendered stereotypes. It seeks to establish a link between the patriarchal and feudal psyche of the Pakhtun community that feeds the impetus for the social exclusion of women and the widespread practice of *swara*. The chapter will also present recommendations regarding essential socio-legal reforms required to eliminate discriminatory customary practices in northwestern Pakistan. It is imperative to emphasize the importance of implementing these reforms in a culturally sensitive manner that is inclusive and acceptable to local Pakhtun communities.

THE ROLE OF THE *JIRGA* IN DISPENSING JUSTICE

> *Ma khpal badal sal kala pus waghasto Ao khalko owayal Che dera tundi de wakra (I took my revenge after a hundred years and people say I hurried).*
>
> —Pakhtu proverb

The Pakhtun belt of Pakistan is a hotspot of radical extremist militant groups that has perpetrated violent acts costing thousands of lives, both of civilians and of the armed forces. Embroiled in a conflict with non-state actors who have challenged the writ of the state, successive governments have not been able to provide the majority of the population with a fair and operative structure of governance to bring an end to human rights abuses, especially those of women and the marginalized.

The Frontier

The northwest of Pakistan, typically known as the Frontier of Pakistan, comprises of the province of Khyber Pakhunkhwa (KPK). The valleys and crests of the mountains of the Afghanistan-Pakistan border are home to the Pakhtun tribes. Perceived to be opposed to urban and modern Pakistan, the Pakhtun society is very conservative and celebrated for their deeply rooted tribal identity and lineage (*Pakhtunwali*). Pukhtuns' love for their freedom, egalitarianism among social class, and pride in tribal lineage has ensured the preservation of their own territory, language, and particular traditions separate from the state system.[5] Typically, this is a society that places emphasis on pride (*Wiaarh*), honor (*Nang*), and clanship (*Azizwali*). It is not uncommon for a Pakhtun of a particular confederacy to have knowledge of their genealogical relation to other members of the tribe.[6] This strengthens their communication ties and encourages them to mediate in times of conflict and eventually reach an acceptable settlement.

Through the recently passed 25th Amendment of the Constitution of Pakistan, KPK merged with Federally Administered Tribal Areas (FATA) to bring the semiautonomous tribal borderland under the umbrella of the Constitution in order to extend fundamental rights and all legislation to the citizens. The legal framework of KPK is intertwined with conflict, dualism, and compromise. This hybrid system is shaped with three overlapping mechanisms of dispute resolution which include: (1) the state's formal legal system, (2) the analogous Islamic institution of governance, and (3) the informal justice system out of the state's patronage (*jirga*).

The Politics of Legal Pluralism in Pakistan

Simply put, legal pluralism is the existence of more than one legal system within a jurisdiction.[7] According to John Griffiths, this concept includes "*diverse and often contested perspectives on law, ranging from the recognition of differing legal orders with the nation-state, to a more far reaching and open ended concept of law that does not necessarily depend on state recognition for its validity.*"[8] Building on this concept, Saima Jasam states that legal pluralist theory involves a hierarchy of systems that may be established through a special legal order that specifically deals with dispute resolution of particular class or type of people, outside the writ of formal courts.[9] Legal pluralism is found in different parts of the world in divergent political

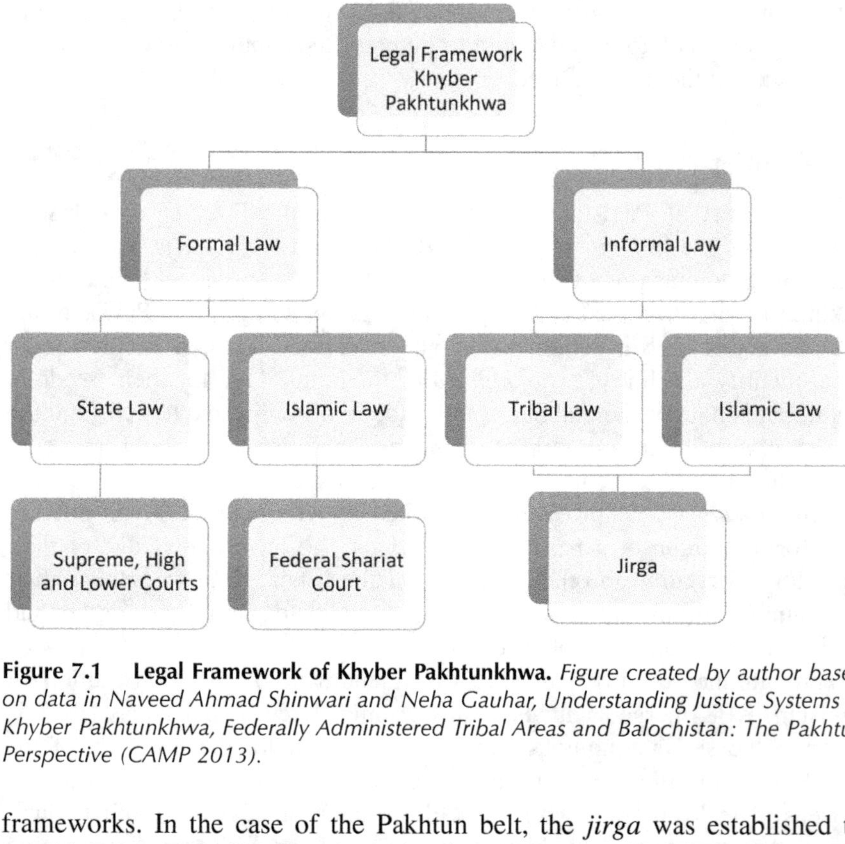

Figure 7.1 Legal Framework of Khyber Pakhtunkhwa. *Figure created by author based on data in Naveed Ahmad Shinwari and Neha Gauhar, Understanding Justice Systems of Khyber Pakhtunkhwa, Federally Administered Tribal Areas and Balochistan: The Pakhtun Perspective (CAMP 2013).*

frameworks. In the case of the Pakhtun belt, the *jirga* was established to provide community justice that accommodates cultural differences of the indigenous society. Furthermore, the legitimacy of the customary fora can be accounted to the fact that they are "procedurally acceptable" and "geographically, financially and linguistically accessible."[10] Having said that, in reality, there is a constant conflict between the centralized formal law and decentralized informal justice especially on the subject of gender discrimination and anti-women practices. Subsequently, the focus will now be on the plural legal order in Frontier which includes: (1) "Islamic" branch of the formal legal system and (2) the informal system (Pakhtun *Jirga*), both functioning parallel to the high and lower judiciary.

Islamization' of Legal Framework

Born out of religious tensions and differences, Pakistan was the first nation to be founded as an Islamic state.[11] Paradoxically, Muhammad Ali Jinnah, the founding father of Pakistan envisaged a modern and secular state with equal rights for all.[12] However, soon after attaining independence, the nation's ruling politico-religious parties managed to transform it into a theocratic state.[13] To begin with, the Objectives Resolution in 1949[14] significantly redrew the parameters of the new state by sharing a general commitment to create an Islamic society based on principles of sharia.[15]

However, two decades later, General Zia-ul-Haq's military coup in 1977 engineered the first serious attempts to "Islamize" the legal system of Pakistan. Under Article 203C of the Constitution, 1973, the Federal Shariat Court was created to fundamentally transform the legal fora. For the first time in the nation's judicial history, a parallel institution was set up to evaluate the compatibility of an extensive array of legislation with Islamic jurisprudence in line with the Holy Quran and sunnah.[16] With a separate jurisdiction and judiciary, the court has the power to amend or repeal laws that are inconsistent with Islamic law initiated through a petition filed by a citizen or a government authority or even a motion commenced on its own. Furthermore, the Federal Shariat Court has jurisdiction over all *Hudood* cases,[17] with its decision binding on the high courts as well as the lower courts of Pakistan.[18] Zia did not revise the pluralistic character of Pakistan's legal framework, but managed to branch out the judicial institution into two independent divisions, an Islamic and secular division. Therefore, the ordinary formal courts were not substituted by the emergence of the Federal Shariat Court but functions parallel to it with separate jurisdictions.

Justice through the Pakhtun Jirga

In *Pashto* diction, the term "*jirga*" refers to both a practice and an institution. *Jirga* serves as a traditional institution that incorporates local *Riwaj* (customs), principles of sharia in dispute settlement.[19] This institution is head by a body of village elders whose collective decision is binding on all parties to the dispute.[20] Basically, it comprises a gathering or meeting of elders, often including *Maliks* (heads of dominant tribes) and influential members, convened by an intermediary to resolve both civil and criminal disputes through mediations, consultations, and evidence gathering; ultimately delivering verdicts based on consensus from both parties.[21] The informal system does not have a monolithic form, their practices differ from region to region according to their unique statutory and community norms.[22] Furthermore, these non-state bodies have been prevalent for centuries especially in the rural segments; however, there is evidence of their existence even in urban pockets of Pakistan.

The informal *jirga* deals with a wide range of issues faced by the Pakhtun population, beginning with disputes involving inheritance, honor crimes to tribal clashes and murders. Despite the option to access the formal judiciary, Pakhtuns prefer to approach the local *jirga* for dispute resolution, as their decisions are mostly compatible with customary practices and religious sentiments. According to Mumtaz A. Bangash, the *jirga* encourages mediation and negotiation in order to ensure just and equitable decisions, while giving voice to the weaker segments of the Pakhtun tribe.[23] This view will be contested in the next section, where it will be argued that the *jirga* system is inherently biased toward vulnerable groups that include women and girls.

This system of parallel justice is popular due to the lack of faith in the efficiency and effectiveness of the formal justice system. A survey of representative respondents in the Pakhtun belt reveals that more than two-third (68.5 percent) confirmed that Pakhtun *jirga* is the most effective system of dispute resolution.[24] This illustrates that the populace of KPK rely on the informal justice system for dispute resolution. This can be attributed to the fact that the *jirga* ensures fast and cheap justice to its people, in a culturally sensitive approach that promotes restorative justice and peace in the community.[25] At other levels, the underprivileged and disempowered segment of the society simply cannot decipher and/or meaningfully seek recourse to the formal judiciary, due to its alien language, unscrupulous lawyers, inadequately trained judges, convoluted and outdated laws, together with weak governance suffering from rampant corruption.[26]

Despite the growing legitimacy of the *jirga* system, human rights activists have repeatedly condemned their practice at national and international platforms.[27] In 2019, hearing a petition filed by the National Commission on the Status of Women, chief justice of Pakistan at the time, Mian Saqib Nisar, in a landmark judgment held that *jirgas* were unlawful as they violated human rights guaranteed by the Constitution. However, the judgment allows the informal system to operate "within the permissible limits of the law" to the extent of arbitration, mediation, negotiation, or reconciliation forums in civil disputes if both parties gave their consent.[28] However, today, jirgas are still relied on as a forum of dispute resolution.

THE INTERTWINING OF ISLAMIC, STATE, AND TRIBAL CUSTOMARY LAW: THE STATUS OF WOMEN IN THE PAKHTUN BELT

> *Khaza da kor da ya the gor (For a women it is either the house or the grave).*
>
> —Pakhtu proverb

The lives of many women living under tribal laws informed by the tradition of Pakhtunwali are marked by fear. This state of fear is bred by the "patriarchal, patrilineal and patrilocal"[29] social paradigm of Pakhtun society, where a woman is perceived as a "symbolic vessel"[30] or repository of her husband, father or brother's honor. Consequently, a Pakhtun woman is confined within the sanctity of the four walls of her home, forced to abide by the religious, ethical, and moral codes prescribed by the community, proscribing her freedom of choice, movement, and opportunity. Pakthun women live in constant fear, because their fate rests in the hands of the male members of their families. From birth onward, Pakhtun women are rarely given the opportunity to make their own decisions regarding significant choices which impact their entire lives: education, marriage, the number of children they bear, their mobility, in essence, their ability to use their voice to express their own needs, aspirations, desires.

The Role of *Pakhtunwali* in Perpetuating Gender Inequality: The Comparative Analysis of Law, Religion, and Custom

Traditional notions of *Pakhtunwali* have been interpreted and applied to implement, defend, and reinforce patriarchal ideals. *Pakhtunwali* with an admixture of sharia has been used to establish a women's subservient position in the social hierarchy.[31] Akbar Ahmed and Zeenat Ahmed categorically divide the role of Pakhtun women into two models. The first model covers the concept of *Mor*, the mother, reflecting on their piety and high status in the society. The second model is based on the concept of *Tor*, or the color "black," signifying dishonor and shame. The boundary that distinguishes between these two models is blurred and transition from one model to another can be set off by a single "alleged" dishonorable act considered to be a transgression of the moral code enshrined in *Pakhtunwali*.[32] Therefore, this "layered"[33] identity of Pakhtun women restricts her within the shackles of customs and creates impenetrable obstacles that surpass any legal framework or Islamic jurisprudence.

Pakhtunwali, a centuries-old fusion of social, cultural, economic, and religious dogmas,[34] disempowers women and positions them at the bottom of the dominance-submission dynamic common to patriarchal societies. To begin with, women are denied the right to inherit or own property in the Pakhtun belt.[35] Under the custom of *Tarboor*, the nearest male relative or relatives inherits all property, leaving women completely financially and socially dependent upon the men in their families.[36] This *Riwaaj* serves to keep wealth within the family, and clearly contradicts Islamic principles[37] and the legislations[38] enacted to guarantee women's right to inheritance.

Within the sphere of marriage, Pakhtun women are denied all rights enshrined both in the religion of Islam and the Constitution of Pakistan. Their identity, derived from their fathers, is automatically transferred to their husbands.[39] Violence within the domestic space, in particular within the home of the husband and his family, is common and at times severe, resulting in death.[40] Women in the tribal belt are more likely to be subjected to domestic violence in comparison to women in other provinces. This was stated in the findings of recent research, which reported that approximately 59 percent of rural women in Khyber Pakhtunkhwa were exposed to physical abuse since the age of 15.[41] At one level, these alarming statistics can be attributed to the high rate of illiteracy and underdevelopment[42] in the region; however, the role of *Pakhtunwali* in perpetrating the acceptance and practice of violence cannot be denied.

Furthermore, divorce is considered a "social impossibility";[43] consequently, women who attempt to seek divorce risk being killed.[44] Therefore, women in physically and psychologically abusive marriages have no recourse to law or an avenue to escape the torment they are subjected to. The legal framework of the state has extensive laws that allow women to seek divorce in line with notions of Islamic law,[45] hence, once again, the law of the land is undermined and totally in conflict with *Riwaaj*, the dominant tradition in Pakhtun culture.

The tribal code revolves around *zan, zar, zameen* (woman, wealth, and land) and encourages men to go to great lengths to protect the notion of honor attached to these symbols of wealth and possession.[46] These cultural values have given birth to customary practices including *swara*, *walwar*, and *xhag*. The traditional practice of *swara* is prevalent in various parts of the Pakhtun belt and is entrenched in Pakistan's tribal culture. The custom calls for a girl to be given away in marriage as compensation for a crime committed by her father, brothers, or uncles.[47] The custom of *swara* forms the central subject of our discussion and will be examined and analyzed in-depth at a later stage of the chapter.

Walwar

Pakhtun women are usually not entitled to being in possession of independent identities and are viewed as economic assets by their families. Even a women's marriage is seen as a "bargain between two families"[48] often strengthening tribal and political alliances.[49] The custom of *walwar*, also known as *Sar Paisa* ("bride price"), is frequently practiced in the tribal regions of Pakistan. This Pakhtun custom involves the payment of tangible items (cattle, gold) or money paid by the groom to the bride's family.[50] Traditionally, *walwar* was given as a gift, with the aim to bring families together and by easing the financial burdens of the bride's family associated with raising a girl and bearing her wedding expenses.[51] Today, this practice appears to have been "commercialized" through the commodification of women as "marketable" members of families, losing much of its conventional value.[52] The significance of this ancient, indigenous custom has been distorted by being morphed into a list of demands made by the bride's family. It now appears that a man "buys" his wife as a commodity, with her price exclusively determined by her beauty, health, age, and the family's monetary status.[53] Poverty-stricken families are more vulnerable to giving away their girls in order to survive. Therefore, women are sometimes trafficked or forced into prostitution under the guise of this custom.[54] *Walwar* reinforces the normative structuring of tribal society that gives an inferior status to women in Pakhtun society. The impact of this iniquitous custom on young women is catastrophic, as it reduces them to chattels, devoid of an independent and empowered existence. This "object of value" will be sold to the highest bidder, regardless of his age, marital status, or intent.[55] This practice is not compatible with Islamic principles, which requires the payment and inclusion of *mahr*,[56] in the Nikkah contract.

Xhag

In the Pakhtun belt, women are considered the guardians of familial honor and often sacrificed to preserve their honor in the eyes of the tribal community. This is evident in the custom of *xhag* (call), an ancient tribal practice, although in decline, but still common where *Pakhtunwali* prevails. *Xhag* involves a man declaring his claim over a woman for marriage; typically, a Pakhtun man forces the girl's family to give her hand in marriage by firing a gun and shouting out the girl's name outside her house.[57] This custom is a reflection of the mindset that Pakhtun males have a birthright to marry their female cousins, even if their match is incompatible. The region is testament to the sufferings of countless Pakhtun women, forced to marry criminals, mentally challenged males or men as old as their fathers.[58] This custom further limits conjugal rights of women, as refusal to adhere to agreement may be revenged by killing the girl or her family members. Other than depriving women of their fundamental rights, this custom also breeds lifelong enmities between families and tribes and results in bloodshed as this coerced agreement is considered a direct insult to the honor of the girl's family.[59] Lastly, this custom is against untainted Islamic values, as it is prohibited to oppress or force a woman into marriage or to obtain her consent through coercion.[60]

Tor

Aside from the above-mentioned discriminatory norms that degrade women and render them voiceless, women in the tribal belt are also exposed to grave dangers of practices that are widespread in all four provinces of Pakistan. The practice of *tor* (black) or the custom of killing women (and men) if suspected of violating tribal or family honor.[61] It is estimated that a thousand women are killed in the name of honor annually in Pakistan, a figure that constitutes 25 percent of honor-based murders around the world.[62]

Discrepancies and ambiguities in the legal system also grant perpetrators the freedom to kill with impunity. The *Hudood* Ordinances and the implementation of the Criminal Law (Fourth Amendment) *Qisas* and *Diyat* Ordinance 1991[63] allow the *wali* (heir) of the victim to "pardon" the perpetrator and/or receive *diyat* (monetary payment as compensation).[64] Commonly, honor killings are committed by the men of the victims family, this allows them to escape imprisonment based on an ambiguity created by an Islamic principle.

The Denial of Rights: Access to Justice for Pakhtun Women

These customary practices are frequently sanctioned or safeguarded by the tribal *jirga*.[65] Commonly known as an egalitarian system of dispensing justice,[66] the informal justice system excludes a woman's voice in its decision-making process.[67] Presently, the *jirga* system fails to be representative and inclusive of half of its population, women can only be represented by their male relatives to advocate on their behalf.[68] Consequently, in disputes that concern the violation of women's fundamental rights, their fate would ultimately rest in the hands of the tribal elders or the men in her family. This causes more concern in cases where the perpetrators of crime are related to the victim, thus allowing them to easily twist the facts and escape punishment; this is very relevant to the discriminatory practices discussed earlier, especially honor killing. Consequently, women suffer from gender disparities and unfair dictates at every level in the Pakhtun society. Despite having the option to access the state institutions for justice, ironically, women still blindly follow and support the rigid principles of *Pakhtunwali*.[69] This could be linked to the low level of education and awareness regarding their fundamental rights and the protections guaranteed by the legal framework of Pakistan. Most of their knowledge derived from the men of the family or social networking through weddings and funerals or during fetching water from the well or nearby *gudar*;[70] therefore, they are not exposed to independent sources of information.

THE DARK SIDE OF *PAKHTUNWALI*: THE PRACTICE OF *SWARA* IN NORTHWESTERN PAKISTAN

Pakhtun sowal na kawee, ao chay kawee no khor ta hoom odreegee (A Pakhtun does not beg, but if he stoops he will even beg from his sister).

—Pakhtu proverb

Examining the situation of Pakhtun women within the legal framework of Pakistan and Islamic sharia, the practice of *swara* can be seen as a menace deleteriously affecting many women and girls belonging to either the rugged tribal villages or to the bustling metropolis of Peshawar. In a year, approximately 180 cases of *swara* surfaces; however, local journalists believe that hundreds of cases are unreported and concealed from the eyes of the media.[71] The abhorrent practice of *swara* calls for settling of blood feuds through the practice of giving away girls in marriage to an aggrieved family as compensation for a crime committed by the male heirs of the "gifted" girl's family.[72] The crimes range from situations where an individual murders an individual from another family, or a man elopes with a girl from another family, or merely an accusation of committing adultery.[73] In each instance, the punishment involves the giving away of a daughter or a sister in recompense for crimes the young women did not commit.

Human Rights Critique

The tradition of *swara* dates back 400 years, when two Pakhtun tribes of Mianwali scuffled in a protracted conflict that took the life of more than 800 people.[74] The besieged *Nawab* (regional governor) called on a *jirga* of tribal elders representing both sides to prevent further violence. It was then collectively decided to settle the crimes by giving their familial girls as *qisas*[75] to compensate for the lives lost.

Historically, Pakhtun women were perceived as a symbol of peace and at times the only hope of reconciliation between warring tribes. According to Muhammad Ali Babakhel, the practice of sending women to the aggrieved family was metaphoric gesture of forgiveness.[76] He further explains that traditionally the aggrieved tribe treated these women with utmost respect and sent them back with a *chadar* (veil) and gifts signifying honor; women were never retained permanently.[77] Over time, this practice became accepted as local tradition and was passed on over generations and across many tribes among the Pakhtun "nation."[78] Having said that, today, *swara* is closer to the concept of *badl*, which essentially consists of acts of vengeance taken in pursuit to defend their family "honor." Parallels have been drawn between *swara* and the ancient Egyptian fable "Bride of Nile" where a girl was thrown into the River Nile to prevent it from flooding;[79] and in KPK, where girls are given away to the victim's family to prevent escalation of the conflict and ultimately save the community.

Currently, *swara* is practiced as an indigenous mechanism of conflict resolution by the informal *jirga* to bring in an attempt to end lifelong enmities, outside the writ of state law.[80] Arguably, *jirgas* aim to preempt and curtail tension between families or tribes and endeavor to restore harmony by sacrificing the individual rights of girls to the collective needs of society.[81] In a recent interview, a tribal elder explained that the rationale behind this custom is that it is hoped that children born in *swara* wedlock will keep peace among tribes and families.[82]

The sanctity of the practice is embedded in *Pakhtunwali*'s positioning of women as "lesser," coupled with the weaknesses of the formal judiciary that leaves Pakhtun communities with little recourse to modern, legal institutions and maintains the primacy of the *jirga* as the alternate and informal body of dispute settlement. More importantly, the cultural acceptance of *swara* serves as the undertone that legitimizes the practice since most of the Pakhtun society have chosen to turn a blind eye toward the heavy price paid by girls given away as *swara* in an unceremonious marriage.[83]

As a constant reminder of loss to the bereaved family, the girl given as *swara* is sentenced to a lifetime of oppression in the home of the "enemy." According to advocate Khalil ur Rehman, "the woman is traded like an animal. Once married, she is little better than a slave."[84] The Human Rights Commission of Pakistan (HRCP) describes *swara* as "virtual death penalty" for victims of this heinous crime.[85] Arguably, the practice of *swara* is a contemporary form of sexual slavery.[86] Furthermore, this practice indiscriminately incarcerates girl children and sometimes even girls who have not yet been born. Therefore, families will receive a "lifetime slave"[87] due to the girl's young age. These victims are denied some of the basic human rights as result of the social stigma attached to their existence. Amnesty International has exposed the consequences of this custom, finding that a majority of *swara* brides suffer from unbelievable psychological and physical abuse, with no hope or recourse to justice.[88]

The Legal and Religious Status of *Swara*

One of the factors that led to the prevalence of this discriminatory practice is the fact that Pakhtun women fail to grasp the very meaning or concept of having *rights*, as theirs have been historically curtailed under a corrupted "guise of religion"[89] and *riwaj*. According to a recent survey conducted in KPK, only 27 percent female respondents claimed to have knowledge of the fundamental rights protected by the Constitution whereas less than 50 percent had awareness of domestic legislation that prohibited *swara*.[90]

Fundamental Rights Enshrined in the Constitution and Swara

The Constitution of Pakistan safeguards certain indispensable fundamental human rights against state interference. Articles 8-28 of the Constitution unequivocally grant all citizens their inherent rights and inculcate regulatory mechanisms to protect and promote these substantive freedoms. In particular relevance to *swara* is Article 9 that guarantees the security of life and freedom of liberty to every citizen.[91] Girls given away in *swara* are forced to marry against their will and face social imprisonment that restricts their liberty for the rest of their lives. Furthermore, *swara* also contravenes Article 4 that provides for the right of all citizens to enjoy the protection of law and to be treated in accordance with the law. *Swara* also stands in direct conflict with Article 25 that indubitably and unambiguously prohibits discrimination based on gender.[92]

State Laws Addressing Swara

To begin with, there was a legal vacuum in relation to regulating *swara* crimes in Pakistan, as there was no law in place to explicitly deal with women given in marriage as compensation for a crime committed by her male relative(s). The only legal tools available to address this subject were jurisdictional legislation that outlawed child marriages in Pakistan. Having said that, this legal embargo would only apply in cases where the *swara* victim is still a child. Firstly, Section 5 of the Child Marriage Restraint Act 1929 holds responsible the parent or guardian of the minor contracted in a child marriage.[93] Secondly, Section 2 (vii) The Dissolution of Muslim Marriages Act 1939, theoretically speaking, is the most vital instrument to liberate underage girls captive under the custom of *swara*. Under this provision, a minor girl under the age of 16 given in marriage by her father or guardian can be entitled to dissolve the marriage before the age of 18, given that the marriage has not been consummated.[94] In reality, however, the flawed Act fails to effectively provide victims with any legal redress. Thirdly, Section 5 (1) The Muslim Family Laws Ordinance 1961 aims to monitor the culturally embedded custom of child marriage, as it requires the registration of all marriages solemnized under Muslim law.[95]

Following decades of activism and struggle, the discriminatory custom of *swara* was unequivocally declared illegal for the first time through the Criminal Law Amendment Act 2004.[96] This Act amended Section 310 of the Pakistan Penal Code (PPC) and states that in murder cases under the Islamic principle of *qisas*,[97] the aggrieved family may choose to pardon the murderer and accept compensation in return provided that a girl is not given in marriage or otherwise in *Budla-e-sulah*.[98] Section 310 A strictly prohibits *swara* and those found guilty of involvement in such offenses will face imprisonment of up to ten years. The law further incriminates those indirectly involved in *swara* marriages, including parents or guardians, tribal elders that ruled (through *jirga*) in favor of *swara* marriages, and the marriage registrar, and/ or local mullah.

Section 310 has been replaced by the Prevention of Anti-Women Practices (Criminal Law Amendment) Act 2011[99] that aimed to strengthen the legal mechanisms in place to eradicate harmful customary practices against women in Pakistan. Under this regulation, lawmakers have explicitly included the terms "*wani*" and "*swara*" in addition to *Badle-sulah* to ensure that provincial variations of this traditional practice cannot escape the grasp of the law. Having said that, the amended provision fails to provide a definition of the terms "*wani*" and "*swara*" or the words "custom" or "practice," leaving its understanding to the comprehension and knowledge of law enforcement agencies and the judiciary.

Furthermore, in cases where the court and police are reluctant to include certain acts within the ambit of this crime, this would allow perpetrators to evade criminal liability. The exclusion of other regional terms used to identify these forced marriages such as *sung-chati* and *khoon-baha*[100] causes confusion for the district administration and the police to identify and report this crime.

The Criminal Law Amendment Act 2011 introduces a prerequisite that for the law to be applicable a girl should be given in exchange of settling a "civil or criminal" dispute. This considerably narrows down the applicability of this legal provision to a situation where the girl is forcefully married for this specific purpose. Another gap is that the amended Section 310 only holds those who "give" girls in marriage responsible; in most cases, these are the family members. This creates a legal ambiguity, because the groom and his family are not penalized despite their equal part in carrying out this crime. Even though this law also implicates those who "compel" the girl into a marriage, in order to ensure effective implementation of the law and eradication of this custom, it is essential that every party that directly or indirectly facilitates this crime is held accountable.

It is also noteworthy that in comparison to the Criminal Law Amendment Act 2004, this provision is non-cognizable. This means that the police authorities are required to take permission of the court before arresting the culprit(s),[101] giving the parties involved ample time to flee in order to avoid prosecution. Furthermore, the punishment for a person convicted under this section has been reduced from ten years to seven years. Therefore, despite being termed as a non-bailable offense, under Section 497 of Criminal Procedure Code,[102] the alleged criminal arrested for a non-bailable offense with a punishment of less than ten years can be released on bail.

The chief justice of the Peshawar High Court has also pointed out the present loopholes in the recently amended provision of the PPC and has requested the federal and provincial governments to enact special laws to eliminate *swara* in the region.[103] Lastly, as the law does not apply retrospectively, *swara* victims, who were married before the enactment of this legislation, will have no grounds for legal proceedings.[104]

The collective study of the historical background and current legislative stagnancy exposes deeply powerful gender dimensions in both legislation and sociocultural norms in many parts of the country.

The Position of Swara in Islam

One of the main justifications behind the acceptance and practice of discriminatory customs in northwestern Pakistan is the concept that the basic precepts of *Pakhtunwali* are in line with Islamic jurisprudence; this necessitates an analysis of the linkages between tribal law and sharia, particularly in reference to *swara*. Professor Mashood Baderin rightly identifies the notion of "Islamic culture" in Muslim nations that is highly applicable to the current discussion. He argues that various negative local cultures have influenced Islamic culture despite its incompatibility with sharia.[105] This Islamic culture is derived from the social environment and based on the concept of "honor and shame."[106] Over time, these cultural practices have interwoven in Muslim communities and recognized as genuine Islamic norms.[107]

Therefore, lines between religious and cultural practices are constantly blurred in this region, this was evident in the survey conducted in the Pakhtun belt by a Pakistani NGO where 50 percent of the respondents believed that *jirgas* applied admixture of sharia and *riwaj* in dispute resolution and 19 percent of the respondents answered that *jirgas* made their decisions based purely on an understanding of Islamic law.[108]

A study of the main sources of Islamic law demonstrates that sharia does not support the practice of *swara*. Reportedly, in pre-Islamic era, Arabs practiced a tradition where retribution for a murder demanded the blood of a person higher in rank to that of the murderer, for example, a free man was to be killed for a slave and man for a woman.[109] However, this practice was refuted by the revelation of verses 178–179 of *Surah al-Baqrah* that prohibits passing on the burden of one's crime to another. According to Islamic law, punishments should be "punitive, retributive, reformative and act as a deterrent,"[110] and no one should bear another's liability.[111] Given this emphasis, it is clear that a woman or minor cannot be held accountable for a crime committed by her guardians, while the offender goes scot-free. In addition, the Quran firmly prohibits the concept of collective punishment and states that only the offender should be incriminated for the crime he/she committed and no one else should be punished in his place.[112] The Quran also prescribes clear ways of dispute settlement between feuding parties and stresses on "justice" to always be the overriding principle while resolving disputes. The harsh practice of *swara* completely rejects this injunction. Furthermore, the Quran also speaks of kindness and equality, both principles that are not found in *swara* marriages.[113]

There is plenty of evidence in the *sunnah* of the Holy Prophet that contravenes the practice of compensation marriages. To begin with, reconciliations based on illegitimate methods are rejected in Islam. As narrated by Abu Huraira and Zaid bin Khalid Al-Juhani, a *Bedouin* had paid a ransom of 100 sheep and a slave girl to save his son who had committed *zina*. The Prophet (PBUH) decided that the sheep and slave girl should be returned and the son should be punished according to principles of sharia.[114]

Islamic scholars based in Pakistan unanimously agree that forced marriages are un-Islamic. During an interview, renowned Islamic scholar, Dr. Anis Ahmed explains that "in cases where a girl is coerced into a marriage, it's not *Nikah* but *Nikah bil jabar* (forced marriage), which is prohibited in Islam."[115] Echoing this view, Dr. Khalid Zaheer states that *Nikah* is a binding agreement between a man and woman to live as husband and wife, based on free consent of both parties. The fact that both the bride and the bridegroom must consent to the *Nikah* before it is solemnized points to the necessity of this condition. In *swara*, on the other hand, the bride is forced to marry a man without her free consent.[116]

Undoubtedly, the above is illustrative of the fact that contrary to popular belief that the discriminatory practice of *swara* is backed by religious principles and values, this custom infringes principles of sharia and a girl or a woman cannot be given as *swara* under any circumstances. Consequently, it is safe to conclude that religion has been misinterpreted or even completely obfuscated and Islamic law has been rendered subservient or even irrelevant to the social and cultural mores of the Pakhtun belt. Any challenge to the rigid code of conduct, *Pakhtunwali*, is judged to be a "detour from the path of piety."[117]

HUMAN RIGHTS INTERVENTIONS

Despite the negligence of the state institutions in addressing *swara*, activists and non-state bodies have stepped forward to fill this void and efforts to deter locals from succumbing to compensation marriages. The section below will present two such case studies.

Samar Minallah's Battle against *Swara*

The lens of Samar Minallah's camera has revealed the dark side of culture and the shadow it has cast on the lives of Pakhtun women in Pakistan. Blending film with social activism, Ms. Minallah has successfully highlighted the underreported custom of *swara* through her debut documentary *Swara: Da Zhwand Mairman* (*Swara*: A Bridge over Troubled Waters). To catalyze transformative change, Ms. Minallah's documentaries are culturally sensitive and filmed in local dialects to be accessible to the local masses.[118]

Ms. Minallah successfully mobilized policy-makers to join hands with her in the campaign against *swara*, which resulted in the legislation of the Criminal Amendment Act 2004 that outlawed *swara* in Pakistan.[119] In the journey of her fight against this tribal practice, Ms. Minallah filed a petition of public interest litigation against *swara* in the Supreme Court of Pakistan over a decade ago.[120] Consequently, the Supreme Court took a suo motu notice under Article 184 (3) of the Constitution that held the custom of giving girls in marriage as compensation, as "unconstitutional, unlawful and un-Islamic."[121] In addition, the court asked police forces to provide protection to girls from forced marriages of *swara.* Inspector generals of police in all regions were directed to take immediate action against those who encouraged and supported this custom.[122] In a separate ruling, the Supreme Court ordered for committees to be established around the country to provide legal support to victims.[123] As a result of the judicial activism, sixty-five minor girls were saved from being handed over as *swara* in different parts of the country.[124]

Community Appraisal and Motivation Programme (CAMP): Using Jirga to Reform Jirga

CAMP is a local nongovernmental organization based in Pakistan that has been working over the past decade to promote human rights, peace and security in the Pakhtun belt of Pakistan.[125] In its initiative to strengthen the rights of women, CAMP initiated a campaign against the inequitable customs of *swara*, *walwar*, and *xhag*, which have been considered sacrosanct for centuries.

On May 29, 2012, CAMP held a historic and exemplary Grand *jirga of* its kind in Islamabad chaired by the governor of KPK where more than 800 tribal elders and traditional *Qazis* announced the ban on these inhumane practices against women in the region. The effects of this customary ban have been widespread, and tribal elders reported over twenty *swara* cases that were prevented in less than a year after its announcement.[126]

Given below are three examples that involved *swara* decisions in the *jirga*:[127]

Case 1

Malik Najaf Ali (tribal elder) from Orakzai Agency stated that as signatories to the decision of the Grand *jirga*, his *jirga* stopped a family from giving their daughter as *swara* to resolve their protracted conflict and instead asked the responsible party to pay Rs. 2.5 million. Furthermore, the tribal elder was also of the opinion that Pakhtun women, especially educated segment, felt more secure and free after the ban held on the custom of *swara*, as now they did not fear being forced into marriages under social pressure.

Case 2

Sanab Gul (tribal elder) from FR Lakki Marwat reported that a *jirga* was convened to resolve a dispute that concerned the murder of five people in Tajoori village. The tribal elders in these cases held that the aggrieved parties should receive a compensation of Rs.1.5 million, along with two girls from the accused's family in the presence of fifteen people to swear upon the Quran as witnesses. Fortunately, due to the ban on *swara* imposed by the Grand *jirga*, tribal elders were allowed to intervene and save the lives of two innocent girls.

Case 3

According to Sheikh Jahanzada (tribal elder) from Bajaur Agency, in order to settle an eighty-year-old feud, one party demanded three underage girls as *swara*. However, the tribal elders leading the *jirga* declared that *swara* is an un-Islamic practice and has been prohibited by the Grand *jirga*. Therefore, the *jirga* decided that ten large flour bags and one cow should be given to the victim's family as compensation.

CONCLUSION

> *Pakhtu wata, Pakhtu Khwala, ao Pakhtu Pala (Speak Pakhtu, Do Pakhtu and Honour Pakhtu).*
>
> —Pakhtu proverb

This chapter attempted to highlight the customary practice of *swara* that has not made its place in the human rights discourse in the national and international fora. The purpose was to also engage in a comparative analysis of human rights of Pakhtun women in formal law, sharia, and tribal customs. The analysis has helped us map a number of conclusions that restate the hypostasis that practice of *swara* is implicitly and explicitly upheld by the patriarchal construct of the *Pakhtunwali* endorsed under the precarious guise of religion and overlooked by law.

Recommendations

Over the past decade, there has been a paradigm shift in the women rights legislation and mechanisms to strengthen the role of women in Pakistan and protect them from oppressive cultural practices. Feminist academics and activists have successfully critiqued legal loopholes and proposed for a way forward in curbing gender-based violence in the public and private spaces. In context of *swara* and other traditional norms against women in Pakistan, parliamentarians and human rights workers urge lawmakers to take strict actions against the tribal *jirga* as they reflect the failure of the state to uphold rule of law in Pakistan.[128]

The Sukkur Bench of the Sindh High Court has explicitly declared informal mechanisms unlawful in province[129] and the Supreme Court has declared *jirgas* to be unconstitutional.[130] Despite these significant legal steps taken, community-based systems are in place de facto in all four provinces of Pakistan. Therefore, to eradicate these negative trends in the society, legal reform should be supported by strengthening public institutions to effectively implement the law. Consequently, recognizing the legitimacy and popularity of the *jirga*, there is a need to adopt a new angle toward the approaches to eradicate unjust practices such as *swara* in the Pakhtun society; therefore, this chapter proposes the following key recommendations:

I. Do-no-harm approach: In order to bring sustainable and positive change in customary practices in KPK, it is imperative to include the voices of all stakeholders into the reform process. It has been evident that the Pakhtun community has rightly rejected all campaigns that are severely critical of *Pakhtunwali* and impose change from the outside. Therefore, it is necessary to design culturally sensitive campaigns and programmes that support locally owned and led change.

II. Public-private partnership: Referring back to the success of the CAMP's Grand Jirga to ban *swara*, such social initiatives can have a greater impact if endorsed by the state. Therefore, it is essential to create opportunities for public-private partnership in combating *swara* at a provincial level.

III. Sensitization of *Jirga* members: Acknowledging the impracticality of banning the *jirga* system, instead of eradicating this system which is widely trusted within Pakthun community, this parallel system of dispute resolution should be reformed to make it accessible to all segments of the community. To begin with, stakeholders managing conflict and delivering traditional justice should be sensitized and educated on fundamental human rights inherent in the Constitution and sharia, in particular, rights of women and children. Religion can be used as a catalyst for social reform in the Pakhtun society.[131] As Pakhtuns give more weight to Islamic principles to that of statutory norms, therefore, denial of any linkage between Islamic principles and discriminatory practices can effectively intervene in cases of *swara*.

IV. Encouraging women *Jirga*: The improvement of access to justice for women requires the *jirga* to be a representative and inclusive of women participation. Keeping in mind the conservative structure of the region, this can be achieved by establishing women *jirgas* that exclusively deal with disputes involving women. An exemplary community-based organization in Swat has set up such a *jirga*, known as *Khwaindo Tolana* (sister's group), that stands up to the wave of injustices and violence against women in their community.[132] Based on this success, state and non-state bodies should establish, support, and monitor other women-led *jirgas* in different constituencies.

V. Changing mindset through education: To break the shackles of obsolete and prejudiced cultural practices, the state and civil society also has to introduce educational reforms to create indispensable awareness regarding human rights and to alter the patriarchal interpretations of sharia that has sustained the practice of *swara*. This needs to happen together with creating economic opportunities to prevent underprivileged families from falling prey to this vicious custom.

VI. Adjudicators of civil dispute: *Jirgas* are mostly condemned for resolving criminal cases based on notions that conflict with human rights standards. Therefore, the state can limit the function of this restorative institution to merely civil disputes in an attempt to achieve social reconciliation while eliminating the risk of infringing fundamental rights in line with the Supreme's Court decision on *swara* marriages.

GLOSSARY

Adl	Justice
Badl	Revenge
Ghairat	Honor
Diyat	Blood money
Hadith	Sayings of Prophet Mohammad (PBUH)
Hujra	A place for guests and gatherings for the male population in the community. *Hujra* is usually attached to the house of a local leader.
Huquq	Rights
Izzat	Honor
Jirga	Refers to the practice and to the institution in KP, FATA, and Balochistan. A *Jirga* is a gathering of elders, convened by an intermediary (*Jirgamaar*, see below) between contesting parties, to hear the arguments of the parties.
Jirgamaars	The leader of a *Jirga* who hears the arguments of the plaintiffs.
Karo Kari	Literally meaning black in Sindh. The term is used to describe a man and woman who are charged with an illicit relationship

Maher	Dower
Maliks	Tribal elders
Nang	Honor
Nikkah	Marriage contract
Nizam-e-Adl	System of governance based on sharia law in Malakand
Pakhtun	Ethnic group
Pakhtunwali	The inherited moral and social code of Pakhtun society
Panchayat	Informal dispute resolution through community mediation in Punjab
Pakhtu	Language
Pardah	Veil
Qazi	Judge
Riwaj	Tradition
Sarkari	Official
Sharia	Islamic code of life
Shariat	Islamic code of life
Swara	The giving of young women and girls in marriage as a method of resolving conflict; this is also known as *Badal-i-Sulh, Sang Chati, Khoon baha,* and *Vani*
Wali	Guardian
Walwar	Bride price
Xhagg	Man's declaration of claim over a woman for marriage
Zina	Adultery

NOTES

1. Tribal elders convening the *Jirga* proceedings.
2. The way of the Pakhtuns.
3. VOA, "Pakistani family fights Tradition of *swara*" (2012) watch https://www.youtube.com/watch?v=nvLWsIw028c
4. Sehrish Wasif, "Survey Find 77% of marriages made in Traditional Exchanges" *Tribune*, February 12, 2013,http://tribune.com.pk/story/506066/survey-finds-77-of-marriages-made-in-traditional-exchanges/
5. Akhbar Ahmed, *The Thistle and the Drone* (Thomson Press, 2013) 51.
6. Nancy Tapper, *Bartered Brides* (CUP, 1991) 45.
7. Michael Barry Hooker, *Legal Pluralism: an Introduction to Colonial and Neo-Colonial Laws* (CP, 1975) 2.
8. Ibid, 2.
9. Saima Jasam, "Cultural Violence, Legal Pluralism and Women's Rights" in *Scratching the Surface: Decomaracy, Tradition, Gender,* ed. Jennifer Bennet (HBF, 2007), 75.
10. Leigh Toomey, "Building Complementary Customary and State Legal Systems." *LDR* 3, no. 1 (2010): 157.
11. Christinan Jones-Pauly and Dajani Tuwan, *Women Under Islam: Gender, Justice and the Politics of Islamic Law* (I.B. Tauris, 2011), 216.
12. Zeba Mir-Hosseini and Vanja Hamzic, *Control and Sexuality, The Revivial of Zina Laws in Muslim Contexts* (RS, 2010), 156.

13. Farida Shaheed, "Contested Identities: Gendered Politics, Gendered Religion in Pakistan" *TWQ* 31, no. 6 (2010): 851.

14. Siobhan Mullally, "Nearly as May be: Debating Women's Human Rights in Pakistan" *SLS* 14(2005): 341.

15. Ibid, 341.

16. Article 203 D, Constitution of Pakistan 1973.

17. Ibid.

18. Article 203 G, Constitution of Pakistan 1973.

19. Interview with Malik Abdul Razaq Afridi, Zakha Khel clan of Afridi Tribe, Khyber Agency (June 2014).

20. Bruce Benson, "Pashtunwali: Law for the lawless, defense for the stateless" *IRLE* 37 (2014): 108–120.

21. Hassan Yousafzai and Ali Gohar, *Towards Understanding Pukhtun Jirga: An Indigenous Way of Peacebuilding and More* (JPI, 2005), 18.

22. Shaheen Sardar Ali and Javaid Rehman, *Indigenous Peoples and Ethnic Minorities of Pakistan Constitutional and Legal Perspectives* (Curzon, 2001), 50.

23. Mumtaz Bangash, "Jirga: Speedy justice of Elders," *Khyber*, December 26,2004, http://www.khyber.org/culture/a/Jirga_-_Speedy_Justice_of_Elde.shtml

24. Naveed Ahmad Shinwari and Neha Gauhar, *Understanding Justice Systems of Khyber Pakhtunkhwa, Federally Administered Tribal Areas and Balochistan: The Pakhtun Perspectiv*e (CAMP 2013), 43.

25. CAMP and Saferworld, *Jirga Justice and Conflict Transformation* (2012).

26. Osama Siddique, *Pakistan's Experience with Formal Law: An Alien Justice* (CUP, 2013), 174.

27. Katharine Houreld, "In Pakistan, ancient and modern justice collide" *Reuters,* March 3, 2013, http://in.reuters.com/article/2013/03/13/pakistan-jirgas-idINDEE92C0HM20130313

28. "SC holds jirgas violative of Pakistan's world commitments" *Dawn*, January 17, 2019 https://www.dawn.com/news/1458038

29. Tahira Khan, *Beyond Honour: A Historical Materialist Explanation of Honour Related Violence* (Oxford University Press, 2006), 137.

30. Mazna Hussain "Take my Riches, Give me Justice: A Contextual Analysis of Pakistan's Honor Crimes Legislation" *HJLG* 29 (2006): 223.

31. Shaeen Sardar Ali, *Gender and Human Rights in Islam* (KLI, 1999), 182.

32. Akbar S Ahmed and Zeenat Ahmed, "*Mor and Tor: Binary and Opposing Models of Pakhtun Womanhood*" in *The Endless Day*, ed. T. Scarlett Epstein (Pergamon Press, 1981), 32.

33. Sardar Ali, *Gender and Human Righ*ts, 173.

34. Khan, *Beyond Honour: A Historical Materialist Explanation of Honour Related Violence*, 236.

35. Naila Aman Khan, "Socio-Economic and Political Status of Women in FATA- The Process of Development and Phenomenon of Militancy" *TIGAH*, no. 2(2012): 1.

36. Akbar S. Ahmed, *Pakhtun Economy and Society: Traditional Structure and Economic Development in a Tribal society* (RR, 2012), 182.

37. The Qu'ran states 'There is a share for men and a share for women from what is left by parents and those nearest related, whether, the property be small or large-legal share' (*Al Nisa* 4:7).

38. Article 23 of the Constitution of Pakistan 1973, recognizes the right of all citizens including women to own property. In addition, Inheritance laws in Pakistan are based on Sharia and codified in the Family Laws Ordinance 1961, and the West Pakistan Muslim Personal Law (Shariat) Application Act (V of 1962); see, World Justice Project, *Women's Inheritance Rights to Land and Property in South Asia* (RDI, 2009).

39. Naveed Shinwar, *Understanding Jirga in FATA* (CAMP, 2012).

40. M. Maqbool Khan Wazir, "Violence against Women: Violation of Right of Life of Women in FATA" *PJC*, no. 2 (2010): 2.

41. Murtaza Haidar, "The continued abuse of the Pashtun woman.", *Dawn,* February 19, 2014, http://www.dawn.com/news/1088086

42. Sarfaraz Khan and Samina, "Patriarchal Social and Administrative Practices in Federally Administered Tribal Areas (FATA), Pakistan: A Case for Gender Inclusive Reforms," *Area Study Center* (Peshawar University, 2009) www.asc -cent ralasia.edu.pk/Issue_65/02_Patriarchal_Social_and_Administrative.html.

43. Ahmed, *Pakhtun Economy and Society: Traditional Structure and Economic Development in a Tribal Society*, 250.

44. Samia Sarwar was murdered by her parents outside her lawyers office; See, Marvi Sirmed, "Pakistan: Die my daughter, die quickly" *Asian Human Rights Commission,* June 6, 2014, http://www.humanrights.asia/opinions/columns/AHRC -ETC-013-2014.

45. Symphonious to Islamic Law, the legal framework in Pakistan provides women a right to divorce under Section 8 of Muslim Family Law Ordinance 1961 and Dissolution of Muslim Marriages Act 1939 See, Karin Carmit Yefet, "The Consitution and Female-initiated Divorce in Pakistan: Western Liberalism in Islamic Garb.", *HJLG* no. 34,(2011): 554.

46. Maliha Zia, *Honour Killings in Pakistan and Compliance of Law* (Aurat Foundation, 2012).

47. *Swara: The Human Shield* (Ethnomedia, 2006).

48. Khalid Ashraf, *Tribal People of West Pakistan: A Demographic Study of Selected Population* (PU, 1962) 52.

49. Fredrik Barth, *Political leadership Among Swat Pathans* (the Athlone, Press 1965) 107.

50. Ahmed, *Pakhtun Economy and Society: Traditional Structure and Economic Development in a Tribal society,* 284.

51. Samar Minallah, "Bride for Sale" *Newsline,* November,10, 2003, http://www .newslinemagazine.com/2003/11/bride-for-sale.

52. Ibid, 52.

53. Khan, Socio-Economic and Political Status of Women in FATA- The Process of Development and Phenomenon of Militancy.

54. Samar Esapzai, "Pakistan: Sex Trafficking in Relation to Marriage Customs in Kyber Pakhtunkwa" *A safe world for women*, January 2013, http://www.asafeworldforwomen.org/safe-world-blogs/sesapzai/3709-kpk-marriage-customs.html .

55. Minallah, "Bride for Sale."

56. Mahr is dowry paid to the wife by the husband. The Qur'an states "And give to the women (whom you marry) their mahr (obligatory bridal money given by the husband to his wife at the time of marriage) with a good heart…" [al-Nisaa' 4:4]

57. Azim Afridi, "Pashtun Customs Related to Weddings" *Khyber,* November 11, 2002, http://www.khyber.org/culture/a/Pashtun_Customs_Related_to_Wed.shtml.

58. Abubakar Siddique, "Ghag: The Pashtun Custom of Men Forcing Marriage Proposals on Women" *The Atlantic,* December 9, 2012, http://www.theatlantic.com /international/archive/2012/12/ghagh-the-pashtun-custom-of-men-forcing-marriage -proposals-on-women/266059/.

59. Syed Irshad Hussain, "Conflict Management at the Grassroots in FATA" *TIGAH,* no. 1 (2012): 132.

60. Ameer Ali, "*Muhammedan Law: The Law Relating to Succession and Status*" (APLD, 1965), 241.

61. Khan "Socio-Economic and Political Status of Women in FATA- The Process of Development and Phenomenon of Militancy."

62. Amnesty International, *Pakistan: Honour Killings of Girl and Women* (September, 1999).

63. Nasira Iqbal, "Legal Pluralism in Pakistan and its Implications" in *Scratching the Surface: Democracy, Traditions, Gender,* ed. Jennifer Bennett (Heinrich Boll Foundation, 2007), 104.

64. Are Knudsen, *License to Kill: Honour Killings in Pakistan* (Chr. Michelsen Institute, 2004).

65. In the Lal Jamilla case, a government official raped a 16-year-old mentally handicapped girl. The police handed over the girl to the local Jirga, who decided to shoot her in public to restore their lost honor. See; 'Teenage Rape Victim Executed for Bringing 'Shame' to her Tribesmen' *Guardian,* April, 18, 1999, http://www.theguardian.com/world/1999/apr/18/theobserver7.

66. Ali, *Gender and Human Rights in Islam*, 182.

67. Khan, *Beyond Honour: A Historical Materialist Explanation of Honour Related Violence*, 232.

68. Shinwari and Gauhar, *Understanding Justice Systems of Khyber Pakhtunkhwa, Federally Administered Tribal Areas and Balochistan: The Pakhtun Perspective*, 44.

69. Akbar and Ahmed, *Mor and Tor: Binary and Opposing Models of Pakhtun Womanhood*, 30.

70. Spring water source (secluded) specifically meant for women to fetch water.

71. Gillian Felix, "Every Three Seconds, A Girl is Traded As a Swara" *Plain Talk Book Marketing,* July, 24, 2013 http://www.plaintalkbm.com/swara/.

72. Ali, *Gender and Human Rights in Islam*, 180.

73. Ethnomedia, *Swara: The Human Shield.*

74. Arshad Munir and Ghulam Ali Khan, "A Social Custom 'Vani': Introduction and Critical Analysis," *ALADWA* 40, no. 28 (2010): 37.

75. Under Sharia, Qisas means retribution for murder.

76. Muhammad Ali Babakhel, *Swara, the Price of Honour* (AF, 2003).

77. Ibid.

78. Ethnomedia,*Swara: The Human Shield.*

79. WCLRF, *Bad Painful Sedative* (2004).

80. Mohammad Ali Babakhel, *Swara the Price of Honour* (Aurat Foundation, 2003).

81. Samar Minallah, "Judiciary as a Catalyst for Social Change," *PJWS* 14, no. 2 (2007): 119.

82. Interview tribal elder Malik Razzaq.

83. Minallah, "Judiciary as a Catalyst for Social Change."

84. Declan Walsh, "Traded like animals - the blood feuds settled with 'gift' of a wife." *The Guardian,* April 21, 2006, http://www.guardian.co.uk/world/2006/apr/21/pakistan.declanwalsh.

85. Zofeen Ebrahim, "Death Penalty: Swara Killings in Pakistan Continue" *IPS,* September, 27, 2006, http://www.ipsnews.net/2006/09/death-penalty-swara-killings-in-pakistan-continue/.

86. Amnesty International, Pakistan, *Violence against Women in the Name of Honour* (1999).

87. AGEHI Resource Centre, "*Understanding Adolescent and youth RH issues in Pakistani Context; perspectives from the advocates, activists, academicians scholars and practitioners*" (SACHET, 2008).

88. *"Afghanistan: Women Still under Attack: A Systematic Failure to Protect"* (Amnesty International, 2007).

89. Rahat Imran, "Legal Injustices: The Zina Hudood Ordinance of Pakistan and Its Implications" *WJIWS* 7, no. 2 (2005): 80.

90. Neha Gauhar and Fareeha Sultan, *Honour Crimes in Pakistan Unveiling Reality and Perception* (CAMP, 2014).

91. Article 9 of the Constitution of Pakistan, 10 April 1973, available at http://www.pakistani.org/pakistan/constitution

92. Article 25 of the Constitution of Pakistan, 10 April 1973, available at http://www.pakistani.org/pakistan/constitution

93. Child Marriage Restraint Act (Pakistan) 1929.

94. The Dissolution of Muslim Marriages Act (Pakistan) 1939.

95. Contrary to this law most marriages (including Swara marriages) are not registered in the region under discussion. See, VIII of 1961, Muslim Family Laws Ordinance (Pakistan) 1961.

96. Criminal Law (Amendment) Act (Pakistan) 2004 (I of 2005).

97. Criminal Law Amendment Act (n 97).

98. 310 PPC defines Badl-i-sulh as the mutually agreed compensation according to Sharia to be paid or given by the offender to a *Wali* in cash or in kind or in the form of movable or immovable property.

99. Section 310 A now states that 'Whoever gives a female in marriage or otherwise compels her to enter into marriage, as badal-e-sulh, wanni, or swara or any other custom or practice under any name, in consideration of settling a civil dispute

or a criminal liability, shall be punished with imprisonment of either description for a term which may extend to seven years but shall not be less than three years and shall also be liable to fine of five hundred thousand rupees.'

100. In Sindh the practice of giving girls to settle disputes is known as *Sung-Chati* and *Khoo-n-Baha* in Balochistan.

101. Waseem Ahmad Shan, "Superior courts focus on helping swara, vani victims" *Dawn,* March 25, 2012, http://www.dawn.com/news/705527/superior-courts-focus-on-helping-swara-vani-victims

102. Code of Criminal Procedure (Pakistan) Act No V July, (1898).

103. Minallah, "Judiciary as a Catalyst for Social Change."

104. Riffat Butt, *Lacunas in Pro-Women Legislation in Pakistan* (NCA, 2013).

105. Mashood A Baderin, "Islam and the Realization of Human Rights in the Muslim World: A Reflection on Two Essential Approaches and Two Divergent Perspectives," *MWJHR* 4, no. 1 (2007): 1.

106. Christine Mallouhi, *Miniskirts, Mothers and Muslims* (Lion Hudson, 2004), 21.

107. A. Al-Hibri, "Islam, Law and Custom: Refining Muslim Women's Rights" *AUJILP* 12 (1997): 1.

108. 2140 respondents were interviewed in KPK and Pakhtun dominated regions in Balochistan, See Shinwar and Gauhar,*Understanding Justice Systems of Khyber Pakhtunkhwa, Federally Administered Tribal Areas and Balochistan: The Pakhtun Perspective*.

109. Reported by Ibn Abi Hatim (RA) and Ibn Katheer (RA).

110. Samuel Lane, *Stealing Innocence: child marriage and gender inequality in Pakistan* (Plan, 2011), 13.

111. Qu'ran *Al- Fatir* 18.

112. Also see, Qu'ran *Al Nisa'* 135, 93.

113. Qur'an, *Al-Nisa'* 4:19.

114. Sahih al-Bukhari 2695, Book 53, Hadith 6.

115. Interview with Professor Dr. Anis Ahmed, Vice President of International Islamic University Islamabad, April 2014.

116. Interview with Dr. Khalid Zaheer, vice president of Al-Mawrid, August 2014.

117. Imran, "Legal Injustices: The Zina Hudood Ordinance of Pakistan and Its Implications."

118. Amna R. Ali, "Profile: Documentary Filmmaker Samar Minallah Khan," *Newsline*, January, 1, 2012, http://www.newslinemagazine.com/2012/02/profile-documentary-filmmaker-samar-minallah-khan/

119. "Samar Minallah Khan," *Vital Voices*, http://www.vitalvoices.org/node/2681

120. Samar Minallah v. Federation of Pakistan, Const.P. No. 16/2004.

121. Minallah, "Judiciary as a Catalyst for Social Change."

122. Azam Khan, "Tribal Decisions: SC Declared 'Jirgas' Unconstitutional" *Tribune,* March 27, 2012, http://tribune.com.pk/story/356123/tribal-decisions-sc-declares-jirgas-unconstitutional/

123. Mohammad Karam, "SC Orders Legislation Against Vani," *Daily Times,* April, 25, 2006, http://archives.dailytimes.com.pk/national/25-Apr-2006/sc-orders-legislation-against-vani

124. "Samar Minallah Khan," *Women have wings,* http://womenhavewings.org/whw-courage-award15/

125. Community Appraisal and Motivational Programme, http://camp.org.pk/about-us/

126. Interview with Mr. Shinwari, CEO CAMP, September 2014.

127. Taken from interviews from tribal elders, while working with CAMP, Islamabad, August 2013.

128. "Rights Activists Urge SC to Ban Jirga System" *Tribune,* May, 31, 2012, http://tribune.com.pk/story/386606/parallel-courts-rights-activists-urge-sc-to-ban-jirga-system/

129. Ardeshir Cowasjee, "A First Step" *Dawn*, May 2, 2004, http://www.dawn.com/news/1072875/a-first-step

130. Dawn, "SC holds jirgas violative of Pakistan's world commitments."

131. Interview Feryal A. Gauhar, activist and filmmaker, June 2014.

132. 'Jirga in Swat, by the Women, for the Women' *The Hindu,* July 12, 2013, http://www.thehindu.com/todays-paper/tp-international/jirga-in-swat-by-the-women-for-the-women/article4907043.ece

REFERENCES

Afridi, Azim, "Pashtun Customs Related to Weddings" *Khyber*, November 11, 2002.

Ahmed, Akhbar and Ahmed, Zeenat, "*Mor and Tor: Binary and Opposing Models of Pakhtun Womanhood.*" in *The Endless Day*, edited by T. Scarlett Epstein. Pergamon Press, 1981.

Ahmed, Akbar, *The Thistle and the Drone*. Thomson Press, 2013.

Akbar, S. Ahmed, *Pakhtun Economy and Society: Traditional Structure and Economic Development in a Tribal society*. RR, 2012.

Ali, Ameer, *Muhammedan Law: The Law Relating to Succession and Status.* APLD, 1965.

Ali, Amna, "Profile: Documentary Filmmaker Samar Minallah Khan", *Newsline*, January, 1, 2012 .

Ali, Rabia, *The Dark Side of Honour: Women Victims of Pakistan.* Shirkat Gah, 2001.

Asma Jilani v The Government of Punjab. PLD, 1972, SC 139.

Aurat Foundation, *Beyond Denial: Annual Report 2012 on Violence against Women in Pakistan, A Qualitative Review of Reported Incidents.* Aurat Foundation, 2012.

Aurat Foundation, *Legislative Quotas for Women: A Global and South Asian Overview of Types and Numbers.* Aurat Foundation, 2012.

Aurat Foundation, *Pakistan NGO Alternate Report on CEDAW.* Aurat Foundation, 2012.

Ayaz, Erum, *Peace and Development in FATA through Economic Transformation.* Tigah, 2012.

Babakhel, Muhammad Ali, *Swara, the Price of Honour.* Aurat Foundation, 2003.

Baderin, Mashood, "Islam and the Realization of Human Rights in the Muslim World: A Reflection on Two Essential Approaches and Two Divergent Perspectives", *MWJHR* 4, no. 1 (2007): 1.

Bangash, Mumtaz, "Jirga: Speedy Justice of Elders", *Khyber*, December, 26, 2014.

Butt, Riffat, *Lacunas in Pro-Women Legislation in Pakistan.* NCA, 2013.

CAMP and Saferworld, *Jirga Justice and Conflict Transformation.* 2012.

Felix, Gillian, "Every Three Seconds, A Girl is Traded As a Swara" *Plain Talk Book Marketing,* July, 24, 2013.

Gauhar, Neha, *Honour Crimes in Pakistan Unveiling Reality and Perception.* CAMP, 2014.

Gilani, Hina, "Violence against Women: the Legal Systems and Institutional Responses in Pakistan", in *Violence, law and women's rights in South Asia,* edited by Goonsekere, S. Sage Publications, 2004.

Haidar, Murtaza, "The Continued Abuse of Pashtun Women", *Dawn,* February 21, 2014.

Hamid, Hussain Muhammad, *Frontier Crimes Regulation: A Case Study of Reform Process.* Tigah, 2012.

Hassan, Ali Dayn, "Pakistan: Objective Reality", *Dawn* , August 6, 2010.

Houreld, Katharine, "In Pakistan, Ancient and Modern Justice Collide", *Reuters,* Islamabad, March 14, 2014.

HRCP, S*tate of Human Rights in Pakistan.* 2012 and 2013.

Human Rights Watch, *Crime or Custom? Violence against Women in Pakistan.* 1999.

Iqbal, Nasira, "Legal Pluralism in Pakistan and its Implications" in *Scratching the Surface: Democracy, Traditions, Gender,* edited by Jennifer Bennett. Heinrich Boll Foundation, 2007.

Jasam Saima, "Cultural Violence, Legal Pluralism and Women's Rights" in *Scratching the Surface: Democracy, Traditions, Gender,* edited by Jennifer Bennett. Heinrich Boll Foundation, 2007.

Karam, Muhammad, "SC Orders Legislation Against Vani" *Daily Times,* April, 25, 2006,

Karvan Community Development Organization, *A study of Vanni.* 2006.

Khan, Asghar, *Islam, politics and the state: the Pakistan experience.* Zed Books, 1985.

Khan, Tahira, *Beyond Honour: A Historical Materialist Explanation of Honour Related Violence.* Oxford University Press, 2006.

Knudsen, Anna, *License to Kill: Honour Killings in Pakistan.*(Chr. Michelsen Institute, 2004.

Lane, Samuel, *Stealing Innocence: Child Marriage and Gender Inequality in Pakistan.* Plan, 2011.

Minallah, Samar, "Bride for Sale" *Newsline,* November, 10, 2003.

Minallah, Samar, "Judiciary as a Catalyst for Social Change", *PJWS* 14, no. 2 (2007):119.

Mir-Hosseini, Zeba and Hamzic, Vanja, *Control and Sexuality, The Revivial of Zina Laws in Muslim Contexts.* RS, 2010.

Mullally, Siobhan, "Nearly as May be: Debating Women's Human Rights in Pakistan" *SLS* 14 (2005): 341.

Munir, Arshad and Khan, Gulam Ali, "A Social Custom 'Vani': Introduction and Critical Analysis", *ALADWA* 40, no. 28 (2010): 37.

Role of Tribal Jirga in Violence against Women. PDI, 2005.

Samar Minallah v. Federation of Pakistan, Const.P. No. 16/2004.

Sardar, Shaheen Ali, *Gender and Human Rights in Islam and International Law: Equal Before Allah, Unequal Before Man?* Kluwer Law International, 2000.

Sardar, Shaeen Ali and Rehman, Javed, *Indigenous Peoples and Ethnic Minorities of Pakistan Constitutional and Legal Perspectives.* Curzon, 2001).

Shah, Waseem, "Superior courts focus on helping swara, vani victims" *Dawn,* March 25, 2012.

Shinwari Naveed, *Understanding Iirga: Legality and Legitimacy in Pakistan's Federally Administered Tribal Areas.* CAMP, 2011.

Shinwari, Naveed and Gauhar, Neha, *Understanding Justice Systems of Khyber Pakhtunkhwa, Federally Administered Tribal Areas and Balochistan: The Pakhtun Perspective.* CAMP, 2013.

Shirkat Gah, *Obstructing Progress: Growing Talibanisation and Poor Governance in Pakistan, Shadow Report.* 2013.

Siddique, Osama, *Pakistan's Experience with Formal Law: An Alien Justice.* CUP, 2013.

Swara: The Human Shield. Ethnomedia, 2006.

Toomey, Leigh, "Building Complementary Customary and State Legal Systems." *LDR* 3, no. 1 (2010): 157.

Walsh, Declan, "Traded Like Animals—The Blood Feuds Settled With 'Gift' of a Wife." *The Guardian,* April 21, 2006.

Warriach, Sohail, "Honour Killings and the Law in Pakistan" in *Honour – Crimes, Paradigms, and Violence Against Women* edited by Lynn Welchman and Sara Hossain. Oxford University Press, 2005.

Wasif, Sehrish, "Survey Find 77% of marriages made in Traditional Exchanges" *Tribune*, February 12, 2013.

World Justice Project, *Women's Inheritance Rights to Land and Property in South Asia.* RDI, 2009.

Yousafzai, Hassan and Gohar, Ali, "*Towards Understanding Pukhtun Jirga: An Indigenous Way of Peacebuilding and More.*" (JPI, 2005), 18.

Zia, Maliha, *Honour Killings in Pakistan and Compliance of Law.* Aurat Foundation, 2012.

Chapter 8

Taking Children's Rights Seriously

Is Pakistan Ready?

Adnan Sattar[1]

In 1988, British philosopher Onora O'Neil famously critiqued the idea of children's rights based partly on the premise that children lack autonomy to claim rights.[2] This position can be challenged on both empirical and conceptual grounds. Children as young as 10 and 11 years of age have shown a capacity for rational decision making as documented, for example, by David Nasaw in his history of American "newsies" at the turn of the nineteenth century.[3] Not all children lack the maturity to make choices. And denying all of them the status of rights-holder is arbitrary.[4] Taking off from Philip Aries's thesis that childhood is a modern construct, which emerged in Europe between the fifteenth and eighteenth centuries,[5] scholarship on childhood now recognizes the extent to which children's lives and expectations about their roles and competencies vary across time and space.[6]

That said, autonomy as a prerequisite for rights is a "partial expression of why people count and why we matter to each other."[7] Further, if we make autonomy the basis of rights, the status of smaller children becomes suspect. Here, instead of sliding into anti-foundationalist nihilism, we could ground children's rights in their unique ontological status, which is both privileged and precarious: privileged in the sense that children come into the world with "unique capacities which mark them out from the rest of the natural world,"[8] and precarious because all children are vulnerable to abuse and harm. Children's rights refer to conditions necessary for children to survive and live lives of dignity in the present and in the future. Both temporal domains are worth remembering because there has been a tradition in Western thought as well as in Islamic philosophy under the influence of Aristotelian teleology to view children as *becomings*, adults on probation as it were, rather than *beings* existing here and now.[9] Policy pronouncements casting children instrumentally as future of the nation echo this same truncated view.[10]

I begin with a theoretical primer because there is a tendency within human rights movement to shun philosophical debates as unnecessary at best and disruptive at worst. In the global South, the ideology of human rights and children's rights is either adopted as a matter of faith or dismissed offhand as a product of Western cultural imperialism. My contention is that when we lack a firm theoretical ground to stand on, we are prone to making half-backed and self-defeating moves as practitioners.

In juridical terms, conceptualizing children as persons means recognizing them as subjects rather than objects of authority or adults in the making. In a landmark 1967 decision, the US Supreme Court declared that children were persons within the scope of the 14th Amendment, entitled to due process in delinquency proceedings.[11] However, when called upon to decide whether a state's failure to protect a child from private violence constituted a violation of the substantive part of the 14th Amendment (life, liberty, or property), the court answered in negative.[12] The decision echoed a deep-seated intellectual commitment to a minimal state. Earlier in 1972, the court held that the Wisconsin law mandating the Amish community to send children to school beyond the elementary level violated the Free Exercise clause of the First Amendment.[13] Justice William Douglas dissented. He took issue with the majority's focus on the interests of the parents and the state. On his account, where "the child is mature enough to express potentially conflicting desires, it would be an invasion of the child's rights to permit such an imposition without canvassing his views."[14] Justice Douglas's dissent foreshadowed what is now Article 12 of the Convention on the Rights of the Child (hereinafter "CRC"), adopted by the General Assembly in 1989, and which has since become the most widely ratified international treaty.

The conceptual challenges highlighted above constitute the frame within which I shall reflect on some salient aspects of children's rights and children's protection from abuse and violence in Pakistan. How is the child positioned in relation to those entrusted with her care? What value is placed on children's interests and wishes in matters that concern them? Has the historical conceptualization of children as property of parents given way to a new understanding of children as subjects? Is the notion of the state's *parens patre* powers[15] to protect children from abuse articulated and operationalized adequately in law and in practice?

In the first section below, I sketch some key features of CRC, highlighting helpful benchmarks as well as tensions written into the text. Section II contextualizes children's rights within Pakistan's legal framework. Section III offers a close reading of court proceedings and judgments surrounding a recent case of a maid, 10-year-old Tayyaba, subjected to violence at a judge's residence. Bringing into spotlight some unanswered questions surrounding the case, the discussion examines children's right to freedom from violence and exploitation with reference to power relations embedded in the family, society, and the state. In conclusion, I share some general theoretical points on how to comprehend extant problems and to chart a way forward.

CHILDREN'S RIGHTS UNDER CRC

The CRC traverses a range of freedoms as well as children's welfare interests. The convention shuns a strict binary between civil and political rights on the one hand, and economic, social, and cultural rights on the other, which was written into international law at the end of World War II.[16] CRC began its journey as a declaration of the General Assembly in 1959.[17] Drafted through the 1980s, during a period in which human rights came of age, CRC is a textual embodiment of the broad church approach. The thematic breadth is simultaneously a source of CRC's strength and its weakness. By accommodating diverse viewpoints, it garnered unprecedented endorsement. However, embracing an array of views also exacts a cost in terms of leveling down of standards.

The Committee on the Rights of the Child (hereafter "CRC Committee") has designated certain provisions as general principles animating the convention.[18] These are nondiscrimination (Art. 2) the principle of the best interests of the child (Art. 3), child's survival and development (Art. 6), and the right to be heard. Article 3, paragraph 1, arguably the linchpin of the convention, provides that:

> In all actions concerning children, whether undertaken by public or private social welfare institutions, courts of law, administrative authorities or legislative bodies, the best interests of the child shall be a primary consideration.

While the word "shall" signifies this requirement's mandatory nature, the best interests of the child are cast as "*a* primary consideration," not *the* primary consideration.[19] In this sense, the principle is less stringent than the corresponding provision in the 1959 Declaration, which provided that "in the enactment of laws" for the child's protection and development, the best interests of the child shall be *the* paramount consideration. At the same time, the operational reach of the "best interests principle" in CRC is broader as it relates to "all actions concerning children" and not just legislative enactments.

Article 12, another of the four general principles of CRC, and one of its innovative features, requires state parties to "assure to the child who is capable of forming his or her own views the right to express those views freely in all matters affecting the child." The child's right to be heard is contingent on adult assessment of which the child is "capable of forming views" and which matters affect the child. Another curious aspect of CRC is that it incorporates not only the duties of parents but their rights over children as well. Article 5 is particularly far-reaching. It requires that "States Parties shall respect the responsibilities, rights and duties of parents . . . to provide, in a manner consistent with the evolving capacities of the child, appropriate direction and guidance in the exercise by the child of the [Convention rights]." Article 14, which guarantees respect for "the right of the child to freedom of thought, conscience and religion," circumscribes that freedom with an obligation to respect the "rights and duties of the parents . . . to provide direction to the child in the exercise" of this right.[20] The travaux préparatoires indicate that the reference to parental rights and duties was added, at least in part, due to the opposition of some Islamic countries to a much stronger version which contained the child's "freedom to have or to adopt a religion of his choice."[21] Bangladesh was of the opinion that the proposal ran counter to Islam as it appeared "to infringe upon the sanctioned practice of a child being reared in the religion of his parents."[22] A note from Morocco stated that "the rule adopted in Moroccan legislation is that the child shall follow the religion of his father."[23]

The criticism of CRC on account of its allegedly ethnocentric contents needs to be tempered in light of the role played in its drafting by Asian and African countries.[24] The problems in the text relate more to the potential means of social control inserted into it from an adult-centric perspective. Ashleigh Barnes has argued that CRC tells a story of childhood in which the child is happily nestled within the family. Drawing on the provisions of CRC which give parents the primary responsibility for the care of the child and make the child dependent on the adult for her physical needs and internal life (freedom of thought and conscience), Barnes suggests that "the family in the CRC is defined as not just the presence of an adult and a child, but rather the presence of an adult positioned over a child."[25] This story comes unstuck where parents shun the role assigned to them as is the case with those involved in trafficking their children. We will return to this point. Suffice it to mention that although CRC is a normative landmark, it is far from perfect. We should not foreclose the debate on its merits and demerits. While exploring children's rights in context, we might need to push beyond CRC into new directions, looking fruitfully perhaps at other jurisdictions, or blazing a new trail, if needed.

CHILDREN'S RIGHTS IN THE CONTEXT OF PAKISTAN'S CONSTITUTIONAL AND LEGAL SYSTEM

Pakistan ratified CRC on November 12, 1990, and the Optional Protocols on the Involvement of Children in Armed Conflict, and on the Sale of Children,

Child Prostitution and Child Pornography on July 5, 2011. The country is not a party to the Third Optional Protocol, which entered into force in April 2014, providing a procedure for children to submit complaints to CRC Committee regarding specific violations.

It is sometimes argued that ratification of a treaty in dualist states like Pakistan does not automatically confer domestic legal effect. The relationship between international and domestic law today is much more diverse. In South Africa, Article 39 of the Constitution directs the courts to "consider" international law. The UK's Human Rights Act makes domestically applicable the rights protected in the European Convention on Human Rights.[26] Further, across common aw jurisdictions, courts interpret domestic law in harmony with international law. In *Smith v. Secretary of State for Work and Pensions and Another*, for example, the House of Lords was called upon to determine the basis for child support calculation following parental separation. Invoking Article 27 of CRC which enjoins states to "take all appropriate measures to secure the recovery of maintenance for the child from the parents or other persons having financial responsibility for the child," Baroness Hale noted:[27]

> Even if an international treaty has not been incorporated into domestic law, our domestic legislation has to be construed so far as possible so as to comply with the international obligations which we have undertaken. When two interpretations of these regulations are possible, the interpretation chosen should be that which better complies with the commitment to the welfare of children which this country has made by ratifying the [CRC].

One general obligation, which is expressed in varying formulations in human rights instruments, is that a state aligns its legislative framework and administrative practices with the treaty in question. Article 4 of CRC sets out that obligation has been a subject of the CRC Committee's General Comment No. 5 issued in 2003.[28] Pakistan is also bound by the doctrine of *pacta sunt servanda*, embodied in Article 26 of the Vienna Convention on the Law of Treaties, requiring that treaties be performed in "good faith."

These general points are worth noting because Pakistan has yet to enact a comprehensive statute protecting children's rights along the lines of Children Act, 1989, in England, or South Africa's Children Act, 2005. The ratification of CRC by Pakistan has had some impact on legislative framework. One example is the Juvenile Justice System Ordinance 2000, and the successor legislation, the Juvenile Justice System Act, 2018. In line with CRC, the law defines the child as a person below the age of 18, establishes separate juvenile courts, and prohibits the imposition of a death sentence on a child.[29]

However, there are several other substantive areas where domestic law lacks a specific provision corresponding to CRC rights. Examples include the right of the child to be heard and the right to play. Domestic jurisprudence is patchy and devoid of reasoning regarding the relationship between international law and domestic law. More often than not, courts fail to consider international and comparative jurisprudence. Occasional references made to international instruments are tokenistic, rarely shedding light on substantive legal questions at hand. Let me illustrate with an example.

In a 2002 public interest litigation before the Lahore High Court, the question was whether the de facto conversion of a dilapidated public park into a hawkers' market and a parking lot constituted a violation of "Fundamental Rights" guaranteed under the 1973 Constitution of Pakistan.[30] Finding the cantonment authorities at fault, Justice Fakhar-un-Nisa Khokhar stated that any administrative authority or elected representative was not empowered by law "to convert any place, which is meant for public purpose" into a commercial enterprise and "in any manner deprive the inhabitants/citizens of that locality from their fundamental rights ensured by the [Constitution] for enjoying recreation [at a children's park] established for the interest of public at large."[31] The judgment fails to point out a specific constitutional right that was being violated. That is understandable since Pakistan's Constitution does not contain a right to recreation. Although the court's order directing authorities to "remove all sorts of material on the children park, fill up the dug ground with soil, restore the boundary of children park forthwith" constituted a welcome outcome from the perspective of children, it also represented a lost opportunity in terms of providing legal clarification.[32] The court could have grounded its decision in the CRC principle of the best interests of the child as a paramount consideration in all matters concerning children (Article 3.1), and the right to rest, play, and recreation (Article 31.1).

Pakistan's constitutional framework and the legal system are underpinned by multiple normative frameworks, including the legacy of British colonialism, Islam, and modern human rights and welfare principles. When the British arrived in India, there existed an ensemble of customary legal traditions and informal mechanisms. The colonial authorities set out to transform them gradually in light of changing context. However, the move toward a secular mode of governance expediently left aside personal laws of Hindus, Muslims, and other communities to appease patriarchal power.[33] Family law in Pakistan is still structured around that legacy. The Indian Penal Code, 1860, not only codified crimes and punishment, but also formalized a system of repressive legality by recasting political activity and dissent as offenses against the state and public tranquility. The Pakistan Penal Code (PPC), subjected to ruthless Islamization under General Zia ul Haque in the 1980s, retains an indelible colonial imprint. Some positive changes have come about. The Protection of Women (Criminal Laws Amendment) Act, 2006, for instance, separated the offenses of *zina* (extra-marital consensual sex) and rape following years of struggle by feminist groups. The age of criminal responsibility was enhanced after repeated urgings by human rights bodies from 7 years to 10 years in 2016.[34] But repressive provisions, rooted in Victorian morality and sanctioned by local culture, still survive. Section 89, for example, provides a defense to a charge of assault on a child under 12 years of age if it is an "act done in good faith for benefit of a child."[35]

It has been claimed that the 1973 Constitution provides a "comprehensive Bill of Rights."[36] That is hyperbole. The catalog of rights falls short of accommodating many of Pakistan's international obligations. The nondiscrimination provision mentions "sex" as the prohibited ground,[37] but omits other vectors of discrimination such as "race, colour, sex, language, religion, political or other opinion, national, ethnic or social origin, property, disability, birth or other status."[38] Article 14(4) defines torture narrowly to cover only "extraction of evidence," excluding other purposes of torture outlined in the Convention against Torture (CAT), namely, "intimidating, punishing, obtaining information from the individual being subjected to pain or a third-party or for any reason based on discrimination of any kind."[39] The Constitution also lacks an explicit prohibition of cruel, inhuman, or degrading punishment and treatment enshrined in Article 16 of CAT and in various other human rights instruments and domestic constitutions. Globally, courts have used the prohibition to invalidate corporal punishment and censure various forms of abuse directed against children.[40]

The 18th Constitutional Amendment enacted in 2010 restored the supremacy of the Parliament and shifted significant legislative powers to provinces. The amendment introduced Article 25-A, obligating the state to "provide free and compulsory education to all children of the age of 5 to 16 years." Article 11 (3), which prohibits employing children below the age of 14 years in a factory, mine or hazardous work, was left untouched. The discrepancy in the age limit is odd given that the state has committed to providing free and compulsory education to everyone at least until the age of 16. It is one of several examples of the state taking away from one hand what it offers from the other. There is certainly force in the argument that children's education and work are not always mutually incompatible. In taking up work, a child may in fact be exercising her agency.[41] However, that perspective is hard to reconcile with certain forms of work, which, by definition, impinge negatively on the child's health and education.

There is no evidence that the drafters of the 18th Amendment consulted children or looked into children's best interests as a primary consideration. If they had, they would perhaps have inserted into the Constitution some provision comparable to Section 28 of the Constitution of South Africa. That section defines a child as every person under the age of 18,[42] and states that "a child's best interests are of paramount importance in every matter concerning the child."[43] Substantive rights include: the right to identity; to family care or alternative care; basic nutrition, shelter, health care and social services; protection from neglect, abuse and exploitation; right not to be detained except as a measure of last resort; to have a state-appointed legal counsel; and, freedom from involvement in armed conflict. Reading this provision together with CRC, the Constitutional Court of South Africa has, besides other measures, invalidated a law which imposed a blanket ban on foreigners adopting children born in South Africa,[44] and directed courts to consider the best interests of the child before imposing a sentence on a primary care giver.[45]

In its concluding observations on the fifth periodic report submitted by Pakistan, the CRC Committee expressed a concern that following the devolution of power to provinces, the standards and services relating to the protection of children varied considerably and lacked coordination.[46] This criticism is misplaced because it seems to suggest that under the centralized governance system, child protection standards were uniformly high. That is certainly not the case. If anything, devolution has created space for federating units to introduce stronger standards. For example, the government of Sindh, responding to a long-standing demand of human rights bodies—and despite vicious opposition by religious groups—introduced Sindh Child Marriage Restraint Act, 2013. The law prescribed 18 years as the minimum age for marriage for both boys and girls. In doing so, it set a benchmark against which local NGOs and international actors judge other provinces.[47] It is another story that legislative advances are not always matched by resource commitments and enforcement mechanisms. For instance, the District Monitoring Committees mandated to report violations of the Sindh Child Marriage Restraint Act, 2013, exist only on paper.[48]

Deeper conversations about children's status as citizens and social actors and about adult-child relationships are still missing in public discourse. There are inspiring prototypes of children's movements elsewhere that have yet to take root in Pakistan.[49] With the increasingly shrinking space for free expression and association in the country, this seems like a forlorn hope for now. The crackdown against NGOs, which began in 2015 at the behest of security agencies, has intensified since Imran Khan's Pakistan Tehreek-i-Insaf assumed power in 2018, following polls marred by serious allegations of rigging.[50]

THE OTHER SIDE OF SILENCE: TAYYABA CASE IN CONTEXT

Toward the end of December 2016, mainstream and social media were awash with pictures of a girl with a bruised face and a swollen eye. It transpired that

Tayyaba, around 10, was a maid at the residence of a lower court judge, Raja Khurram Ali Khan, in Islamabad. Originally from a village near the industrial city of Faisalabad, Tayyaba's father had "sent" her through an intermediary to Islamabad against a payment of 18,000 rupees. A next-door neighbor had taken the photographs of the injured Tayyaba on her cell phone. The woman had, on another occasion, found Tayyaba locked out, shivering in bitter Islamabad cold. This time around, Tayyaba told the neighbor that she had been beaten up and exposed to a burning stove by Maheen Zafar, the judge's wife for losing a broom.[51]

A day after the publication of Tayyaba's pictures and the ensuing uproar on media, then chief justice of the Supreme Court, Saqib Nisar, took *suo motu* notice[52] and ordered an inquiry on December 28, 2016. Tayyaba was rescued by the police next day from the judge's house although Raja Khurram Ali, through his official assistant, had filed a report claiming that the girl had gone missing.[53]

A first investigation report was lodged following Tayyaba's medical examination and her statement before a magistrate. Following the Supreme Court order, a single judge bench of the Islamabad High Court initiated the trial. Maheen Zafar and Raja Khurram Ali were both charged under the penal code's Section 342 (wrongful confinement) and 328-A (cruelty to a child).[54] Maheen Zafar faced additional charges under Sections 337-A and 337-F (intentionally causing hurt and injury) and Section 506 (criminal intimidation), and her husband under Section 201 for "causing disappearance of evidence." Meanwhile, Tayyab's father, who had not seen her in months and came to know about the incident through TV, approached the court claiming that he had reached a "compromise" with the defendants. He did not want the proceedings to continue. The court refused to accept the compromise.[55]

There is no evidence on record whether Tayyaba had received psychological help or whether the court had appointed *a guardian ad litem* to represent her best interests.[56] Relying on alleged discrepancies in Tayyaba's recounting of the incident before the assistant commissioner and during cross-examination, and the prosecution's reliance on medical and circumstantial evidence, the court acquitted the defendants of the charges of wrongful confinement, intentional causing of hurt, and criminal intimidation.[57] It did, however, find the couple guilty of "willfully neglecting a child" (Section 328-A, "Cruelty to a Child"), reasoning that even if Tayyaba's injuries had been caused accidently (the defense had claimed she had fallen off stairs), they had neglected her in not providing medical treatment. The judge handed down a one-year sentence to both the defendants, the minimum available under Section 328-A.[58]

The couple appealed against the conviction and the sentence. In a connected petition, the state challenged their acquittal on other charges. The

Division Bench of the High Court upheld the conviction under Section 328-A, and enhanced the sentence to the maximum possible imprisonment of three years. The court further convicted Maheen Zafar of intentionally causing hurt, ordering her to pay a *daman* (compensation) of Rupees 500,000 to Tayyaba "for the agony which she had to suffer."[59] That is not the end of the legal story.

On appeal, the Supreme Court modified the judgment of the Division Bench of the High Court. It maintained the conviction under Section 328-A, while setting aside the enhancement of sentence from one year to three years.[60] The decision angered human rights activists and media outlets. A report by the BBC seemed to suggest that the decision by the Supreme Court evinced a lack of sympathy for Tayyaba.[61] In reality, the apex court overturned the sentence because the Division Bench of High Court was not competent to hear an appeal for enhancing a sentence imposed by another bench of the same court.[62] Simultaneously, the Supreme Court ruled that the trial court had made serious errors in failing to appreciate the evidentiary value of the testimony of a child witness who was also a "victim" of a crime. The trial court, it said, had misinterpreted the law on the burden of proof in cases where the defendant has exclusive knowledge of events that happened behind closed doors, "and practically impossible for the prosecution to prove."[63] The court further clarified that given sufficient evidence against the appellants, the state could seek enhancement in sentences by filing a separate appeal with the Supreme Court.

What matters more than the quantum of the sentence awarded to Maheen Zafar and her husband is the narrative constructed around the Tayyaba case. Throughout the proceedings, the courts did not make a single reference to CRC. The Supreme Court missed an opportunity to point out how the domestic law and policy fell short of procedural requirements set out in Article 9 of CRC for protecting the "child from all forms of physical or mental violence." It was only in 2018 that a law was enacted in Islamabad to protect children "from mental and physical violence."[64] The state's failure at the time Tayyaba's case came to light in providing procedures for "prevention and identification, reporting, referral, investigation, treatment and follow-up of instances of child maltreatment and for judicial involvement" was one which the apex court should have highlighted.[65]

Tayyaba was rescued because she had been seen with an injured face. For a child in her position being visible before institutions and agents of the state is not easy. You have to expose your wounds. You have to come out with a bruised body and a swollen face to be recognized as somebody. Before her pictures came into circulation, Tayyaba was, for all practical purposes, a *filius nullius*, a child of nobody.

The interrogation record summarized in the High Court and Supreme Court judgments does not indicate if anyone had sought Tayyaba's consent before dispatching her to Islamabad. Are we to assume that a "parent's rights" over their children extend to the kind of transaction which Tayyaba was subjected to? Feminist writers have shed light on how the conceptualization of women as property of fathers, family, and community perpetuates their marginalization.[66] Scholars have yet to comment on how the same dynamics underpin the oppression of children in Pakistan.

In May 2018, weeks after the Division Bench of the Islamabad High Court had delivered its judgment in Tayyaba's case, the government—then led by Pakistan Muslim League (N)—rushed the Prevention of Trafficking in Persons Act, 2018, through the Parliament.[67] The law repealed the 2002 Prevention and Control of Human Trafficking Ordinance which did not cover instances of internal or domestic trafficking.[68] Although the parliamentary debates do not indicate that Tayyaba's case influenced the passage of the Act, it is significant to note that in the appeal judgment, Islamabad High Court's Justice Ather Minallah had characterized Tayyaba's case as one involving trafficking. He suggested that Tayyaba's employment as a domestic help amounted to trafficking in terms of Article 3(c) of the Protocol to Prevent, Suppress and Punish Trafficking in Persons, Especially Women and Children, supplementing the United Nations Convention against Transnational Organised Crime. The Protocol designates the recruitment, transportation, transfer, harboring or receipt of a child for the purpose of exploitation as trafficking regardless of the child's consent or lack thereof.[69] Curiously, however, the judgment failed to note that Pakistan is not a party to the protocol. It would have been more apt for the court to refer to Pakistan's positive obligation under CRC's Article 36 to take all appropriate national, bilateral, and multilateral measures to prevent the abduction of, the sale of or traffic in children for any purpose or in any form. It would have been equally relevant for the court to highlight Pakistan's duty to suppress the sale of children under the Optional Protocol to CRC on the Sale of Children, Child Prostitution and Child Pornography. The Optional Protocol defines the sale of children as any act or transaction whereby a child is transferred by any person or group of persons to another for remuneration or any other consideration. The 2018 Prevention of Trafficking in Persons Act is indeed a welcome development as it was expressly enacted to protect women and children, and included in the definition of trafficking acts of recruiting, harboring, transporting, providing or obtaining another person for compelled labor or commercial sex. However, the law was way too late in the coming. Its protective ambit did not reach Tayyaba in time despite prior urgings by the CRC Committee that Pakistan needed to criminalize and prevent domestic trafficking.[70]

While taking *suo motu* notice of the Tayyaba case, Chief Justice Saqib Nisar had reportedly remarked that poverty compelled parents to sell their children into bonded labor. That is a rather idle comment coming from the top judge. The law does not recognize a defense of deprivation at a criminal trial. Why should we then suggest even implicitly that poverty could serve as an explanation for the selling of a child?[71] In the Tayyaba case, the prosecution did not press for charges of forced labor, bonded labor, or slavery despite the fact that Tayyaba's father had given her away against an advance payment (*peshgi*), a practice prohibited under law.[72] Having ratified the CRC Optional Protocol on the Sale of Children, Pakistan is also obligated to criminalize "any act or transaction whereby a child is transferred by any person or group of persons to another for remuneration or any other consideration."[73] The prosecution did not raise this argument before the courts in Tayyaba's case.

In August 2020, the government banned child domestic work in Islamabad, an ad hoc measure which is being honored in the breach. Child labor laws in the capital or in the provinces do not list children's work in private households as a form of hazardous work. In light of Tayyaba's case, and other cases which have since been reported,[74] there is an argument that at least live-in domestic work should be categorized as a form of work "which, by its nature or the circumstances in which it is carried out, is likely to harm the health, safety or morals of children."[75] There are forces pitted against this proposition, not least middle-class elites who benefit from cheap and unregulated labor. It is also a misguided assertion sometimes made by privileged Pakistanis or NGOs insulated from children's lives that poverty is the sole determinant of child labor. Children sometimes opt to work for want of meaningful alternatives; for example, where schools are congested and teachers do not show up.[76]

Earlier in 2015, a writ petition filed before the Lahore High Court catalyzed the adoption by the Punjab Assembly of the Domestic Workers' Act, 2019. Disposing of the petition in February 2019, the High Court endorsed the law as a "positive step towards protection of domestic workers."[77] The court passed over in silence several problematic aspects of the legislation. The law was drafted following consultations with experts and NGOs as directed by the court. However, children did not participate at any stage. Further, as one member of the committee set up to advise the labor department told this author, there was a consistent attempt on the part of some "stakeholders" to keep the law toothless as it concerned *chaddar aur chardiwari*, that is, privacy of women and the four walls of her home.[78] The provisions of the Act bear out this skepticism.

The law restricts the prohibition of child domestic work to those under the age of 15. Older children can still be engaged on part-time basis for "light work."[79] That may be a sensible step except that the law does not lay down a viable mechanism to ensure that "light work" does not turn into exploitative drudgery. Labor inspectors, who are woefully low in numbers, can inspect a house only on the direction of a Dispute Resolution Committee.[80] No such committee or an appellate authority has been constituted. All domestic workers are entitled to a letter of employment, a weekly holiday, and maternity benefits. However, the law does not recognize the right of domestic workers to unionization or collective bargaining, which could be a powerful tool for preventing exploitation and safeguarding children's right to work with dignity.

While Tayyaba and other live-in maids are particularly vulnerable to exploitation, that does not mean children escape abuse within the walled gardens of the family. There are loving parents, and there are those who manipulate, spank, and batter their children. Pakistani society has a "regime of truth," which does not brook criticism of the institution of the family and the myth of benign parenthood.[81] Elaborate defense mechanisms are built up to hide toxic forms of child-rearing. Children are socialized into believing that parents must be obeyed. The abuses that children experience for their "own good" result in behavioral problems that become hard to resolve.[82]

There have been no reported convictions of parents under Section 328-A of PPC. The Punjab Destitute and Neglected Children Act, 2004 (note the pejorative terminology!), seeks to protect children in begging, homeless children, those found in brothels, and those in the care of "a parent or guardian who is unfit or *incapacitated* to exercise control over the child" and "a child who is *beyond control*."[83] The law does not clarify what constitutes "control" or "incapacity." A Child Protection Court may pass an order to place a "destitute or neglected" child to an institution or to "a suitable person."[84] There is no mechanism for the review of such "orders."[85] The law does not specify remedies should a child suffer mistreatment in institutional care. The concept of "the best interests of the child" or the "right to be heard" are not mentioned.

Child protection laws in other provinces use slightly different terminology although they too have blind spots. The Khyber Pakhtunkhwa Child Protection and Welfare Act, 2010, enshrines the best interests of the child as a primary consideration in "all actions either by public or private bodies, for [the] protection, survival, development and participation of children."[86] It sets up child protection courts empowered to pass care and custody orders for children at risk. Courts are required to obtain a child's views before passing an order.[87] They must decide cases within four months, embodying the "no-delay principle," considered a crucial component in child protection and custody proceedings. Disappointingly though, the Act borrows from the Punjab legislation, including in the list of "children at risk," a child who has a parent "unfit or incapacitated to exercise control,"[88] and a child who is beyond parental control.[89] The rhetoric of children's rights sits absurdly alongside a tacit commitment to repressive child-rearing practices.

This contradiction emerges starkly in the provisions concerning corporal punishment. For an action to fall within the range of prohibited corporal punishment, it has to involve a "*high degree* of pain or discomfort" administered for "discipline, correction and control, changing behaviour or in the belief of educating or bringing up the child, that either results in or has a high likelihood of resulting in injury, psychological harm, maldevelopment or deprivation."[90] Section 44 reproduces the PPC provision on "cruelty to a child" albeit with a significant cop-out. The prohibition of cruelty and neglect does not extend to parents. A proviso follows providing that "some reasonable punishment," administered in "good faith" by "the person having lawful control or protective care of the child as parents normally would do for the betterment of the child [shall] not be deemed an offence."[91] It is hard, then, to characterize this law as anything but a disingenuous sop to human rights bodies.

CONCLUSION

I began this chapter with a plea for reflexivity on how we conceptualize children's rights. Recognizing children as persons in their own right has profound practical and policy implications. It prompts us to see children's lives more clearly, directing attention to their survival and protection interests as well as their agency and voice. CRC goes some distance toward capturing such a holistic viewpoint. However, being a product of negotiation and cultural contestation, it carries some tensions and paradoxes. The child is placed in a power-matrix within which parents and adults have a dominant role. Yet, even as we remain alert to the unfinished business of standards-setting, CRC could be an important normative resource in nudging society and the state toward a more child-centric paradigm.

From the standpoint of children, the ratification of CRC has brought some substantive and symbolic gains. Pakistan's international legal commitments provide a reference point for critiquing policy and practice, and, potentially, grounds for litigation. But, as we have seen, the country has yet to catch up with other jurisdictions such as South Africa where CRC has played a much more central role in reshaping law and securing rights through courts. The law—as stated on paper and as interpreted by courts—is more than a means of resolving disputes and dispensing justice. As Carol Smart has pointed out, writing from a feminist perspective, the law is also "an instrument of truth," a site for constructing and legitimizing extant norms and power relations.[92]

What we have seen with reference to the Tayyaba case—and other developments in the domestic law on child protection—is that the law offers only a partial view of children's realities. And, it is marked by unexplained fissures and contradictions. This becomes evident when the state fails to prevent internal trafficking and selling of children as domestic help, and when prosecutors and judges edit out the role of parents and families in perpetuating exploitative practices. When the state intervenes to regulate potentially hazardous forms of child labor, it offers too little too late. As is the case with the 2019 Punjab law on domestic work, children are denied participation or the right to unionize.

Edmund Burke once said that the law "must coerce like a man but cajole like a woman, chastise like a father but indulge us like a mother."[93] This necessarily self-divided character is revealed where the law prescribes custodial sentences for petty theft but only paltry fines for the exploitation of child labor. Contradictions also animate the legal discourse where it simultaneously condemns corporal punishment and offers a cop-out to parents and legal guardians in the form of the defense of reasonable chastisement.

Children's rights are intertwined with technologies of power and domination. Power is posited here in the Foucauldian sense as a diffuse and heterogenous phenomenon. It concerns the control of resources as well the ability to name and describe realities. Children in Pakistan continue to be objects of power and authority at multiple sites from the family and school to workplace to courts and welfare institutions. Things are done to children rather than with them. Children are thought to owe respect to adults and not the other way around.

As the experiences of other historically oppressed groups suggest, power never concedes much without a struggle. Children's rights, it is sometimes naively asserted, are above politics. In truth, one reason why legally guaranteed rights atrophy into false promises is that they are not adequately politicized. Children's rights must be put fairly and squarely on the centerstage of politics. They must be articulated in terms of demands for children's participation in all matters, big or small, and for redistribution of resources necessary for their protection from violence and exploitation.

NOTES

1. The author would like to acknowledge research support provided by Zahra Bajwa, research assistant at Shaikh Ahmad Hassan School of Law, Lahore University of Management Sciences.
2. Onora O'Neil, 'Children's Rights and Children's Lives' (1998) 98 *Ethics* (April) 445–463. Cf. Michael D.A. Freeman, 'Taking Children's Rights More Seriously', in Philip Alston, Stephen Parker and John Seymour (eds) *Children, Rights and the Law* (Clarendon 1992) 52–71.
3. David Nasaw, *Children of the City: At Work and at Play* (OUP 1985).
4. David Archard, *Children, Rights and Childhood* (Routledge 1993) 80–82
5. Philip Aries, *Centuries of Childhood: A Social History of Family Life* (Alferd A. Knopf 1962).

6. Alison James, 'From the Children's Point of View: Issues in the Social Construction of Childhood', in Catherine Panter-Brick (ed) *Biosocial Perspectives on Children* (Cambridge University Press 1998) 45–65.

7. Tom D. Campbell, 'The Rights of the Minor: as Person, as Child, as Juvenile, as Future Adult', in Alston, Parker and Seymour (n 2) 1–23.

8. Bhikkhu Parekh, 'Finding a Proper Place for Human Rights', in Kate E. Tunstall (ed.) *Displacement, Asylum, Migration: The Oxford Amnesty Lectures 2004* (OUP 2006) 17–43, 19.

9. See Avner Gil'adi, *Children of Islam: Concepts of Childhood in Medieval Muslim Society* (Macmillan 1992) 42–59.

10. See, for example, Government of Pakistan, *National Education Policy—2017-2025* (GoP 2017) 68, 107.

11. In re Gault, 387 U.S. 1 (1967).

12. *DeShaney v. Winnebago County*, 489 U.S. 189 (1989).

13. *Wisconsin v. Jonas Yoder*, 406 U.S. 205 (1972).

14. Ibid at p. 242 (William Douglas J. Dissenting in part).

15. *Parens patriae* (literally father of the nation) is the doctrine that the state has the power to act in protection of the weak and powerless, namely minors and persons with mental disorders. On the historical evolution and the application of the doctrine in child custody law, see Sarah Abramowicz, 'Note: English Child Custody Law, 1660-1839: The Origins of Judicial Intervention in Parental Custody' (1999) 99 *Columbia Law Review* 1344.

16. See Adnan Sattar, *Criminal Punishment and Human Rights: Convenient Morality* (Routledge 2019) 150–168.

17. G.A. res. 1386 (XIV), 14 U.N. GAOR Supp. (No. 16) at 19, U.N. Doc. A/4354. This document itself had an antecedent in the 1924 Geneva Declaration of the Rights of the Child, adopted by the League of Nations.

18. General Comment No. 5, 'General measures of implementation of the Convention on the Rights of the Child', UN Doc CRC/GC/2003/5, para 12.

19. Emphasis added. Michael Freeman, *A Commentary on the United Nations Convention on the Rights of the Child, Article 3* (Brill 2007) 60.

20. Art 14 (2).

21. See Report of the Working Group to the Commission on Human Rights, UN Doc. E/CN.4/1983/62, paras 52–57.

22. UN Doc. E/CN.4/1986/39, annex IV.

23. UN Doc. E/CN.4/1987/WG.1/WP.35.

24. See Sonia Harris-Short, 'Listening to the Other - The Convention on the Rights of the Child', (2001) 2 *Melbourne Journal of International Law* 304.

25. Ashleigh Barnes, The Trafficking of Children: A Counter-Narrative to the CRC's Construction of Care (2013) 9 (2) *Socio-Legal Review* 51.

26. See Sections 2, 3 and 4 of the Human Rights Act, 1998.

27. [2006] UKHL 35, at para 78.

28. CRC Committee, General Comment No. 5, 'General Measures of Implementation on the Rights of the Child', UN Doc. CRC/GC/2003/5.

29. Concerns have been expressed though about the absence of age determination protocols, leading to some children being tried and sentenced as adults. See, CRC Committee, 'Concluding Observations to the Fifth Periodic Report Submitted by Pakistan', UN Doc CRC/C/PAK/CO/5, 11 July 2016, para 25.

30. *Manzoor Bhatti v Executive Officer, Cantonment Board Multan and another* PLD 2002 Lahore 412.

31. Ibid para 5.

32. Ibid para 7-A.

33. See *Governing Islam: Law, Empire, and Secularism in Modern South Asia* (Cambridge University Press 2018).

34. Pakistan Penal Code, 1860, sections 82 and 83 as amended by Act 10 of 2016.

35. The defense does not extend to a charge of murder or attempted murder or causing of grievous hurt.

36. Mehreen Kasuri Raza, 'Reviewing the Law of Public Interest Litigation', in Werner Menski (ed) *Public Interest Litigation in Pakistan* (Pakistan Law House 2000) 64–105, 72.

37. Constitution (Eighteenth Amendment) Act, 2010 did omit the word 'only'. The provision previously read: 'There shall be no discrimination on the basis of sex alone'.

38. Article 2(1), CRC.

39. Art 1 (1), Convention against Torture and Other Cruel, Inhuman or Degrading Treatment or Punishment.

40. See, for example, *A v United Kingdom* (1999) 27 EHRR 611 [The European Court of Human Rights finding that the UK had violated the prohibition of ill-treatment by permitting a defense of reasonable chastisement to a stepfather accused of beating up the applicant]; *Christian Education South Africa v Minister of Education* (CCT4/00) [2000] ZACC 11; 2000 (4) SA 757 [Upholding a ban on corporal punishment in schools as a permissible limitation on parents' freedom of religion and a requirement under the prohibition of ill-treatment]

41. See, for example, Ali Khan, *Representing Children: Power, Policy and the Discourse on Child Labour in the Football Manufacturing Industry of Pakistan* (OUP 2007) 13, 178–181; Olga Nieuwenhuys, 'From Child Labour to Working Children's Movements' in Jens Qvodrtrup et al (eds) *The Palgrave Handbook of Childhood Studies* (Palgrave 2009) 289–300.

42. Section 28(3).

43. Section 28(2).

44. *Minister of Welfare and Population Development v Fitzpatrick and Others* 2000 (3) SA 422 (CC).

45. *S v M (Centre for Child Law as Amicus Curiae)* [2007] ZACC 18; 2008 (3) SA 232 (CC).

46. CRC Committee (n 29) para 10.

47. See recommendations put forward to Pakistan during the third cycle of the UPR. Human Rights Council, 'Report of the Working Group on the Universal Periodic Review—Pakistan', UN Doc. A/HRC/37/13, 29 December 2017. Recommendation

152.276 (Denmark); 152.277 (Namibia); 152.278 (Belgium). See also CEDAW Committee, 'Concluding observations on the fifth periodic report of Pakistan', CEDAW/C/PAK/CO/5, 10 March 2020, paras 49–50.

48. Oxfam, 'Creating Spaces to take Action on Violence against Women and Girls: Mid-Term Review Report - Pakistan', 20 June 2019, p. 25.

49. Examples include Bhima Sangha in India, African Movement of Working Children and Youth in West Africa, and MANTHOC in Peru. See Nieuwenhuys (n 40), and Karl Hanson and Arne Vandaele, 'Working Children and International Labour Law: A Critical Analysis', (2003) 11 *International Journal of Children's Rights* 73.

50. Shandana Khan Mohmand, 'Pakistan's Closing Civic Space' (April 2020) *Current History* 146.

51. These details are drawn from court records as summed by the Islamabad High Court in a judgment delivered on 4 June 2018, dismissing an appeal by Khan and his wife against their conviction and enhancing the sentence awarded by a single-judge bench of the same court. *Raja Khurram Ali Khan and Another v. Tayyaba Bibi and Another* 2019 YLR 98, paras 2-5. Same details with variations in the chronology of events can be found in the Supreme Court appeal decision. *Raja Khurram Ali Khan v Tayyaba Bibi (Minor)* PLD Supreme Court 146, paras 5–9.

52. The Supreme Court of Pakistan has derived *suo motu* (on its own motion) powers from Article 184(3) of the Constitution, which authorizes the court to make a wide range of orders 'if it considers that a question of public importance with reference to the enforcement of any of the Fundamental Rights' is involved. However, the court took *suo motu* actions sparingly until the tenure of Justice Iftekhar Chaudry (2005–2013). During Chaudry era, and subsequently, under Chief Justice Saqib Nisar (2016–2019), *suo motu* powers became the anchor of an increasingly interventionist court.

53. *Raja Khurram Ali Khan v Tayyaba Bibi (Minor)* PLD Supreme Court 146, para 5.

54. Section 328-A was added to PPC via Act 10 of 2016, section 5.

55. See Section 345, Code of Criminal Procedure, 1898.

56. A *guardian ad litem* is a person appointed by a court for the conduct of legal proceedings on behalf of a minor.

57. *The State v Maheen Zafar and Another* 2018 IHC 33 [PLJ 2018 Cr.C. 664) at paras 17–18.

58. Ibid para 21.

59. *Raja Khurram Ali Khan and Another v. Tayyaba Bibi and Another* 2019 YLR 98, para 35.

60. *Raja Khurram Ali Khan v Tayyaba Bibi (Minor)* PLD Supreme Court 146.

61. BBC, 'Tayyaba Abuse Case: Pakistan Judge and Wife's Sentences Cut', 10 January 2020. Available: https://www.bbc.com/news/world-asia-51060569

62. See Section 411-A (2), Criminal Procedure Code, 1898.

63. *Raja Khurram Ali Khan v Tayyaba Bibi (Minor)* PLD Supreme Court 146, paras 43-54.

64. Islamabad Capital Territory Child Protection Act, 2018.

65. CRC Article 9(2).

66. See, for example, Sadia Toor, 'The Political Economy of Moral Regulation in Pakistan: Religion, Gender and Class in a Postcolonial Society', in Leela Fernandes (ed) *Routledge Handbook of Gender in South Asia* (Routledge 2014) 129–142.

67. See National Assembly of Pakistan, 'Assembly Debates - Friday, the 18th May, 2018', pp. 173–178; The Senate of Pakistan, Official Debates - Tuesday, May 15, 2018 (277th Session) Volume VI, No. 12 (Nos. 01–12) pp. 18–36.

68. The Ordinance under Section 2, sub-section h, defined trafficking restrictively as 'obtaining, securing, selling, purchasing, recruiting, detaining, harbouring or receiving a person, notwithstanding his implicit or explicit consent, by the use of coercion, kidnapping, abduction, or by giving or receiving any payment or benefit, or sharing or receiving a share for such *person's subsequent transportation out of or into Pakistan'*. Emphasis added.

69. *Raja Khurram Ali Khan and Another v. Tayyaba Bibi and Another* 2019 YLR 98, at para 12.

70. See Committee on the Rights of the Child, Concluding Observations to Pakistan's Combined Third and Fourth Reports', 15 October 2009, UN Doc CRC/C/PAK/CO/3-4, paras 95-96; 'Concluding Observations on the Fifth Periodic Report of Pakistan', 11 July 2016, UN Doc CRC/C/PAK/CO/5, paras 75–76.

71. On this point see Ashleigh Barnes's commentary on a deeply problematic judgment by the Supreme Court of India in *Vishal Jeet v. Union of India* 1990 SCR (2) 861. Barnes (n 25) 92–99.

72. See Bonded labour System (Abolition) Act 1992, enacted following a Supreme Court decision in *Darshan Masih v State* PLD 1990 SC 513. Provinces have since enacted laws which mostly follow the terms of the 1992 Act prohibiting *peshgi.* Bonded labor is left undefined. Guidance could have been drawn from the Supplementary Convention on the Abolition of Slavery, 1956. It does not outlaw all forms of work against an advance. Rather, it prohibits services against a loan when the value of those services as 'reasonably assessed is not applied towards the liquidation of the debt'.

73. Article 2(2).

74. See, The News, 'Editorial: Justice for Zohra', 4 June 2020.

75. Article 3(d), ILO's Worst Forms of Child Labour Convention, 1999 (No. 182). Pakistan ratified the Convention in 2001. In failing to regulate child domestic work, Pakistan also violates Article 32 (1) of CRC, which prohibits hazardous forms of child labour.

76. Khan (n 41) 181–195.

77. *Subay Khan v Secretary of Labour, Government of the Punjab* PLD 2019 Lahore 119 at para 32.

78. Author's conversation with Dr. Muhammad Azeem, Assistant Professor, LUMS.

79. Section 3.

80. As of 2017, Punjab had only 130 labor inspectors. See Bureau of International Labour 'Findings on the Worst Forms of Child Labour—2017', p. 5. CRC Committee has also identified lack of inspection as a reason for exploitation of child domestic workers in Pakistan. See CRC Committee (n 28) para 71.

81. See Michael Foucault, *Power/Knowledge* (Harvester 1980) 131.

82. Alice Miller, *Breaking Down the Walls of Silence: The Liberating Experience of Facing Painful Truth* (Basic Books 2009).

83. Section 3(k). Emphasis added.

84. Section 28.

85. Contrast this with England's Children Act, 1989. Section 26 'Review of cases and inquiries into representations', which also requires that a local authority while reviewing a case will seek the views of the child concerned.

86. Section 2(b).

87. Section 16(2).

88. Section 2(iv).

89. Section 2(vii).

90. Section 2(m). Emphasis added.

91. Section 44.

92. Carol Smart, 'Law's body, the Sexed Body, and Feminist Discourse', 17 (1990) 11 *Journal of Law and Sociology* 194.

93. Cited in Terry Eagleton, *Holy Terror* (OUP 2005) 49.

Part III

Chapter 9

Pakistan's Death Penalty Law[1]

Satvinder S. Juss

INTRODUCTION

Some years ago, Andrew Novak undertook a comprehensive worldwide study of state executions and came to the conclusion that "[t]he death penalty is in rapid and irreversible retreat everywhere in the English-speaking world, even in the most intransigent holdouts like Texas and Singapore." So robust were his findings that he was even able to say that it "has declined even faster than this, to the point of extinction in the Commonwealth." In fact, Novak could even declare how "[a]cross the Commonwealth, the mandatory death penalty is in decline in favour of a capital sentencing regime that delegates sentencing discretion to a trial judge."[2] Increasingly, worldwide, there was recognition by countries that "the death penalty, as the ultimate expression of state power, must be treated with great care."[3] A subsequent report from Amnesty International, however, dashed all hopes of a new dawn when it referred to "a killing spree" of state executions taking place across the world.[4] If there has been a reemergence of the death penalty now, it is because it is seen as the ultimate answer to the rising scourge of terrorism and insurgency.[5] It is, however, Pakistan which arguably breaks the record in the number of its inmates awaiting execution. One in four people on death row worldwide is Pakistani.[6] One in eight people executed by the state worldwide is Pakistani.[7]

A person in Pakistan, convicted of a capital offense, will on average spend eleven years on death row before dying.[8] Conditions in Pakistan's jails are appalling, with overcrowding and lack of medical care being rife throughout the country.[9] Amnesty International reports, however, a drop of 77 percent in executions from sixty in 2017 to at least fourteen in 2018.[10] And yet, Pakistan remains at the top of the death penalty league among states internationally, and sits alongside countries like China, Iran, Saudi Arabia, and Vietnam.[11]

This may come as a surprise. At the time of Pakistan's independence in 1947, only two crimes carried the death penalty, and these were the obvious ones of murder and treason.[12] How has the number grown so exponentially since then? It grew dramatically under the rule of General Muhammad Zia-ul-Haq in the 1970s and 1980s.[13] In 2008, Pakistan imposed an informal moratorium on the death penalty, halting all executions nationwide. This lasted until 2014. But then there was the attack by the Taliban in that year at the Army Public School in Peshawar in which 149 people, including 132 school children, were killed. This prompted the government to bring back this severest of all punishments.[14]

Initially, the death penalty was reserved exclusively for terrorist offenses under the National Action Plan.[15] Terrorism was after all what had led to the suspension of the moratorium. However, three months later, other offenses were included as well, the most controversial being that for the offense of blasphemy.[16] People started once again being sent to the gallows by the government, their families incurring massive costs and social stigma, in the process.[17] Against this background, this analysis into Pakistan's death penalty will firstly focus on its use of capital punishment in the context of international norms and practices around the world. Second, it will analyze the role of religion and culture in this debate. Third, it will consider the two prominent crimes which carry the death penalty, namely, terrorism and blasphemy. Finally, there will be an inquiry into what best explains Pakistan's use and justification of capital punishment.

INTERNATIONAL NORMS AND PRACTICES

It is as well to begin by remembering that Pakistan is not oblivious to the observance of human rights norms under international law. Indeed, it has signed up to such obligations. When the Universal Declaration of Human Rights, which is the right to "life, liberty and security of person" in Article 3, was put to vote at the newly created General Assembly on December 10, 1948, it was Pakistan that, along with forty-seven other countries, had voted in favor.[18] Article 3 therein is not aimed solely at abolishing the death penalty. It fits into wider philosophical, sociological, and legal considerations that were present after World War II when the document was written. Hernán Santa Cruz, a Chilean lawyer who worked on drafting the Universal Declaration of Human Rights, pointed out that a driving force behind Article 3 and other such provision was the belief that "the interests of the individual [came] before those of the state."[19] The Chinese Third Committee representative Peng-Chun Chang also confirmed at the time that it constituted an implementation of the first part of the French revolutionary tripartite motto of

"*Liberté, égalité, fraternité*."[20] This is to say nothing of the fact that, practically speaking, one cannot enjoy the rights set forth in the subsequent articles if one is not alive. And yet, it remains ironic that Article 3 has had very little effect on the legal status of capital punishment globally.

Most countries have prescribed death as a punishment at some time or other in their history, so at an international level the abolition of the death penalty could not occur on the basis of a "one-size-fits-all method."[21] Nothing evidences this more than the fact that although around the time of World War II, 24 percent of the countries between 1940 and 1949 had abolished the death penalty, this had dipped slightly to 23.6 percent of countries in the following decade, but then went down even more in the 1960s to only 19.5 percent of countries which had abolished death as a punishment.[22] What had happened was that the rapid decolonization that followed World War II, which created vastly more independent states by the 1960s, saw many of them keep the death penalty on their statute books as an inherited colonial rule. Moreover, abolition goes hand in hand with democratization. Just because countries have become liberated does not mean that they would readily relinquish a tool of colonial oppression. For instance, Romania only abolished capital punishment in 1990 as a direct result of the Revolution of December 1989 which brought an end to the communist dictatorship.[23] Not all states, however, managed to smoothly transition from being under colonial rule to fully functioning democracies. This is what accounts for the delay in abolition. South Africa, despite gaining independence from the British Empire in 1961, only got rid of the death penalty and Apartheid simultaneously many decades later in the 1990s.

Added to this was the complication that those tasked with drafting the follow-up human rights successor documents to the Universal Declaration, namely the two International Covenants of the 1960s, the principal one of which was the International Covenant on Civil and Political Rights 1966[24] (ICCPR), eventually conceded that despite the abolitionist tendencies of some countries, an outright call for removing the death penalty from all judicial systems worldwide could potentially weaken the document if states dropped their support for it. The result was that whereas Article 6 of the ICCPR guarantees the right to life, it also guarantees under Article 6.2, the right of a state that has not yet abolished the death penalty to impose such a punishment. This is not to ignore the notable *caveat* in Article 6.2, namely that the "sentence of death may be imposed only for the most serious crimes." The difficulty with this, however, is that the ICCPR provides no guidance for what constitutes a "most serious crime."[25] Pakistan signed the ICCPR in April 2008, and it entered into force in 2010. The government has not become a signatory to the Second Optional Protocol to the International Covenant on Civil and Political Rights 1989, aiming at the abolition of the death penalty.[26] This would, as its name suggests, have committed Pakistan to the abolition of the death penalty for all ordinary crimes, with there being only exceptions under Article 2.1 for "a most serious crime of a military nature committed during wartime," thus severely limiting its use, as a prelude to abolition.

Several decades later, the Commission on Human Rights passed a resolution offering up some direction away from nonviolent crimes,[27] and notwithstanding the absence of any guidance within the International Covenant on Civil and Political Rights, most countries have now indeed concluded that "the most serious [of] crimes" constitutes murder, as well as some treason and/or terrorism offenses. The United States, for instance, used to sentence people to death for rape, partly as a state-sponsored continuation of the lynchings of black men accused of attacks on white women in the Southern States.[28] But following the Supreme Court case of *Coker v. Georgia*[29] in 1977, the punishment was removed nationwide for the rape of an adult, and for the rape of a minor in 2008 thanks to the case of *Kennedy v. Louisiana*.[30] While these decisions did not expressly mention the International Covenant on Civil and Political Rights—and *Coker v. Georgia* makes only a brief footnote reference to the fact that "out of 60 major nations in the world surveyed in 1965, only three retained the death penalty for rape where death did not ensue"[31]—there is no doubt that national judiciaries have had to grapple with questions of proportionality, especially when imposing an irreversible punishment. In *Kennedy v. Louisiana*, it was a question of whether execution for child rape could be considered "cruel and unusual punishment" under the 8th Amendment to the Constitution,[32] not wholly dissimilar to the task of asking whether a given crime is "the most serious," as both are a careful exercise in proportionality.

RELIGION AND CULTURE

So how does Pakistan approach these issues of proportionality when considering the death penalty? The question is important not least in the light of its commitments under Article 6.2 of the International Covenant on Civil and Political Rights? Astonishingly, Pakistan has no less than twenty-seven offenses which carry the death penalty. These include not just murder but such diverse crimes as kidnapping, drug trafficking, sabotage of the railway system, rape, sexual intercourse outside of marriage, and even something called an assault on the modesty of women.[33] Such a wide range of offenses clearly call into question the genuine application of "a most serious crime" standard to the application of the death penalty. Many seeking to understand Pakistan's use of the death penalty may be quick to look to the obvious fact that over 96 percent of the country's population is Muslim.[34] Article 2 of the Constitution prescribes Islam as the state religion, and this has then transcribed itself into the rest of the legal system. Although, the country has an adversarial Common Law-based system inherited from the one in place under the British Raj before independence, there are many elements of sharia law (which is the primary source of Islamic Law based on the Quran as the "words of God") and the *Sunnah* (words of the Prophet)) throughout the legal system.[35] Yet, it need not have been so. If Pakistan's legal system has the imprimatur of Islam today, this is primarily as a result of the rule of General Muhammad Zia-ul-Haq, who pushed for an "Islamification" of Pakistan's judiciary, and even amended the Constitution of Pakistan to include the establishment of the Federal Shariat Court in 1980.[36] This court, based in Islamabad, is tasked with ensuring that any law passed is in line with *sharia law*.

While the Quran does grant a right to life, there is an exception if death is ordered by a court of law, whereby the religion of Islam makes clear: *"Do not kill a Soul which Allah has made sacred except through the due process of law"* (6:151).[37] This is taken up by Article 9 of the Pakistani Constitution, which states that "No person shall be deprived of life or liberty save in accordance with law." Two of the six crimes that fall under *Hadd* or *Hudud*, in other words, crimes that pose a threat to Islam, carry a non-discretional death sentence, namely illicit sexual relations and highway robbery.[38] Intentional crimes to the person fall under *Quisas*, governed by the more discretionary principle of "an eye for an eye, a tooth for a tooth," thus justifying the taking away of not just the life of murderers but in appropriate cases, quite literally, the amputation of corresponding parts of body as punishment. Traditionally, executions are to be public so as to enhance deterrence and are to be done by stoning or by a sword.[39] Be that as it may it is as well to bear in mind how the initial basis for the state taking away life in Islamic law is in the form of an injunction against its use. What is said in 6:151 is that life is "sacred," as given by "Allah" and that for that reason mankind is expressly enjoined "Do not kill a Soul"—but that where that is to be done it must be very much as an exception and only after "due process of law." This being so, it is not beyond the realms of possibility for Islam to be a basis for eventual abolition. After all, if sharia law, as divine law, is part of Muslim morality, then with changing values (e.g., abolition of slavery or continual removal of cruel, inhuman and degrading punishments), Islamic law can be brought in conformity with human rights laws. Even so the argument has been made that, on the basis of "cultural relativism," non-Western countries may, due to their traditional and cultural differences with the West,[40] render themselves immune from Western standards because of the equal validity of all cultures and practices, so that the widespread use of the death penalty in Islamic countries may be justified. If that is so then Pakistan should be allowed a wider margin of appreciation when determining the "the most serious [of] crimes" due to the role of Islam's teachings in its legal system. The underlying assumption here is that human rights are a Western construct which may not be compatible with the socio-political fabric of all nations.

This argument may be rejected at once. First, the drafting of the Universal Declaration of Human Rights was done by the Drafting Committee whose members included those of Chinese, Lebanese, and Indian nationality, to name but a few. Second, cultural relativists are, whether intentionally or not, presenting non-Western countries as a monolith, but there is more to the picture than merely "Western" and "non-Western" approaches to human rights. Countries outside of Europe and North America do not stand in a united block,[41] much like countries within those two regions do not all share the same views. One need look no further than the fact that the United States, while by all accounts the "leader" of the Western world, continues to routinely execute prisoners, yet all European Union countries abolished the practice decades ago. Third, even within smaller geopolitical blocks, there is a lack of agreement on the use of the death penalty, and to pretend otherwise is misguided at best and dangerous at worse. For instance, Mauritania has not executed anybody since 1987,[42] while Saudi Arabia has executed at least 122 prisoners within the first six months of 2019 right up to July 10, 2019.[43] As both these countries are Islamic countries, and both no doubt have *Hadd* or *Hudud* and *Quisa* crimes occurring within their borders, surely if cultural relativism was valid factor in this situation, we would have expected to see executions at a similar rate, proportional to their respective populations. Fourth, the theory of cultural relativism, which incorrectly identifies all Islamic countries as having a monolithic stance on such fundamental issues as that of the death penalty, is also one which incorrectly implies a consensus within individual countries.

Thus, while a majority of Pakistani citizens may support the death penalty, there are still individuals and groups that are actively working within the country to stop executions, such as *Justice Project Pakistan*, whose research and activism is referenced throughout this chapter. To present Pakistan itself as a homogenous block on this issue is a worrying exercise in the denial of agency of all those working tirelessly to stop executions in the country—a phenomenon described by James Wyman as "cultural stereotyping."[44] This lack of consensus within Pakistan is long-standing. It can be located historically to its founding moment. In 1959, Pakistan supported a move by the General Assembly to invite the Economic and Social Council to conduct a study on the use of capital punishment worldwide,[45] a move that would be unlikely to take place today, six decades later. Yet, this goes to show that a country's policy stance can easily evolve over time, so that any statement about its position must keep this in mind. For all these reasons, while it is no doubt important to be aware of how religion and culture shape any country's approach to the death penalty, particularly in a country like Pakistan, it is essential that we do not fall into a "cultural stereotyping." Capital punishment is complex, and while officials and others may use religion as a front, the real reasons behind a country's choice to execute its citizens almost always go beyond just religious or cultural ones, as we will now see.

TWO PROMINENT DEATH PENALTY CRIMES

We will now consider two crimes which attract the highest number of death penalty sentences in Pakistan, namely, terrorism and blasphemy.

Terrorism

The key piece of terrorism-related legislation in Pakistan is the Anti-Terrorism Act. It came into force in 1997 after being passed by the National Assembly and Senate, under the government of Nawaz Sharif.[46] It had propitious timing, following as it did, an attack in Lahore in January of that same year. Mehram Ali, member of the Shia extremist group Sipah-e-Muhammad Pakistan (later labeled a terrorist organization), set off a bomb near to a courthouse. It killed twenty-three people, including two Sunni leaders of Sipah-e-Sahaba Pakistan, an anti-Shia organization, who were on trial at the time, as well as a journalist and police officers. Ali was tried and sentenced to death by the newly created Anti-Terrorism Court, and appealed to the Anti-Terror Appellate Tribunal. His appeal eventually made its way to the Supreme Court of Pakistan on issues of constitutional compatibility with the new legislation, but judges upheld the conviction and Mehram Ali was executed not too long afterward on August 11, 1998.[47] What is interesting, however, is that despite upholding the sentence of death, the judges of the Supreme Court found that sections of the Anti-Terrorism Act 1997 flew in the face of Pakistan's Constitution, in that the newly created courts were not subject to the same rules as the other courts in the nation's judicial system. This concerned such fundamental questions of due process as the tenure of judges and the rules of evidence. As a direct result of the ruling in *Mehram Ali v. Federation of Pakistan*, the government issued the Anti-Terrorism (Amendment) Ordinance in October 1998, which disbanded the Anti-Terror Appellate Tribunals, with the effect that all appeals hereafter would be handled by the existing regular high courts.[48]

The Anti-Terrorism Act 1997 also had a key role, aside from establishing the new courts, of defining terrorism, which it did in Section 6(1) as either where:

> The use or threat is designed to coerce and intimidate or overawe the Government or the public or a section of the public or community or sect or create a sense of fear or insecurity in society.
>
> or
>
> The use or threat is made for the purpose of advancing a religious, sectarian or ethnic cause, or intimidating and terrorizing the public, social sectors, media persons, business community or attacking the civilians, including damaging property by ransacking, looting, arson or by any other means, government officials, installations, security forces or law enforcement agencies, provided that nothing herein contained shall apply to a democratic and religious rally or a peaceful demonstration in accordance with law.

In other words, offenses must have an element of inciting fear in some degree of the public. Section 6(2) then listed eighteen actions which, if they fell within the remits of Section 6(1), could be considered terrorism, but a list to which the government could add at any point without parliamentary consultation.[49] The list included an act that "involves grievous damage to property," or one which "incites hatred and contempt on religious, sectarian or ethnic basis" or one which "involves extortion of money." Once again, it would appear that these did not fall under the concept of "the most serious crimes" as mandated by Section 6.2 of the International Covenant on Civil and Political Rights. Less controversially, but no less importantly, Section 7 of the Anti-Terrorism Act 1997 outlined three acts, namely actions causing death of another, kidnapping for ransom or hostage-taking and hijacking, which were punishable by death or life imprisonment.

Not surprisingly, the Anti-Terrorism Act 1997 has been widely criticized by rights groups for its egregious vagueness. All murders to a greater or lesser degree spur "a sense of fear or insecurity in society," and this is so even if the murders are carried out for reasons other than terrorism, such as personal revenge. Although the UN General Assembly has yet to arrive at a single definition[50] itself, this vagueness allows for many cases that may not meet an objective threshold for terrorism which could be tried as such. And yet, in 2014, it was estimated that there were more than 17,000 cases pending under the Anti-Terrorism Act,[51] and report the same year by Justice Project Pakistan and Reprieve found that anywhere between 10 percent and 40 percent of the people on death row were there having been convicted of terrorist offenses, but with huge variations from region to region.[52] As if this was not enough, of the 546 cases heard in the five-year period up to 2019, the Supreme Court of Pakistan acquitted the death penalty of 467 people.[53] That is a staggering clemency rate of over 80 percent!

Nevertheless, despite the Supreme Court's frequent interventions, many cases fall through the judicial safety-net unchecked, and Pakistan ends up regularly executing juveniles[54] and those with mental illness. This is despite the fact that Chapter 34 of the Pakistani Code of Criminal Procedure makes clear that if "the accused is of unsound mind and consequently incapable of making his defense," then special provisions are to be made for them in their trial. This is consistent with international law under which states are enjoined not execute those suffering from mental disorders. The Commission on Human Rights has even issued a resolution underscoring this in 2003.[55] However, it is now abundantly clear that misdiagnosis and a lack of awareness of mental illness is all too common in Pakistani courts, "mak[ing] it difficult for mentally ill defendants to get a fair trial."[56] Even though, as the 2003 resolution[57] affirms, that the execution of anybody under the age of 18 is unlawful, and as such provided for in Pakistan's national legislation, nevertheless, in a country where just one out of every three births is officially registered,[58] determining a person's age can be quite challenging. Perhaps one of the most shocking illustrations is the case of *Ghulam Qadir* and *Ghulam Sarwa*, two brothers who were acquitted by the Supreme Court in 2016 for a murder that took place in 2002. However, when officials were sent to deliver the good news, they discovered that the pair had in fact been hanged a year earlier, and no one had let their families or lawyers know.[59]

One other distressing case that also escaped the judicial safety-net is that of Shafqat Hussain. In 2004, Hussain was working as a watchman in a Karachi apartment block. When a seven-year-old boy who lived in the apartment went missing, Hussain was charged with his kidnapping and murder under the Anti-Terrorism Act of 1997. Quite what this had to do with "terrorism" is unclear. Nevertheless, he was sentenced to death by an Anti-Terrorism Court. His family stated that he was only 14 at the time of the crime. This would have meant that he was ineligible for the death penalty. There were also questions surrounding his confession to the crime. His lawyers maintained that he was tortured by police.[60] Eventually, the authorities were led to the body of the victim. Despite pressure from various international rights groups such as Amnesty International and Reprieve, as well as from the United Nations,[61] Hussain was hanged after multiple postponements in August 2015—which was just eight months after the Peshawar school massacre. That fact is not without significance. After all, it was the terrorism-related death charges which were the first to be green-lighted when the moratorium on the death penalty was lifted in 2014 under the National Action Plan.[62]

This followed the dreadful Peshawar school massacre. The attack, which started in the morning of December 16, 2014, claimed the lives of 148 people.[63] Of these, 132 were children, aged between 8 and 18 years old.[64] They were killed in the fourth most deadly school massacre in modern history. The gunmen, who numbered seven, were all non-Pakistani,[65] belonging to the Taliban terrorist group, and claimed that by attacking the school, they were avenging the attacks which had been carried out earlier in 2014 by the army in the nearby Federally Administered Tribal Areas of North-Western Pakistan.[66] But there was also an added dimension. The school was an Army Public School, so many of the pupils there had parents who worked in the military. The general consensus which arose in the immediate aftermath was that the army had not done enough to stop the attack. They had failed to protect the people who now looked to the government for action. Said Alam Mehsud, a resident of Peshawar, summarized the feeling well when he said, "[t]he army's quick response force failed to thwart a terror attack in the cantonment. The government should either provide protection to the citizens or allow us to fight against these beasts."[67] The people on the whole had little doubt that terrorism was one of the "most serious crimes." Given this widespread sentiment, Prime Minister Nawaz Sharif brought back the ultimate punishment in the name of protecting the people.

The key question, however, is whether the lifting of the moratorium has led to the rates of terrorism or of murder actually going down at all in the country. This was after all the intended aim of the move, which was to protect citizens from further attacks and to quell their fears of a worsening situation. Unfortunately, the evidence in the ensuing years does not bear this out. For one thing, Pakistan's murder rate was already in decline in 2014.[68] Thereafter, for the next 2 ½ years from December 2014 to May 2017, the province of Punjab carried out 83 percent of all executions nationwide, of some 382 prisoners, and saw a drop of only 9.7 percent in the murder rate there.[69] By contrast, the neighboring province of Sindh saw a 25 percent drop in their murder rate, and that was after the Sindh Province having carried out only eighteen executions, which amounted to just 4 percent of the total deaths in that same period.[70]

Confronted with figures like these, one has to question the efficacy of the death penalty in deterring murder and terrorism rates. A closer look reveals that the real reason why a province like Punjab is sending people to the gallows has nothing to do with deterrence, but with the fact that twenty-five of the twenty-seven prisons in Punjab are overcrowded, so that the more the burden of overcapacity that a prison suffers from, the more executions it is shown to have carried out.[71] The lack of economic prosperity is reason why most people commit crimes. There is a striking inverse correlation between the sum of homicide and terrorist casualties, and the growth of Pakistan's gross domestic product (GDP) per capita.[72] Many individuals commit murder or involve themselves in acts of terrorism for reasons of economic desperation, and not because of a lack of state-imposed consequences for their actions.

Blasphemy

If Pakistan criminalizes blasphemy, it is not alone.[73] Around one in three countries worldwide do so in some way, shape, or form,[74] and they include nations as diverse as Russia, India, and Northern Ireland. Only Iran and Pakistan, however, explicitly mandate death as a punishment, although executions on these grounds are known to happen in many other jurisdictions. In Saudi Arabia, while no punishment for offenders is prescribed within the blasphemy laws themselves, offenders are left to the mercy of judicial discretion, where they may be subject to punishments that range from imprisonment to flogging, and sometimes even death, as was the case with Sabri Bogday from Turkey in 2007, although eventually an appeal to the King was allowed and he was released.[75] The Quran, however, does not prescribe punishment for blasphemy. It encourages a "discourse" with those who speak ill of the Prophet leaving punishment only in the hands of Allah himself. This raises the question why such severe punishments are being met out on this basis.[76]

The Quran guarantees freedom of religion so that the verse Al-Baqara (2:256) clearly states that "There should be no compulsion in religion." This is despite the fact that throughout Islam there is an extremely high level of respect for the Holy Prophet, not just because he was the one to whom Allah revealed himself, but also because, for Muslims, "you have in Allah's Messenger an excellent example (role-model) to follow" [Al-Ahzab (33:21)]. Thus, the Quran strongly condemns any insults made to the Holy Prophet so that verse Al-Mujadila (58:20) makes it clear that "Lo! those who oppose Allah and His messenger, they will be among the lowest." What is significant, nevertheless, is that the Quran does not suggest any earthly punishments for those who engage in blasphemy, as this is to be left to Allah, who "is severe in punishment" [Al-Anfal (8:13)], be that in this life or the next. What the Quran does enjoin fellow human beings to do is to engage in a nonviolent reaction with the offender, directing other Muslims that "When you hear God's revelations disbelieved in and mocked at, do not sit with them until they enter into some other discourse; surely then you would be like them" [An-Nisa' (4:140)]. That being said, this has not prevented extensive discussions from taking place among scholars in Islamic jurisprudence about the appropriate form of punishment in law for those guilty of blasphemy.

In Pakistan, the offense of blasphemy falls under Section 295 and Section 298 of the Penal Code, which deal with cases of "Injuring or defiling a place of worship, with Intent to insult the religion of any class" and "uttering words, etc., with deliberate intent to wound religious feelings" respectively. Punishments can be severe so as to include fines and prison sentences ranging from one year to life. Only one offense, at section 295C, carries the death penalty. This covers the "Use of derogatory remarks, etc., in respect of the

Holy Prophet," so that "Whoever by words, either spoken or written, or by visible representation or by any imputation, innuendo, or insinuation, directly or indirectly, defiles the sacred name of the Holy Prophet Muhammad (peace be upon him) shall be punished with death, or imprisonment for life, and shall also be liable to fine." This law was reviewed by the Federal Shariat Court in *Muhammad Ismail Qureshi v. Pakistan*, but although the judgment found that the provision "was repugnant to the fundamental principles of Islam," astonishingly, this was only in so far as it allowed punishments other than death.[77] The implication in this was that the ultimate punishment must be the only option available for those who degrade the Holy Prophet. This suggests that in the eyes of many Pakistanis, blasphemy is, without a shred of doubt, one of "the most serious crimes."

The ruling is unfortunate for it overlooks the colonial origins of the penal code. An indigenous law may well have been very different because it would not have been concerned exclusively with matters of law and order.[78] In the penal code, which was designed to subject the population to rigorous control, Section 295-A punishes any utterance with the "deliberate and malicious intention of outraging the religious feelings of any class of the citizens [of Pakistan], by words, either spoken or written, or by visible representations insults the religion or the religious beliefs of that class" with up to ten years in prison and/or a fine. The provision, however, was introduced in the 1920s by the British Raj following an incident in Punjab. A publisher called Mahashe Rajpal had released a book that mocked the marriages of the Prophet. This was, however, in response to a pamphlet published by Muslims that portrayed the Hindu goddess Sita as being a prostitute. Rajpal was arrested but eventually acquitted, as there was no law under which he could be charged. He was, as it happened, eventually murdered by a Muslim man, Ghazi Ilm-ud-Din, who was then himself given the death penalty for his crimes.[79] Ghazi Ilm-ud-Din received great praise from fellow Muslims for his actions.[80] Section 295-C, along with the other blasphemy-related clauses in the Penal Code, was introduced after independence from British India, and it added the punishment of death for blasphemy.

A good litmus test of how the penalty of death came to be administered for blasphemy can be found in the conduct of the *Asia Bibi* case after the 2014 Peshawar terror attack had taken place. In 2009, Bibi, a Roman Catholic, was living with her husband and five children in Sheikhupura in Punjab, close to the city of Lahore. Her family was the only Christian household in the village, having lived there since Partition.[81] She worked as a farmhand collecting falsa berries, when in June 2009, an argument erupted between her and the other farmhands initially over drinking water, in which Bibi allegedly then made derogatory remarks against the Holy Prophet. She is said to have later confessed to her guilt at a public meeting called in the village. A

FIR (First Information Report) was filed against her under Section 295-C at the local police station on June 19, 2009.[82] The local trial court found her guilty on November 8, 2010, and sentenced her to death. This sentence was upheld four years later in the Lahore High Court. On November 24 of that same year, an appeal was filed to the Supreme Court of Pakistan. With the Peshawar army school attack having taken place in December of that year, shortly afterward Pakistan began executing people again with a renewed zeal. To its credit, the apex court decided on July 22, 2015, to suspend Bibi's death sentence. In so doing, it avoided being drawn into the frenzied drive toward state executions on grounds of "terrorism." Asia Bibi's appeal remained suspended for the duration of her appeal and this gave her much-needed time. In October 2018, the Supreme Court of Pakistan reversed the decisions of the lower courts, and her death sentence was overturned. The seriousness of her situation should not, however, be underestimated. She had spent more than eight years on death row. Most of this was in solitary confinement. It is unsurprising, therefore, that Asia Bibi and her family were upon release granted asylum in Canada which was rumored to have been done under a new identity.[83]

Asia Bibi's case, despite her eventual release and grant of sanctuary in Canada, raises some troubling questions. First, she narrowly escaped being sent to the gallows, and had this happened then she would have been the first woman to have been put to death under Pakistan's blasphemy laws.[84] That is a chilling thought. Second, while it is ultimately the law that saved her, the fact that her case went through the legal system at all is highly unusual and noteworthy in itself. In a country where public feeling around blasphemy runs so high, many accused of the crime are killed extrajudicially before they get the right to savor a fair trial. Indeed, there is a sobering reminder of this by the Supreme Court judges themselves in the judgment when they draw attention to the fact that since 1990, no less than sixty-two people who were alleged to have committed blasphemy have been murdered before they received any sort of official trial.[85] Third, what saved Asia Bibi was the lobbying by her family, which allowed her case to receive a huge amount of international attention. Many rights groups, such as Human Rights Watch and Amnesty International, launched campaigns to mount pressure on Pakistani authorities. Questions were asked not only at Prime Minister's Question Time in the United Kingdom,[86] but several other governments spoke out as well, including the Pope. Offers for asylum came flooding in from around the world, including from Italy's Deputy Prime Minister Matteo Salvini. Salvini had said of Bibi's case that "[he] want[ed] women and children whose lives are at risk to be able to have a secure future, in our country or in other Western countries, so [he] will do everything humanly possible to guarantee that [for Bibi]."[87] Ironically, he was in other respect strongly opposed to the arrival of

Muslim asylum seekers to Italy and the European Union. Fourth, Asia Bibi was a Christian.

It has routinely been pointed out that Pakistan's blasphemy laws are disproportionately used against minorities.[88] The National Commission for Justice and Peace, a Catholic Human Rights organization, found that of 1,335 people accused under one or more clauses of the blasphemy laws since 1987, that 633 were Muslim, 494 Ahmadis, 187 Christian, and 21 were Hindu.[89] However, what is significant here is that only 1.6 percent of the population is listed as Christian,[90] and yet they represent over 14 percent of blasphemy accusations. Christians are disproportionately targeted. This overlooks the fact that other religions too are protected under blasphemy laws, apart from Islam, so that while Sections 295-B and 295-C pertain specifically to Islam, there are other clauses such as Section 295-A, which encompass insults to any and all religion.[91] Indeed, historically, Pakistan inherited the Indian Penal Code wherein religious offenses applied to all religions and were public order offenses. It was only in the time of General Zia that specific offenses targeting Ahmadis and protecting Islam were introduced.

This is important because in his judgment Judge Asif Saeed Khan Khosa did spend time talking about the possibility that Bibi was provoked into insulting the religion of her Muslim coworkers after her own religion was attacked by them. He was quite clear that "insulting the appellant's religion by her Muslim co-workers was no less blasphemous." He reiterated the reference to freedom of religion to be found in Article 20-A of Pakistan's Constitution in a manner which would have surprised most ordinary citizens in Pakistan, namely, that "Subject to law, public order and morality—every citizen shall have the right to profess, practice and propagate his religion." Interestingly, he also referenced such protection in the Promise to St. Catherine, a charter of rights the Holy Prophet had conferred to Christians in 628 AD which "declared that Christians, all of them, were [the Holy Prophet's] allies and he equated ill treatment of Christians with violating God's covenant]."[92] This leaves no doubt that despite their minority status in Pakistan, Christians have the right to practice their religion without insult to it.

These insightful and highly perspicacious observations of Justice Khosa do not, nevertheless, dispel worries about how a case like that of Asia Bibi was ever brought against her in the first place. These worries were shared by no less than three of the judges who were troubled by "contradictions [that were] sufficient to cast a shadow of doubt on the prosecution's version of facts." These ranged all the way from such matters as the timing of the public meeting, that was called in the village following the incident in the field, to the rank of the police officer who dealt with the incident, because only a Superintendent of Police or one of higher rank is permitted to investigate a section 295-C incident.[93] The judges were concerned with Bibi's extrajudicial confession, which she gave at the public meeting, where she was alone, "tensions were running high," and the situational environment was overall "intimidating." Such elements were not uncommon in extrajudicial scenarios that emerge in blasphemy cases. Accordingly, the evidence for a conviction, particularly in a death penalty case, was wholly inadequate.

The judgment, nevertheless, failed to make strong criticism of Pakistan's blasphemy laws or indeed of the country's use of the death penalty in general. Given their grave reservations about the way in which the *Asia Bibi* case had been brought, this is regrettable. In fact, being aware of the huge controversy to which their judgment would give rise, the judges spent a considerable amount of time at the start of their opinions reaffirming their commitment to, and the necessity for, the legislation in question. This is all the more unfortunate given that the *Asia Bibi* case did not sadly stay within the confines of the courtroom. Blasphemy, as the judges observed, "infuriates Muslims to an intolerable limit," which no doubt explains why two prominent politicians were killed after they spoke out in favor of Asia Bibi. These were the governor of Punjab Salman Taseer, and the Minister for Minorities Affairs Shahbaz Bhatti,[94] who was the only Christian in the government at the time. In a series of events reminiscent of the killing of Mahashe Rajpal,[95] the killer of Salman Taseer was none other than his own bodyguard, Mumtaz Qadri. Although he was in turn executed for the murder of his former boss on February 29, 2016,[96] such was the government's apprehension in doing so that there was speculation around the fact that authorities had chosen to execute him on a leap day, in the hope of making it harder for his supporters to commemorate the anniversary of this death.

Government fears were not without foundation because forty days later, at the end of the Chehlum mourning period, tens of thousands of supporters of Qadri gathered and then marched through Islamabad from the outskirts. A bus station and cars were burned, roads were closed, cellular coverage had to be blocked and armed forces called in to disperse a sit in.[97] This was precisely the type of "extremely serious law and order situation, with grievous, disastrous consequences" that the Supreme Court warned about in Bibi's case.[98] To this day, many people visit Qadri's grave daily, and a Barelvis mosque was erected in Islamabad in his name. The mosque, however, was struggling to keep up with demand to such an extent that it had to raise funds to double in size.[99] When in October 2018 the Supreme Court had the audacity to declare Asia Bibi to be innocent of the crime of blasphemy, major demonstrations took place up and down the country, bringing it to a standstill. Many of the demonstrations were led by the right-wing conservative Islamist political party Tehreek-e-Labbaik (TLP) that was set up by Qadri's supporters following his death. Up to 5,000 TLP supporters were arrested,[100] including 2 prominent leaders. In short, given how hard it is to overstate how big an impact allegations of blasphemy have on the structure of everyday life in Pakistan, it is difficult to see how the removal of the death penalty can be countenanced by any political party for this offense. Indeed, it is arguably even hard to rely upon judicial morality, where the whole moral fabric of the society (including the judiciary) is so determined to punish the alleged blasphemer. This is clear from the Supreme Court judgment in *Zaheer-ud-din v. The State* (1993) SCMR 1718, which has been described by one scholar as "a problematic decision" because "not only does it confirm the legality of the continued persecution of members of the Ahmadiyya community, . . . but it also attempts to establish a new interpretation of the scope and the limits of fundamental rights in Pakistan."[101]

CONCLUSION

Is capital punishment in Pakistan here to stay? Or can it some day be abolished? For cases of terrorism and blasphemy, it seems to fit under the "most serious crimes" standard of Article 6.2 of the ICCPR even though the use of capital punishment in Pakistan pre-dates it. With both blasphemy and terrorism, however, the death penalty is applied in less than a principled way[102] in a disproportionate manner to the "other," be that a religious "other" or a socioeconomic "other." For Pakistan, when the "other" is not punished, this results massive law and order problems in the country as a whole. To this there are serious economic and human costs. By issuing death sentences so readily, the Pakistani judiciary routinely demonstrates a willingness to sacrifice the "other" for the sake of law and order. This need not be so surprising. In "Discipline and Punishment," Foucault described an economic and social balance between the cost of repression and the cost of misdemeanors.[103] Punishing the "other" comes at little cost due to the concerned person's already removed status in society, the punishment makes huge savings for the maintenance of the "rule of law."

Others, such as Sherman, have gone beyond Foucault, and pointed out how former colonies like Pakistan had a "coercive network of the colonial state" in place of the "rule of law."[104] This is perhaps best epitomized by the infamous "Bloody Code," of which Anderson writes, "the scale of judicial reprisals seen in Empire [. . .] had no parallel in nineteenth-century Britain," whereby the death penalty was used to "consolidate imperial rule and to eradicate resistance."[105] The legacy of this is still very much felt in Pakistan today, despite the passage of more than seventy years since independence, and this is so also in other countries that were formerly under colonial rule. In fact, a striking illustration of this postcolonial "coercive network" is that among

Commonwealth countries, the rate of abolition is nearly 45 percent lower than among non-Commonwealth countries.[106] That is a sobering thought.

The remaining question is how might Pakistan's attitude toward the death penalty evolves in the coming years. The question is important in relation to eliminating the scourge of corruption which is endemic in the country. In 2018, *Transparency International* ranked Pakistan 117th out of 180 countries, with a score of just 33 out of 100.[107] Kenya, albeit with a lower score of 27 out of 100,[108] recently suggested punishing corruption with the death penalty in the name of deterrence.[109] This proposal was severely criticized by Amnesty International, as it stressed that "[t]here is no credible evidence that the death penalty deters corruption—or any other crime."[110] Arguments centered on the ineffectiveness of the death penalty as a deterrent do not travel far in countries which use it, however, and so the question is whether Pakistan could one day even expand its usage to include crimes of corruption. Might this be done in the name of promoting the rule of law? If this happens, the pressure to do so may well come from China.

In October 2018, Mussarat Jamshed Cheema from the Pakistan Tehreek-e-Insaf (PTI) said that her party was working on introducing a bill that would punish corruption by making it a capital offense.[111] Speaking to *The Express Tribune*, she cited China's policy of executing those found guilty of "economic crimes."[112] This is telling of the strong diplomatic, economic, and military ties that have arisen in recent years between Pakistan and China,[113] which have only become stronger as China has developed into a global superpower. Pakistan has been at the forefront of China's Belt and Road Initiative (BRI), a project stretching over around seventy countries and carrying an estimated price tag of 1 billion US dollars.[114] To date, China has invested billions of dollars in projects ranging from railways to the deep-water port of Gwadar in the Southwest of the country as part of the China-Pakistan Economic Corridor.[115] Beijing has been willing to cooperate with Pakistan, which is after all a nuclear armed-nation with which it shares a 438 kilometer long border, on military issues too with the result that it recently shared access to the Beifou satellite navigation system.[116]

Prime Minister Imran Khan, upon coming to office in August 2018, had already within the space of a year paid two visits to China, describing the country as, "our closest friend."[117] All this goes on to show that Pakistan's increased closeness to China could result in the former drawing inspiration from the latter, and to expanding its use of the death penalty to incorporate "economic crimes" as well, in much the same way as China does at present. If that happens, Pakistan will continue to face no drastic international sanctions. As long as countries such as the United States and China continue to deploy the punishment with such zeal themselves, there will unfortunately be no pressure upon it to desist in its use.

Change will ultimately have to come from internal pressure alone—and that road may well be a very long one.

NOTES

1. I am grateful to the research assistance of Ms. Eliška Stroehlein in the preparation of this chapter and to Professor Javaid Rehman for his thoughtful observations on this chapter, as well as to Marva Khan and Adnan Sattar for their comments. Needless to say, all errors are mine.

2. Andrew Novak, *"The Abolition of the Mandatory Death Penalty in India and Bangladesh: A Comparative Commonwealth Perspective,"* 28 Pac. McGeorge Global Bus. & Dev. L.J. 227 (2014) at p. 227 Available at: https://scholarlycommons.pacific.edu/globe/vol28/iss2/6

3. Andrew Novak, *The Global Decline of the Mandatory Death Penalty: Constitutional Jurisprudence and Legislative Reform in Africa, Asia, and the Caribbean* (Ashgate, 2014) at p. 1.

4. The report shows how an alarming number of countries resorted to the death penalty in a flawed attempt to stop crime and terrorism in 2014. Their 68-page Report, published in early 2015, shows that at least 778 executions were carried out globally in 2013, of which 538 were in Iran and Iraq alone, amounting to two-thirds of the world's total. This showed an increase of 682 executions in 2012 an increase of 15 percent. Available at https://www.amnestyusa.org/pdfs/DeathSentencesAndExecutions2014_EN.pdf

5. Pakistan, after a self-imposed moratorium since March 2008, took to state executions at the end of March 2014 with the zeal of a newly converted zealot after the horrifying Taliban school attack which killed 132 children. In six months and by June 2015 it had performed 150 executions outnumbering Saudi Arabia, with the largest death row in the world. (see Doug Bolton, *"Pakistan performs 150 executions in six months, more than Saudi Arabia" The Independent*, Tuesday, 9 June 2015. Available at http://www.independent.co.uk/news/world/asia/pakistan-performs-150-executions-in-six-months-more-than-saudi-arabia-10306668.html#)

6. Sughra Bibi, Qian Hongdao, Najeed Ullah, Muhammad Bilawal Khaskheli and Hafiz Abdul Rehman Saleem *'Excessive Use of Death Penalty as Stoppage Tool for Terrorism: Wrongful Death Executions in Pakistan'* (2019) *Journal of Law, Policy and Globalization*, 81. pp 42–52.

7. Ibid.

8. Ibid.

9. *'A "most serious crime" Pakistan's unlawful use of the death penalty'* (September 2016) Allard K. Lowenstein International Human Rights Clinic Yale Law School

10. '*Death penalty in 2018: Facts and figures*' (Amnesty International, 10 April 2019) https://www.amnesty.org/en/latest/news/2019/04/death-penalty-facts-and-figures-2018/ Accessed 10 October 2019.

11. Ibid.

12. '*Death Row*' (Justice Project Pakistan) https://www.jpp.org.pk/death-row/ Accessed 10 October 2019.

13. Ibid.

14. Sughra Bibi, Qian Hongdao, Najeed Ullah, Muhammad Bilawal Khaskheli and Hafiz Abdul Rehman Saleem *'Excessive Use of Death Penalty as Stoppage Tool for Terrorism: Wrongful Death Executions in Pakistan'* (2019) *Journal of Law, Policy and Globalization*, 81. pp. 42–52.

15. Ibid.

16. Pakistan Penal Code S-295 C was originally inducted in 1986. This carried death penalty for blasphemy as an alternative punishment. However, a Federal Shariat Court Judgment in 1991 removed the alternative punishment, making death penalty as mandatory punishment for this offense.

17. Sughra Bibi, Qian Hongdao, Najeed Ullah, Muhammad Bilawal Khaskheli and Hafiz Abdul Rehman Saleem *'Excessive Use of Death Penalty as Stoppage Tool for Terrorism: Wrongful Death Executions in Pakistan'* (2019) *Journal of Law, Policy and Globalization*, 81. pp. 42–52.

18. *'Yearbook of the United Nations 1948-1949 Part 1 Chapter 5 Social, Humanitarian and Cultural Questions'* p. 535.

19. Danchin, Peter '*Article 3: Life, Liberty & Security of Person*' (The Universal Declaration of Human Rights Peter Danchin CSHR/ CCNMTL) http://ccnmtl.columbia.edu/projects/mmt/udhr/article_3.html Accessed 22 July 2019.

20. Ibid.

21. Neumayer, Eric '*Death penalty: the political foundations of the global trend toward abolition*' (2008) *Human Rights Review*, 9 (2). pp. 241–268.

22. Ibid.

23. Ibid.

24. Adopted and opened for signature, ratification and accession by General Assembly resolution 2200A (XXI) of 16 December 1966 entry into force 23 March 1976, in accordance with Article 49. (Available at https://www.ohchr.org/en/professionalinterest/pages/ccpr.aspx. The other Covenant was *International Covenant on Economic, Social and Cultural Right*s, Adopted and opened for signature, ratification and accession by General Assembly resolution 2200A (XXI) of 16 December 1966 entry into force 3 January 1976, in accordance with article 27 (Available at https://www.ohchr.org/en/professionalinterest/pages/cescr.aspx)

25. See, UN Human Rights Committee (HRC), *General comment no. 36, Article 6 (Right to Life)*, 3 September 2019, CCPR/C/GC/35 . The Human Rights Committee has emphasized in their understanding most serious crimes is restricted to intentional killing. The Committee has also made a number of highly significant observations as to how violations of other rights, for example, violations of the right to fair trial renders an execution arbitrary and violation of Article 6.

26. Adopted and proclaimed by General Assembly resolution 44/128 of 15 December 1989. (Available at https://www.ohchr.org/en/professionalinterest/pages/2ndopccpr.aspx)

27. Office of the High Commissioner for Human Rights resolution 2003/67, *The question of the death penalty.*

28. Day, Meagan, '*This landmark Supreme Court case outlawed the death penalty for rape*' (Timeline, 6 October 2016) https://timeline.com/death-penalty-for-rape-935969eb3a2d Accessed 22 July 2019.

29. *Coker v. Georgia* 433 U.S. 584 (1977).

30. *Kennedy v. Louisiana*, 554 U.S. 407 (2008).

31. *Coker v. Georgia* 433 U.S. 584 (1977) at Footnote 4.

32. Day, Meagan, '*This landmark Supreme Court case outlawed the death penalty for rape*' (Timeline, 6 October 2016) https://timeline.com/death-penalty-for-rape-935969eb3a2d Accessed 22 July 2019.

33. See, "*A 'Most Serious Crime': Pakistan's Unlawful Use of the Death Penalty*"—A report by Justice Project Pakistan, in collaboration with the Yale Law School's Allard K. Lowenstein International Human Rights Clinic (September 2016) at p.4 (Available at https://law.yale.edu/sites/default/files/area/center/schell/2016_09_23_pub_dp_report.pdf)

34. Misachi, John, 'Religion in Pakistan' (World Atlas, 22 August 2018) https://www.worldatlas.com/articles/religious-beliefs-and-freedoms-in-pakistan.html Accessed 22 July 2019.

35. Schabas, William, '*Islam and the Death Penalty*' (2000) *William & Mary Bill Rights Journal*, 9(1). pp. 223–236.

36. See Part VII, Chapter 3A: Federal Shariat Court, of the *Constitution of Pakistan*, at section 203C (Available at http://www.pakistani.org/pakistan/constitution/part7.ch3A.html)

37. See, Schabas, William, '*Islam and the Death Penalty*' (2000) *William & Mary Bill Rights Journal*, 9(1). pp. 223–236.

38. "Hadd." in *The Oxford Dictionary of Islam*, edited by John L. Esposito (Oxford Islamic Studies Online) http://www.oxfordislamicstudies.com/article/opr/t125/e757 Accessed 22 July 2019. It is worth noting, however that the understanding of *Hud* crimes has varied as some jurists regard theft, alcohol consumption and apostasy as Hudud offenses (and within some jurisdictions carrying a potential death penalty).

39. Schabas, William, '*Islam and the Death Penalty*' (2000) *William & Mary Bill Rights Journal*, 9(1). pp. 223–236.

40. Wyman, James, '*Vengeance Is Whose: The Death Penalty and Cultural Relativism in International Law*' (1997) *Journal of Transnational Law Policy*, 6. pp. 543–570.

41. Ibid.

42. '*Mauritania: Mandatory Death Penalty for Blasphemy*' (Human Rights Watch, 4 May 2018) https://www.hrw.org/news/2018/05/04/mauritania-mandatory-death-penalty-blasphemy Accessed 22 July 2019.

43. '*Bloody rise in Saudi Arabia: 122 executions in the first half of 2019*' (European Saudi Organisation for Human Rights, 8 July 2019), https://www.esohr.org/en/?p=2371 Accessed 22 July 2019.

44. Wyman, James, '*Vengeance Is Whose: The Death Penalty and Cultural Relativism in International Law*' (1997) *Journal of Transnational Law Policy*, 6. pp. 543–570.

45. Schabas, William, '*Islam and the Death Penalty*' (2000) *William & Mary Bill Rights Journal*, 9(1). pp. 223–236.

46. Kennedy, Charles, '*The Creation and Development of Pakistan's Anti-terrorism Regime, 1997-2002*', Religious Radicalism and Security in South Asia, (2004). pp. 387–411.

47. 'Pakistan hangs sectarian bomber' (BBC News, 11 August 1998), http://news.bbc.co.uk/1/hi/world/south_asia/149215.stm Accessed 22 July 2019.

48. Kennedy, Charles, '*The Creation and Development of Pakistan's Anti-terrorism Regime, 1997-2002*' pp. 387–411.

49. Hasan, Ali Dayan '*Destroying Legality: Pakistan's Crackdown on Lawyers and Judges*' (Human Rights Watch, 18 December 2007) https://www.hrw.org/report/2007/12/18/destroying-legality/pakistans-crackdown-lawyers-and-judges Accessed 22 July 2019.

50. Schmid, Alex '*The definition of terrorism*' (2011) The Routledge Handbook of Terrorism Research, pp. 39-158.

51. Sughra Bibi, Qian Hongdao, Najeed Ullah, Muhammad Bilawal Khaskheli and Hafiz Abdul Rehman Saleem '*Excessive Use of Death Penalty as Stoppage Tool for Terrorism: Wrongful Death Executions in Pakistan*' (2019) *Journal of Law, Policy and Globalization*, 81. pp. 42–52.

52. '*Terror on death row: The abuse and overuse of Pakistan's anti-terrorism legislation*' (Justice Project Pakistan and Reprieve, December 2014) https://reprieve.org.uk/wp-content/uploads/2014/12/2014_12_18_PUB-Pakistan-Terror-Courts-Report-JPP-and-Reprieve.pdf Accessed 22 July 2019.

53. Sughra Bibi, Qian Hongdao, Najeed Ullah, Muhammad Bilawal Khaskheli and Hafiz Abdul Rehman Saleem '*Excessive Use of Death Penalty as Stoppage Tool for Terrorism: Wrongful Death Executions in Pakistan*' (2019) *Journal of Law, Policy and Globalization*, 81. pp. 42–52.

54. See, Urooj Tarar, 'Rotting in the dark—the forgotten children of Pakistan: An in-depth analysis of the juveniles prisoners of Pakistan and the conditions they live in' (Daily Pakistan Global, 17 March 2018) https://en.dailypakistan.com.pk/opinion/rotting-in-the-dark-the-forgotten-children-of-pakistan/. Also see, Pakistan: Juvenile and Justice System Ordinance 2000.

55. Office of the High Commissioner for Human Rights resolution 2003/67, *The question of the death penalty*.

56. '*Mentally Ill Prisoners*' (Justice Project Pakistan) https://www.jpp.org.pk/mentally-ill-prisoners/ Accessed 22 July 2019.

57. Office of the High Commissioner for Human Rights resolution 2003/67, *The question of the death penalty*.

58. UNICEF Data https://data.unicef.org/country/pak/# Accessed 22 July 2019.

59. Sughra Bibi, Qian Hongdao, Najeed Ullah, Muhammad Bilawal Khaskheli and Hafiz Abdul Rehman Saleem '*Excessive Use of Death Penalty as Stoppage Tool for Terrorism: Wrongful Death Executions in Pakistan*' (2019) *Journal of Law, Policy and Globalization*, 81. pp. 42–52.

60. '*Terror on death row: The abuse and overuse of Pakistan's anti-terrorism legislation*' (Justice Project Pakistan and Reprieve, December 2014) https://reprieve

.org.uk/wp-content/uploads/2014/12/2014_12_18_PUB-Pakistan-Terror-Courts-Report-JPP-and-Reprieve.pdf Accessed 22 July 2019.

61. Boone, Jon '*Pakistan hangs Shafqat Hussain despite claim he was a child at time of crime*' (The Guardian, 4 August 2015) https://www.theguardian.com/world/2015/aug/04/pakistan-hangs-shafqat-hussain-claim-child-crime Accessed 22 July 2019.

62. Kaphle, Anup 'Pakistan announces a national plan to fight terrorism, says terrorists' days are numbered' (The Washington Post, 24 December 2014) https://www.washingtonpost.com/news/worldviews/wp/2014/12/24/pakistan-announces-a-national-plan-to-fight-terrorism-says-terrorists-days-are-numbered/?utm_term=.8fa52bde37b7 Accessed 22 July 2019.

63. Zulfiqar Ali and Shashank Bengali, '*Pakistan raises death toll in Peshawar school attack to 148*' (Los Angeles Times, 17 December 2014) https://www.latimes.com/world/afghanistan-pakistan/la-fg-families-grieve-peshawar-pakistan-20141217-story.html Accessed 22 July 2019.

64. Ibid.

65. Roberts, Rachel, '*Pakistan: Three years after 140 died in the Peshawar school massacre, what has changed?*' (The Independent, 15 December 2017) https://web.archive.org/web/20180304021728/http://www.independent.co.uk/news/world/asia/pakistan-peshawar-school-shooting-massacre-what-has-changed-happened-three-years-a8113661.html Accessed 22 July 2019.

66. Zulfiqar Ali and Shashank Bengali, '*Pakistan raises death toll in Peshawar school attack to 148*' (Los Angeles Times, 17 December 2014) https://www.latimes.com/world/afghanistan-pakistan/la-fg-families-grieve-peshawar-pakistan-20141217-story.html Accessed 22 July 2019.

67. Ibid.

68. '*Counting executions*' (Justice Project Pakistan, 6 July 2017) https://www.jpp.org.pk/report/counting-executions/ Accessed 15 October 2019.

69. Ibid.

70. Ibid.

71. Sughra Bibi, Qian Hongdao, Najeed Ullah, Muhammad Bilawal Khaskheli and Hafiz Abdul Rehman Saleem '*Excessive Use of Death Penalty as Stoppage Tool for Terrorism: Wrongful Death Executions in Pakistan*' (2019) *Journal of Law, Policy and Globalization*, 81. pp 42-52

72. Ibid.

73. See, *Cornell Center on the Death Penalty Worldwide* Death Penalty Database https://www.deathpenaltyworldwide.org/country-search-post.cfm?country=Pakistan

74. Joelle Fiss and Jocelyn Getgen Kestenbaum '*Respecting Rights? Measuring The World's Blasphemy Laws*' (United States Commission on International Religious Freedom, July 2017) https://www.uscirf.gov/sites/default/files/Blasphemy%20Laws%20Report.pdf Accessed 23 July 2019.

75. Khan, Ghazanfar Ali 'Freed Turkish barber reaches home' (Arab News, 28 January 2009) http://www.arabnews.com/node/320422 Accessed 23 July 2019.

76. For a wide-ranging discussion, see N Cox, 'Judging Blasphemy Law:' *Journal of Law and Religion* (2020) 35(1) 33.

77. *Mst. Asia Bibi v. The State etc.* in the Supreme Court of Pakistan (Appellate Jurisdiction) Criminal Appeal No.39-L of 2015

78. See, *"On Trial: The Implementation of Pakistan's Blasphemy Laws"* (November 2015) *International Commission of Jurists* (Available at https://www.icj.org/wp-content/uploads/2015/12/Pakistan-On-Trial-Blasphemy-Laws-Publications-Thematic-Reports-2015-ENG.pdf)

79. Kumar, Girja *'The Book on Trial: Fundamentalism and Censorship in India'* (Har-Anand Publications, 1997).

80. Ali, Umer '*Until we start denouncing Ilm-ud-din's legacy Mumtaz Qadris will keep sprouting up in Pakistan*' (The Nation, 10 October 2015) https://nation.com.pk/10-Oct-2015/until-we-start-denouncing-ilm-ud-din-s-legacy-mumtaz-qadris-will-keep-sprouting-up-in-pakistan Accessed 23 July 2019.

81. Guering, Orla '*Pakistani Christian Asia Bibi 'has price on her head*'' (BBC News 7 December 2010) https://www.bbc.co.uk/news/world-south-asia-11930849 Accessed 23 July 2019.

82. *Mst. Asia Bibi v. The State etc.* in the Supreme Court of Pakistan (Appellate Jurisdiction) Criminal Appeal No.39-L of 2015.

83. Sherwood, Harriet '*Asia Bibi begins new life in Canada - but her ordeal may not be over*' (The Guardian 8 May 2019) https://www.theguardian.com/world/2019/may/08/asia-bibi-begins-new-life-in-canada-but-her-ordeal-may-not-be-over Accessed 23 July 2019.

84. '*Pakistan frees woman facing death penalty for blasphemy*' (RTÉ News 31 October 2018) https://www.rte.ie/news/world/2018/1031/1007672-pakistan-blasphemy/ Accessed 23 July 2019.

85. *Mst. Asia Bibi v. The State etc.* in the Supreme Court of Pakistan (Appellate Jurisdiction) Criminal Appeal No.39-L of 2015

86. 'PMQs: Theresa May is asked about Asia Bibi case in Pakistan' (BBC News 31 October 2018) https://www.bbc.co.uk/news/av/uk-politics-46045217/pmqs-theresa-may-is-asked-about-asia-bibi-case-in-pakistan Accessed 23 July 2019.

87. Pullella, Philip *'Italy says will help Pakistani woman in blasphemy case leave her country'* (Reuters 6 November 2018) https://uk.reuters.com/article/uk-pakistan-blasphemy-italy/italy-says-will-help-pakistani-woman-in-blasphemy-case-leave-her-country-idUKKCN1NB1W4 Accessed 23 July 2019.

88. For some useful insights, see J Rehman and S Berry, 'Is "Defamation of Religions" Passé?' 44 *George Washington International Law Review* (2012) pp. 431–472.

89. '*"As good as dead" The impact of the blasphemy laws in Pakistan*' (Amnesty International 2016) https://www.refworld.org/pdfid/585a41704.pdf Accessed 23 July 2019.

90. Misachi, John, '*Religion in Pakistan*' (WorldAtlas, 22 August 2018) https://www.worldatlas.com/articles/religious-beliefs-and-freedoms-in-pakistan.html Accessed 22 July 2019.

91. See, *"On Trial: The Implementation of Pakistan's Blasphemy Laws"* (November 2015) *International Commission of Jurists* (Available at https://www.icj.org/wp-content/uploads/2015/12/Pakistan-On-Trial-Blasphemy-Laws-Publications-Thematic-Reports-2015-ENG.pdf)

92. *Mst. Asia Bibi v. The State etc. in the Supreme Court of Pakistan (Appellate Jurisdiction) Criminal Appeal No.39*-L of 2015.

93. *Mst. Asia Bibi v. The State etc.* in the Supreme Court of Pakistan (Appellate Jurisdiction) Criminal Appeal No.39-L of 2015.

94. Taseer, Shehrbano '*Pakistan has abdicated its responsibilities*' (The Guardian 2 March 2011) https://www.theguardian.com/commentisfree/2011/mar/02/salmaan-bhatti-blasphemy-assassination Accessed 23 July 2019.

95. Ali, Umer '*Until we start denouncing Ilm-ud-din's legacy Mumtaz Qadris will keep sprouting up in Pakistan*' (The Nation, 10 October 2015) https://nation.com.pk/10-Oct-2015/until-we-start-denouncing-ilm-ud-din-s-legacy-mumtaz-qadris-will-keep-sprouting-up-in-pakistan Accessed 23 July 2019.

96. '*Salman Taseer murder: Pakistan hangs Mumtaz Qadri*' (BBC News 29 February) https://www.bbc.co.uk/news/world-asia-35684452 Accessed 23 July 2019.

97. Haider, Irfan '*Nearly 2000 pro-Qadri protesters continue sit-in outside Parliament*' (Dawn, 27 March 2016) https://www.dawn.com/news/1248261 Accessed 23 July 2019.

98. *Mst. Asia Bibi v. The State etc.* in the Supreme Court of Pakistan (Appellate Jurisdiction) Criminal Appeal No.39-L of 2015 .

99. Boone, Jon '*Pakistan mosque built to honor politician's killer to double in size*' (The Guardian, 30 April 2014) https://www.theguardian.com/world/2014/apr/30/pakistan-mosque-killer-mumtaz-qadri-salaman-taseer Accessed 23 July 2019.

100. '*Tehreek-e-Labbaik: how blasphemy case in Pakistan brought down hardline religious party*' (The Conversation, 18 July 2019) http://theconversation.com/tehreek-e-labbaik-how-blasphemy-case-in-pakistan-brought-down-hardline-religious-party-119800 Accessed 23 July 2019.

101. For a critique, see Prof. Martin Lau at https://www.soas.ac.uk/cimel/materials/intro.html)

102. See, Concluding observations on the initial report of Pakistan (Human Rights Committee CCPR/C/PAK/CO/1 (2017), para 18: Also of relevance is para 23 of the above report: anti-terrorism courts and para 33 & 34 (on blasphemy). Concluding observations on the fifth periodic report of Pakistan (2016): CRC/C/PAK/CO/5, paras, 24, 25, 26.

103. Sherman, Taylor C. '*Tensions of colonial punishment: perspectives on recent developments in the study of coercive networks in Asia, Africa and the Caribbean*' (2009) *History Compass*, 7 (3). pp. 659–677.

104. Ibid.

105. Anderson, Clare '*Execution and its Aftermath in the Nineteenth-Century British Empire*' (2015) A Global History of Execution and the Criminal Corpse, pp. 170–198.

106. Kaner, David'The death penalty is a Commonwealth problem' (Open Global Rights, 23 July 2015) https://www.openglobalrights.org/the-death-penalty-is-a-commonwealth-problem/ Accessed 13 October 2019.

107. '*Corruption Perceptions Index [Executive Summary]*' (Transparency International, 2019) https://www.transparency.org/files/content/pages/CPI_2018_Executive_Summary_EN.pdf Accessed 10 October 2019.

108. Ibid.

109. Popoola, Oluwatosin '*Op-Ed: Death penalty is not the solution to corruption in Kenya*' (Amnesty International, 8 June 2018) https://www.amnesty.org/en/latest/news/2018/06/op-ed-death-penalty-is-not-the-solution-to-corruption-in-kenya/ Accessed 7 October 2019.

110. Ibid.

111. Yasif, Rana *'PTI lawmaker for death sentence of corrupt'* (The Express Tribune, 6 October 2018) https://tribune.com.pk/story/1819406/1-pti-lawmaker-death-sentence-corrupt/ Accessed 7 October 2019.

112. Ibid.

113. Irshad, Muhammad Saqib '*One Belt and One Road: Dose China-Pakistan Economic Corridor Benefit for Pakistan's Economy?*' (2015) *Journal of Economics and Sustainable Development*, 6(24). Available at SSRN: https://ssrn.com/abstract=2710352

114. Hillmann, Jonathan '*How Big Is China's Belt and Road?*' (Center for Strategic and International Studies CSIS, 3 April 2018) https://www.csis.org/analysis/how-big-chinas-belt-and-road Accessed 7 October 2019.

115. Strohecker, Karin '*Pakistan says China to make extra $8.5 billion investments in rail, energy*' (Reuters, 23 November 2016) https://uk.reuters.com/article/uk-pakistan-economy-cpec-idUKKBN13I1Y2?il=0 Accessed 7 October 2019.

116. Abi-Habib, Maria *'China's 'Belt and Road' Plan in Pakistan Takes a Military Turn'* (The New York Times, 19 December 2018) https://www.nytimes.com/2018/12/19/world/asia/pakistan-china-belt-road-military.html Accessed 7 October 2019.

117. Khan, Sanaullah '*PM Imran reaches Beijing for second official visit of China*' (Dawn, 25 April 2019) https://www.dawn.com/news/1478336 Accessed 7 October 2019.

Chapter 10

Enforced Disappearances in Pakistan

A Tool of Terror?

Reema Omer

INTRODUCTION

The term "enforced disappearance" encompasses many different situations in the context of Pakistan, ranging from the secret detention and renditions of people accused of carrying out terrorism to the abductions of people allegedly involved in nationalist or separatist struggles in Balochistan and Sindh, and now, to the disappearances, often "short-term," of activists and journalists critical of the state.

In Pakistan, enforced disappearances take place in a context of widespread and systematic human rights violations, which include extrajudicial executions, torture and other ill treatment, arbitrary arrests and detentions, denial of fair trial, and restrictions on the right to freedom of expression. More recently, individuals—particularly those who are critical of the certain state institutions and policies—have also been targeted using laws related to terrorism, sedition, and defamation. The targeted nature of such persecution suggests that enforced disappearances are being used as a political tool by the state to silence dissent and turn its citizens into obedient, unquestioning vassals.

The Supreme Court of Pakistan has called the practice a "crime against humanity" and has directed those responsible be brought to justice. However, the ambit of people subjected to enforced disappearances appears to be widening, and, until now, not a single perpetrator has been held accountable.

ENFORCED DISAPPEARANCE: A GLOBAL PERSPECTIVE

Enforced disappearance is understood as the arrest, detention, abduction, or any other form of deprivation of liberty by state agents, or by persons or groups of persons acting with the authorization, support, or acquiescence of the state, followed by a refusal to acknowledge the deprivation of liberty or by concealment of the fate or whereabouts of the disappeared person. The UN General Assembly has repeatedly described enforced disappearance as "an offence to human dignity" and a grave violation of international human rights law.

According to some accounts, the practice of what we understand as "enforced disappearance" first emerged during World War II. Under the decree known as *Nacht und Nebal* (night and fog) passed in 1941, Adolf Hitler's regime secretly transferred thousands of people accused of "endangering German security" to suppress resistance through intimidation and terror.[1] The International Military Tribunal in Nuremberg categorically referred to the practice as a violation of the laws of war.

In the conventional human rights conception, the international crime of enforced disappearance evolved out of human rights instruments and declarations created in response to "disappearances" perpetrated by dictatorial regimes and military juntas in Latin America during the 1960s, 1970s, and 1980s. In three decades, over 90,000 cases of enforced disappearance were reported from the region.

The practice of enforced disappearance is now a global phenomenon. The UN Working Group on Enforced and Involuntary Disappearances has cases registered from at least 109 countries from all continents.[2] Once considered a practice used by dictatorships, enforced disappearances are now perpetrated in all kinds of political setups as a means of political repression of opponents and human rights defenders; as part of counterterrorism strategies; and in response to organized crime.

ENFORCED DISAPPEARANCES IN PAKISTAN: OVERVIEW

The practice of enforced disappearance has existed in Pakistan since at least the 1980s. According to the UN Working Group on Enforced Disappearances, the first cases of enforced disappearance filed with the Working Group allegedly occurred between the mid-1980s and the mid-1990s, in the northwestern region, "in relation to the conflicts in Afghanistan."[3]

The WGEID also noted:

> A number of other cases were also reported to the Working Group to have taken place in the 1990s and the beginning of the 2000s in relation to the military operations carried out in Karachi and their aftermath (Sindh Province). Most of the cases concerned the alleged disappearance of members of the political party Muhajir Qaomi Movement (MQM), who were allegedly arrested by the police or by other security forces.[4]

Cases of enforced disappearances have been recorded in significant numbers in the early 2000s, beginning with Pakistan's involvement in the US-led "war on terror" in late 2001. Since then, hundreds of people accused of terrorism-related offenses have reportedly been "disappeared" after being abducted by security agencies and detained in secret facilities. The practice continues unabated until today, with spikes in numbers of alleged enforced disappearances every time the military launches an offensive in the northwestern region of Pakistan, notably in the former Federally Administered Tribal Areas (FATA), now constitutionally a part of the Khyber Pakhtunkhwa Province.

Cases of enforced disappearances are also reported in Balochistan, where the practice is used against political activists and people who are considered sympathetic to separatist or nationalist movements in the province. In recent years, there has been a rise of cases of enforced disappearance in Sindh, where political activists have largely been targeted.[5]

Estimates of the overall number of cases of enforced disappearance in Pakistan vary. The Commission of Inquiry on Enforced Disappearances has reported 2,123 unresolved cases until December 2020. The Working Group on Enforced or Involuntary Disappearances has received a total of 1,264 cases, out of which 813 remain outstanding as of 2019.[6] The HRCP, an NGO that documented enforced disappearances in 60 districts of Pakistan, reported nearly 400 cases from 2014 to 2017. Other NGOs claim between 5,000 to 18,000 cases. Even by the most conservative estimates, a significant number of enforced disappearances remain unresolved.

With the "disappearance" in recent years of a number of bloggers, journalists, and activists from different parts of the country, including from Islamabad, enforced disappearance has now become a national phenomenon.

However, the government has failed to bring perpetrators to account in even a single case involving enforced disappearance. On the contrary, in recent years, it has enacted legislation that facilitates the perpetration of enforced disappearance—including by explicitly legalizing forms of secret, unacknowledged, and incommunicado detention—and giving immunity to those responsible.[7]

"Short-Term Disappearances"

One recent evolution in the practice of enforced disappearances in Pakistan is that of "short-term" disappearances, which is a trend that has also been documented in a number of other countries.

In a recent report, the UN Working Group on Enforced or Involuntary Disappearances expressed alarm at the "frightening trend" of "short-term enforced disappearances" in a number of countries around the world. The WGEID described short-term disappearances as "the unacknowledged deprivation of liberty which puts the individual concerned outside the protection of the law for a limited amount of time."[8] It emphasized that "there is no time limit, no matter how short, for an enforced disappearance to occur," and "when a person is disappeared, every anguished minute spent by his or her relatives without news of that person is a minute too long."[9]

The WGEID's commentary echoes the observations of the UN Human Rights Committee. In 2015, responding to a case alleging enforced disappearance before the UN Human Rights Committee, committee member Olivier de Frouville pointed toward the evolution of enforced disappearance since the turn of the century. According to him, in the 1970s, 1980s, and even the 1990s, only a few people survived enforced disappearance. Most of the victims, once placed in secret detention, died after being subjected to torture or were summarily executed. In some countries, victims of disappearances would "reappear" years or even decades later, "completely shattered by the experience of confinement," which included torture and other forms of ill treatment.[10]

Nowadays, he noted, "short-term disappearances have proliferated," where victims are placed outside the protection of the law in secret detention before being released weeks or months later, sometimes after having been tortured and without having been brought in front of a judge.

As discussed earlier, this description captures recent trends in Pakistan. Victims of the practice of "short-term enforced disappearance" include bloggers, journalists, peace activists, and others who are critical of the state.[11] After being interrogated in secret detention for weeks or months and reportedly being subjected to torture and other forms of ill treatment, they are released without being charged with any offense.

Some recent examples include the case of Matiullah Jan, a journalist, who was abducted, and his whereabouts remained unknown for twelve hours before he was released, and Sajid Gondul, who "disappeared" for five days before his return. Circumstances in both these cases suggest the involvement of the state.

In January 2017, four Pakistani activists—Ahmad Waqas Goraya, Asim Saeed, Salman Haider, and Ahmed Raza Naseer—were also "missing." They were released weeks after their abduction. At least three of them have written or spoken about the involvement of the intelligence agencies in their enforced disappearance and have made allegations of torture during their secret detention.[12]

In other cases, people are kept in secret detention outside the legal framework for some time before being handed over to the police, often with a falsified arrest warrant in an attempt to hide the real date of arrest. They may also be detained in internment centers in the former Federally Administered Tribal Areas, now a part of the Khyber Pakhtunkhwa Province.

Reports of the Commission of Inquiry on Enforced Disappearance too highlight this trend. In the last two years alone, the commission has documented dozens of cases where the "disappeared" person has "returned home" after weeks or months of going "missing" or been "traced" in an internment center.

The fact that the victims "reappear" or "return" does not mean these cases can be treated as just another form of arbitrary detention. To be completely cut off from the outside world and be placed beyond the protection of the law has a particularly devastating impact on a person's right to dignity and well-being. This makes the act a serious crime of enforced disappearance, for which the individuals responsible are liable to criminal accountability.

The Commission of Inquiry on Enforced Disappearances, however, considers such cases "resolved" and has failed to take action against perpetrators. Curiously, the commission's terms of reference specify that it may direct the registration of FIRs only in the disappearance of an "untraced" person. This effectively means that once a person subjected to an enforced disappearance is found, the commission no longer has the competency to register FIRs against perpetrators (see section on the COIED below).

NATIONAL LEGAL FRAMEWORK

Enforced disappearance is not recognized as a distinct crime in Pakistan. On the rare occasion that police register criminal complaints in such cases, they do so for the crimes of "abduction" or "kidnapping."[13] Police also register complaints of enforced disappearances under Section 346 of the Penal Code that relates to "wrongful confinement in secret," and prescribes a penalty of two-year imprisonment.

When registering a complaint under these provisions for alleged enforced disappearances, police often refuse to identify members of the security or intelligence forces as the alleged perpetrators. In most cases, such complaints are filed against "unknown persons."

Pakistan's Constitution guarantees the right to life, liberty, and security of a person; the right to a fair trial; and right to freedom from arbitrary arrest and detention as "fundamental rights." Allegations of violations of these constitutional protections, which are necessarily invoked in cases of enforced disappearance, have been challenged at the Supreme Court and high courts as human rights petitions.

Role of the Judiciary

Families of "disappeared" people have also made *habeas corpus* petitions in the high courts and the Supreme Court under Articles 199 and 184(3) of the Constitution respectively, requesting the courts to find out the whereabouts of their "missing" loved ones. Courts have responded by directing concerned authorities to "trace" the whereabouts of "missing persons" and producing them before court. However, despite the defiant attitude and repeated failure of members of security forces to follow directions of the courts in cases of enforced disappearances, the courts have refrained from using its contempt of court powers to compel authorities to implement their orders.

The Supreme Court first took up the issue of the widespread practice of enforced disappearances in Pakistan in December 2005, when it took *suo motu* notice under Article 184(3) of the Constitution of a news report citing the growing numbers of enforced disappearances in the country.[14]

Soon after, the Human Rights Commission of Pakistan (HRCP) petitioned the Supreme Court under Article 184(3) to take notice of more cases of enforced disappearance. The HRCP submitted a list of 148 "missing persons"—individuals allegedly subjected to enforced disappearance—to the Supreme Court.

During the hearings, the Supreme Court acknowledged evidence establishing that many of the "disappeared" were in the custody of the security agencies and summoned high-level military intelligence officials before the Supreme Court to explain the legal basis of the detention and to physically produce the detainees.[15]

As the number of cases of enforced disappearances pending in the Supreme Court steadily grew, the Court directed the government to establish a Commission of Inquiry on Enforced Disappearance to investigate enforced disappearances across Pakistan and to provide recommendations to curb the practice. The government complied with the Court's orders and constituted a commission in 2010.

In October 2012, the Supreme Court issued an interim order in what is known as the "Balochistan Law and Order case." The Court held that there was "overwhelming evidence" implicating the Frontier Corps (a paramilitary force) in cases of "missing persons" and acknowledged that at least a hundred people were still "missing" from Balochistan.[16] The Court also noted that the issue of "missing persons" has "become a dilemma as their nears and dears are running from pillar to post spending their energy despite poverty and helplessness but without any success, which aggravated the mistrust not only on law enforcing agencies but also on civil administration."[17]

A year later, in one its strongest judgments yet on the practice of enforced disappearances, the Supreme Court held in the *Mohabbat Shah* case[18] that the unauthorized and unacknowledged removal of detainees from an internment center amounted to an enforced disappearance. The Court expressed concern at the "kafkaesque workings"[19] of the security forces and held that "no law enforcing agency can forcibly detain a person without showing his whereabouts to his relatives for a long period" and that, currently, there was no law in force in Pakistan that allowed the armed forces to "unauthorizedly detain undeclared detainees." The Court gave reference to a number of international instruments including the DED and ICPPED, and said that the practice of enforced disappearance is considered a "crime against humanity" all over the world.[20] Finally, the Court held that armed forces personnel responsible for the enforced disappearances should be dealt with "strictly in accordance with law."[21]

Notably, the Supreme Court also held that even though Pakistan has not yet become a party to the International Convention for the Protection of All Persons from Enforced Disappearance (ICPPED), principles enunciated in the convention are applicable in Pakistan in the interpretation of other rights such as the right to life.[22]

The government responded by filing for a review of the judgment, asking the court to delete remarks implicating the agencies as such findings could "demoralize the troops."

In March 2014, after repeated court orders, the defense minister lodged FIRs for wrongful confinement against some military officers allegedly responsible for the "disappearances." However, the provincial government reportedly referred the matter to the military for further investigation and possible trial under the Army Act, 1952.[23] Since military trials are secret and not open to the public, what became of the case is not known.

Most recently, in October 2018, the Peshawar High Court (PHC) set aside the convictions of over seventy people who were tried by military courts on various terrorism-related charges. The court ordered their release after finding the proceedings had been conducted in bad faith and that there was effectively no evidence against them.

Significantly, the judgment highlighted the link between enforced disappearances and proceedings before military courts. It described how a number of accused were picked up by security authorities as far back as 2008 and kept in secret detention for many years before their military trials. Even when questioned by the courts, state agencies kept denying any knowledge of their whereabouts, until their names appeared in their press statements about people convicted and sentenced to death. The court indicated that in many cases, the proceedings appeared to have been a way of giving legal cover to the practice of enforced disappearances and secret detentions in internment centers.[24]

The government appealed the PHC judgment before the Supreme Court, where it is still pending.

In a number of cases, courts have directed that family members of individuals allegedly subjected to enforced disappearance be provided compensation "for their failure to trace the whereabouts of a missing person."

The Islamabad High Court delivered one of the most significant judgments in this regard in 2018.[25] The court considered enforced disappearance a violation of a number of fundamental rights and denounced the practice in strong terms:

> Enforced disappearance affects in a complex and profound manner because the person subjected to disappearance is not the only victim. His or her close relatives, particularly those who are dependents, suffer the most. Their anguish and suffering cannot be comprehended because their loved ones are removed from the protection of the law. By removing a person from protection of the law gives the captors the freedom and license to do what they feel like. This creates an environment of uncertainty for the dependents and other family members. The perpetrators get a license to subject the victim to torture, which is otherwise strictly forbidden under the law, and in the case of death it enables them to cause the body to vanish without a trace. The fundamental rights of the victims guaranteed under the Constitution become irrelevant and virtually suspended. It creates anguish, insecurity and fear for the close relatives, exposing them to grave economic and social consequences, particularly if the abductee is the sole breadwinner . . . it results in multiple violations of fundamental rights guaranteed under the Constitution. It is, therefore, one of the most heinous crimes and cannot be justified on any ground whatsoever, particularly under the Constitution of Pakistan. It is definitely a crime which ought to be given the highest priority by the State instrumentalities and functionaries and their conduct and attitude towards the victims must manifest their intent and will as guardians of the fundamental rights of citizens.[26]

The court made a number of directions to the state regarding enforced disappearances, including any complaint that alleged or disclosed characteristics in the nature as that of an enforced disappearance shall be treated by the state as a heinous act and thus dealt with accordingly; public functionaries will have the onus to dispel any impression regarding the involvement of the state or its instrumentalities in an alleged abduction, which they shall discharge by establishing prompt, responsive, and effective investigations; if it is established that the criminal justice system failed in responding promptly, followed by conducting effective investigations into a complaint of a citizen alleging enforced disappearance of a loved one, then the state depending on the facts and circumstances in each case shall become liable to compensate the person if it can be shown that the latter's fundamental rights were infringed; and that the Special Branch, Intelligence Bureau, the Inter Services Intelligence and the Military Intelligence have the duty to collect information and promptly report to the concerned functionaries regarding any incident of abduction of a citizen having the characteristics of an enforced disappearance and to take effective measures in tracing the whereabouts of the victim.

Commission of Inquiry on Enforced Disappearances

The government constituted a Commission of Inquiry on Enforced Disappearances (COIED) in 2010 on the Supreme Court's orders. The mandate of the commission expired in December 2010, and in March 2011, the Interior Ministry formed a new commission to continue its work.

The notification establishing the commission gives it a broad mandate, which include tracing the whereabouts of allegedly enforced disappeared persons; fixing responsibility of individuals or institutions responsible; registering or directing the registration of First Information Reports (FIRs) against named individuals who in the view of the commission were involved either directly or indirectly in the disappearance of an untraced person; recommending Standard Operating Procedures (SOPs) to be adopted by law enforcement and intelligence agencies through which arrests/detentions of a suspected person could be recorded in one database, and recommending SOPs to be adopted by all law enforcement and intelligence agencies through which the arrest/detention of a suspected person could be declared under the provisions of existing Acts/Rules.

The COIED was initially established for six months, but its mandate has since been extended a number of times, most recently in August 2020 for another three years.

The repeated extensions to the commission's mandate seem to indicate it has been a success. Yet many victims' groups—especially from Balochistan—have boycotted the COIED, and other human rights organizations are deeply critical of its work. The UN Human Rights Committee and the UN Working Group on Enforced or Involuntary Disappearances have also expressed concerns about the commission, including the insufficient resources allocated to it and law enforcement agencies' noncompliance with its binding orders.

Performance of the COIED

According to its monthly progress report from January 2021, the commission received sixty-seven new cases in December 2020, bringing the total number of cases received since March 2011 to 6,921.

The largest number of cases received by the commission are from Khyber Pakhtunkhwa (2,942—out of which 291 were reported from the former Federally Administered Tribal Areas), followed by Sindh (1,643), Punjab (1,432), Balochistan (537), Islamabad (300), Azad Jammu and Kashmir (58), and Gilgit Baltistan (9).

Out of the 6,921 cases received by the commission, 4,798 cases have been "disposed of" and 2,123 cases are still pending. According to the commission's monthly reports, cases which the commission categorizes as "disposed of" include those where people had been "traced" (in jails, internment centers, or their homes); where they have been found dead; and where the commission "closed" the case after concluding that they were not cases of enforced disappearance, where the complainant provided an incomplete address, where the complainant withdrew the complainant, or in cases of "non-prosecution" by the complainants.[27]

The commission's monthly reports show that in 857 cases, "missing persons" were eventually found in internment centers, and 535 people were "traced" in prisons. In a number of cases, the "missing persons" were traced in internment centers years after their families registered a complaint before the COIED. Mujahid Ali, for example, was reported as "missing" in January 2015. The Military Intelligence, however, only acknowledged that he was being detained in an internment center in Lakki Marwat in July 2020, more than five years after he went "missing."[28] It should be recalled that irrespective of whether the fate or whereabouts is contemporaneously clarified, a period of unacknowledged detention remains an enforced disappearance, which is a crime under international law.

The commission, however, has not "fixed responsibility" on any person or organization, or directed the registration of FIRs against those responsible for concealing the whereabouts of the disappeared people who were eventually traced in detention centers.

The commission's reports also indicate that in 220 cases, "dead bodies" of missing persons were found, and since the "missing people" were no longer alive, their cases stand disposed of. In a number of such cases, the commission has also stated that the police or other security forces had killed the "missing person" in an "encounter."[29] It should be recalled that the fact that a person subsequently turns up dead has no bearing on whether the crime of enforced disappearance has occurred, though in many cases it will also be indicia of other crimes, such as extrajudicial killing.

Again, the commission's reports are silent on why such an admission of "encounter" was made months or years after the registration of their cases as "missing persons," and what steps, if any, had been taken to fix responsibility on perpetrators.

Failure to Ensure Accountability

In its follow-up report to its mission to Pakistan, the UN Working Group on Enforced and Involuntary Disappearances (WGEID) found "there is a climate of impunity in Pakistan with regard to enforced disappearances, and the authorities are not sufficiently dedicated to investigate cases of enforced disappearance and hold the perpetrators accountable."[30]

This also appears to be true for the COIED. While the commission has made some progress in documenting cases of enforced disappearances and "trace the whereabouts" of a number of disappeared people, it has failed in holding perpetrators accountable.

The COIED's monthly reports are silent on whether it has taken any steps to bring perpetrators of enforced disappearance to justice. The only indication that there had been some progress in this regard is a statement by the chairperson of the commission, Justice (r) Javed Iqbal, to the Senate Human Rights Committee, where he said, "action had been taken against 153 army personnel" in relation to their role in enforced disappearances.[31]

The commission's sole focus on "tracing" people who are "missing" is also visible in the case of Idrees Khattak, a human rights defender, was subject to enforced disappearance in November 2019. His whereabouts remained unknown for more than six months until June 2020, when it was submitted before the commission that he was being tried under the Official Secrets Act (the commission's report does not specify the government agency that acknowledged the detention). Even though Idrees Khattak's whereabouts continue to remain unknown, the commission considers his case "disposed of" and is yet to take action against perpetrators.

The failure of the COIED also demonstrates a larger problem: Though ostensibly formed to provide a measure of public accountability, more often than not, COIs have promoted impunity by diverting investigation of human rights violations and crime through the criminal justice process into a parallel ad hoc mechanism vulnerable to political interference and manipulation. Recent experiences in Pakistan, the South Asia region, and around the world suggest that without substantial reform to existing law and practice, continued use of COIs will not succeed in providing effective remedies to victims of human rights violations.[32]

INTERNATIONAL LEGAL FRAMEWORK

Article 2 of the International Convention for the Protection of All Persons from Enforced Disappearance (ICPPED) defines enforced disappearance as "the arrest, detention, abduction or any other form of deprivation of liberty by agents of the State or by persons or groups of persons acting with the authorization, support or acquiescence of the State, followed by a refusal to acknowledge the deprivation of liberty or by concealment of the fate or whereabouts of the disappeared person, which place such a person outside the protection of the law."[33]

The ICPPED is the leading global instrument setting out international standards on enforced disappearance. It was adopted by consensus at the UN General Assembly in 2006, and now has sixty-three states parties with a further thirty-five states having signed but not yet ratified. The ICPPED builds on and establishes particular treaty obligations building on the UN Declaration on the Protection of all Persons from Enforced Disappearance, which had been adopted with the agreement of all states at the UN General Assembly in 1992.[34]

Pakistan has not yet signed or become a party to the ICPPED. However, as discussed earlier, the Supreme Court of Pakistan has held the principles of the convention were applicable in Pakistan as the convention was inextricably linked with the right to life, guaranteed by Pakistan's Constitution.[35] In addition, Pakistan is a party to other treaties that establish binding obligations protecting against enforced disappearance. These include the International Covenant on Civil and Political Rights (ICCPR) and the Convention Against Torture and Other Cruel, Inhuman or Degrading Treatment or Punishment (CAT). Although enforced disappearance is not expressly mentioned in either treaty, any perpetration of an enforced disappearance inherently involves one or more acts that are prohibited by these treaties. The international bodies mandated to supervise state compliance with these treaties (i.e., the Human Rights Committee and the Committee against Torture) have consequently developed extensive jurisprudence and guidance on the application of the more general treaty provisions to acts of enforced disappearance, including with regards to the right to life, the right to be free from torture and other cruel, inhuman or degrading treatment, the right to liberty and security, and recognition as a person before the law.[36]

Human Rights Committee

The UN Human Rights Committee conducted a review of Pakistan's implementation of the ICCPR for the first time in July 2017.[37]

In its concluding observations, the committee emphasized how the practice of enforced disappearance constituted multiple violations of Pakistan's obligations under the ICCPR expressed its concern at:

> the high incidence of enforced disappearances and extrajudicial killings allegedly perpetrated by the police and military and security forces; the absence of explicit criminalization of enforced disappearances in domestic law; the Actions (in Aid of Civil Power) Regulation, 2011, which provides for detention by the army without warrants or judicial supervision and indefinite detention in military internment centres, and the allegedly high number of persons held in secret detention under the Regulation. It is also concerned by reports that the families of disappeared persons are subjected to threats and intimidation to discourage them from filing cases of enforced disappearance; by the lack of prompt and effective investigation and the very low rate of prosecution and conviction of perpetrators; and by the inadequate remedies and reparation provided for victims and their families. While welcoming the establishment of the Commission of Inquiry on Enforced Disappearances, the Committee remains concerned by the insufficient power and resources allocated to the Commission; the non-compliance with the Commission's orders by the relevant authorities; and the high number of cases brought before the Commission that remain unresolved, with no criminal proceedings brought against perpetrators.

The committee recommended that Pakistan criminalize enforced disappearance and put an end to the practice of enforced disappearance and secret detention and ensure that "all allegations of enforced disappearance and extrajudicial killings are promptly and thoroughly investigated; all perpetrators are prosecuted and punished, with penalties commensurate with the gravity of the crimes; families of disappeared persons and their lawyers and witnesses are protected; and a mechanism is put in place for full and prompt reparation for victims and their families. It should further strengthen the authority and the capacity (financial and personnel) of the Commission of Inquiry on Enforced Disappearances so that the latter can function effectively."

Committee against Torture

Similarly, in its Concluding Observations following the first review of Pakistan's implementation of the convention against Torture and Other Cruel, Inhuman and Degrading Treatment, the Committee against Torture stated that it was deeply concerned at reports that "members of the State party's military forces, intelligence forces, such as the Inter-Services Intelligence agency, and paramilitary forces, such as the Frontier Corps and the Pakistan Rangers, have been implicated in a significant number of cases of extrajudicial executions involving torture and enforced disappearances."

The Committee also expressed concern that "hundreds of enforced disappearances have been reported in recent years in the State party and that the

State party's authorities have not taken adequate steps to investigate the reports and identify those responsible."

The committee recommended that Pakistan "should ensure that enforced disappearance is a specific crime in domestic law, with penalties that take into account the grave nature of such disappearances."[38]

The committee also recommended that Pakistan should:

> ensure that enforced disappearance is a specific crime in domestic law, with penalties that take into account the grave nature of such disappearances. It should ensure that all enforced disappearances are thoroughly, promptly and effectively investigated, suspects are prosecuted and those found guilty are punished with sanctions proportionate to the gravity of their crimes. It should also take measures to strengthen the independence, resources and investigative capacity of the national Commission of Inquiry on Enforced Disappearances to enable it to fulfil its mandate effectively and independently. Furthermore, the State party should implement the advice of the Working Group on Enforced or Involuntary Disappearances, especially with regard to increasing the power of the National Commission of Inquiry on Enforced Disappearances and allocating it adequate resources.

UN Working Group on Enforced and Involuntary Disappearances

On February 26, 2013, the United Nations Working Group on Enforced and Involuntary Disappearances (WGEID) published its report on Pakistan, following the WGEID's visit to the country in September 2012.

The report expressed concern at the continuing practice of enforced disappearances in Pakistan and made a series of recommendations to the government. One of the recommendations was that the crime of enforced disappearance be established and included in the Criminal Code of Pakistan in line with the definition given in the Convention on Enforced Disappearances.[39] The WGEID also recommended that Pakistan review its "constitutional, legislative and regulatory provisions, in particular 'preventive detention' regimes and rules allowing for arrest without warrant," and ensure "deprived of liberty shall be held in an officially recognized place of detention."

In its follow-up report to the Human Rights Council in September 2016, the WGEID regretted that "most of the recommendations contained in its country visit report have not been implemented," and again reiterated the importance of recognizing enforced disappearance as a distinct, autonomous crime.[40]

In its most recent report to the UN Human Rights Council, the WGEID said that it remained concerned that it "unceasingly continues to receive allegations of enforced disappearances in Pakistan."[41]

Other Commitments

The Pakistani government has also committed to criminalize enforced disappearances and bring perpetrators to account on multiple occasions before a number of international forums. This includes accepting recommendations during Pakistan's first and second Universal Periodic Reviews on recognizing enforced disappearance as an autonomous crime.[42]

NO END IN SIGHT?

UN experts have called enforced disappearance "a tool for repression" and a "technique of terror." They have expressed concern that in a number of countries, it is being taught to intelligence and security officers as a response to "legitimate civil strife demanding democracy, freedom of expression or religion."[43]

This, disturbingly, also rings true for Pakistan. In the last few years, there has been a severe clampdown on civil society in the country, and the space for dissent has progressively shrunk. This is due to a number of factors, including repressive laws that are used by the state to silence critical voices. One such law is Section 124A of the Pakistan Penal Code that relates to "sedition" or exciting "disaffection" against the government—a colonial relic that remains a part of Pakistan's criminal law even after independence. Political activists, human rights defenders and journalists have been charged with sedition merely for exercising or demanding their constitutional rights. Other such laws include the Anti-Terrorism Act, 1997, and the Prevention of Electronic Crimes Act, 2016, both of which contain vaguely drafted, oppressive provisions that are easily misused to target critics.

It has become a cliché to speak of a "crisis of impunity," but the phrase is entirely apt in describing the situation in Pakistan, where impunity for human rights violations has become institutionalized and systemized. It is also essential in understanding why the practice of enforced disappearances has persisted and is spreading—both in terms of geographical reach and also the categories of people being targeted.

"Impunity" means the impossibility of bringing violators of serious crimes and gross human rights violations to account, typically because there is an absence of a proper investigation that would lead to the arrest, prosecution, and sentencing of those responsible. It results in concealing the truth; denying victims the right to effective remedy and reparation; and emboldening perpetrators of human rights violations.

Despite the government's claims that it "pursues action against perpetrators who have been involved in enforced disappearances"[44] before international forums, the country's current legal framework has proven to be completely ineffective in responding to such cases—it has failed to reveal the truth, bring perpetrators of the practice to account, and deter similar violations in future. If Pakistan is to stop the practice of enforced disappearances, it must start bringing those responsible for this practice to justice. At the minimum, this would require recognizing enforced disappearance as an autonomous offense (and until such time, prosecuting such acts under existing laws); empowering independent institutions like the National Commission on Human Rights to investigate cases of alleged disappearances, notwithstanding the identity of the perpetrators; ensuring cases of serious human rights violations are only tried by civilian courts, including where members of the security apparatus are allegedly responsible; and as recommended by the WGEID, enacting "clear rules and dedicated institutions . . . to ensure the oversight and accountability of law enforcement and intelligence agencies."

Any progress toward such action, however, has been slow. In August 2018, the Senate's Functional Committee on Human Rights urged the human rights ministry to draft legislation to recognize "enforced disappearance" as a distinct, autonomous offense. A few days later, Minister for Human Rights Shireen Mazari announced that the government is considering tabling a law to criminalize enforced disappearance. Finally, in June 2021, the National Assembly of Pakistan passed a bill including "enforced disappearance" as an offense in the Penal Code, carrying a penalty of up to ten years imprisonment. The Senate, however, has not passed the bill as of July 2021.

Enacting legislation to criminalize enforced disappearances would be an important step to acknowledge that enforced disappearance is unlawful, and recognized as a "heinous crime" by the state. However, a more comprehensive set of reforms—both in law and policy—are required to ensure that perpetrators are brought to justice and victims get remedies and reparation. As illustrated by the *Mohabbat Shah* case referred to above, perpetrators of enforced disappearance escape justice due to a number of reasons including lack of political will to hold those responsible to account; trial of accused in military courts; the lack of oversight for intelligence and security agencies; and often sanction by the highest authorities.

Additionally, as discussed earlier, enforced disappearance must not be seen as a stand-alone problem but understood in a wider context of human rights violations and the silencing of dissent in the country.

Unless this climate of oppression changes and there is political commitment at all levels of the state to respect the rights of people and end the crisis of impunity for perpetrators, there remains a real possibility that even if enforced disappearances are reduced, they will be replaced with some other "technique of terror" and control.

NOTES

1. Tullio Scovazzi and Gabriella Citroni, *Martinus Nijhoff Publishers*, "The Struggle against Enforced Disappearance and the 2007 United Nations Convention," p.4.

2. Report of the Working Group on Enforced or Involuntary Disappearances, UN Doc A/HRC/45/13, August 2020.

3. Report of the Working Group on Enforced or Involuntary Disappearances on its mission to Pakistan, 26 February 2013, UN Doc. A/HRC/22/45/Add.2, para 33.

4. Ibid, para 34.

5. See, for example, "Concerns voiced over rise in 'enforced disappearances' in Sindh," *The News*, 29 July 2017, accessed at: https://www.thenews.com.pk/print/219686-Concerns-voiced-over-rise-in-enforced-disappearances-in-Sindh and *Human Rights Commission of Pakistan*," HRCP's alarm at missing men in SIndh turning up dead," 5 December 2014, accessed at: http://hrcp-web.org/hrcpweb/hrcps-alarm-at-missing-men-in-sindh-turning-up-dead/

6. http://www.undocs.org/A/HRC/45/13

7. See, for example, *International Commission of Jurists*, "Military Injustice in Pakistan", June 2016, accessed at: http://www.icj.org/wp-content/uploads/2016/06/Pakistan-Military-court-Advocacy-Analysis-brief-2016-ENG.pdf.

8. https://www.ohchr.org/EN/NewsEvents/Pages/DisplayNews.aspx?NewsID=20505&+LangID=E

9. https://www.ohchr.org/EN/NewsEvents/Pages/DisplayNews.aspx?NewsID=20416&LangID=E

10. Communication No. 2038/2011, Views adopted by the Committee at its 114th session (29 June-24 July 2015), UN Doc. CCPR/C/114/D/2038/201

11. See, for example, Pakistan: UN expert calls for return of four disappeared human rights and social media activists: https://news.un.org/en/story/2017/01/549202-pakistan-un-expert-calls-return-four-disappeared-human-rights-and-social-media

12. See, for example, Pakistan blogger Aasim Saeed says he was tortured, 24 October 2017, accessed at: https://www.bbc.com/news/world-asia-41662595, "Pakistan activist Waqass Goraya: The state tortured me," 9 March 2017, accessed at: https://www.bbc.com/news/world-asia-39219307, and https://www.bbc.com/urdu/pakistan-42577193

13. Sections 359 to 368 of the Pakistan Penal Code relate to the crimes of "kidnapping" and "abduction." The crime of kidnapping is of two kinds: kidnapping from Pakistan and kidnapping from lawful guardianship, and is punishable with a maximum of seven years imprisonment and a fine. The crime of "abduction" is regulated by section 362 of the Penal Code and is defined as "whoever by force compels, or by any deceitful means induces, any person to go from any place." Section 364 prescribes a punishment of ten years imprisonment for the crime of "kidnapping or abducting in order to murder." Section 365 relates to kidnapping or abducting "any person with intent to cause that person to be secretly and wrongfully confined" and prescribes a punishment of a maximum of seven years imprisonment.

14. Article 184(3) of Pakistan's Constitution enables the Supreme Court to assume jurisdiction over matters involving a question of 'public importance' with reference to the 'enforcement of any of the fundamental rights' of the citizens of Pakistan. It may do so either on the application of party (a petition) or of its own accord (commonly referred to as *suo motu* notice).

15. See, for example, Reema Omer, *Dawn*, "Justice for the disappeared," 29 July 2013, accessed at : https://www.dawn.com/news/1032711/justice-for-the-disappeared

16. Constitution petition no.77 of 2010, para 14.

17. *Ibid*, para 10.

18. HRC No.29388-K/13, 10 December 2013.

19. *Ibid*., para 15.

20. *Ibid.,* para 16. Under international law, an enforced disappearance is a crime against humanity if committed as part of a widespread or systematic attack directed against any civilian population, with knowledge of the attack (See Art. 7, para 1 of the Rome Statute).

21. See *International Commission of Jurists*, "ICJ urges Senate to reject 'Protection of Pakistan' Bill", 14 May 2014, accessed at: http://www.icj.org/icj-urges-senate-to-reject-protection-of-pakistan-bill/, p. 5.

22. *Ibid.*

23. Nasir Iqbal, *Dawn News*, "Main accused will be court-martialled, govt tells SC," 17 April 2014, accessed at: https://www.dawn.com/news/1100408/main-accused-will-be-court-martialled-govt-tells-sc

24. For a detailed analysis of the link between enforced disappearances and military courts, see *International Commission of Jurists*, "Military Injustice in Pakistan," https://www.icj.org/wp-content/uploads/2016/06/Pakistan-Military-court-Advocacy-Analysis-brief-2016-ENG.pdf

25. Mahera Sajid VersusStation House Officer, Police Station Shalimar & 6 others, W. P. No. 2974/2016.

26. Ibid., para 21.

27. As provided in the COIED's progress reports.

28. Progress report of the COIED, June 2020.

29. Progress report of the COIED, January 2020.

30. Report of the Working Group on Enforced or Involuntary Disappearances, Addendum, Follow-up report to the recommendations made by the Working Group, 13 September 2016, UN Doc. A/HRC/33/51/Add.7.

31. "The Chairman Committee (Senator Mustafa Khokhar) inquired if any action had been initiated against those individuals who were thought to be involved in abducting people and depriving missing persons of their liberty. The Committee was apprised that action had been taken against 153 army personnel," as reproduced in "Missing Persons and More Questions," Farhatullah Babar, The Friday Times, accessed at: https://www.thefridaytimes.com/missing-persons-and-more-questions/

32. For a detailed analysis of the COIED's performance and legal framework, see International Commission of Jurists, Entrenching Impunity, "Denying Redress:The Commission of Inquiry on Enforced Disappearances in Pakistan," September 2020,

accessed at: https://www.icj.org/pakistan-commission-of-inquiry-on-enforced-disappearances-has-failed-in-providing-justice-to-victims/

33. Article 2, UN General Assembly, *International Convention for the Protection of All Persons from Enforced Disappearance*, 20 December 2006.

34. UN Commission on Human Rights, *Declaration on the Protection of All Persons from Enforced Disappearance*, 28 February 1992, E/CN.4/RES/1992/29.

35. HRC No.29388-K/13, 10 December 2013.

36. For a detailed discussion, see International Commission of Jurists, "No More Missing Persons: the criminalization of enforced disappearances in South Asia," August 2017, available at: https://www.icj.org/wp-content/uploads/2017/08/South-Asia-Enforced-Disappearance-Publications-Reports-Thematic-Reports-2017-ENG.pdf

37. *UN Human Rights Committee*, "Concluding observations on the initial report of Pakistan," July 2017, UN Doc. CCPR/C/PAK/CO/1.

38. *Committee against Torture*, "Concluding observations on the initial report of Pakistan," 1 June 2017, UN Doc. CAT/C/PAK/CO/1.

39. Report of the Working Group on Enforced or Involuntary Disappearances on its mission to Pakistan, 26 February 2013, UN Doc. A/HRC/22/45/Add.2, p. 20.

40. Report of the Working Group on Enforced or Involuntary Disappearances, Addendum, Follow-up report to the recommendations made by the Working Group, 13 September 2016, UN Doc. A/HRC/33/51/Add.7.

41. http://www.undocs.org/A/HRC/45/13

42. There have been numerous other calls on the Government to recognize enforced disappearance as a distinct crime. For example, the Government constituted a "Task Force on Missing Persons" in 2013 to provide recommendations on how to deal with the prevalent practice. The Task Force submitted its report in December 2013. While the report has not been made public, members of the Task Force have revealed that one of the recommendations in its report was the criminalization of the practice.

43. https://news.un.org/en/story/2011/08/385232-all-states-must-end-heinous-crime-enforced-disappearances-un-demands

44. List of issues in relation to the initial report of Pakistan, Addendum, Replies of Pakistan to the list of issues, CCPR/C/PAK/Q/1/Add.1, 23 March 2017.

Chapter 11

The Use of Special Criminal Courts and Tribunals in Pakistan

Marva Khan

INTRODUCTION

Chapter 1 of the Constitution of the Islamic Republic of Pakistan, 1973 ("Constitution"), grants multiple fundamental rights, some of which are intrinsically essential to Pakistan's criminal procedure. Right to due process of law (Article 10), right to a fair trial (Article 10A), and "dignity of man" (Article 14), are some examples of such rights. Out of these three provisions, Article 10A was introduced via the 18th Constitutional Amendment, 2010. This amendment also introduced two other fundamental rights: the right to information and the right to education.[1]

Conversely, Article 10 of the Constitution, after enlisting protections similar to *Miranda* rights, sets the parameters for preventive detention. In preventive detention, a person, who is deemed to be "acting in a manner prejudicial to the integrity, security or defence of Pakistan or any part thereof, or external affairs of Pakistan, or public order, or maintenance of supplies or services" can be picked up by the state, possibly without being informed about the reason for their detention. Such a person has no right to legal counsel, nor do they have a right to be produced in front of a magistrate. Instead, the detainee is to be produced in front of a Review Board every three months. If the detaining state agency feels that the reasons for detention can further lead to state security threats, they are not bound to inform the Review Board about grounds for arrest either. The infamous *Missing Persons' Case* in the Supreme Court of Pakistan (SC) and the numerous writ petitions filed in across Pakistan's five High Courts illustrate how pervasive the practice of preventive detention is. In the ongoing parliamentary session, the current government also tried to pass an anti-terrorism statute to bolster preventive detention mechanisms further. This makes one ponder about the veracity of rights provided for in Article 10 clauses 1 to 3, when clauses 4 to 9 of the same provision completely override all the aforementioned rights, by retaining the colonial legacy enshrined in the Government of India Acts, and used by the British to control local dissidents in the Indian subcontinent.

Upon a more in-depth evaluation of Pakistan's criminal justice system, one can see that many necessary guarantees provided to defendants by criminal justice systems across common law countries are often missing in the special criminal courts and tribunals established by the government of Pakistan over the years. One recent example of such criticism came from the Supreme Court of Pakistan in the case of *Khawaja Saad Rafique & Khawaja Salman Rafique v. National Accountability Bureau* (2020).[2] In this 87-page judgment, the 2-member bench highlights how the National Accountability Bureau (NAB), created through the NAB Ordinance in 1999 by the then-president, General Musharraf, not only infringes upon the concept of separation of powers but has been recurrently used for political victimization. The procedure in NAB Courts is fundamentally inconsistent with principles of prosecution, as the burden of proof is placed on the defendant, rather than the prosecution. While this is a very significant jurisprudential development, it is pertinent to note that in 2001, the Supreme Court dismissed constitutional challenges brought against NAB and NAB Ordinance in the case of *Khan Asfandyar Wali v. Federation of Pakistan, PLD 2001 SC 607.*

Trends similar to the usage of preventive detention and NAB functionality are also evident in other special criminal courts. Another example of constitutional curtailment of fundamental rights was the four-year civilian jurisdiction granted to military courts in Pakistan via the 21st and 23rd Constitutional Amendments. This was granted under the twenty-point agenda of the National Action Plan (NAP).[3] The NAP was the government's response to a terrorist attack on the Army Public School, Peshawar, in December 2014.

In recent years, the notion of Pakistan being a police state has grown stronger. The abridgment of rights including fair trial and due process became more acceptable after the NAP was introduced. This was done on the pretext of temporary measures instituted for capturing and prosecuting terrorists, and curbing terrorism in Pakistan. However, as the appeals from these forums illustrated, a nexus developed between preventive detention and the military courts, further exacerbating Pakistan's *Missing Persons' Cases*.[4] What is even more problematic about the operations under preventive detention and prosecution by military courts is that only data sources available is the information selectively released by the government or the Inter-Services Public Relations (ISPR).[5] While cases emanating from these platforms have been challenged at the level of the High Courts and Supreme Court, most of these judgments are not reported, hence only secondary sources are available for analysis and perusal. Despite the lack of information about these adjudications, what information is publically available reflects blatant violations of the most basic fundamental rights. One reason for this, however, is that both these platforms fall within constitutionally acceptable exceptions to fundamental rights, as the chapter shall discuss in subsequent sections. The other cause of concern with military courts is the fact that the state granted judicial powers to what can be termed as a tribunal or a quasi-judicial body at best.

In addition to the state garnering more powers on the pretext of national security, there has been resurgence in the activities by NAB, a creation of the former dictator Pervez Musharraf, particularly since the current ruling party, Pakistan Tehreek-e-Insaf, came to power in 2018. While this is a statutory body created by a presidential ordinance, it is vital in illustrating the role of how usurpation of separation of powers and clash of institutions has resulted in blatant violations of fundamental rights by NAB, including the absence of free trial and due process. I have picked this particular platform among all the other special statutory courts that exist primarily because the consequent result of NAB's functionality has been similar to preventive detention and trial by military courts, *sans* the death penalty. Because NAB can retain defendants for a far longer time and make it significantly difficult to seek bail, and for other reasons discussed subsequently, NAB is starkly different from the regular criminal justice system. It has been used to curb dissent and limit the influence of the opposition parties and other critics of the state. It has also been used as a tool for limiting freedom of expression in the country. Even though NAB primarily deals with white-collared crimes, the impact of this institution is quite extreme.

This chapter will first analyze the basic protections provided by the Constitution to a person engulfed in the criminal justice system. The rights discussed include the safeguards to arrest and detention under Article 10, right to fair trial and due process under Article 10A, and the inviolable right to dignity enshrined under Article 14 of the Constitution. Next, the chapter shall discuss the creation and functionality of preventive detention, four-year long civilian jurisdiction exercised by military courts, and NAB in Pakistan from the lens of access and provision of aforementioned rights to defendants being prosecuted in these parallel criminal justice systems. The chapter shall also highlight how subversion of rights has been made easier through constitutional immunity granted to military courts and functionality of preventive detention. While such immunity is not extended to NAB, it still exercises broad punitive powers due to absence of a proper separation of powers within the institution itself. The chapter also discusses the special court that tried General Musharraf's treason case as the only outlier in this schematic. The subsequent ruling declaring the composition of this special court as invalid was a return to the previously existing balance.

It is important to note here that the creation of special courts in Pakistan is not a recent phenomenon. Special courts have been created during the life of the current Constitution for the purposes of accountability in cases of corruption and misappropriation, courts for speedy trials,[6] and courts of specialist nature such as consumer courts, GBV courts, labor courts, and so on. The focus of this chapter is to analyze the specialist forums being used pervasively in the current times, and assess where they stand when measured against constitutionally protected fundamental rights, namely, Articles 10, 10A, and 14 of the Constitution. Article 212B of the Constitution, which now stands repealed, allowed for the creation of special courts for the trial of heinous offenses. However, the state seems to have accelerated its efforts for increasing reliance on special adjudicating forums on the criminal side despite repealing of this provision.

FUNDAMENTAL RIGHTS

Before delving into a discussion on the functionality of special courts, one must analyze the fundamental rights enshrined in the Constitution, against which the courts' functionality is being assessed.

Part 1 Chapter 1 of the Constitution entails the bill of rights in Pakistan.[7] The first two clauses of Article 10 of the Constitution, titled "Safeguards to arrest and detention," pertain to widely recognized constitutional protections to defendants, namely being informed about reasons for arrest, right to consult and be defended by a legal counsel,[8] and the right to be produced in front of a magistrate within 24 hours of one's arrest.[9] These rights are also protected under Sections 60, 61, and 81 of the Criminal Procedure Code, 1898. Some rights that are further implied from these provisions include the right to being heard,[10] being afforded the opportunity to cross-examine the witnesses and evidence produced against oneself,[11] produce evidence to defend oneself,[12] the requirement for probable cause,[13] or "grounds of arrest [to] exist before the arrest takes place."[14] This principle is codified in the Criminal Procedure Code, 1898 as well.

Adding to the protections under Article 10(1) and (2), Article 10A was inserted via the 18th Constitutional Amendment, 2010, which reads as follows: "For *the determination of his civil rights and obligations* or in *any criminal charge against him* a person shall be entitled to a fair trial and due process" (emphasis added). The italicized phrases appear to have been lifted verbatim from Article 6 of the European Convention of Human Rights; however, the enumeration of what can be construed as fair trial has been left out of Article 10A.[15] Similarly, while the notion of due process of law was previously interpreted as an implied right by reading Articles 10 and 14 (dignity) together, while incorporating the concept into Article 10A, the drafters left out the phrase "of law." It remains to be seen if the courts insinuate any divergent meaning from this drafting exercise. The constitutional courts of Pakistan have been criticized for citing, yet failing, to expound upon the scope of Article 10A in detail, despite citing it in numerous judgments over the last decade.[16]

Article 14(1) reads "[t]he dignity of man and, subject to law, the privacy of home, shall be inviolable." From the text of the provision, it appears that it grants protection to dignity of all persons as an absolute and inviolable right. Article 14(2), however, prohibits "torture for the purpose of extracting evidence." The lack of an absolute prohibition on torture makes it rather problematic; although constitutional courts have never allowed torture for any purpose. Yet, as discussed later in the chapter, the Supreme Court did turn a blind eye toward allegations of torture raised by family members of those prosecuted by the military courts.

Furthermore, the Constitution grants original jurisdiction to the Supreme Court and the five High Courts of the country to hear matters pertaining to the violation of these, and all other fundamental rights in their original jurisdiction, under Articles 184(3) and 199 respectively. Petitioners can file a writ in the SC when the case pertains to violation of fundamental rights, and the matter is one of public importance.[17] For a case to be filed in one of the five High Courts, the petitioner must be an aggrieved party alleging violation of their fundamental rights by a state entity.[18] Several of the *Missing Persons' Cases*, where the state is deemed as the alleged "abductor," are filed under these two provisions by filing a writ of *habeas corpus*. So there is a constitutional remedy available for violation of all rights, including those found in Articles 10, 10A, and 14. However, these remedies are often denied to those picked up under preventive detention, and those who are prosecuted by military courts and also NAB.

Special Courts and Tribunals

This section will discuss the constitutional framework surrounding preventive detention and military courts, followed by a discussion of how a statutory body like NAB exercises similarly blatant abusive powers, despite falling outside the "national security" narrative. This section also evaluates the special court that tried General Musharraf for treason, and how, for a limited time period, it served as a point of distinction from the other special forums.

Constitutionally Sanctioned Parallel Adjudicating Bodies

Review Board for Assessing Preventive Detention Cases

A "special tribunal" created by the Constitution itself appears to act in subversion of the aforementioned rights. Clauses 3 to 9 of Article 10 provide exceptions to these protections: preventive detention, and the inapplicability of these rights to "enemy aliens." Preventive detention is a colonial legacy, which was retained and codified into the Constitution. Article 10(4) defines the scope of preventive detention as "persons acting in a manner prejudicial to the integrity, security or defence of Pakistan or any part thereof, or external affairs of Pakistan, or public order, or the maintenance of supplies or services." The "protection" afforded to those held under preventive detention is to be produced in front of a Review Board after the passage of three months. The Review Board can extend the detention every three months, for up to twenty-four months. The Review Board is appointed by the chief justice of Pakistan, comprising of a chairman and two other members, all of whom are or have served as Supreme Court or High Court judges, for persons detained under federal laws; while for persons detained under provincial laws, the chief justice of that province's High Court will appoint a three-member bench, all of whom are, or have served as High Court judges.[19]

The composition of the Review Board, that is, seating of former or current judges sit on this Board, it does not automatically grant the Board the same adjudicating powers, nor does it grant the defendants the same statutory and constitutional rights available in regular criminal and constitutional courts in Pakistan. The Review Board is a quasi-judicial forum, and in theory subject to judicial review under Article 199.[20] However, it is also validly accepted as enunciated within Article 10 itself, that the detainee and the Review Board can be denied being informed about the grounds for arrest, and evidence against the detainee, if the state feels that such disclosure will be "against public interest."[21] Furthermore, in the *Missing Persons Cases*,[22] the main state entities to face judicial scrutiny has been the police force, which is often not the one responsible for the detainee. Even in cases where the police might have been used for the initial detention, the internment centers are often not run by them. Furthermore, there are no proper guidelines on whom the responsibility will fall upon if the state fails to produce a detainee in front of the Board itself. Hence even when the grounds for detention are justiciable,[23] the explicit absence of transparency within Article 10 makes it extremely difficult for a detainee to even receive the minimalistic rights attributed to those in preventive detention. So in addition to overly broad scope of preventive detention, the Constitution strips the detainee of all protections against unlawful arrest and detention using the pretext of national security.

Additionally, from the perspective of the framers of the Constitution, the intent of having a strong way out of protections against arbitrary arrests and detentions was further bolstered by the 3rd Constitutional Amendment, 1975, which increased the detention period from one month to three months. Article 10(8) provides some relief to the family of the detainee, by mandating the Review Board to set a "reasonable subsistence allowance" for his family.

However, it was not until recently that the Islamabad High Court ordered the state to actually pay the stipend. As is evident from the *Missing Person's Cases*,[24] far from paying the allowance, the families often have no insight whether their kin were picked up by the state, or met with some other untoward incident. Due to the excessively broad and ambiguous scope of preventive detention, this quickly became a tool for curbing political dissent by the civil and subsequently military powers.

Civilian Jurisdiction of Military Courts in Pakistan

This section evaluates the four-year long tenure of the military courts exercising jurisdiction over civilians in cases pertaining to terrorism in Pakistan.

On December 16, 2014, the Army Public School, Peshawar, was attacked by Taliban, resulting in 141 casualties, 131 of whom were children.[25] As a response to this attack, the government launched the NAP to curb terrorism.[26] The NAP proposed capital punishment for terrorists involved in the incident, thereby resulting in the lifting of the six-year moratorium on death penalty in Pakistan for all convicts.[27] The second point on the twenty-point agenda was to create special courts under the supervision of the army for a period of two years. Subsequently, the Parliament passed the 21st Constitutional Amendment, by virtue of which the already existing military courts were granted civilian jurisdiction to try civilian terrorism suspects.[28] The amendment came with a sunset clause of two years, and was passed unopposed in both houses of the Parliament.[29] It is pertinent to note here that as per Article 63A of the Constitution, all legislative members are bound to vote on party lines on matters pertaining to constitutional amendments.[30] So, as long as all political parties represented in the Parliament are on the same page, passage of a constitutional amendment will in all likelihood go unopposed, since the only opposition can come from independent candidates.

The SC took up challenge against the 21st Amendment, under Article 184(3) of the Constitution. While discussing maintainability of the case in light of an explicit bar of jurisdiction of all courts in matters pertaining to constitutional amendments,[31] the SC ruled that the civilian jurisdiction granted to military courts threatens the independence of judiciary, which is one of the salient features of the Constitution.[32] However, the SC allowed the continuation of the civilian jurisdiction in light of the exigent circumstances. While the SC did find the parallel adjudication system to be problematic, the fact that appeals to High Courts and Supreme Court were allowed, in conjunction with the sunset clause, was deemed satisfactory. The Supreme Court made no effort in their 900-page long judgment, to make it mandatory for due process to be followed during trials in the military courts. The accessibility of due process and fair trial at the level of the High Court and Supreme Court were deemed a sufficient implementation. One may argue that the SC's hands were tied in the matter by virtue of the military courts' adjudication becoming an exception to the chapter on fundamental rights, as stipulated in Article 8 of the Constitution. However, the SC had already stepped outside the bounds of the Constitution that creates the SC itself by ruling on a constitutional amendment. Therefore, by that logic, they could at least mandate greater scrutiny or transparency into the exercise of the civilian jurisdiction of these courts.

The sheer number of rejection and overturning of the convictions by the military courts can be seen as sufficient grounds for contention. However, the SC did not intervene when the Parliament passed the 23rd Constitutional Amendment in 2017, reinstating the civilian jurisdiction of military courts for another two years.[33] The Supreme Court Bar Association filed a challenge in the SC against the extension,[34] nothing became of this application.

Furthermore, the right to fair trial is broader than the mere procedure followed. "The superstructure of the principles of fair trial is built on the premise that justice should not only be done but manifestly and undoubtedly appear to have been done. Every litigant, whether an accused or the prosecution, must have confidence regarding the impartiality and independence of the adjudicator."[35] Thus, the functionality of civilian jurisdiction of the military courts for these four years being shrouded in mystery is sufficient violation of the right to fair trial.

It is also pertinent to note here that via this judgment, the SC departed from its earlier jurisprudence. The Pakistan Armed Forces Ordinance, 1998, allowed civilians to be tried by military courts for civil offenses (offenses not pertaining to the armed forces) under this ordinance. The ordinance was held to be unconstitutional on grounds including how the executive cannot be responsible for carrying out judicial functions.[36] This judgment had only bolstered similar stances taken by the SC in earlier judgments on the matter.[37] One point of distinction vis-à-vis the 21st and 23rd Constitutional Amendments is that they granted this jurisdiction by adding the Pakistan Army Act, 1952, in the First Schedule of the Constitution, and further amended the 1952 Act itself. As per Article 8(3) of the Constitution, in case a law stipulated in the First Schedule contravenes a fundamental right, the law will not be deemed unconstitutional on this ground.

Other than concerns about rights to due process and fair trial being granted in military courts, the contention that is not immune from a challenge here is contravention of separation of powers. Military courts can, at best, be seen as quasi-judicial entity formed for internal regulation of the armed forces and thus cannot be tasked with judicial powers over the civilians. The SC has produced ample precedents to show that a tribunal does not always function as a court, nor will it always be considered as an affiliate of the judicial branch of the state.[38] Factors which must be present for a tribunal to be considered a judicial body include that it "has to determine a dispute relating to a right or liability, recognized by the Constitution or law and is under an obligation to discover the relevant facts, in the presence of the parties, in the light of the evidence produced by them . . . such Tribunals have to be manned, controlled and regulated in accordance with the established judicial principles."[39] As can be seen from the limited information accessible via ISPR, and also through appeals filed against these proceedings discussed below, the military courts did not espouse these principles. Defendants were not afforded a choice of who to appoint as their legal counsel, confessions were often the result of torture; defendants were not given time to defend themselves; and were often presumed guilty.[40]

By 2019, the status of trials of civilians by military courts was as follows:[41]

Number of trials concluded	646
Convictions	641
Death sentences	345
Imprisonment sentences awarded	296
Acquittals	05
Number of convicts executed	56

Source: "Military Injustice in Pakistan: Briefing Paper," January 2019, page 5.

This table illustrates that the propensity of conviction was extremely high in these trials, with a total of only five acquittals during over three years of functionality.

The SC also turned a blind eye toward various allegations of blatant violations of fundamental rights, including usage of torture to obtain confessions in *Said Zaman Khan v. Federation of Pakistan*.[42] This case represented sixteen petitions filed by family members of civilians convicted by military courts during 2015–2016. Some of these convicts had been arrested prior to the civilian jurisdiction being granted to these courts.[43] By dismissing these petitions, the SC inadvertently expanded the scope of the military courts from what was initially perceived.

However, the High Courts were more prudent in protection of rights. In 2018, the Peshawar High Court set aside over seventy convictions, stating that the proceedings had been conducted in bad faith, and/or there was insufficient evidence.[44] The court also held that all petitioners were denied adequate access to legal counsel of their choice, thus denying their basic rights under the Constitution.[45] Furthermore, all confessions produced before the court appeared to have been acquired after the petitioners had spent time in internment camps, and the tone of all these confessional statements was too similar, thus casting shadow of doubt on their legitimacy.[46] The court also highlighted that many of the petitioners were in fact victims of enforced disappearances.[47]

Special Court Constituted for Musharraf's Treason Case

In 1999, the then chief of army staff, General Pervez Musharraf, deposed Prime Minister Nawaz Sharif and his government, and imposed martial law in the country.[48] During his nine-year long presidential regime, General Musharraf imposed another emergency in 2007 as well, while removing sixty-one judges, including the then chief justice of the Supreme Court of Pakistan, Chaudhry Iftikhar.[49] While the SCP validated his first coup,[50] the Court called upon General Musharraf to justify the imposition of the second emergency,[51] which appeared to trample upon the independence of judiciary, and found the emergency to be illegal.[52]

Subsequently, in the National Assembly of Pakistan, the then Prime Minister Nawaz Sharif said that his government intends to file a written request before the SCP to try Musharraf for treason under Article 6 of the Constitution.[53] On November 18, 2013, the SCP accepted the Sharif government's request to set up a special court to try Musharraf under Section 2 of the High Treason (Punishment) Act 1973.[54] On November 19, 2013, Prime Minister Nawaz Sharif approved three High Court judges to form a special court to begin Musharraf's treason trial.[55] This court was constituted under Section 4 of the Criminal Law Amendment (Special Courts) Act, 1976.[56] It is pertinent to note that this was indeed a court, that is, a judicial forum, and not an administrative tribunal. The detailed proceedings were not only public, but also followed regular processes available to all defendants under Articles 10, 10A, 14, and other statutory rights granted under the Code of Criminal Procedure, 1898. In a 2-1 split, the special court found Musharraf guilty of committing high treason and sentenced him to death.[57] This is the only time a former dictator was convicted of committing treason in Pakistan's history. This judgment was lauded by many for taking a stand against a living former dictator, criticized by others for strong tone used by one of the judges,[58] and seen as contemptuous by the armed forces and their sympathizers. Consequently, it did not come as a surprise when two months later, the Lahore High Court ruled that the formation of the special court was unconstitutional on account of failure of the federal government to show proper grounds and a formal decision for filing such a case.[59]

This case is an outlier in the context of this chapter because it represents a clash of institutions. The civilians were not a direct party to this case; but the imposition of the emergency did clampdown on fundamental rights and freedoms available at other times, including parts of Musharraf's regime. From another angle, however, this situation further bolsters the same trend illustrated through most part of this chapter: during the recent years, in the war between the state increasing its powers at the expense of rights of the people, rights tend to be at the losing end.

NAB and NAB Courts

The NAB was created via the National Accountability Ordinance, 1999, by the then-president General Pervez Musharraf. It is pertinent to evaluate NAB for two reasons: the abrasion of separation of powers and absence of due process lies at the core of this institution; and NAB appears to have become a tool for political victimization and state censorship.[60]

This body, headed by the chairman, has powers to investigate and prosecute in its own separate courts, government officials, and private persons on corruption and misappropriation charges, with the exception of persons belonging to the armed forces and judges.[61] The exclusion of the armed forces from the ambit of NAO appears obvious since it was passed by General Musharraf himself (ordinances at this time were not temporally limited, and did not require legislative ratification either). Furthermore, the exclusion of the judiciary from the scope might also be seen as a reward for those who had recently validated Musharraf's coup.

One report summarizes the scope of NAB as "detection, investigation, prosecution, and speedy disposal of cases involving corruption, corrupt practices, misappropriation of property, kickbacks, commissions" and ancillary matters.[62] These have also been deemed as non-bailable offenses,[63] and the chairman of NAB is empowered to add further conditions when bail is sought.[64] NAB also as has its own prisons. In addition to this lack of separation of powers, the NAO places the burden of proof on the defendant rather than the prosecution,[65] something that is in direct contravention of the basic elements of criminal prosecution. Unlike regular criminal cases where the physical remand of an accused is fifteen days,[66] the remand under NAO is ninety days.[67] NAB is also the only entity on the criminal side that allows plea bargains.[68]

Furthermore, as per Sections 2 and 3, the NAO is deemed to have come into force from the first day of January 1985, and shall have effect notwithstanding anything contained in any other law for the time being in force. This is a direct violation of the fundamental protection against retrospective punishment enshrined under Article 12 of the Constitution, 1973. Unlike the Pakistan Army Act and the Protection of Pakistan Act discussed in former sections, the NAO is not listed in the First Schedule of the Constitution. Thus, the immunity under Article 8 of the Constitution does not apply and, consequently, the interpretation and application of NAO must be in line with the fundamental rights listed in the Constitution.

The *vires* of NAO were challenged in the SC soon after its promulgation.[69] However, this was still early during the tenure of General Pervez Musharraf's takeover. Thus, as was expected, while the SC made amendments to various procedural aspects, it retained the more problematic substantive elements, namely allowing the absence of separation of powers between the executive and judicial functions to continue, along with retaining the burden of proof on the defendant at the trial stage.

The prolific use of NAO after Pakistan Tehreek-e-Insaaf came into power after the 2018 general elections led to a lot of hue and cry against the NAB. To pacify public office holders, President Arif Alvi passed an ordinance, which was later tabled as the NAO 2019 Amendment Bill, but could not be passed. By and large, this bill appears to be in favor of public office holders, and tried to offer them protection from the unnecessary abuse of NAB's powers. It also makes a valiant attempt at upholding the fundamental rights of the accused individuals, including right to liberty, right to due process of law, right to fair trial, and right to dignity.

Even though the SC had upheld the NAO, recently in the case of *Khawaja Salman Rafique v National Accountability Bureau*,[70] the SC discussed how the processes followed by NAB in this case against a prominent opposition leader and his brother was "against all norms of justice, fair play and propriety."[71] It explained how the prosecution had failed in furnishing any evidence to corroborate the allegations leveled against the petitioners,[72] and also failed to show the SC why the investigation was initiated against them at all.[73] The SC found that this was

> a classic example of trampling fundamental rights, unlawful deprivation of freedom, and liberty and the complete disregard for human dignity as guaranteed by the Constitution. NAB's conduct throughout this case is a clear manifestation of their utter disregard for law, fair play, equity and propriety. Indeed, curbing loot, plunder and combating corruption is a noble cause. Nonetheless, the means, process and mechanism employed therefor should be within the parameters as prescribed and mandated by the law and not in derogation thereof.[74]

Despite such a damning judgment coming out of the SC, the NAB continues to detain and/or otherwise pester the public.

CONCLUSION

There is a large number of special courts and tribunals in Pakistan. While many of these judicial forums follow principles of separation of powers, and operate in line with the fundamental rights enshrined in Part 1 Chapter 1 of the Constitution of the Islamic Republic of Pakistan, the same does not hold true for all forums, particularly those that have been seen to be used rather pervasively over the last few years. It is easier for the state to do away with rights enforcement entirely when these forums are created by the Constitution itself and/or granted immunity by them, as is the case with the Review Board constituted for assessing people held under preventive detention, and the same is true for the four-year-long civilian jurisdiction granted to military courts in cases pertaining to terrorism and extremism. The fact that both these forums are quasi-judicial bodies further seems to absolve them of the responsibility of protection of citizens' rights. While sometimes the High Courts and the Supreme Court have stepped in to set aside their orders, or to push the state to provide at least some basic legal recourse to the detainees, the SC has also granted validation to these forums, and turned a blind eye toward the atrocities committed by the state under their purview.

A similar judicial stance was apparent pertaining to the NAB as well, until the recent judgment of *Khawaja Salman Rafique v National Accountability Bureau*.[75] While the SC validated the NAB during a dictatorship, it never reverted its opinion on the substantive *vires* of the ordinance. Although now it has accepted that the institute is involved in abuse of powers bestowed upon it under the NAO, NAB's practical dealings in other similar matters remain unfettered.

The only outlier in terms of the special courts was the special court constituted to try General Musharraf for treason. However, when challenged, the Lahore High Court did treat it as the anomaly that it was and declared the composition of the court as invalid.

What one may see from a perusal of these laws and their consequent application is that there is a clear demarcation between the state and its citizens. There is a deep-rooted skepticism on part of the state, which uses jargon like preserving national security, national integrity, curbing terrorism, extremism, and corruption, for devising tools to enhance its own arbitrary powers, at the expense of fundamental rights enshrined in the Constitution. Additionally, even when rights-based cases stem from a clash of institutions, it leads to a further weakening of fundamental rights in Pakistan, particularly the protections against arrest and detention, rights to fair trial and due process, and right to dignity.

NOTES

1. Articles 19A and 25A of the Constitution of Islamic Republic of Pakistan, 1973.
2. Available at https://www.supremecourt.gov.pk/downloads_judgements/c.p._2243_l_2019.pdf.
3. The NAP was drafted by the Ministry of Interior and NACTA, and was later approved by the Parliament. National Counterterrorism Authority (NACTA), "National Action Plan, 2014," https://nacta.gov.pk/nap-2014/.
4. *See* Supreme Court of Pakistan, "Missing persons cases," https://www.supremecourt.gov.pk/missing-person-cases/. *See also* Dawn News, "Military Courts convicted five missing persons," https://www.dawn.com/news/1307086.

5. The ISPR is the media and public relations wing of the Pakistan Armed Forces. *See* ISPR https://www.ispr.gov.pk/.

6. *See* Suppression of Terrorist Activities (Special Courts) Act, 1975; Special Courts for Speedy Trials Act, 1987; Defence of Pakistan Ordinance, 1965; Drugs Act, 1976; Special Courts for Speedy Trials Ordinance 1990; Special Courts for Speedy Trials Ordinance 1991; Special Courts for Speedy Trials Act 1992; Special Courts for Speedy Trials Act 1996; Anti-Terrorism Act 1997; Control of Narcotics Substances Act 1997; Prevention of Anti-National Activities Act, 1974; Special Courts for Speedy Trials Ordinance 1992; establishment of "model courts" for speedy criminal trials by CJP Asif Saeed Khosa, DAWN News, "Model courts in each district to conduct day-today hearings, says CJP," https://www.dawn.com/news/1469115. Furthermore, in *Shugufta Shaheen v. The State through DG NAB*, 2019 SCMR 1106, at para 8, the SC held that lengthy trials contradict the rights of fair trial and due process.

7. Articles 9-28 of the Constitution.

8. *See also* J. Fazal Karim, Judicial Review of public Actions, Volume 2, page 850.

9. *See also Muhammad Bashir v. Ruskhsar,* PLD 2020 SC 334, at para 4.

10. *See Altaf Ibrahim Qureshi and another v. Aam Log Ittehad and others,* PLD 2019 SC 745*; Ishtiaq Ahmed v. Honourable Competent Authority through Registrar Supreme Court of Pakistan,* 2016 SCMR 943*; Ministry of Interior v. Special Court,* PLD 2020 SC 82.

11. Ibid.

12. Ibid.

13. *Muhammad Bashir v SHO*, PLD 2007 SC 539.

14. J. Fazal Karim, Judicial Review of public Actions, Volume 2, page 829.

15. *See also* J. Fazal Karim, Judicial Review of public Actions, Volume 2, page 870.

16. Hassaan Niazi & Noor Bano Khan, "The Price of Protection: The Right to Fair Trial & The Protection of Pakistan Act."

17. Article 184(3) of the Constitution.

18. Article 199 of the Constitution.

19. Clauses pertaining to preventive detention in the current Constitution are substantively similar to their counterpart in the 1962 Constitution of Pakistan (this was the second constitution of the country). The Supreme Court ruling in *Government of West Pakistan v Haider Bux Jatoi*, PLD 1969 SC 210, held that the Review Board is a quasi-judicial body, and is subject to judicial review under Article 199. *See also* J. Fazal Karim, Judicial Review of public Actions, Volume 2, page 868.

20. J. Fazal Karim, Judicial Review of public Actions, Volume 2, page 868. *See also Government of West Pakistan v. Haider Bux Jatoi*, PLD 1969 SC 210.

21. Article 10(5) and (6) of the Constitution.

22. Supreme Court of Pakistan, "Missing persons cases," https://www.supremecourt.gov.pk/missing-person-cases/. *See also* Dawn News, "Military Courts convicted five missing persons," https://www.dawn.com/news/1307086.

23. J. Fazal Karim, Judicial Review of public Actions, Volume 2, page 868.

24. Supreme Court of Pakistan, "Missing persons cases," https://www.supremecourt.gov.pk/missing-person-cases/. *See also* Dawn News, "Military Courts convicted five missing persons," https://www.dawn.com/news/1307086.

25. Dawn News, "APS attack judicial commission report points to security 'fiasco' at school," https://www.dawn.com/news/1581564.

26. "National Action Plan 20 Points" https://www.satp.org/satporgtp/countries/pakistan/document/papers/National_Action_Plan_20_Points.htm.

27. The Washington Post. "Pakistan Announces a National Action Plan To Fight Terrorism Says Terrorists' Days Are Numbered." https://www.washingtonpost.com/news/worldviews/wp/2014/12/24/pakistan-announces-a-national-plan-to-fight-terrorism-says-terrorists-days-are-numbered/?utm_term=.8a9367080ba6. In 2015 alone, Pakistan carried out 333 executions http://hrcp-web.org/hrcpweb/executions-in-2015/, and another 87 in 2016 http://hrcp-web.org/hrcpweb/wp-content/uploads/2016/12/Final-Executions-2016.xlsx-9.pdf. Only 30 percent of these were charged with terrorism, and 17 percent convictions emanated from military courts. See Justice Project Pakistan, "Trial and Error: The overreach of Pakistan's Anti Terrorism Act," pages 1-2.

28. Dawn News, "Parliament passes 21st Constitutional Amendment, Army Act Amendment," https://www.dawn.com/news/1155271. Military courts already existed, and were created by the Pakistan Army Act, 1952. The Amendment amended Article 175, and the First Schedule of the Constitution to include the Pakistan Army Act, 1952 as one of the laws that may legally infringe upon Fundamental Rights enshrined in the Constitution (*See* Article 8 of the Constitution). The Army Act was simultaneously amended to grant them civilian jurisdiction in terrorism cases.

29. Ibid.

30. Any member of parliament who does not vote on party lines will lose their seat.

31. Article 239(5) and (6) grant the Parliament absolute power for constitutional amendments, and explicitly bar the jurisdiction of all courts to hear challenges against them.

32. The Salient Features doctrine is treated by the SC as a derivative of the Basic Structure Doctrine. The SC ruled that federal structure, parliamentary form of government, independence of judiciary, read in line with Islamic Injunctions are the Salient Features of the Constitution of Pakistan. The SC used the Salient Features Doctrine to hear challenges against the passage of the 18th and 19th Constitutional Amendments as well, citing that the amendment of judicial appointment procedure under Article 175A threatened judicial independence.

33. Dawn News, "Military Courts resume in Pakistan," https://www.dawn.com/news/1323974.

34. Dawn News, "SCBA challenges 23rd Amendment in the SC," https://www.dawn.com/news/1327105.

35. *Ministry of Interior v. Special Court*, PLD 2020 SC 82, at para 9.

36. Liaquat Hussain v Federation of Pakistan, PLD 1999 SC 504, at 656- 657.

37. *See* Darwesh M. Arbey v. Federation of Pakistan, PLD 1980 Lahore 206; Niaz Ahmad Khan v. Province of Sindh, PLD 1977 Karachi 605; J. Fazal Karim, Judicial Review of public Actions, Volume 1, page 148.

38. *Sh. Riaz ul Haq Advocate v Federation of Pakistan,* PLD 2013 SC 501.

39. Ibid. *See also* J. Fazal Karim, Judicial Review of public Actions, Volume 1, pages 310-318.

40. *See* Peshawar High Court W.P.536-P of 2018; International Commission of Jurists, "Military Injustice in Pakistan: Briefing Paper," January 2019.

41. These statistics have been taken from International Commission of Jurists, "Military Injustice in Pakistan: Briefing Paper," January 2019, page 5.

42. 2017 SCMR 1249.

43. M Nawaz Wahla, 'Trial of Civilians before Military Courts of Pakistan' (2020) 35 Conn J Int'l L 209.

44. Peshawar High Court W.P.536-P of 2018. *See also* International Commission of Jurists, "Military Injustice in Pakistan: Briefing Paper," January 2019, Page 8-9.

45. Ibid.

46. Ibid.

47. ibid.

48. The New York Times, "Coup in Pakistan; Pakistan Army Seizes Power ours after Prime Minister dismisses his Military Chief," https://www.nytimes.com/1999/10/13/world/coup-pakistan-overview-pakistan-army-seizes-power-hours-after-prime-minister.html.

49. Dawn News, "Gen Muhsarraf's second coup: charge-sheet against judiciary; Media promoting negativism; Country's integrity at stake; Legislature intact," dawn.com/news/274263.

50. Zafar Ali Shah v. General Pervez Musharraf, PLD 2000 SC 868.

51. Dawn News, "SC calls Musharraf to defend November 3 actions," https://www.dawn.com/news/849120/sc-calls-musharraf-to-defend-nov-3-actions.

52. Dawn News, "SC strikes down November 3 Emergency," https://www.dawn.com/news/849047.

53. Article 6 states that the suspension, holding in abeyance, and/or abrogation of the Constitution amounts to high treason. The High Treason Act, 1973, defines the punishment of high treason as death penalty or life imprisonment.

54. Dawn News, "SC agrees to try Musharraf," https://www.dawn.com/news/1056985.

55. Dawn News, "Three-member bench finalized for Musharraf Treason Case," https://www.dawn.com/news/1057196.

56. *See also ibid.*

57. Federal Government of Islamic Republic of Pakistan v. General (R) Pervez Musharraf, 2019, available at https://www.dawn.com/news/1523186.

58. See para 64 of the judgment.

59. "[D]iscretion to direct a trial relating to the offence of high treason exclusively vests in the Executive." *Gen. (R) Pervez Musharraf v. Nadeem Ahmed (Advocate) and others*, PLD 2014 SC 585; The Nation, "LHC terms formation of special court 'unconstitutional' in Musharraf treason case," https://nation.com.pk/13-Jan-2020/treason-case-lhc-reserves-verdict-on-musharraf-s-plea-against-formation-of-special-court.

60. There has been massive censorship by the state on various fronts during the last three years. Geo News is a network that has been critical of the current ruling party and the censorship attempts. Their owner and Editor-in-Chief Mir Shakil ur Rehman has been in NAB custody for 231 days at this point for a case dating back over 40 years. Despite having retrospective effect, NAB does not have jurisdiction over that time period, despite this, he has been unsuccessful in being granted bail.

61. Section 5(m) (clauses iv, vi).

62. Pakistan Institute of Legislative Development and Transparency, "National Accountability Bureau: An Independent Review of Structure and performance," Citizens' Periodic Reports on Performance of State Institutions, April 2015. *See* Sections 9-12 of NAO.

63. Section 9(b).

64. Section 9(c).

65. Section 14. Section 15 of the Protection of Pakistan Act, 2014, also places the burden of proof on the accused, however, due to being listed in the First Schedule of the Constitution, it is not *ultra vires* the Constitution, unlike NAO.

66. Section 167 of the Code of Criminal Procedure, 1898.

67. Section 20.

68. Section 25.

69. *Khan Asfandyar Wali v. Federation of Pakistan*, PLD 2001 SC 607.

70. Available at https://www.supremecourt.gov.pk/downloads_judgements/c.p._2243_l_2019.pdf.

71. ibid at para 18.

72. Ibid at para 19.

73. Ibid at para 35, 36.

74. Ibid at para 48.

75. Available at https://www.supremecourt.gov.pk/downloads_judgements/c.p._2243_l_2019.pdf.

Chapter 12

The Pakistani Judiciary and the Suo Motu Jurisdiction

Waris Husain[1]

INTRODUCTION

Few jurists could describe the sound of judicial overreach but perhaps it can be best exemplified by the clanging of hospital cutlery heard on Pakistan's national news stations as Chief Justice Saqib Nisar conducted a surprise inspection of a government-administered hospital asking administrators in visible disgust "you serve food in this?"[2] The image of a chief justice of Pakistan conducting on-the-spot inspections of hospital or prison facilities likely left many wondering. Undoubtedly, this was not the first time a media-savvy chief justice was dominating the headlines[3] by utilizing a legal concept unknown to much of the world: suo motu.

Over time, but particularly under the leadership of Chief Justice Iftikhar Chaudhry, the Supreme Court has staked out its right to rule over cases on their own cognizance, or rather without satisfying formal requirements like parties approaching the court for relief. The power derives from the constitutional article concerning the power of judicial review for Pakistan's courts over any matter of public importance relating to a fundamental right.[4]

The justification for allowing such an expansive right to the Supreme Court is the severe imbalance of power and access to justice between privileged and underprivileged citizens[5] requiring a method to short-circuit the normal judicial processes as a means to either assist underprivileged citizens or to punish powerful individuals for crimes they have committed. In the words of former chief justice Saqib Nisar, "We [the Supreme Court] have to fight for those people who unfortunately don't have means to get their rights."[6]

While most justices on the apex court agree that there is a right to exercise suo motu jurisdiction, there is little agreement concerning the scope of this power among members of the court.[7] This divergence of opinion is particularly important when one remembers that the ambit of the suo motu powers are not set by a majority of justices, but rather is the exclusive purview of the chief justice of the country.

This means that there has been little consistency regarding the use of suo motu in the last decade as its scope has been set and reset by Chief Justices serving little more than a year or two on the bench as leaders of the Supreme Court. As such, the definition of suo motu changes constantly,

> that the measure of suo motu, too, varies with the size of the Chief Justice's foot. One chief justice is convinced the court must regulate sugar prices. Another is equally convinced it is none of the court's business. One pursues, with great vigour, the building of dams. Another decides it is not dams that are needed, but railways and bridges. And since it is chief justices who constitute Supreme Court benches, it is not uncommon for them to include, in their own bench, judges of similar ideologies.[8]

Since the retirement of Pakistan's leading suo motu judge, Iftikhar Chaudhry, the pendulum between restraint and expansion of suo motu has swung wildly with relatively restrained uses of suo motu by Chief Justices Jillani, Mulk, and Jamali while Chief Justice Nisar's tenure was unprecedented "in the extent of its activism and disregard for formal legal procedures."[9]

Undoubtedly, in order to ensure stability and balance of powers between Pakistan's three branches of government, some sort of rules-based system would be helpful in divesting exclusive control over this power from the chief justice.[10] However, as this chapter will explain, there has been a reluctance by the chief justices of the country to bind their successors to a rules-based system considering how pervasive the personality-based system is in the apex court, which could explain why some have referred to Pakistan's top court as the chief justice's court rather than the Supreme Court. In some ways, the ghost of Chief Justice Chaudhry remains to impact the Court as he once advised junior justices not to create rules limiting suo motu because he "counseled younger judges to consider the time they'd be CJP [Chief Justice of Pakistan] and such [suo motu] power would be handy."[11] By examining both the jurisprudence and the public statements concerning suo motu made by each chief justice since Chaudhry, this chapter will describe the dynamic and ever-changing definition and scope of suo motu in Pakistan. Particularly since Chief Justice Chaudhry's retirement we have seen three eras emerge: the Taciturn Trio (Jillani, Mulk, and Jamali), the Maverick (Nisar), and the Sheriff (Khosa).

THE TACITURN TRIO

Subsequent to Chief Justice Chaudhry's retirement in 2013, Pakistan's Supreme Court came under the leadership of three jurists who ushered in a period of judicial restraint. Yet, since 2007, the Supreme Court became a news-making institution whose members helped bring down a military government and reinstate democratic rule.[12] As such, the Supreme Court enjoyed more public attention and adulation since 2007 than any other time in its history.[13] Yet, criticisms emerged by 2013 when some described Chaudhry's overuse of the suo motu powers as "personal aggrandizement,"[14] which was "overstepping his authority, paralysing government and undermining democracy."[15] At the conclusion of Chaudhry's reign, many hoped that suo motu cases would be decreased and that the next chief justices would speak out against judicial overreach.[16] This was mostly true for Chief Justices Tassaduq Hussain Jillani, Nasirul Mulk, and Anwar Zaheer Jamali who succeeded Chief Justice Chaudry and "used suo motu power sparingly."[17]

Tassaduq H. Jillani

The promotion of Justice Jillani, known as the "gentleman judge,"[18] to the post of chief justice of Pakistan came with demands from Chaudhry's critics that he regulate the overuse of suo motu. Chief Justice Jillani himself raised the issue of judicial restraint relating to suo motu early in his tenure, explaining in a December 11, 2013, speech that "here is a need to consider/determine the limits and contours of jurisdiction under Article 184(3) of the Constitution with a view to discouraging frivolous petitions and to preventing the misuse of jurisdiction by vested interests."[19]

Chief Justice Jillani established a "policy of judicial restraint"[20] which ended "four long years of judicial activism under former chief justice Iftikhar Muhammad Chaudhry...turn[ing] a new leaf by refusing to interfere in politics, governance and economic policymaking."[21] While Chief Justice Jillani was not immune from criticism, some saying that he curtailed the Court's intervention in human rights cases and failed to pursue "aggressive elite accountability,"[22] others say his rule was a "period of blissful sanity."[23]

Significantly, it is important to note that Chief Justice Jillani limited the use of suo motu but did not abolish it completely.[24] In 2013, in the aftermath of a terrorist attack on a church in Peshawar where nearly 100 people lost their lives,[25] a non-governmental organization (NGO) sent a letter to the Chief Justice to take cognizance of the incident.[26] In the past, the Supreme Court has been reluctant to take up issues relating to religious minorities potentially fearing violent blowback from either extremist groups or their political surrogates in the country. Despite this history and his overall practice of judicial restraint, Chief Justice Jillani took up the case regarding the attack on the Christian church and included in his suo motu relief other religious minorities like Hindus whose places of worship were threatened or destroyed in the past.[27]

In *S.M.C. No. 1* or *Justice Helpline and others v. Attorney General of Pakistan*,[28] the Supreme Court held that the government was providing insufficient protection to religious minorities and should form a religious minority committee with members from the impacted groups to create long-term solutions to the lethal security threats and discrimination these groups face. In a law review article written by Chief Justice Jillani about the seminal case, he explained that he took up the case because failing to do so would "be tantamount to abdication of our constitutional mandate as custodians of people's rights." He explained that:

> The court was of the view that minorities in Pakistan, as in several transitional democracies, are a vulnerable section of society because of their social and economic limitations. They cannot effectively espouse their grievances and, to them, the constitutional guarantees are mere hollow promises signifying nothing in practical terms. They and their places of worship have been subjected to violence. Their dilemma is exasperated both by the absence of sufficient political will to provide remedies and by a weak law enforcement machinery. This is further compounded by a lack of empathy in the general public."[29]

Particularly, on the counter-majoritarian role of the court and using suo motu in order to address inaccessibility to justice for minorities, Chief Justice Jillani wrote

> Courts have traditionally been viewed as conservative institutions that preserve the status quo. But I have always believed that superior courts, particularly the supreme courts, in a democracy can be catalysts for social change through such judgments . . . (this case) underpin(s) the belief that the judiciary can eliminate discrimination and bias through its judgments and thereby promote tolerance, which is one of the important elements of democracy. The supreme court in a democracy must protect liberal institutions.[30]

While the reasoning put forward by Chief Justice Jillani in the *Justice Helpline* case may seem to contradict his overall restrained view on judicial power, the two concepts can be seen as complimentary. With an issue as difficult as religious freedom in Pakistan, progress can only be made by a Supreme Court that reserves its political capital and energy on those particular cases rather than adopting an overall hostile attitude toward the political branches of government through the overuse of suo motu as exercised by

Chief Justice Chaudhry. Despite this political calculation, the adoption of judicial restraint by Jillani, and the passage of six years, much of the *Justice Helpline* judgment remains unenforced and unimplemented by the political branches.[31]

Regardless of the result in this particular case, Chief Justice Jillani laid down an approach adopted by two of his successors by limiting the use of suo motu to one or two cases per year that raised particularly sensitive issues, rather than the dozens of suo motu cases taken from 2007 to 2013 including those relating to the price of consumer products like samosas and sugar.[32]

Nasirul Mulk

In July 2014, Chief Justice Nasirul Mulk took the reins of the apex court from Chief Justice Jillani and served for thirteen months. Known as the "democrat judge,"[33] Chief Justice Mulk enjoyed the reputation of being "noncontroversial, nonpartisan, flawless, impartial and unbiased," having "no passion or penchant whatsoever for judicial activism," as described by one writer.[34] This was demonstrated in Chief Justice Mulk's farewell speech to Chief Justice Jillani, during which he stated that "Institutions need to work in harmony with one another and it is their constitutional duty to desist from undue interference in the functioning of other pillars of the state."[35]

During his tenure, Chief Justice Mulk "carried forward the police of judicial restraint of his predecessor . . . staying away from the affairs of other institutions, taking few suo motu notices and focusing the attention on disposing cases of ordinary litigants."[36] Where Chief Justice Chaudhry was accused of "meddling in government affairs"[37] or "encroached upon the constitutional powers of the legislature and the executive,"[38] Chief Justice Nisar "is credited with adopting the policy of 'judicial restraint.' "[39] Not only did Chief Justice Nisar use the suo motu sparingly, he also overruled a prior suo motu decision by the Court "wherein the federal government's power to appoint heads of different state's departments was encroached."[40]

While Chief Justice Nisar minimized the Supreme Court's use of suo motu and the confrontational approach to dealing with political branches, he did utilize suo motu powers in two particular cases. Following up on Chief Justice Jillani's judgment in the minorities' rights case, he "took suo motu notice of the Kot Radha Kishan incident in which a Christian couple was allegedly beaten to death by a mob and their bodies were burnt in a brick kiln on allegations of blasphemy."[41] Following the lynching, Nasir Saeed working for the Center for Legal Aid, Assistance and Settlement stated that

> unfortunately the government has always been hesitant to take action and bring those responsible for church attacks, the burning of Christian towns and

> villages, and the killing and burning of Christians alive, to justice. Therefore, Christians have lost hope for justice from the present government, *but after the suo motu notice by Chief Justice Nasirul Mulk, their hopes for justice for Shama, Shahzad and their unborn child have been raised.*" (Emphasis added)[42]

During hearings for the case, recorded as *Constitutional Petition 94 of 2014*, the Court was "shocked" by the response from the police authorities in the Kot Radha Kishan case where "police did nothing to disperse the crowd that lynched a Christian couple." The police's failure to take action caused Chief Justice Mulk to state that "at least police could have resorted to aerial fire to disperse the crowd to save the Christian couple."[43]

Additionally, Chief Justice Mulk took suo motu in a second case relating to the gang rape and murder of a mother and daughter in the Sindh Province.[44] After reading about the incident in an Urdu-language newspaper, the Chief Justice called on the inspector general of Sindh Police, advocate general of Sindh, and the National Commission on the Status of Women to provide a report concerning the incident and what the Sindh's law enforcement bodies would do to bring justice to the victims.[45]

Chief Justice Mulk followed the path set by Chief Justice Jillani by exercising overall restraint under Article 184(3) of Pakistan's constitution and limiting the Court's use of suo motu. Yet, both justices retained and used this suo motu power in select cases involving victims from marginalized communities who have historically been denied access to the justice system. This stands in contradiction to Chief Justice Chaudhry whose use of suo motu was less focused on particularly disenfranchised groups, and was more generally confrontational with the political branches. For Chief Justice Jillani, the victims for which he used suo motu belonged to religious minority communities and the perpetrators were violent extremists who attacked their worship houses with impunity from state officials failing at their duty to protect religious minorities. The same can be said for the Kot Radha Kishan case where Chief Justice Mulk focused on victims from the Christian community and state officials who, again, failed in their duty to protect citizens from violence. The second suo motu decision by Chief Justice Mulk focused on women, another marginalized community often subject to violence without judicial recourse in Pakistan.

Anwar Zaheer Jamali

Following Chief Justice Mulk's tenure, Justice Anwar Zaheer Jamali was promoted to lead the apex court and served for fifteen months in the role.[46] Following the trend set by Chief Justices Jillani and Mulk, Chief Justice

Jamali distanced himself from Chief Justice Chaudhry's hyper-activism and "adopted a policy of judicial restraint, mostly avoiding taking notice of executive failures."[47]

Jamali's tenure was summarized by Babar Sattar as follows: "CJP [Chief Justice of Pakistan] Jamali didn't employ suo motu much. But when he did it mostly had to do with things around his hometown."[48] While one writer found that Chief Justice Jamali took twenty suo motu notices, only a few were concluded by him, with "most of the suo motu cases . . . taken up during his time [being] still sub judice."[49]

One of these home-state cases involved the alleged "political interference" in the administration of Sindh's police force which came to light in the aftermath of the kidnapping of the Sindh High Court's Chief Justice son.[50] Another case which attracted the suo motu powers of the chief justice came in the aftermath of a suicide bombing targeting the legal community in Quetta. The attack left nearly sixty of the most senior lawyers in the province dead, which many feared meant that "[a] generation of lawyers has been wiped out in Quetta, and it will leave Baluchistan, in more ways than one, lawless."[51] Chief Justice Jamali took suo motu notice of the case after reviewing a note written by the Supreme Court's registrar who was concerned that the government had failed to provide security to the people of Quetta which "constitutes violation of fundamental right of life and liberty guaranteed under Article 9 of the Constitution."[52]

Despite the appreciation for Chief Justice Jamali's restraint, some critics argued that he left "office without leaving a weight legacy,"[53] while others criticized his judgment in the *Hajj Policy*[54] case in 2016. Interestingly, for the issue of suo motu, while Chief Justice Jamali limited its use by the Supreme Court, he recognized that Pakistan's election tribunal vested with suo motu powers to investigate allegations of misconduct or wrongdoing by political figures.[55]

A trend which emerged from both instances where Chief Justice Jamali did use suo motu powers relates to protecting the physical security of the legal community, whether it is lawyers in Quetta or the son of the Chief Justice of Sindh's High Court. These cases came at the same time as Chief Justice Jamali was improving relations between lawyers at the bar and judges at the bench, which suffered under Chief Justice Chaudhry's leadership.[56] These facts seen together demonstrates that Chief Justice Jamali utilized his suo motu powers to unify and protect the legal community despite serious and persistent threats faced by the community. Overall, while Justice Jamali used suo motu in some other cases than those listed above, his tenure "was more or less a continuation of the 'judicial restraint' policy adopted by his two predecessors—Justice (retd) Tassaduq Hussain Jilani and Justice (retd) Nasirul Mulk."[57]

CONCLUSION

All three chief justices that followed Chaudhry's tenure committed themselves to limiting the court's use of suo motu, and saving the "suo motu card" for extreme cases or scenarios. For Justices Jillani and Mulk, suo motu was the right tool to use in cases involving victims from disenfranchised communities who are usually unable to seek justice for their mistreatment. For Justice Jamali, the suo motu power was to be used in physical defense of the legal community itself. All three chief justices established a multiyear era of restraint, but all three unfortunately were not able to create binding rules about the use of suo motu which would bind their successors. The failure to systematically restrain chief justices from abusing or overusing their suo motu power left the door open for a hyper-activist chief justice like Saqib Nisar to return the court back to the intense era of Chief Justice Chaudhry.

THE MAVERICK: SAQIB NISAR

In the aftermath of the Supreme Court being led by three jurists who created provisional limits to their suo motu powers, Chief Justice Saqib Nisar was promoted to lead Pakistan's judiciary in December 2016 and served in that capacity for two years.[58] Nisar's term was longer than his three predecessors but his rate of taking on suo motu cases outpaced them, particularly during his second year. Interestingly, Nisar had been known as a judge that avoided hyper-activism by the court as "[j]udicial restraint and a modesty about the constitutional role of judges were the hallmarks of his approach."[59]

Chief Justice Nisar's tenure started "in a measured, circumspect manner," but eventually exceeded the Chaudhry court's hyper-activist approach in his second year. During his final year, Chief Justice Nisar emulated the approach of Chief Justice Chaudhry:

> calling politicians, bureaucrats and ordinary citizens to court and unleashing thunderous remarks from the bench makes everyone sit up, makes hourly tickers (not just headlines) and people take you more seriously . . . Chief Justice Nisar's tenure came to be increasingly characterised by populist measures (be it dams, healthcare facilities, schools or national airlines) that stretch the definitions of what we consider normal judicial conduct.[60]

As one writer summarized, Nisar used suo motu "to launch inquiries ranging from the payment of sugar cane farmers by mills and increases in milk prices to allegations of corruption in the running of the country's railways and national airline," which some political parties stated "smacks of judicial overreach."[61] Some argued that Nisar's court had actually exceeded the kind of hostile interventionist policies of the Chaudhry court due to the "frequency and the absence of a strictly legal justification for the Supreme Court's involvement."[62]

The frequent accusation of "delving into matters clearly outside the judiciary's domain" came from academics, jurists, and practitioners alike when reviewing Chief Justice Nisar's suo motu decisions.[63] The most discussed example of judicial overreach is likely the critiques related to the water dam fund which was created by Chief Justice Nisar after a suo motu hearing on the Kalabagh Dam in July 2018.[64] The chief justice was concerned about the issue of water scarcity in the country and wished to have his legacy on the bench center "around the mission to address the country's water scarcity."[65] This culminated in hearings and eventually directions from the Supreme Court to begin "immediate work on the construction of Diamer-Bhasha and Mohmand dams."[66] Significantly, the Court decided to crowdfund the project, appealing "to the general public to donate for the cause," and "[a]n account was opened with the apex court's registrar to collect donations—instructions were given that the donors will not be asked for the source of income."[67] In some instances, lawyers representing litigants requesting extended adjournments were "granted their requests in return for donations."[68] In addition, the chief justice made international trips and television appearances to encourage Pakistanis around the world to donate to the dam fund appearing alongside associates of the prime minister while serving as the top judge of the country.[69]

While Chief Justice Nisar explained that his purpose in creating the fund was to raise awareness about Pakistan's water shortage, "it is difficult to find a strictly judicial justification for the creation of the dam fund," and the effort seemed to be "uninformed by the unintended consequences of a judicial intervention in policy matters."[70] This failure to understand the limits of judicial power when it comes to mega-projects and policy decisions is likely one of the reasons the dam fund was abandoned by the Supreme Court after Nisar's term and has been left incomplete.[71]

The use of suo motu to extend the Supreme Court's control over policy issues otherwise handled by political branches went far beyond water dams to include investigations into money laundering and offshore assets, the murder of a child, land encroachment, hospital management, water company liability, population growth, police personnel transfers, and the moral character of a politician.[72]

At the start of his tenure, Chief Justice Nisar publicly expressed support for regulating the suo motu powers, but in order to "avoid fetters on suo motu powers," he refused to create new Supreme Court rules and "kicked it towards the judicial side."[73] Simply put, the chief justice could have moved swiftly with the "SC's rule-making power" but left the question open for future litigation which could never happen.[74] Despite good intentions in the beginning of his tenure to regulate suo motu, improve case disposal rates, and improving the lower judiciary, CJ Nisar's leadership turned into a "reign of suo motus" which caused "tremendous damage to the majesty of law [and] to certainty as an ideal of the rule of law."[75]

THE SHERRIFF: ASIF SAEED KHOSA

In January 2019, Justice Asif Saeed Khosa was promoted to lead the Supreme Court of Pakistan, serving a tenure of twelve months.[76] When Justice Khosa was promoted to chief justice, he

> inherited a hyper-activist Supreme Court frequently accused of judicial overreach under the stewardship of his controversial predecessor, Saqib Nisar. At the time, the top court was routinely branded with making populist decisions at the expense of adherence to the law and with unduly interfering in the work of the government while neglecting its own duties.[77]

Before taking the helm of the Supreme Court, Justice Khosa received public attention for his involvement in the *Panamagate* case related to allegations of money laundering against Prime Minister Nawaz Sharif.[78] Justice Khosa's aggressive posturing in the case led many to criticize his decision "as having deprived a democratically-elected prime minister of his fundamental rights of due process and fair trial . . . [and Justice Khosa] allowed his zeal for moral accountability to trump due process, amounting to a dangerous precedent."[79] This decision led many to fear that Chief Justice Khosa may adopt a confrontational policy with political branches when he was promoted.

Yet, much like his predecessors Chief Justices Jillani, Mulk, and Jamali, Khosa delivered a speech before his promotion that set out his plan to adopt a policy of judicial restraint.[80] Chief Justice Khosa explained that he would use suo motu powers "very sparingly and only in respect of larger issues of national importance where either there is no other adequate or efficacious remedy available or the available constitutional or legal remedies are ineffective or are rendered incapacitated."[81] He went on to discuss how the relationship between the judiciary and other branches of government had suffered in the past due to the politicized nature of disputes handled by the Supreme Court:

> Let us discuss the alleged encroachment of the executive domain by the judiciary through interference in matters of policy, the alleged excessive use

of its constitutional jurisdiction in matters which are administrative in nature and how best the judiciary can return to its normal but effective adjudicatory role.[82]

During his tenure, Chief Justice Khosa focused on procedural and structural reforms to the criminal justice system in Pakistan. He argued that the invocation of suo motu by the highest court of the land in criminal incidents led to delays, deprived the defendants of appeal to a higher court, and such "pre-mature interventions" weakened the role of lower courts as an integral part of the judicial process.[83]

He delivered on his promise to curtail the use of suo motu and stabilizing relations with the executive branch by not interfering with "executive affairs" and by not taking "a single suo motu notice on governance issues."[84] Senior counsel Aitzaz Ahsan explained that "Chief Justice Khosa tries his best to have a steady hand in affairs and is not in favour of taking suo motu notices."[85]

There was one exception: Chief Justice Khosa utilized his suo motu powers relating to the reappointment of the chief of army staff. In the final month of his leadership of the Supreme Court, the chief of army staff was reappointed and petitions challenging this action were submitted to the Court.[86] Subsequently, when petitioners allegedly withdrew their complaints, Chief Justice Khosa took cognizance of the issue.[87] This was unlike other suo motu cases that were based on news clips or personal letters read by the chief justice of Pakistan as this case involved litigious parties at some point.

Outside of his singular invocation of suo motu powers, Chief Justice Khosa followed the path to restraint laid out by former chief justices Jillani, Mulk, and Jamali or the "Taciturn Trio." Yet, Chief Justice Khosa differed from the trio in one major way: he tried to create rules and systematize the Court's future use of suo motu. Unlike his quiet predecessors, Chief Justice Khosa was more like a sheriff attempting to lay down a system and rules for the exercise of the Court's power.

As Babar Sattar explains, Chief Justice Khosa held Supreme Court administrative meetings to discuss the need for suo motu rules.[88] These rules were created through proposed amendments to the Supreme Court Rules of 1980 and even though they were not adopted or made public, their drafting demonstrated Chief Justice Khosa's commitment to "structuring and regulating" the Court's powers under 184(3).[89] Some who have seen the amended Supreme Court Rules of 1980 explained that they create the first-ever appeals system for suo motu cases and they require the Chief Justice to seek the advice of two senior justices before invoking suo motu.[90] These two changes would radically transform Pakistan's Supreme Court, yet

> [t]he big challenge . . . is to evolve consensus among the Supreme Court judges, who have had a different approach in exercising public interest jurisdiction in the past. It is debatable whether all judges will be unanimous in structuring the chief justice's discretionary powers in initiating public interest litigation.[91]

Divergence of opinion by various Justices on the bench may have been one of the reasons the amendments to the Supreme Court Rules were not adopted. Despite this, many hope that these draft rules will be made public one day, opening the door for a robust discussion on what rules and limits could be institutionally applied to the Supreme Court's suo motu jurisdiction.

Following Chief Justice Khosa, in December 2019, Justice Gulzar Ahmed was promoted to lead the Court until February 1, 2022.[92] As Chief Justice Ahmed will be leading Pakistan's judiciary for two years, it is significant to note that he has not made any major statements concerning the regulation of suo motu powers. However, Chief Justice Ahmed raised his first suo motu notice surrounding the government's response to the COVID-19 pandemic.[93] The role of the courts in dealing with the pandemic remains unsettled around the world. Yet, some have pointed to the fact that "[j]udicial overreach at this time would pose to be an obstacle,"[94] particularly with the Pakistani judiciary's recent history of interfering with the substantive work of the political branches. Chief Justice Ahmed has been accused of attempting to micromanage a particularly complicated policy issue, which is "problematic as it transfers power from the elected public representatives to the unelected bench who cannot be held accountable by the people."[95] Some have expressed their fear that the COVID-19 decision may foretell Chief Justice Ahmed following the example of Chief Justice Nisar in amplifying suo motu powers during his last year as chief justice of Pakistan.

THE FUTURE OF THE COURT

There are two methods to chart the potential future of suo motu powers by Pakistan's Supreme Court. The first method recognizes that the control of suo motu by the chief justice will persist over time, which requires analysts to examine the personal record and jurisprudence of each of the upcoming chief justices. The second method suggests that suo motu can only be regulated when rules are laid down to bind all future chief justices without reference to their personal views.

For the first method, one must look to the speeches and past judgments of junior justices on the Supreme Court in order to understand how they might use suo motu powers. The example of Chief Justice Nisar demonstrates that past actions and public statements may not be the sole indicator of a chief justices use of suo motu considering he began his tenure with restraint but ended with a hyper-active posture toward the political branches.

The future of suo motu under the personality model currently in place is complicated because "it can be said that future chief justices have also varying approaches to public interest litigation,[96]" which means each chief justice will leave their individual mark on the use of suo motu. For Justice Umar Ata Bandial, who will become chief justice in February 2022 and will serve nearly two years leading the apex court: he was "part of the bench led by Justice Saqib Nisar" during many of the suo motu cases.[97] This indicates that Chief Justice Bandial would be open to continuing the use of suo motu where he deems appropriate. Following Bandial, Justice Qazi Faez Isa is likely to become the next chief justice from September 2023 to October 2024. Many have argued that Justice Isa is one of the more independent judges on the apex court and objected in the past to Chief Justice Nisar's overuse of suo motu.[98] This indicates that the suo motu powers may be reserved for a handful of extreme cases much like the Taciturn Trio, with a particular potential focus on issues in Baluchistan, Justice Isa's home province. Lastly, Justice Mansoor Ali Shah will take power from August 2025 until November 2027, potentially serving a two-year term. Justice Shah is also known for his independence and groundbreaking administrative work as chief justice of the Lahore High Court.[99] Yet, much like Chief Justice Khosa, Justice Shah is an expert in judicial administration and his focus remains on "reforming the judicial system,"[100] which indicates that he may attempt to revive Chief Justice Khosa's initiative to create rules for the use of suo motu by amending the Supreme Court Rules of 1980.

While the above shortly summarizes the future of suo motu under individual control, legal scholars have argued that this power should be vested in the Supreme Court as an institution rather than in the chief justice as a personality. Sattar points out that Article 176 of Pakistan's constitution states that the Supreme Court is composed of both the chief justice and the junior judges and that "Article 184(3) [including suo motu] powers are powers of the SC and not those of the CJ Article 175."[101] The current improvisational use of suo motu based on the personalities of the chief justice is partly why many suo motu decisions remain unimplemented and have not provided justice to victims in the case.[102] The refusal to regulate the Court's use of suo motu is often justified as a means to ensure judicial independence or ensure that the Court can take corrupt politicians to task. Yet, Sattar answers these justifications with the following:

> After a decade of experience with suo-motu powers one can safely say that its net benefit has been close to zero. None of the high-profile suo-motu cases led to sustainable reform of structures of governance or accountability of individuals

> shamed by the SC . . . Suo motus must be regulated in the interest of the trichotomy of power, legal certainty, due process and fair trial. The refusal to regulate suo-motu powers is simply about power. It isn't about judicial independence or protecting the institution against evil.[103]

Therefore, while the needful action of any upcoming chief justice is to remove their own exclusive control over suo motu and share it with their junior justices, this has not occurred since the outburst of suo motu under the Chaudhry court. Likely, there is little agreement among the future chief justices concerning suo motu, but this is even more reason that predictable rules are necessary for the court to continue providing justice to disenfranchised or disadvantaged citizens. While some political analysts have suggested that these rules be imposed upon the chief justice through a legislation passed by parliament,[104] this may be interpreted as violating the independence of the judiciary and be deemed illegitimate by the Supreme Court itself.[105]

This leaves the one potential option being an amendment to the Supreme Court Rules of 1980 as suggested by Chief Justice Khosa. Such an amended set of rules would bind all chief justices to limits on suo motu, and the power of suo motu would be vested in the Supreme Court as a whole rather than in the personality of the chief justice. Another potential solution posed by jurists is that the Court could regulate its definition of terms "fundamental rights" and "public interest" in Article 184(3): "it is the confusion and ambiguity around the limits of this constitutional provision that allow its use indiscriminately . . . his can be avoided by clearly defining what constitutes fundamental rights and what does not."[106]

Until either the Supreme Court Rules are amended or jurisprudence is created that limits the definition of terms in Article 184(3), jurists and policymakers will be subject to massive shifts in the Supreme Court's exercise of powers, and the personality analyses of each chief justice would be the only method to anticipate the Court's future policy on suo motu.

NOTES

1. Adjunct Professor, Howard University School of Law. Senior Staff Attorney, American Bar Association Center for Human Rights

2. Gandhara, Pakistan's Emboldened Judiciary Poses Headache For Ruling Party Ahead of Polls, May 29, 2018. Available at https://gandhara.rferl.org/a/pakistan-emboldened-judiciary-poses-headache-for-ruling-party-ahead-of-polls/29257227.html (last accessed on Dec. 19, 2020).

3. Saad Sayeed, Incoming Pakistan Chief Justice opens new era for powerful court, Reurters, Jan. 17, 2019. Available at https://www.reuters.com/article/us-pakistan-court/incoming-pakistan-chief-justice-opens-new-era-for-powerful-court

-idUSKCN1PB1AE (last accessed Dec. 19, 2020). ("Nisar's high media profile has drawn parallels with Iftikhar Chaudhry, a chief justice who initially won plaudits for helping oust military ruler Pervez Musharraf in 2008, but was later criticized for overstepping his constitutional remit.")

4. Pakistan Constit. Article 184 (3).

5. Saad Sayeed, Incoming Pakistan Chief Justice opens new era for powerful court, Reurters, Jan. 17, 2019. Available at https://www.reuters.com/article/us-pakistan-court/incoming-pakistan-chief-justice-opens-new-era-for-powerful-court-idUSKCN1PB1AE (last accessed Dec. 19, 2020). ("[Chief Justice] Nisar himself has said his suo motu cases and frequent public appearances to inspect development projects and facilities such as schools and hospitals were aimed at protecting the poor.")

6. Pakistan's Emboldened Judiciary Poses Headache For Ruling Party Ahead Of Polls, Reuters, May 29, 2018. Available at https://gandhara.rferl.org/a/pakistan-emboldened-judiciary-poses-headache-for-ruling-party-ahead-of-polls/29257227.html (last accessed on Dec. 19, 2020).

7. Hasnaat Malik, Divide on use of suo motu powers, Express Tribune, Feb. 10, 2019. Available at https://tribune.com.pk/story/1907256/divide-use-suo-motu-powers (last accessed on Dec 19, 2020).

8. Salahuddin Ahmed, Regulating Suo Motu and Chief Justices Powers, Dawn, April 16, 2020 (available at https://www.dawn.com/news/1549624) (last accessed on Dec. 19, 2020).

9. Saad Sayeed, Incoming Pakistan Chief Justice opens new era for powerful court, Reurters, Jan. 17, 2019. Available at https://www.reuters.com/article/us-pakistan-court/incoming-pakistan-chief-justice-opens-new-era-for-powerful-court-idUSKCN1PB1AE (last accessed Dec. 19, 2020).

10. Babar Sattar, Back to the Suo Motu, Available at https://www.thenews.com.pk/print/646553-back-to-the-suo-motu (last accessed Dec 19, 2020). ("with a decade of judicial overreach with no visible benefit accruing to the people in whose name the power is exercised, the need to structure suo-motu power is writ large…")

11. Babar Sattar, Back to the Suo Motu, Available at https://www.thenews.com.pk/print/646553-back-to-the-suo-motu.

12. See generally Law Library of Congress, Suspension and Reinstatement of the Chief Justice of Pakistan: From Judicial Crisis to Restoring Judicial Independence?" Available at https://www.loc.gov/law/help/pakistan/justice.php#f19 (last accessed Dec. 19, 2020).

13. See Gallup, Pakistan's Troubled State," May 2011. Available at https://news.gallup.com/poll/157055/pakistan-troubled-state.aspx (last accessed on Dec 19, 2020). ("The judicial system saw an increase in confidence after the two-year Lawyer's Movement ended with Chief Justice of the Supreme Court, Iftikhar Muhammad Chaudhry, being restored to his post in March 2009.") See also, Yale Review of International Studies, Dictatorial Tendencies: Chaudhry and Pakistan's Supreme Court, January 2014. Available at http://yris.yira.org/essays/1236#_edn17 (last accessed on Dec. 19, 2020) citing to Christine Fair, Addressing Fundamental Challenges in The Future of Pakistan, ed. Stephen Cohen, Brookings Institution Press

2011 at 93. Available at http://sanipanhwar.com/The%20Future%20of%20Pakistan.pdf (last accessed Dec. 19, 2020) ("According to a 2009 national poll, Pakistanis had 'high expectations' that courts would be independent of political or military influences…because they believed that the courts could advocate and defend economic needs and basic rights.")

14. Jon Boone, Pakistan's chief justice Iftikhar Chaudhry suffers public backlash, Guardian, August 28, 2013. Available at https://www.theguardian.com/world/2013/aug/28/pakistan-judges-backlash-ftikhar-haudhry (last accessed Dec 19, 2020).

15. Katharine Houreld, Pakistan's top judge, feared by some, to pass seat to gentle successor, Reuters, Nov. 19, 2013. Available at https://www.reuters.com/article/pakistan-justice-idINDEE9AH0G920131119 (last accessed Dec. 19, 2020).

16. Jon Boone, Pakistan's chief justice Iftikhar Chaudhry suffers public backlash, Guardian, August 28, 2013. Available at https://www.theguardian.com/world/2013/aug/28/pakistan-judges-backlash-ftikhar-haudhry (last accessed Dec 19, 2020).

17. Hasnaat Malik, SC yet to determine suo motu's parameters, Express Tribune Dec. 9, 2019. Available at https://tribune.com.pk/story/2114648/sc-yet-determine-suo-motus-parameters (last accessed on Dec. 19, 2020).

18. Katharine Houreld, Pakistan's top judge, feared by some, to pass seat to gentle successor, Reuters, Nov. 19, 2013. Available at https://www.reuters.com/article/pakistan-justice-idINDEE9AH0G920131119 (last accessed Dec. 19, 2020).

19. Sabir Shah, History of voluntary court initiatives in Pakistan, India, US, The News, Aug. 25, 2015. Available at https://www.thenews.com.pk/print/58379-history-of-voluntary-court-initiatives-in-pakistan-india-us (last accessed Dec 19, 2020).

20. Business Standard, Pak SC Chief Justice Jillani to vacate Supreme Court's helm, June 30, 2014. Available at https://www.business-standard.com/article/news-ani/pak-sc-chief-justice-jillani-to-vacate-supreme-court-s-helm-114063000530_1.html (las accessed Dec. 19, 2020.)

21. Hasnaat Malik, From Judicial Activism to Judicial Restraint, Express Tribune, Dec. 31 2014. Available at https://tribune.com.pk/story/814921/2014-from-judicial-activism-to-judicial-restraint (last accessed Dec. 19, 2020).

22. Faisal Siddiqi, Rainbow Supreme Court, Dawn, Aug 25, 2015. Available at https://www.dawn.com/news/1202670/newspaper/newspaper/column (last accessed Dec 19, 2020.)

23. Babar Sattar, Back to the Suo Motu, Available at https://www.thenews.com.pk/print/646553-back-to-the-suo-motu (last accessed Dec. 19, 2020).

24. I.A. Rehman, SC and minority rights, Dawn, April 11, 2019. Available at https://www.dawn.com/news/1475329 (last accessed on Dec. 19, 2020.) ("During his seven-month tenure, the court took suo motu notice of only a couple of cases in 2013 and one case in 2014.")

25. Zahir Shah Sherazi, Twin church blasts claim 80 lives in Peshawar, Dawn, Sept. 22, 2013. Available at https://www.dawn.com/news/1044668 (last accessed Dec. 19, 2020).

26. Justice Tassaduq Hussain Jillani, The Interplay of Majority and Minority Religious Rights and the Role of the Judiciary, 2017 *B.Y.U. L. Rev.* 901, 905–10 (2017).

27. I.A. Rehman, SC and minority rights, Dawn, April 11, 2019. Available at https://www.dawn.com/news/1475329 (last accessed on Dec. 19, 2020.) ("During his seven-month tenure, the court took suo motu notice of only a couple of cases in 2013 and one case in 2014.")

28. S.M.C. No.1 of 2014 and C.M.A. Nos. 217-K/2014 IN S.M.C. No.1/2014 et al., Pakistan: Supreme Court, 19 June 2014, available at: https://www.refworld.org/cases,PAK_SC,559e57644.html [accessed 19 December 2020]

29. Justice Tassaduq Hussain Jillani, The Interplay of Majority and Minority Religious Rights and the Role of the Judiciary, 2017 *B.Y.U. L. Rev.* 901, 905–10 (2017).

30. Justice Tassaduq Hussain Jillani, The Interplay of Majority and Minority Religious Rights and the Role of the Judiciary, 2017 *B.Y.U. L. Rev.* 901, 905–10 (2017).

31. I.A. Rehman, SC and minority rights, Dawn, April 11, 2019. Available at https://www.dawn.com/news/1475329 (last accessed on Dec. 19, 2020.)

32. Jon Boone, Pakistan's chief justice Iftikhar Chaudhry suffers public backlash, Guardian, August 28, 2013. Available at https://www.theguardian.com/world/2013/aug/28/pakistan-judges-backlash-ftikhar-haudhry (last accessed Dec 19, 2020). "The court regularly involves itself in other matters of public policy, at various times ordering the almost insolvent government to slash prices of sugar, flour and gas." See also Junaid Ashraf, Muhammad, Muhammad, Faiza and Hopper, Trevor (2019) Accounting signifiers, political discourse, popular resistance and legal identity during Pakistan Steel Mills attempted privatization. Critical Perspectives on Accounting, 60. pp. 18-43. ISSN 1045-2354. Available at http://sro.sussex.ac.uk/id/eprint/76638/3/PSM%20Paper%20January%2017%202017%20%281%29.pdf (last accessed on Dec. 20, 2020). Quotation from Justice Shabbar Raza Rizvi "Today the Supreme Court is … fixing prices of everything from CNG to samosas [snacks]. Doing so makes the CJP behave like Mughal emperor Akbar who used to fix the wheat prices. The mindset of the CJP has therefore become that of a ruler ... not of a judge."

33. Nasir Iqbal, Justice Nasirul Mulk- a 'democrat' judge, Dawn, May 30, 2018. Available at https://www.dawn.com/news/1410626 (last accessed Dec 19, 2020).

34. Tariq Butt, Sanity prevails, at last, The News International, May 29, 2018. Available at https://www.thenews.com.pk/amp/322925-sanity-prevails-at-last (last accessed on Dec. 19, 2020).

35. Nasir Iqbal, Justice Nasirul Mulk- politically neutral, Dawn, May 28, 2018. Available at https://www.dawn.com/news/1117415 (last accessed on Dec 19, 2020).

36. Hasnaat Malik, Supreme Court's year of transition, Express Tribune, Dec. 30, 2015. Available at https://tribune.com.pk/story/1019061/supreme-courts-year-of-transition (last accessed on Dec 19, 2020).

37. Hasnaat Malik, Tenure well served: CJ Nasirul Mulk retires after eventful stint, Express Tribune, Aug. 16, 2015. Available at https://tribune.com.pk/story/938940/tenure-well-served-cj-nasirul-mulk-retires-after-eventful-stint?amp=1 (last accessed on Dec. 19, 2020).

38. Nasir Iqbal, Justice Nasirul Mulk- politically neutral, Dawn, May 28, 2018. Available at https://www.dawn.com/news/1117415 (last accessed on Dec 19, 2020)

39. Hasnaat Malik, Tenure well served: CJ Nasirul Mulk retires after eventful stint, Express Tribune, Aug. 16, 2015. Available at https://tribune.com.pk/story/938940/tenure-well-served-cj-nasirul-mulk-retires-after-eventful-stint?amp=1. (last accessed on Dec 19, 2020). See also Courting The Law, Chief Justice Nasirul Mulk Retires, Jawwad Khawaja Takes Over as Head of Apex Court, Aug. 17, 2015. Available at https://courtingthelaw.com/2015/08/17/updates/chief-justice-nasirul-mulk-retires-jawwad-khawaja-takes-over-as-head-of-apex-court/ (last accessed Dec. 19, 2020).

40. Hasnaat Malik, Tenure well served: CJ Nasirul Mulk retires after eventful stint, Express Tribune, Aug. 16, 2015. Available at https://tribune.com.pk/story/938940/tenure-well-served-cj-nasirul-mulk-retires-after-eventful-stint?amp=1 (last accessed on Dec 19, 2020).

41. Irfan Haider, SC takes suo motu notice of Christian couple's lynching, Dawn, Nov 22, 2014. Available at https://www.dawn.com/news/1146175 (last accessed on Dec. 19, 2020).

42. Premier Christian News, Pakistan Supreme Court intervenes over killing of Christian couple, Nov. 24, 2014. Available at https://premierchristian.news/en/news/article/pakistan-supreme-court-intervenes-over-killing-of-christian-couple (last accessed on Dec. 19, 2020).

43. Nasir Iqbal, SC orders action against police over Kot Radha Kishan incident, Dawn, Dec. 17, 2014. Available at https://www.dawn.com/news/1151374 (last accessed on Dec 19, 2020).

44. SAMAA TV, CJP takes suo-moto notice over burning of Ghotki women, April 2015. Available at https://www.samaa.tv/news/2015/04/cjp-takes-suo-moto-notice-over-burning-of-women-in-ghotki/ (last access on Dec 19, 2020).

45. SAMAA TV, CJP takes suo-moto notice over burning of Ghotki women, April 2015. Available at https://www.samaa.tv/news/2015/04/cjp-takes-suo-moto-notice-over-burning-of-women-in-ghotki/ (last access on Dec 19, 2020).

46. Syed Irfan Raza, Justice Jamli takes oath as Chief Justice of SC, Dawn, Sept. 11, 2015. Available at https://www.dawn.com/news/1206224/justice-jamali-takes-oath-as-chief-justice-of-sc (last access on Dec 19, 2020).

47. Hasnaat Malik, CJP takes a break on suo motu action, Express Tribune, Feb. 6, 2018. Available at https://tribune.com.pk/story/1627439/no-suo-motu-notices-earlier-ones-resolved-cjp (last access on Dec. 19, 2020).

48. Babar Sattar, Back to the suo motu, The News International, April 19, 2020. Available at https://www.thenews.com.pk/print/646581-back-to-the-suo-motu (last accessed on Dec. 19, 2020).

49. Hasnaat Malik, CJP to retire today: Justice Anwar Jamali's tenure defined by judicial restraint, Express Tribune, Dec. 29, 2016. Available at https://tribune.com.pk/story/1279155/cjp-retire-today-justice-anwar-jamalis-tenure-defined-judicial-restraint (last accessed Dec. 19, 2020).

50. SAMAA TV, CJ takes suo motu notice of alleged political interference in Sindh police, June 2016. Available at https://www.samaa.tv/news/2016/06/cj-takes-suo-motu-notice-of-alleged-political-interference-in-sindh-police/ (last accessed on Dec. 19, 2020).

51. Max Bearak, An entire generation of a city's lawyers was killed in Pakistan, Washington Post, Aug. 9, 2016. Available at https://www.washingtonpost.com/news/worldviews/wp/2016/08/09/an-entire-generation-of-a-citys-lawyers-was-killed-in-pakistan/ (last accessed Dec. 19, 2020).

52. Dawn, CJP Jamali takes suo motu notice of Quetta carnage, Aug 31, 2016. Available at https://www.dawn.com/news/1281133 (last accessed Dec. 19, 2020).

53. Hasnaat Malik, CJP to retire today: Justice Anwar Jamali's tenure defined by judicial restraint, Express Tribune, Dec. 29, 2016. Available at https://tribune.com.pk/story/1279155/cjp-retire-today-justice-anwar-jamalis-tenure-defined-judicial-restraint (last accessed Dec. 19, 2020).

54. Sohail Khan, SC restores 50pc quota of private Haj tour operators, The News International, May 4, 2016. Available at https://www.thenews.com.pk/print/117370-SC-restores-50pc-quota-of-private-Haj-tour-operators (last accessed Dec 19, 2020).

55. Rai Hassan Nawaz vs. Muhammad Ayub, 2017 PLD Supreme Court 70 (2016). ("The election tribunal is therefore vested with a suo motu power to scrutinise, inter alia, false or incorrect statements made by a returned candidate in respect of his own assets and liabilities and those of his spouse or his dependents.") See also Hasnaat Malik, Election tribunal vested with suo motu powers, says Supreme Court, Express Tribune, Dec. 28, 2019. Available at https://tribune.com.pk/story/1276972/election-tribunal-vested-suo-motu-powers-says-supreme-court (last accessed Dec 19, 2020.)

56. Hasnaat Malik, CJP to retire today: Justice Anwar Jamali's tenure defined by judicial restraint, Express Tribune, Dec. 29, 2016. Available at https://tribune.com.pk/story/1279155/cjp-retire-today-justice-anwar-jamalis-tenure-defined-judicial-restraint (last accessed Dec. 19, 2020). (Ali Zafar, former president of the Supreme Court Bar Association: "He has also maintained good relations with the bar and has always given preference to its opinion.")

57. Hasnaat Malik, CJP to retire today: Justice Anwar Jamali's tenure defined by judicial restraint, Express Tribune, Dec. 29, 2016. Available at https://tribune.com.pk/story/1279155/cjp-retire-today-justice-anwar-jamalis-tenure-defined-judicial-restraint (last accessed Dec. 19, 2020).

58. Tariq Butt, Next CJ to stay in office for two years and 18 days, The News International, Dec. 12, 2016. Available at https://www.thenews.com.pk/print/171451-Next-CJ-to-stay-in-office-for-two-years-and-18-days (accessed on Dec. 19, 2020).

59. Waqqas Mir, Judicial restraint was Saqib Nisar's hallmark — then the dam broke, Dawn, Dec. 21, 2019. Available at https://www.dawn.com/news/1458321 (last accessed Dec. 19, 2020).

60. Waqqas Mir, Judicial restraint was Saqib Nisar's hallmark — then the dam broke, Dawn, Dec. 21, 2019. Available at https://www.dawn.com/news/1458321 (last accessed Dec. 19, 2020).

61. Gandhara, Pakistan's emboldened judiciary poses headache for ruling party ahead of polls, May 29, 2018. Available at https://gandhara.rferl.org/a/pakistan-emboldened-judiciary-poses-headache-for-ruling-party-ahead-of-polls/29257227.html (last accessed Dec. 19, 2020).

62. Saroop Ijaz, Chief Justice Saqib Nisar: Judging too much, Herald Dawn, Feb. 20, 2019. Available at http://herald.dawn.com/news/1398778?fbclid=IwAR1e8TeqJojsUP07o78gd7iY6iIPW62el_RBNMML_5ByhaH_9RrjovEh2sg (

63. Zaki Rahman, A man of the law to the core, Justice Khosa will be a hard act to follow, Dawn, Dec. 21, 2019. Available at https://www.dawn.com/news/1522773 (last accessed Dec. 19, 2020); Waqqas Mir, Judicial restraint was Saqib Nisar's hallmark — then the dam broke, Dawn, Dec. 21, 2019. Available at https://www.dawn.com/news/1458321 (last accessed Dec. 19, 2020).

64. Express Tribune, Justice Nisar's legacy: Fate of the dam fund, Jan. 17, 2019. Available at https://tribune.com.pk/story/1890122/justice-nisars-legacy-dam-fund (last accessed Dec. 19, 2020).

65. Express Tribune, Justice Nisar's legacy: Fate of the dam fund, Jan. 17, 2019. Available at https://tribune.com.pk/story/1890122/justice-nisars-legacy-dam-fund (last accessed Dec. 19, 2020).

66. Express Tribune, Justice Nisar's legacy: Fate of the dam fund, Jan. 17, 2019. Available at https://tribune.com.pk/story/1890122/justice-nisars-legacy-dam-fund (last accessed Dec. 19, 2020).

67. Express Tribune, Justice Nisar's legacy: Fate of the dam fund, Jan. 17, 2019. Available at https://tribune.com.pk/story/1890122/justice-nisars-legacy-dam-fund (last accessed Dec. 19, 2020).

68. Saroop Ijaz, Chief Justice Saqib Nisar: Judging too much, Herald Dawn, Feb. 20, 2019. Available at http://herald.dawn.com/news/1398778?fbclid=IwAR1e8TeqJojsUP07o78gd7iY6iIPW62el_RBNMML_5ByhaH_9RrjovEh2sg (last accessed Dec. 19, 2020).

69. Geo TV, CJP to embark on dam fund-raising trip to Britain from today, Nov. 20, 2018. Available at https://www.geo.tv/latest/219049-cjp-to-embark-on-dam-fund-raising-trip-to-britain-from-today (last accessed Dec. 19, 2020).

70. Saroop Ijaz, Chief Justice Saqib Nisar: Judging too much, Herald Dawn, Feb. 20, 2019. Available at http://herald.dawn.com/news/1398778?fbclid=IwAR1e8TeqJojsUP07o78gd7iY6iIPW62el_RBNMML_5ByhaH_9RrjovEh2sg (last accessed Dec. 19, 2020).

71. Saad Sayeed, Incoming Pakistan Chief Justice opens new era for powerful court, Reuters, Jan. 17, 2019. Available at https://www.reuters.com/article/us-pakistan-court/incoming-pakistan-chief-justice-opens-new-era-for-powerful-court-idUSKCN1PB1AE (last accessed Dec. 19, 2020) ("projects like building of dams have been undertaken only to be left in the middle of nowhere.")

72. Express Tribune, The power of suo motu, Jan. 17, 2019. Available at https://tribune.com.pk/story/1887380/power-suo-motu (last accessed Dec. 19, 2020).

73. Babar Sattar, back to the suo motu, The News International, April 19, 2020. Available at https://www.thenews.com.pk/print/646553-back-to-the-suo-motu (last accessed Dec. 19, 2020)

74. Babar Sattar, back to the suo motu, The News International, April 19, 2020. Available at https://www.thenews.com.pk/print/646553-back-to-the-suo-motu (last accessed Dec. 19, 2020)

75. Babar Sattar, back to the suo motu, The News International, April 19, 2020. Available at https://www.thenews.com.pk/print/646553-back-to-the-suo-motu (last accessed Dec. 19, 2020)

76. Dawn, Justice Asif Saeed Khosa sworn in as 26th Chief Justice of Pakistan, Jan. 18, 2019. Available at https://www.dawn.com/news/1458297 (last accessed Dec. 19, 2019).

77. Zaki Rahman, A man of the law to the core, Justice Khosa will be a hard act to follow, Dawn, Dec. 21, 2019. Available at https://www.dawn.com/news/1522773 (last accessed Dec. 19, 2020).

78. Nasir Iqbal, Khosa-led bench to hear Panama Papers petitions, Dawn, Jan 3, 2017. Available at https://www.dawn.com/news/1305681 (last accessed Dec 19, 2020).

79. Zaki Rahman, A man of the law to the core, Justice Khosa will be a hard act to follow, Dawn, Dec. 21, 2019. Available at https://www.dawn.com/news/1522773 (last accessed Dec. 19, 2020).

80. Complete Text of Address by Justice Asif Saeed Khosa at the full court reference for CJP Nisar, Dawn, Jan. 17 2019. Available at https://www.dawn.com/news/1458118/complete-text-of-address-by-justice-asif-saeed-khosa-at-full-court-reference-for-cjp-nisar (last accessed Dec. 19, 2020).

81. Complete Text of Address by Justice Asif Saeed Khosa at the full court reference for CJP Nisar, Dawn, Jan. 17 2019. Available at https://www.dawn.com/news/1458118/complete-text-of-address-by-justice-asif-saeed-khosa-at-full-court-reference-for-cjp-nisar (last accessed Dec. 19, 2020).

82. Complete Text of Address by Justice Asif Saeed Khosa at the full court reference for CJP Nisar, Dawn, Jan. 17 2019. Available at https://www.dawn.com/news/1458118/complete-text-of-address-by-justice-asif-saeed-khosa-at-full-court-reference-for-cjp-nisar (last accessed Dec. 19, 2020).

83. Tariq Butt, First-ever suo motu notice during 11-month incumbency of CJP Khosa, The News International, Nov. 27, 2019. Available at https://www.thenews.com.pk/print/575041-first-ever-suo-motu-notice-during-11-month-incumbency-of-cjp-khosa (last accessed Dec 19, 2020).

84. Hasnaat Malik, Past decade: How judiciary played role in shaping Pakistan's politics, Express Tribune, Jan. 1, 2020. Available at https://tribune.com.pk/story/2128343/1-judiciary-played-role-shaping-countrys-politics (last accessed Dec. 19, 2020).

85. Dawn, Why has PML-N leadership not rushed to court with their 'undeniable evidence'?: Aitzaz Ahsan, July 10, 2019. Available at https://www.dawn.com/news/1493057 (last accessed Dec 19, 2020).

86. Tariq Butt, First-ever suo motu notice during 11-month incumbency of CJP Khosa, The News International, Nov. 27, 2019. Available at https://www.thenews.com.pk/print/575041-first-ever-suo-motu-notice-during-11-month-incumbency-of-cjp-khosa (last accessed Dec 19, 2020).

87. Tariq Butt, First-ever suo motu notice during 11-month incumbency of CJP Khosa, The News International, Nov. 27, 2019. Available at https://www.thenews.com.pk/print/575041-first-ever-suo-motu-notice-during-11-month-incumbency-of-cjp-khosa (last accessed Dec 19, 2020).

88. Babar Sattar, Back to the Suo Motu, Available at https://www.thenews.com.pk/print/646553-back-to-the-suo-motu. (last accessed Dec 19, 2020).

89. Babar Sattar, Back to the Suo Motu, Available at https://www.thenews.com.pk/print/646553-back-to-the-suo-motu. (last accessed Dec 19, 2020).

90. Hasnaat Malik, CJP shares with judges' draft for amending SC rules, Express Tribune, Dec. 18, 2019. Available at https://tribune.com.pk/story/2120700/1-cjp-shares-judges-draft-amending-sc-rules (last accessed Dec. 19, 2020).

91. Hasnaat Malik, CJP shares with judges' draft for amending SC rules, Express Tribune, Dec. 18, 2019. Available at https://tribune.com.pk/story/2120700/1-cjp-shares-judges-draft-amending-sc-rules (last accessed Dec. 19, 2020).

92. Saqib Virk, Justice Gulzar to be sworn in as 27th chief justice of Pakistan on Dec 21, Express Tribune, Dec. 4, 2019. Available at https://tribune.com.pk/story/2111608/1-justice-gulzar-sworn-27th-chief-justice-pakistan-dec-21 (last accessed Dec. 19, 2020).

93. Haseeb Bhatti, CJP Ahmed takes suo motu notice of measures taken to battle coronavirus, Express Tribune, April 10, 2020. Available at https://www.dawn.com/news/1548098 (last accessed Dec. 19, 2020).

94. The News International, Supreme Court's remarks against SAPM health: Crises when power is wielded without responsibility, says Aitzaz, April 15, 2020. Available at https://www.thenews.com.pk/print/644713-supreme-court-s-remarks-against-sapm-health-crises-when-power-is-wielded-without-responsibility-says-aitzaz (last accessed Dec. 19, 2020).

95. Saad Sayeed, Incoming Pakistan Chief Justice opens new era for powerful court, Reurters, Jan. 17, 2019. Available at https://www.reuters.com/article/us-pakistan-court/incoming-pakistan-chief-justice-opens-new-era-for-powerful-court-idUSKCN1PB1AE (last accessed Dec. 19, 2020).

96. Public interest litigation is a category of cases permitted by Article 184 (3), the Court's suo motu power is also based out of this article in the constitution.

97. Hasnaat Malik, SC yet to determine suo motu's parameters, Dec. 9, 2019. Available at https://tribune.com.pk/story/2114648/sc-yet-determine-suo-motus-parameters (last accessed Dec. 19, 2020).

98. Hasnaat Malik, SC yet to determine suo motu's parameters, Dec. 9, 2019. Available at https://tribune.com.pk/story/2114648/sc-yet-determine-suo-motus-parameters (last accessed Dec. 19, 2020).

99. Courting the Law, Justice Syed Mansoor Ali shah to take oath as chief justice Lahore high court today, Available at https://courtingthelaw.com/2016/06/28/updates/justice-syed-mansoor-ali-shah-to-take-oath-as-chief-justice-lahore-high-court-today/ (last accessed Dec. 19, 2020). ("He has helped in revamping Punjab Judicial Academy in order to strengthen judicial training and has also led initiatives like case management and court automation across Punjab. Justice Shah is currently working on setting up the first Alternative Dispute Resolution (ADR) Centre in Lahore for the benefit of litigants.)

100. Hasnaat Malik, SC yet to determine suo motu's parameters, Dec. 9, 2019. Available at https://tribune.com.pk/story/2114648/sc-yet-determine-suo-motus-parameters (last accessed Dec. 19, 2020).

101. Babar Sattar, limits of courts powers?, Dawn, May 12, 2018. Available at https://www.thenews.com.pk/print/315593-limits-of-court-powers (last accessed Dec 19, 2020).

102. Babar Sattar, Back to suo motu, Dawn, April 19, 2020. Available at https://www.thenews.com.pk/print/646581-back-to-the-suo-motu (last accessed Dec. 19, 2020).

103. Babar Sattar, Back to suo motu, Dawn, April 19, 2020. Available at https://www.thenews.com.pk/print/646581-back-to-the-suo-motu (last accessed Dec. 19, 2020).

104. Hasnaat Malik, SC yet to determine suo motu's parameters, Dawn, Dec. 9, 2019. Available at https://tribune.com.pk/story/2114648/sc-yet-determine-suo-motus-parameters (last accessed Dec. 19, 2020). ("If the judiciary itself does not regularise the public interest jurisdiction then the parliament may take up the issue, which may become source of tension among institutions.")

105. See Generally Saroop Ijaz, Judicial Appointments in Pakistan: Full Circle, *LUMS Law Journal*, Vol. 1. Available at https://sahsol.lums.edu.pk/law-journal/judicial-appointments-pakistan-coming-full-circle which explains that the Supreme Court's reversal of the 18th Amendment was in part due to the Amendment allowing for Parliament to have a substantive role in judicial appointments which have traditionally been left exclusively in the hands of the judiciary itself. The independence of the judiciary was a primary reason for over[1]turning the provisions in the 18th Amendment relating to the appointment of judges).

106. Saroop Ijaz, Chief Justice Saqib Nisar: Judging too much, Herald Dawn, Feb 20, 2019. Available at https://herald.dawn.com/news/1398778 (last accessed Dec. 19, 2020).

Index

About the Contributors

Satvinder S. Juss, PhD (Cantab.), FRSA, teaches at King's College London. A Barrister-at-Law of Gray's Inn, he has been on the Panel "A" of the Government of Wales panel of advocates and on Panel "A" of the Equality & Human Rights Commission. He has written extensively on human rights and constitutional law, as well as on international refugee law. He sits as a deputy judge of the Upper Tribunal in London.

Dr. Muhammad Danyal Khan is serving as a lecturer in law at University Gilani Law College (UGLC), Bahauddin Zakariya University Multan. Dr. Khan is interested in teaching and research in areas of intellectual property, human rights, and administrative laws. With almost twelve years of an active career in teaching and research, he has earned best teacher awards and has been published several times in world-renowned peer-reviewed journals under the umbrella of ScienceDirect, Walters & Kluwer, and Brill-Nijhoff. The qualifications include PhD Law from Brunel University London, after winning a prestigious doctoral scholarship from Punjab Higher Education Commission. He has earned LLM (Corporate Law), LLB (Hons.), and BA from International Islamic University Islamabad. Dr. Khan has played an active role in the inception of LLM and PhD programs at the UGLC during his service, this included curricula development, and its implementation. Dr. Khan aspires to teach with passion, produce impactful research, and administrate effectively in the field of legal education.

Adrija Ghosh is a consultant (Research) at Project 39A, National Law University, Delhi, India.

Dr. Waris Husain is the senior staff attorney for South and Southeast Asia with the ABA Justice Defenders Program. Prior to joining the center, Dr. Husain was a policy analyst at the US Commission on International Religious Freedom covering the South Asia region. He is an adjunct professor of international law at the Howard University School of Law. Dr. Husain received his SJD degree from American University Washington College of Law in 2017, specializing in constitutional and comparative law. His dissertation focused on the development of judicial review in the Supreme Courts of Pakistan, India, and the United States which was published by Routledge South Asia in 2017. Dr. Husain received his JD from the Howard University School of Law in 2011 and his LLM at American University Washington College of Law, specializing in international human rights and international business in 2013.

Uzair J. Kayani is acting head of the Department of Law & Policy at SAHSOL, LUMS. He teaches Law and Economics, Regulatory Agencies, Business Law, Torts, Public International Law, and Game Theory. His research in related areas has appeared in US law journals and edited volumes.

Mr. Kayani has served on the Public Private Partnership Board of the government of Punjab. He has trained the Lahore High Court research cell to assist the Punjab Judiciary. He served as the general secretary the Legal Education Committee of the Lahore High Court Bar Association. He has previously served on the Environmental Advisory Board of the government of Punjab and the Climate Change Commission formed by the Lahore High Court. Professor Kayani has also trained the district judiciary at the Punjab Judicial Academy and advised the federal and provincial governments on legal and policy matters.

Marva Khan is an assistant professor of Practice at the Shaikh Ahmad Hassan School of Law, Lahore University of Management Sciences, Pakistan. Marva Khan holds an LLM degree from Harvard Law School, prior to which she completed her BA-LLB from the Lahore University of Management Sciences. She is the cofounder of the Pakistani Feminist Judgments Project and she is also the founding member and coeditor of the LUMS Law Journal. Marva completed her LLM from Harvard Law School and BA-LLB from LUMS. She is currently working as a co-PI on a project aiming to improve inclusion of PWDs and improving issues pertaining to sexual harassment in educational institutions. Her areas of interest include constitutional law, particularly functioning of the judiciary, human rights, and gender.

Mr. Yasser Latif Hamdani is a barrister of Lincoln's Inn and an advocate of the High Courts of Pakistan. He was the counsel in the YouTube Case which eventually led to the unblocking of YouTube in Pakistan. Mr. Hamdani was subsequently a visiting fellow at Harvard Law School's Human Rights Program, where he researched the legal and constitutional discrimination against Ahmadis in Pakistan. Mr. Hamdani received his BA from Rutgers University in New Jersey in 2002, LLB from Quaid-e-Azam Law College of the Punjab University in Pakistan and LLM from University of Management and Technology Pakistan. He is also an author of three books: *Jinnah Myth and Reality* (2012), *Between Worlds, a Pakistani's Quest to Forge Meaning* (2016), and *Jinnah a Life* (2020). Mr. Hamdani also writes for various national and international publications on law, history, and current affairs. He is an Asia Society 21 Fellow for his work to promote peace between Pakistan and India.

Reema Omer currently serves as a senior international legal advisor (South Asia) at the International Commission of Jurists (ICJ). She did her LLM specializing in public international law at the University of Cambridge in 2009 as a Commonwealth scholar. Reema is a member of the Human Rights Commission of Pakistan and writes regularly for national and international publications on issues related to international law, human rights, and the rule of law. Some of her publications include: *Transgender Persons (Protection of Rights) Act: A briefing paper* (2020); *A primer on international human rights law and standards on the right to freedom of thought, conscience, religion, or belief* (2019); *Challenges to Freedom of Religion or Belief in Myanmar* (2019); *Challenges to Freedom of Religion or Belief in Nepal* (2018); *"No More Missing Persons": The Criminalization of Enforced Disappearances in South Asia* (2017); and *Authority without Accountability: The struggle for justice in Pakistan* (2013).

Javaid Rehman is a professor of International Human Rights Law at Brunel University, London, and the United Nations Special Rapporteur on the human rights situation in the Islamic Republic of Iran.

Adnan Sattar is an assistant professor at Lahore University of Management Sciences, Department of Law and Policy. His research and teaching interests lie in human rights, rights of the child, and the interface between criminal justice, and social justice. He is the author of *Criminal Punishment and Human Rights: Convenient Morality* (2019).

Maleeha Sattar is a teaching fellow at the Department of Governance and Global Studies, Information Technology University, Lahore. She has done MPhil in Development Studies from PIDE, Islamabad. She has also been working as a development practitioner and monitoring and evaluation consultant on projects dealing with broader areas of health and livelihoods of Afghan refugees, skill development of rural youth in South Punjab, improving service delivery standards for maternal and neonatal child healthcare program, and designing and ensuring the efficacy of Advocacy, Communication and Social Mobilization (ACSM) activities in rural areas of Pakistan. She has also worked for the Citizen Foundation Pakistan. Her forthcoming publication is based on her fieldwork which analyzes learning poverty resulting from language-based marginalization in Pakistan.

www.ingramcontent.com/pod-product-compliance
Lightning Source LLC
LaVergne TN
LVHW011808200926
848484LV00005B/1101